23 **creator** [krɪˋetɚ] 名 C 創造者，創

- Matthew Groening is the **cre**
animated series *The Simpso*
馬修．葛林是熱門卡通《辛普森家庭

24 **crew** [kru] 集合名詞 ❶ 全體機員；❷ 一組工作人員　同義 staff 全體人員

❶ All of the passengers as well as the **crew** died in the plane crash.
所有乘客與機組人員都在空難中罹難。

❷ The maintenance **crew** will fix any mechanical problems that arise with a rental car. 維修人員會檢修出租車輛的所有問題。

25 **critic** [ˋkrɪtɪk] 名 C 批評家，評論家　同義 reviewer 評論家

- Hannah is a film **critic** who writes for a weekly magazine.
漢娜為一家週刊寫影評。

26 **darling** [ˋdɑrlɪŋ] 名 C ❶ 親愛的（人）
形 ❷ 心愛的，寵愛的；❸ 漂亮的，迷人的

- dear 親愛的
- -ling 名 表「與……有關者」

❶ **Darling**, can you pass me the remote control?
親愛的，你可以把遙控器拿給我嗎？

❷ Tomorrow afternoon, Mr. and Mrs. Wang will host a birthday party for their **darling** daughter. 明天下午，王氏夫婦將為愛女舉行一個生日派對。

❸ What a **darling** necklace! It looks great with that dress!
這條項鍊好漂亮！而且和那件衣服很配！

02 Jobs and People
職業與人物 (2)

3

01 **dealer** [ˋdilɚ] 名 C ❶ 業者，商人；❷ 發牌者，莊家

- deal 動 交易
- -er 名 表「人」

❶ Mr. Collins is an art **dealer**; his job is to buy and sell artwork. 柯林斯先生是一名藝術商，他的工作是買賣藝術品。

❷ The **dealer** passed out five cards to each poker player.
莊家發給每位玩家五張牌。

02 **designer** [dɪˋzaɪnɚ] 名 C 設計者，構思者，設計師

- de- 表「完全」
- sign 符號
- -er 名 表「人」

- Andrew enrolled in an art school because he wanted to be a fashion **designer**.
安德魯想當時裝設計師，所以進了藝術學院。

03 **detective** [dɪˋtɛktɪv] 名 C 偵探

・detect 動 察覺
・-ive 名 表「有……特性的」

- The **detective** asked Mrs. Wheeler when she last saw her neighbor, Mr. Po.
  偵探詢問魏勒太太，最近一次看到鄰居柏先生是什麼時候。

04 **editor** [ˋɛdɪtɚ] 名 C ❶ 主編；❷ 編輯；❸（影片等的）剪接師

・edit 編輯
・-or 名 表「人」

❶ Mr. White is an **editor** for a local newspaper; he decides which stories and pictures are printed in the paper.
懷特先生是一間地方報社的主編，他決定該份報紙的圖文內容。

❷ The **editor's** job is to prepare books for publication by checking and correcting the text. 編輯的工作是校對和訂正內容，讓書得以付梓。

❸ Alex is not only a professional drummer, but also a renowned movie **editor**. 艾力克斯不僅是職業鼓手，也是有名的電影剪接師。

05 **elderly** [ˋɛldɚlɪ] 形 年長的，上了年紀的　形 old 老的

・elder 較年長的
・-ly 形 表「……性質的」

- Marion started a tour company that takes **elderly** people on trips. 馬莉恩開了一家接洽銀髮族的旅行社。
- The government decided to build a retirement village for the **elderly** in the southern part of the country.
  政府決定在國內南部興建一座銀髮族的退休村。

06 **engineer** [ˏɛndʒəˋnɪr] 名 C 工程師，技師

・engine 引擎
・-eer 名 表「……人」

- Nicole was happy to learn that she passed the exam and is now a certified mechanical **engineer**.
  妮可很高興得知她通過考試，成為一位有執照的機械工程師了。

07 **exception** [ɪkˋsɛpʃən] 名 C ❶ 例外（的人或事物）；❷ U 除去，除外

・except 把……除外
・-ion 名 表「行為的結果」

❶ Although most people in the office caught a cold, Chester was an **exception**. He was in good health at the time.
之前辦公室裡頭大部分的人都感冒了，除了賈斯特。他當時很健康。

❷ With the **exception** of the children, everyone must take a night shift to guard the camp from intruders.
除了兒童以外，每個人都要輪值夜班、看守營地，防範外人進入。

08 **fanatic** [fəˋnætɪk] 名 C 狂熱者，盲信者　同義 enthusiast 熱衷者

- Johnson is a health food **fanatic**; he buys only organic foods.
  強森是一個養生食品狂。他只買有機食品。

09 **folk** [fok] 名 C ❶ 人，人們；❷ 雙親，親屬 ❸ 形 民間的，通俗的

❶ Titus doesn't live with his **folks**, but they talk on the phone every day. 提特斯沒和家人一起住，但他每天都會和家人通電話。

❷ My new neighbors are great **folks**; they are very friendly and helpful. 我的新鄰居人很好，親切又熱心助人。

❸ In Taiwan, ginger is a **folk** medicine used to cure colds. 在台灣，生薑被當作用來治療感冒的偏方。

10 **follower** [ˋfɑləwɚ] 名 C 追隨者，信徒，擁護者

・follow 動 跟隨
・-er 名 表「人」

● Harvey is an environmental activist who has attracted many **followers**. 哈威是一名環保運動人士，吸引了眾多的追隨者。

11 **founder** [ˋfaʊndɚ] 名 C 創立者，締造者

・found 建立
・-er 名 表「人」

● Christopher's grandfather was the **founder** of our community hospital. 克里斯多夫的祖父，是我們社區醫院的創辦人。

12 **genius** [ˋdʒinjəs] 名 C 天才，英才

● Zaha Hadid's architectural designs are truly works of **genius**. 薩哈．哈帝的建築設計作品真是天才。

4

13 **guardian** [ˋgɑrdɪən] 名 C ❶ 保護者，守護者，管理員；❷ 監護人

・guard 守衛
・-ian 名 表「……的人」

❶ Policemen are viewed as **guardians** of the people. Their job is to protect us from criminals and other dangerous types. 警方被視為人民的保姆。他們的職責在於保護好人不受壞人的傷害。

❷ Bruce became his niece's legal **guardian** after his brother's death. 布魯斯在哥哥死後，成了姪女的合法監護人。

14 **hairdresser** [ˋhɛrˏdrɛsɚ] 名 C 髮型師，美髮師

・hair 髮
・dress 梳理
・-er 名 表「人」

● Virgil's girlfriend is a **hairdresser**; she trims his hair every month. 維吉爾的女友是美髮師，她每個月都會幫他修剪頭髮。

15 **historian** [hɪsˋtorɪən] 名 C 歷史學家

・history 歷史
・-an 名 表「精通……的人」

● Lillian needs to consult **historians** for a screenplay she is writing about ancient Rome. 莉莉安自己寫的古羅馬電影劇本，要請歷史學家審閱才行。

16 **host** [host] 名 C ❶ 主人；❷（廣播、電視的）節目主持人
動 ❸ 主辦；❹ 主持

❶ Edmund, the **host**, introduced me to the other guests at the party. 派對的主人艾德蒙介紹其他客人給我認識。

❷ Flora is a famous TV talk show **host**. Her job is to introduce and interview the guests.
弗蘿拉是一位知名的電視脫口秀主持人，她的工作是訪問受邀來賓。

❸ Taipei **hosted** the 2009 Deaflympics. This was the first international event organized by city hall.
台北主辦了 2009 年的聽障奧運會。這是市政府第一次舉辦的國際賽事。

❹ *The Oprah Winfrey Show* is a popular television program **hosted** by Oprah Winfrey.
《歐普拉脫口秀》是一個非常受歡迎的電視節目，由歐普拉．溫芙蕾所主持。

17 **hostess** [ˋhostɪs] 名 C ❶ 女主人；❷ 空中小姐

- host 名 主人
- -ess 名 表「女性」

❶ The **hostess** considered it her duty to make her guests feel at home. 那位女主人認為讓賓客感到舒適自在是她的責任。

❷ Our **hostess**, Ms. West, made sure we were comfortable on the airplane. 我們班機上的空服員魏斯特小姐，讓我們感到賓至如歸。

18 **housekeeper** [ˋhaʊsˏkipɚ] 名 C 女管家，勤務工女領班

- house 房子
- keep 整理
- -er 名 表「人」

● Christopher needs a **housekeeper** to take care of his household affairs.
克里斯多夫需要一名管家來料理家中的大小事。

補充 timekeeper 計時器；計時員；peacekeeper 維持和平的人

19 **housewife** [ˋhaʊsˏwaɪf] 名 C 家庭主婦

- house 房子
- wife 妻子

● Gretchen is a thrifty **housewife** who knows how to find good bargains. 格麗卿是位節儉的家庭主婦，很清楚去哪裡買物美價廉的東西。

20 **humanity** [hjuˋmænətɪ] 名 U ❶ 人性，人道；❷（總稱）人，人類

- human 人
- -ity 名 表「性質，狀態」

❶ The prisoners of war were treated with **humanity**. The guards were kind and tried to limit their suffering.
戰俘受到人道的對待。衛兵善待他們，並盡量免去他們的痛苦折磨。

❷ Gilbert is still optimistic about the future of **humanity** in this increasingly mechanized world.
在這個愈來愈機械化的世界裡，吉伯特還是對人類的未來感到樂觀。

21 **humankind** [ˋhjumən͵kaɪnd] 集合名詞 人類 同義 mankind 人

- human 人
- kind 種類

- A sense of right and wrong separates **humankind** from the beasts. 人類有是非對錯，不同於動物。

22 **identification** [aɪ͵dɛntəfəˋkeʃən] 名 U ❶ 身分證明；❷ 認出，識別

- identity 名 身分
- -fy 動 表「……化」
- -tion 名 表「結果」

❶ Leah always carries two kinds of **identification**, her ID card and a driver's license.
莉亞隨身都會帶著身分證和駕照這兩種身分證明文件。

❷ I quickly found my luggage, as I had put a colorful tag on it for easy **identification**. 我很快就找到了我的行李，因為我在行李上綁了一個彩色的吊牌，很容易就可以認出來。

23 **identity** [aɪˋdɛntətɪ] 名 U ❶ 身分；❷ 特性

❶ The police discovered the **identity** of the murderer by DNA analysis. 警方比對 DNA，找出了兇手。

❷ The fishing village has preserved its distinct **identity** and thus attracts a lot of tourists.
這座漁村仍保有特殊風貌，也因此吸引了許多觀光客。

補充 identity card (=ID card) 身分證；identity theft 身分盜竊

24 **idol** [ˋaɪdḷ] 名 C 偶像

- Tammy doesn't understand how some **idols** become so popular.
泰美不了解有一些偶像怎麼會那麼受歡迎。

25 **immigrant** [ˋɪməgrənt] 名 C (移入)移民，僑民

- im- 表「向……內」
- migrate 移居
- -ant 名 表「人」

- As thousands of new **immigrants** from Southeastern Asia have moved to Taiwan for work or marriage, we should try our best to help them adjust to our society. 隨著數以千計的移民從東南亞移入台灣工作或結婚，我們應該盡可能幫助他們適應我們的社會。〔97 年指測〕

26 **individual** [͵ɪndəˋvɪdʒʊəl] 形 ❶ 個人的；❷ 個別的 ❸ 名 C 個人

- in- 不
- divide 分開
- -al 形 表「關於……的」

❶ You may have the car designed to meet your **individual** needs, but it will cost you a lot of money.
你可以將車子設計得符合你個人的需求，但這會花上你一大筆錢。

❷ Good teachers respect the **individual** characteristics and needs of their students; at the same time, they treat everyone as equals. 一位好的老師必須尊重每位學生的個別差異與需求，並平等對待每個人。

❸ The singing contest is open to teams as well as **individuals**.
這個歌唱比賽不僅向團體、也向個人開放報名。

03 Jobs and People
職業與人物 (3)

5

01 **infant** [ˋɪnfənt] 名 C 嬰兒

- Beverley specializes in designing clothes for **infants**.
貝芙麗專門設計嬰兒服。

02 **inspector** [ɪnˋspɛktɚ] 名 C 檢查員，視察員，督察員

- inspect 檢查
- -or 名 表「人」

- An **inspector** from headquarters unexpectedly visited Prince's branch office today.
一名總部的督察員，在今天無預警地前往普林斯的分部視察。

03 **inventor** [ɪnˋvɛntɚ] 名 C 發明家，發明者，創作者

- invent 發明
- -or 名 表「人」

- Harvey is a very productive **inventor** with more than 100 patents. 哈威是位非常多產的發明家，已申請有上百件的專利品。

04 **junior** [ˋdʒunjɚ] 形 ❶ 年紀較輕的 ❷ 名 C（中學或大學的）三年級生

❶ Kevin just graduated from law school and is a **junior** partner at the firm. 凱文剛從法學院畢業，是那間公司的新夥伴。

❷ All **juniors** are asked to take an aptitude test before their last year of high school. 在中學的最後一年，所有的三年級學生都要做性向測驗。

相關片語 **be . . . years somebody's junior/ be somebody's junior (by . . .)** 比某人小……歲

- She married a man seven years her junior, which stunned all of her friends. 她嫁給一個比她小七歲的男人，讓她所有的朋友都很吃驚。

05 **knight** [naɪt] 名 C 騎士

- Because of Sang's loyalty to the king, he was made a **knight**.
桑對國王忠心耿耿，所以受封為騎士。

相關片語 **a knight in shining armor** 救人（尤指婦女）的男子

- Jenny looked around the bar for a knight in shining armor to save her from this awful date.
珍妮在酒吧裡尋找她的救援騎士，拯救她遠離這場糟糕的約會。

06 **labor** [ˋlebɚ] 名 U ❶ 勞工，勞方；❷ 勞動

❶ There is a shortage of skilled **labor** in the woodcarving field.
木雕這一行，人才短缺。

❷ So-called traditional manufacturing industries such as clothing, shoe, and furniture factories require intensive **labor**.
所謂的傳統製造業，是指那些像是衣服、鞋子和家具等需要密集勞力的產業。

補充 Labor Day 勞動節

07 **liar** [ˋlaɪɚ] 名 C 說謊的人　動 lie 說謊

- Levi sometimes exaggerates, but he is definitely not a **liar**.
李維有時會誇大其辭，但他絕不是個騙子。

08 **librarian** [laɪˋbrɛrɪən] 名 C 圖書館館長，圖書館員

- library 名 圖書館
- -ian 名 表「專家」

- Dennis is a **librarian** trained in library science and engaged in library services.
丹尼斯受過圖書館學訓練，是目前在圖書館服務的館員。

相關字 libraries 圖書館的電腦查詢系統

09 **lifeguard** [ˋlaɪf͵gɑrd] 名 C（海上、游泳池的）救生員

- life 生命
- guard 守衛

- A **lifeguard**'s job is to rescue swimmers who are in danger. 救生員的工作是拯救遭遇危險的游泳者。

10 **madam** [ˋmædəm] 名 夫人，太太（=**ma'am**）

- May I help you carry your luggage upstairs to your room, **madam**? 這位女士，我幫您把行李提上樓、拿到您的客房好嗎？

11 **maid** [med] 名 C 女僕

- The **maid** serves Mr. Wattson breakfast every morning at 7 o'clock. 女僕每天早上七點會送早餐給華森先生。

12 **majority** [məˋdʒɔrətɪ] 名 C 多數，過半數，大多數

- major 主要的
- -ity 名 表「性質，狀態」

- The **majority** of Mariel's readers are young adults who live in the city. 梅麗爾大部分的讀者是住在城市的年輕人。

相關片語 **in the majority** 占多數

- Women are in the majority in the teaching profession. 教職中女性占多數。

13 **manager** [ˋmænɪdʒɚ] 名 C 主任，經理

- manage 管理
- -er 名 表「人」

- Jenny, the store **manager**, is in charge of sales.
商店經理珍妮負責業務銷售。

補充 general manager 總經理；stage manager 舞台監督

6

14 **mankind** [mæn`kaɪnd] 名 U 人類

・man 人
・kind 類

- Cindy uses the word "humankind" instead of "**mankind**" out of respect for women.
  辛蒂避開「男人」而用「人」這個字以表對女性的尊重。

15 **merchant** [`mɝtʃənt] 名 C 商人

- Since ancient times, **merchants** have traveled frequently through this area with their merchandise.
  從古時候開始，商人就常帶著貨物行經此區。

16 **millionaire** [ˌmɪljən`ɛr] 名 C 百萬富翁 (=millionary)

・million 百萬

- In the twenty-first century, being a billionaire is much more glamorous than being a **millionaire**.
  在二十一世紀，成為億萬富翁遠比百萬富翁來得更誘人。

17 **miner** [`maɪnɚ] 名 C 礦工

・mine 名 礦
・-er 名 表「人」

- Frank's grandfather was one of the first gold **miners** to settle in this valley. 法蘭克的祖父是第一批定居於此村的採金礦工。

18 **minority** [maɪ`nɔrətɪ] 名 C ❶ 少數；❷ 少數派，少數群

・minor 少數的
・-ity 名 表「性質，狀態」

❶ This morning, most of the students came to school on time; only a **minority** were late.
今天早上，大部分的學生都準時到校，只有少數學生遲到。

❷ Mr. Markey found he was in the **minority** when he spoke out against the government's new tax policy.
馬其先生在發言反對政府的新稅制時，發現自己是反對的少數人。

相關片語 **in the minority** 處於少數的

- Boys are typically the minority in ballet classes.
  在芭蕾舞課堂上，男孩是稀有動物。

19 **mob** [mɑb] ❶ 名 C 烏合之眾，暴民　❷ 動 成群圍住，蜂擁進入

❶ The police tried to break up the **mob** by spraying the people with water. 警方向群眾噴灑水柱，以驅散暴民。

❷ Two days before Christmas, customers **mobbed** the department store to buy gifts for friends and families.
聖誕節前兩天，消費者蜂擁擠進百貨公司，去採購親友的禮物。

20 **nanny** [`nænɪ] 名 C 保母

- A **nanny's** job is to take care of young children in their own home. 保母的工作就是去孩童的家中照顧他們。

21 **native** [ˋnetɪv] 名 C ❶ 本地人，本國人
形 ❷ 天生的，祖國的；❸ 本土的，土生的

❶ I am not a **native**; I am just a visitor. 我不是本地人，我是遊客。

❷ Derek is a **native** Spanish speaker, and now he is learning Arabic.
德瑞克的母語是西班牙語，他現在在學阿拉伯語。

❸ The koala is **native** to Australia. 無尾熊是澳洲特有的動物。

22 **nickname** [ˋnɪkˏnem] ❶ 名 C 綽號　❷ 動 給……取綽號

❶ Duncan's **nickname** was once Smiley, but now he should be called Grumpy. 鄧肯以前的綽號叫「笑笑」，但現在應該叫他「臭臉」。

❷ Cheney used to be skinny, so he was **nicknamed** string bean.
錢尼以前很瘦，所以有「竹竿」的外號。

23 **novelist** [ˋnɑvḷɪst] 名 C 小說家

- novel 名 小說
- -ist 名 表「做……的人」

- Felicia collects books written by her favorite **novelists**. 費莉西維收集自己最喜愛的小說家們寫的書。

24 **operator** [ˋɑpəˏretɚ] 名 C ❶ 操作者，技工；❷ 接線生

- operate 操作
- -or 名 表「人」

❶ Without the **operator's** manual, Anna doesn't know how to use the new dishwasher.
沒有新洗碗機的使用手冊，安娜不知道要怎麼操作。

❷ I called this afternoon, and the **operator** put me through to Room 101. 我今天下午打了電話，然後接線生就幫我轉接到 101 房。

25 **orphan** [ˋɔrfən] 名 C 孤兒　名 orphanage〔總稱〕孤兒；孤兒院

- Joanne became an **orphan** after both of her parents died in a car accident. 瓊安在父母雙雙死於車禍後成了孤兒。

26 **pal** [pæl] 名 C 伙伴，好友

- Ms. Walker and Mr. Lear have been pen **pals** for three decades, but they have never met in person.
渥克小姐與李爾先生是三十年的筆友了，但他們從未見過面。

補充 pen pal 筆友

27 **pianist** [pɪˋænɪst] 名 C 鋼琴家，鋼琴演奏者　名 piano 鋼琴

- piano 鋼琴
- -ist 名 表「人」

- Leo, who learned to play the piano from his mother, is now a professional **pianist**.
里歐現在是職業鋼琴家，他的鋼琴是跟他媽媽學的。

04 Jobs and People
職業與人物 (4)

7

01 **pilot** [ˋpaɪlət] 名 C ❶ 飛行員，駕駛員；❷ 舵手，領航員
動 ❸ 給（船等）領航

❶ Patrick is training to be a **pilot** at a flight school.
派屈克在飛行學校學習飛行駕駛。

❷ Old Joe used to be a **pilot** on the Mississippi. He guided at least 10 ferries across the river every day.
老喬過去是密西西比河的領航員，一天最少會引領十艘渡船過河。

❸ Ivan's job is to **pilot** foreign vessels into port.
艾文的工作是引領國外船隻入港。

02 **pioneer** [͵paɪəˋnɪr] 名 C ❶ 拓荒者；❷ 先驅者，開拓者
動 ❸ 開創，當先驅

- peon 勞工，散工
- -eer 名 表「與……有關的人」

❶ Josefina's ancestors were among the earliest **pioneers** to reach the West Coast.
約瑟芬娜的祖先是最早一批抵達西海岸的拓荒者。

❷ The company is a **pioneer** in the fashion industry. It created the concept of high fashion designs.
這家公司是時尚界的先驅，提出了高級時尚的概念。

❸ The new AIDS treatment was **pioneered** by doctors in an American hospital. 這項新的愛滋病療法由美國一家醫院的醫師們首創。

03 **plumber** [ˋplʌmɚ] 名 C 水管工

- plumb 鉛錘
- -er 名 表「人」

- The toilet is leaking again, so we have to call the **plumber**. 廁所又漏水了，我們得打電話叫水電工來。

04 **publisher** [ˋpʌblɪʃɚ] 名 C 出版者，出版商

- publish 發行
- -er 名 表「人」

- Edgar has already signed a contract with his **publisher** for his next novel. 愛德格已經和出版商簽訂他的下一本小說。

05 **refugee** [͵rɛfjʊˋdʒi] 名 C 難民，流亡者

- refuge 避難，庇護
- -ee 名 表「與……有關的人」

- The **refugees** from the flooded area have been transferred to neighboring states.
水災災區的難民已經轉送至鄰近的幾個州安置。

06 **representative** [ˌrɛprɪˋzɛntətɪv] ❶ 名 C 代表 ❷ 形 代表性的，典型的

❶ Tyler was elected as a **representative** of his community. 泰勒當選為社區代表。

❷ Today, skinny models are considered the ideal; however, they are not **representative** of most women. 時下瘦骨如柴的模特兒被認為是完美典範，但是他們不代表大多數的女性。

- re- 再
- present 呈現
- -ative 形 表「有……性質的」

07 **researcher** [riˋsɝtʃɚ] 名 C 研究員，調查者

- re- 表「再……」
- search 尋找
- -er 名 表「人」

● After working as an assistant **researcher** in a lab for three years, Liz finally qualified for a promotion.
麗茲在一間實驗室當了三年的研究助理之後，終於得到了晉升。

08 **scout** [skaʊt] ❶ 名 C 童子軍 ❷ 動 偵察，搜索

❶ As a **scout**, Perry was sent to explore nearby water sources.
派瑞身為童子軍，被派去勘查附近的水資源。

❷ The boys are **scouting** the area, trying to find a place to set up their tent. 男孩們搜索這個區域，想找個紮營的地方。

09 **shepherd** [ˋʃɛpɚd] 名 C 牧羊人

- sheep 羊
- herd 放牧人

● Peter is a **shepherd** who guides a flock of sheep to a different grassy meadow each day.
牧羊人彼德每天要趕羊群到不同的茂盛草地上去吃草。

補充 sheep dog 牧羊犬

10 **slave** [slev] 名 C ❶ 奴隸；❷ 擺脫不了某種習慣或影響的人

❶ Nicolas refused to work as a **slave** all his life.
尼可拉斯不願一輩子做牛做馬。

❷ Elvira is a **slave** to fashion; she cannot live without trendy clothes and shoes. 艾薇拉是流行狂，沒有潮服潮鞋，她就活不下去啦。

相關用法 名 **slavery** 奴役

● Centuries ago, some Africans were captured and sold into slavery; they were compelled to do hard labor and were ill-treated for the rest of their lives. 幾世紀前，一些非洲黑人被抓去當奴隸賣掉，被迫一輩子作苦力，境遇悽慘。

11 **spy** [spaɪ] ❶ 名 C 間諜，密探 ❷ 動 暗中監視，刺探

❶ The U.S. government recruited and trained many **spies** in Russia during the Cold War. 冷戰期間，美國政府在蘇俄招募、培訓了許多間諜。

❷ The agent was sent to **spy** on the officer and collect secret information about him.
那名特務被派去暗中監視那位官員，並收集對方的機密資料。

12 **staff** [stæf] 集合名詞 Ⓒ ❶（全體）職員，（全體）工作人員；❷ 幕僚，參謀人員

❶ The boss likes her **staff**; she thinks all her employees are excellent. 這名老闆喜歡她的員工；她覺得他們每一個人都很優秀。

❷ The president relied on his **staff** to make routine decisions.
總統依賴幕僚來做例行的決策。

13 **stepchild** [ˋstɛp͵tʃaɪld] 名 Ⓒ 結婚時夫或妻已有的孩子

- step- 表「繼」
- child 小孩

● Madeline treats her **stepchild** well even though he is not her biological son.
瑪德琳對她的繼子很好，雖然他不是她的親生兒子。

8

14 **stepfather** [ˋstɛp͵fɑðɚ] 名 Ⓒ 繼父

- step- 表「繼」
- father 父親

● Joe is the **stepfather** of the twins. 喬是那對雙胞胎的繼父。

15 **stepmother** [stɛp͵mʌðɚ] 名 Ⓒ 繼母

- step- 表「繼」
- mother 母親

● Kenny and his **stepmother** never talk to each other.
肯尼沒和他的繼母說過話。

16 **survivor** [sɚˋvaɪvɚ] 名 Ⓒ 倖存者；殘存物

- sur- 超過；之上
- viv 表「活著」
- -or 名 表「人」

● The **survivors** of the fire were immediately taken to a nearby hospital.
火災的倖存者立刻被送往附近的一家醫院急救。

17 **tutor** [ˋtjutɚ] 名 Ⓒ 家庭教師

● Gregory is thinking about hiring a **tutor** to help his son learn Russian. 葛格瑞在考慮請一位家教來幫兒子上俄文。

18 **twin** [twɪn] ❶ 名 Ⓒ 雙胞胎（之一） ❷ 形 孿生的

❶ Al, the father of the **twins**, was swept away in the flood and is still missing. 那對雙胞胎的父親艾爾在水災中被沖走，至今下落不明。

❷ The boy standing over there is Darnell's **twin** brother. They do look alike. 站在那裡的男孩是達尼爾的孿生兄弟，他們長得很相像。

19 **victim** [ˋvɪktɪm] 名 Ⓒ ❶ 受害者，受災者；❷ 遇難者，犧牲者

❶ The **victims** of the flood have been in the shelter since yesterday.
水災災民從昨天就被安置在一間避難所了。

❷ All of the passengers were likely killed in the plane crash; however, some of the **victims** have not been identified yet.
所有乘客可能在墜機中喪生。其中一些罹難者的身分尚未獲得確認。

20 **youngster** [ˋjʌŋstɚ] 名 C 年輕人

- young 形 年輕的
- -ster 名 表「……者」

● Grandpa Jones, who is 90 years old, thinks everyone he meets is a **youngster**.
鍾斯祖父已經九十歲了，在他眼中每個人都是年輕人。

21 **settler** [ˋsɛtlɚ] 名 C 移居者，殖民者，開拓者

- settle 安頓
- -er 名 表「人」

● Reginald's grandparents were among the earliest European **settlers** in America.
雷金納的祖父母是最早一批抵達美洲的歐洲移民。

22 **translator** [trænsˋletɚ] 名 C 譯者，翻譯家

- translate 動 翻譯
- -or 名 表「人」

● Paula needs a **translator** to write the Korean subtitles for her film. 寶拉需要一名翻譯，幫她的影片加上韓文字幕。

23 **typist** [ˋtaɪpɪst] 名 C 打字員，打字者

- type 打字
- -ist 名 表「做……的人」

● Jeffery works as a **typist** in the court.
傑弗瑞在法院當打字員。

24 **vegetarian** [͵vɛdʒəˋtɛrɪən] 名 C 素食者

- vegetable 蔬菜
- -arian 名 表「某類型的人」

● Bob is a **vegetarian**; he does not eat meat or fish. 鮑伯是一名素食者，他不吃肉，也不吃魚。

25 **virgin** [ˋvɝdʒɪn] ❶ 名 C 處女 ❷ 形 未開發的，未經利用的

❶ Jennifer is quite proud that she remained a **virgin** until her marriage. 珍妮佛很自豪自己在婚前都保有處女之身。

❷ The **virgin** land is still in its natural state; it has not been used or changed by humans. 這片處女地仍處於原始狀態，還沒有被人類開發過。

26 **volunteer** [͵vɑlənˋtɪr] 名 C 自願參加者，志願者，志工

- voluntary 自願的
- -eer 名 表「與……有關的人」

● Belinda is responsible for organizing **volunteers** in her community. 蓓琳達負責組織社區的志工隊。

27 **witness** [ˋwɪtnɪs] 名 C ❶ 目擊者；❷ 證人

- wit 知道
- -ness 名 表「性質或狀態」

❶ The policeman asked the **witness** to describe what happened during the accident.
警方要求那位目擊者描述意外發生時的情況。

❷ Antoine was called as a defense **witness** in the trial of Mr. Werner, his neighbor. 在鄰居魏納先生的案件裡，安東以被告證人的身分被傳喚出庭。

05 Human Body 人體 (1)

9

01 **abdomen** [ˋæbdəmən] 名 C **腹部**　同義 belly 腹部

- After eating the meal, Gwendolyn felt a dull pain in her **abdomen**; it was likely a stomachache.
  在吃完飯後，關德琳的腹部感到隱隱作痛，感覺上像是胃痛。

02 **ache** [ek] 動 ❶ **(持續性的)疼痛**；❷ **極為想念，渴望**　名 C ❸ **疼痛**

❶ When it turns cold, my grandma always complains that her knees **ache**. 只要天氣一變冷，我阿嬤就會說她膝蓋痛。

❷ After studying in the United States for two years, Jenny **ached** for home. 在美國求學兩年之後，珍妮渴望回家。

❸ Bill gets an **ache** in his lower back when he sits all day.
比爾只要一整天坐著，下背部就會酸痛。

03 **bare** [bɛr] ❶ 形 **裸的；光禿禿的**　❷ 動 **使赤裸，露出**；❸ **揭露**

❶ In ancient times, the people of Central America built huge stone pyramids with their **bare** hands.
在古代，中美洲人徒手建造了巨大的石砌金字塔。

❷ After the wildfire, the hill was **bare** of vegetation.
在那場野火過後，山丘變得光禿禿，毫無草木。

❸ Seeing the stranger approach, the dog **bared** its teeth and growled. 看到陌生人接近，那隻狗露出牙齒咆哮。

相關片語 **be bare of** 沒有……

- The house they lived in was almost bare of furniture.
  他們住的房子幾乎沒有家具。

04 **belly** [ˋbɛlɪ] 名 C **腹部，肚子**

- Until her sister was born, Gabriella couldn't understand why her mother's **belly** was so big.
  嘉布麗拉在妹妹出生後，才了解媽媽之前的肚子為什麼會那麼大。

補充 bellybutton 名 肚臍

05 **breast** [brɛst] 名 C **乳房，胸部**

- The newborn baby stopped crying when he started suckling his mother's **breast**. 那個新生寶寶吸到母乳之後就不哭了。

06 **breath** [brɛθ] 名 ❶ U 呼吸，氣息；❷ C（呼吸的）一次，一口氣

❶ After running for 20 minutes, George was out of **breath**.
在跑了二十分鐘之後，喬治喘得上氣不接下氣。

❷ Whenever Lauren feels anxious or nervous, she takes a few deep **breaths**. 蘿倫只要感到不安或緊張，她就會做幾次深呼吸。

相關片語 ❶ **catch one's breath** 喘氣；❷ **hold one's breath** 屏息而待

❶ The child stopped running to catch his breath.
小孩暫停跑步，讓自己喘口氣。

❷ The audience held its breath as the magician opened the box.
魔術師打開箱子的時刻，觀眾屏息以待。

07 **breathe** [brið] ❶ 動 呼吸，呼氣，吸氣；❷ 呼吸，吸入　名 breath 呼吸

❶ With the invention of scuba, people are able to **breathe** underwater. 水肺的發明，讓人類可以在水底下呼吸。

❷ Killer whales need to **breathe** about every 10 minutes, or they will die. 殺人鯨每十分鐘左右就需要呼吸水面的空氣一次，不然會死亡。

08 **brow** [braʊ] 名 C 眉毛　同義 eyebrow 眉，眉毛

- With his raised **brows** and open mouth, the man was unable to hide his surprise. 那個男子露出目瞪口呆的表情，掩不住驚訝之情。

補充 knit/wrinkle one's brows 某人皺眉頭

09 **cheek** [tʃik] 名 C 臉頰

- Molly puts sunblock on her **cheeks** and nose before she goes out on sunny days. 茉莉在出太陽的日子要出門之前，會在臉頰和鼻子上塗防晒乳。

10 **chest** [tʃɛst] 名 C 胸，胸膛

- Andy felt a pain in his **chest** for many days before finally seeing a doctor. 安迪在就醫之前，胸口已經連續痛好幾天了。

11 **circulate** [ˋsɝkjə͵let] 動 ❶ 使傳播，使流傳；❷ 使循環；❸ 傳播，流傳；❹ 循環

> ‧circle 圓；循環
> ‧-ate 動 表「使成為」

❶ Simon was **criticized** for circulating rumors and gossip about the rich and famous. 賽門因散布富商名流的謠言和八卦而遭致非議。

❷ The fans in the air conditioning unit **circulated** cool air throughout the building. 空調系統中的風扇讓冷空氣可以在整棟大樓裡流通。

❸ The rumor **circulated** very quickly; soon everyone in the company had heard it. 謠言傳得很快，很快地公司裡所有人都知道了。

❹ Exercising can help your blood **circulate** through the body.
運動有助於全身的血液循環。

12 **circulation** [ˌsɝkjəˋleʃən] 名 U ❶ 循環；❷（貨幣、消息等的）流通，傳播

❶ If you exercise regularly, your blood **circulation** will improve and you will feel more energetic.
規律的運動可以改善血液循環，讓人的精神變好。

‧ circulate 動 循環
‧ -ion 名 表「行為」

❷ At the end of last year, police found a large number of forged coins in **circulation**. 去年底，警方發現大量的假幣在流通。

相關片語 ❶ **in circulation** 在流通的 ❷ **out of circulation** 不再流通的
❸ **withdraw/remove from circulation** 停止（貨幣）流通

- The old version of the NT$1,000 bill has been taken out of circulation.
舊版的千元鈔票已經不再流通。
- The Treasury Department plans to remove older coins from circulation and replace them with new ones.
財政部計畫停止舊版錢幣的流通，以新版取代。

10

13 **conscious** [ˋkɑnʃəs] 形 ❶ 有知覺的；❷ 意識到的；❸ 刻意的，故意的

❶ The old man passed out, but he was **conscious** and sitting up by the time help arrived.
老人突然昏倒，但等到救援來時又恢復了知覺，從地上爬了起來。

❷ As the woman walked in the dark alley, she was **conscious** of being followed. 那名女子走在暗巷時，意識到有人跟蹤她。

❸ Marcel made a **conscious** effort to speak more clearly in public.
瑪瑟兒努力讓自己在公開場合談話時口齒清晰。

相關用法 名 **consciousness** 知覺

- The man lost consciousness after being wounded and doesn't remember what happened next. 男子受傷後失去知覺，不知道之後發生了什麼事。

相關片語 ❶ **be conscious of N / V-ing** 意識到
❷ **make a conscious effort** 努力
❸ **self-conscious**（因顧慮外表或表現）不安的，害羞的，刻意的

❶ I was very conscious of the importance of a healthy diet in controlling my weight. 我在控制體重時，很留意飲食健康的重要性。

14 **digest** [daɪˋdʒɛst] 動 ❶ 消化（食物）；❷ 消化　名 digestion 消化

❶ Morris likes to sit calmly for 30 minutes after eating to help **digest** his meal. 莫里斯喜歡在飯後靜地坐 30 分鐘，好幫助消化食物。

❷ Mary has a stomachache and needs to eat food that is easy to **digest**. 瑪麗胃痛，需要吃容易消化的食物。

15 **digestion** [də`dʒɛstʃən] 名 U 消化，消化作用

- Frank thinks that chewing a betel nut after a meal helps his **digestion**. 法蘭克認為，飯後嚼檳榔可幫助消化。

・digest 動 消化
・-ion 名 表「動作」

16 **drowsy** [`draʊzɪ] 形 ❶ 昏昏欲睡的，困倦的；❷ 懶散的，無活力的

❶ Since Randy was feeling **drowsy**, he asked May to drive the rest of the way home.
朗迪很睏，他請梅接手繼續開車回家。

・drowse 打瞌睡
・-y 形 表「性質，狀態」

❷ Dad fell asleep while listening to the radio on a **drowsy** summer afternoon. 在一個令人昏昏欲睡的夏日午後，爸爸邊聽著廣播就睡著了。

相關用法 動 **drowse** 打瞌睡

- The dog lay on the ground drowsing in the sun.
那隻狗躺在地上，在陽光下打瞌睡。

17 **drunk** [drʌŋk] 形 ❶ 喝醉酒的；❷ 為（擁有權勢等而）飄飄然

❶ After three hours in the bar, the man was so **drunk** he couldn't speak clearly. 在酒吧裡待了三個鐘頭之後，這個男人已經醉得語無倫次了。

❷ **Drunk** with power, the military commander directed his troops to assault the village. 那名軍隊司令權欲薰心，揮軍進犯村莊。

相關片語 ❶ **drunk on (alcohol, etc.)** 喝……而喝醉
❷ **be drunk with/on something** 沉迷於，醉心於

❶ He was drunk on whiskey. 他喝威士忌喝醉了。

18 **elbow** [`ɛlboʊ] ❶ 名 C 肘　❷ 動 用手肘推擠著前進

❶ Whenever Faye goes skateboarding, she wears protective pads on her knees and **elbows**. 菲只要去玩滑板，就會在膝蓋和手肘套上護膝和護肘。

❷ There were so many people in the train station that Carina had to **elbow** her way through the crowd.
火車站裡有很多人，柯琳娜得用手肘在人群中推擠著前進。

相關片語 **elbow one's way through/past/into something**
用手肘推擠著穿過……

19 **energetic** [͵ɛnɚ`dʒɛtɪk] 形 ❶ 精力旺盛的，精神飽滿的；❷ 有力的，積極的

❶ The **energetic** boy keeps running around and yelling; he never seems to get tired. 這個精力充沛的男孩一直又跑又叫，好像都不會累。

・energy 活力
・-(t)ic 形 表「具有……特性的」

❷ Ernest is an **energetic** fundraiser who has raised lots of money for the charity. 恩斯特募款積極，他為慈善機構募到了很多捐款。

20 **facial** [ˋfeʃəl] 形 臉的，面部的

- face 臉
- -al 形 表「關於……的」

- Bernard is a good poker player because he can control his **facial** expressions.
  柏納德是一位很好的撲克牌玩家，因為他在玩牌時能控制自己的臉部表情。

21 **feature** [ˋfitʃɚ] 名 C ❶ 面貌，相貌；❷ 特徵，特色；❸（報紙等的）特別報導

- fact 事實
- -ure 名 表「動作，過程」

❶ Curtis is a man of mystery; his facial **features** rarely reveal his emotions. 柯帝士是謎樣的人物，喜怒幾乎不形於色。

❷ The most distinctive **feature** of the elephant is its long trunk.
大象最明顯的特徵是長長的鼻子。

❸ The day after Michael Jackson died, the newspaper ran a special **feature** on the superstar.
麥克傑克森逝世隔天，這份報紙刊登了這位超級巨星的特別報導。

22 **fist** [fɪst] 名 C 拳頭

- When Samuel gets angry, he usually clenches his hands into **fists**. 薩繆爾生氣時，通常會緊握拳頭。

23 **flesh** [flɛʃ] 名 U 肉，肌肉

- Keith's dog kept gnawing on the bone, even after the **flesh** was gone. 那根骨頭都沒肉了，基斯的狗還是一直咬著不放。

相關片語 **flesh and blood** 血肉之軀

- I'm only flesh and blood, like anyone else. 我只是血肉之軀，和大家一樣。

補充 in the flesh 在現實中出現；本人

24 **forehead** [ˋfɔr͵hɛd] 名 C 額頭

- fore- 表「前部」
- head 頭

- Dale denied that he was going bald; instead, he claimed that his **forehead** was growing.
  戴爾不認為自己要禿頭了，他辯稱是他的額頭愈來愈高。

25 **gene** [dʒin] 名 C 基因

- Scientists have shown that our **genes** determine the color of our skin, hair, and eyes. 科學家證實我們的基因決定了皮膚、頭髮和眼睛的顏色。

26 **heel** [hil] 名 C ❶（鞋等的）後跟；❷ 腳後跟

❶ Sabrina was embarrassed when the **heel** broke off her boot, causing her to fall. 莎賓娜因為靴子鞋根掉了，摔了一跤，讓她覺得好窘。

❷ An arrow hit Achilles' **heel** and brought him down.
一枝箭射中阿基里斯的腳跟，讓他倒地不起。

補充 high heels 高跟鞋

06 Human Body 人體 (2)

11

01 **jaw** [dʒɔ] 名 C 下顎，下巴

- During their recent excavation, the archaeologists found a bone from the lower **jaw** of an ancient human.
考古學家在最近的挖掘中，發現了一塊遠古人類的下顎骨。

02 **kidney** [ˋkɪdnɪ] 名 C 腎臟

- Joanna donated one of her **kidneys** to save the life of her child.
瓊安娜捐了一顆腎臟來拯救自己孩子的性命。

03 **knuckle** [ˋnʌkḷ] 名 C 指關節

- Philip busted the **knuckles** on his left hand during the brutal fight in the alley. 在那場街頭火拼中，菲利浦弄斷了他的左手指關節。

04 **limb** [lɪm] 名 C（四）肢

- After sitting at her desk for hours, Linda stood up and stretched her **limbs**. 在書桌前坐了四個小時之後，琳達站起身來，伸展一下四肢。

05 **liver** [ˋlɪvɚ] 名 C 肝臟

- The doctor recommended that Leona stop drinking alcohol because of her weakened **liver**. 醫生說李奧娜的肝功能不佳，最好戒酒。

06 **lung** [lʌŋ] 名 C 肺臟

- When Eva learned that she had won the lottery, she yelled at the top of her **lungs**. 伊娃得知自己中了樂透頭彩時，她驚聲大叫。

07 **muscle** [ˋmʌsl̩] 名 ❶ C 肌肉；❷ U 體力　形 muscular 肌肉的

❶ Brian works out regularly to develop the **muscles** in his arms and legs. 布萊恩定期運動，以鍛鍊手部和腿部的肌肉。

❷ Terrie didn't have enough **muscle** to open the jar, so her brother opened it for her. 德莉的手臂力量不夠大，打不開罐子，所以她哥哥幫她打開。

08 **mustache** [ˋmʌstæʃ] 名 C 髭，髯髭，小鬍子

● Much to his son's embarrassment, Mr. Bishop has worn a handlebar **mustache** since 1999.
比夏先生從 1999 年就開始蓄的翹八字鬍，讓他兒子覺得很窘。

09 **physical** [ˋfɪzɪkl̩] 形 ❶ 身體的，肉體的；❷ 物質的

- physic 醫學
- -al 形 表「關於……的」

❶ Extreme sports challenge the **physical** capabilities of the human body. 極限運動挑戰人類的體能極限。

❷ Dragons exist only in people's minds; they are not found in the **physical** world. 龍只存在於人類的想像中，在這個物質世界裡是看不到的。

10 **pregnancy** [ˋprɛgnənsɪ] 名 U 懷孕

- pregnant 形 懷孕的
- -cy 名 表「狀態」

● Neil's wife took a **pregnancy** test, but she hasn't told him the result yet. 奈爾的妻子用了驗孕棒，但她還沒告訴奈爾測試的結果。

11 **pregnant** [ˋprɛgnənt] 形 懷孕的，懷胎的

● Evelyn is **pregnant** with her first child. 伊芙琳懷了第一胎。

相關片語 **be heavily pregnant** 即將臨盆

12

12 **sex** [sɛks] 名 ❶ U 性別；❷ C 男性，女性　形 sexual 性別的；性的

❶ After a close inspection, Nelson determined the **sex** of his experimental mice. 尼爾森精細檢查實驗老鼠後，判斷出了老鼠的性別。

❷ The actor attracts fans of both **sexes**; women as well as men find him very attractive.
這位男演員的粉絲男女都有，不僅是女性，連男性都覺得他很有魅力。

13 **sexual** [ˋsɛkʃʊəl] 形 ❶ 性的；❷ 兩性的

- sex 名 性別
- -al 形 表「關於……的」

❶ Chad finds it difficult to discuss **sexual** matters with his children. 查德覺得難以啟齒和孩子談性的問題。

❷ My grandfather clings to **sexual** stereotypes; he believes men should support families and women should take care of children.
我爺爺對兩性有刻板印象。他認為男人應該養家，女人應該照顧小孩。

14 **stomach** [ˋstʌmək] 名 C 胃

- Drinking alcohol on an empty **stomach** is not wise; you should eat something first. 空胃喝咖啡不太好，你最好先吃點東西。

相關片語 **have no stomach for** 對……沒有胃口，對……沒有興趣

- Daisy decided to skip the slasher movie, as she has no stomach for violence. 黛西決定不看血腥片，她對暴力沒興趣。

15 **strength** [strɛŋkθ] 名 U 力量，力氣；C 長處，好處

・strong 強壯的
・-th 名 表「性質，狀態」

❶ After the operation, the weakened patient didn't have the **strength** to walk. 那個病人手術後很虛弱，沒有力氣走路。

❷ One of the **strengths** of the plan is its feasibility; another advantage is its cost. 這項計畫的一項優勢是它的可行性，另一項則是成本較低。

16 **sweat** [swɛt] ❶ 名 U 汗，汗水 ❷ 動 出汗

❶ Amanda's T-shirt was dampened with **sweat**, and she really wanted to shower. 阿曼達的 T 恤被汗浸濕了，她好想沖個澡。

❷ The patient has a high fever, and he is **sweating** heavily. 這名病人發高燒，正在大量出汗。

補充 No sweat! 很簡單的事

17 **temperature** [ˋtɛmprətʃɚ] 名 U ❶ 體溫；❷ 溫度，氣溫

・temper 脾氣
・-ate 形 表「有……性質或狀態的」
・-ure 名 表「動作」

❶ The doctor took Fanny's **temperature** and found she had a high fever. 醫生幫芬妮量了體溫，發現她在發高燒。

❷ The **temperature** rose by 10 degrees; it was very hot outside. 氣溫上升了十度，外頭十分炎熱。

18 **thirst** [θɝst] 名 U ❶ 渴；❷ (單數) 渴望　形 thirsty 口渴的

❶ After hiking all day without drinking any water, the students sat down by the stream to quench their **thirst**. 遠足了一整天都沒喝水，學生們在溪邊坐下，灌水解渴。

❷ The professor has a **thirst** for knowledge; she always wants to learn more. 這名教授求知欲強烈，她總是想學習更多。

19 **tissue** [ˋtɪʃʊ] 名 C ❶ (動植物的) 組織；❷ 紙巾，衛生紙

❶ The study shows how toxic substances in cigarette smoke act on lung **tissues**. 這個研究顯示香菸的煙所產生的有毒物質，如何對肺部組織起作用。

❷ Can I borrow some **tissues** to wipe my camera lens?
我可以借幾張面紙擦拭相機鏡頭嗎？

20 **tummy** [ˋtʌmɪ] 名 C（兒語）肚子，胃

- The little boy said he had a **tummy** ache, so his mother rubbed his belly gently. 那個小男孩說他肚子痛，所以他媽媽輕輕地揉揉他的肚子。

21 **visible** [ˋvɪzəbḷ] 形 可看見的

- vision 視力，視覺
- -ible 形 表「能……的」

- The distant mountains are barely **visible** from Jill's office window because of the dense smog.
從潔兒的辦公室窗戶往外望去，濃霧讓人幾乎看不到遠方的山。

22 **vision** [ˋvɪʒən] 名 U ❶ 視力，視覺；❷ C 夢想，遠景；❸ U 洞察力，眼光

❶ Marshall has poor **vision**; he has to wear glasses to read.
馬歇爾的視力很差，他得戴眼鏡來閱讀。

❷ Suzanne's positive **vision** of humanity keeps her working for peace across national boundaries.
蘇珊對人性有很正面的看法，這支撐著她能繼續為國際和平而奔走。

❸ We need a leader with great **vision**, someone who thinks about the future with imagination and intelligence.
我們需要一個有遠見的領袖，他要能以創造力和智慧來思考未來。

23 **wrist** [rɪst] 名 C 手腕

- The woman is wearing a jade bracelet on her **wrist**.
這名女子在手腕上戴了一只玉鐲。

24 **wrinkle** [ˋrɪŋkḷ] 名 C ❶ 皺紋；❷（衣物等的）皺摺 ❸ 動 起皺紋，皺起來

❶ The old woman's face is lined with **wrinkles**.
這名老婦人的臉上布滿了皺紋。

❷ Ethel hangs her blouse in the bathroom while she showers in order to get the **wrinkles** out. 艾瑟兒在浴室沖澡時，把短上衣掛在一旁除皺。

❸ These pants will **wrinkle** in the dryer and will need to be ironed before they are worn.
這些褲子在烘乾的過程中會皺掉，所以在穿之前要燙一下。

07 Activities
活動 (1)

13

01 **abandon** [əˋbændən] 動 ❶ 拋棄，遺棄；❷ 放棄，中止

❶ Bianca had to **abandon** the ship when it started to sink.
船開始沉沒時，碧恩卡只好棄船逃生。

❷ Since it was raining heavily, we **abandoned** the idea of taking a walk along the river. 由於外面雨下得很大，所以我們放棄在河邊散步的主意。

02 **accompany** [əˋkʌmpənɪ] 動 ❶ 陪伴；❷ 隨著……發生，伴有；❸ 為……伴奏或伴唱

❶ Lila **accompanied** her best friend on a long vacation to Asia.
麗樂陪她一個姐妹淘去亞洲度了個長假。

❷ A thunderstorm is often **accompanied** by strong winds and heavy rain. 暴風雨經常伴隨著強風和豪雨來襲。

❸ During the show, the singer was **accompanied** by a guitarist.
在那場表演中，一名吉他手替歌手伴奏。

03 **accomplish** [əˋkɑmplɪʃ] 動 完成，達到　名 accomplishment 成就

- Bradley **accomplished** all of his goals before going home.
布拉德利回家前，完成了自己所有的工作。

04 **accomplishment** [əˋkɑmplɪʃmənt] 名 ❶ U 完成，實現；❷ C 成就，成績

❶ Despite the **accomplishment** of this project, it was not finished on time. 這個計畫雖然完成了，但也逾時了。

❷ Construction of the Hsuehshan Tunnel was an impressive **accomplishment** that required a lot of hard work. 雪山隧道的興建是一項非凡的成就，是辛勤施工所得到的結果。

- accomplish 完成
- -ment 名 表「結果」

05 **achieve** [əˋtʃiv] 動 ❶ 實現，完成；❷ 到達，贏得

❶ Stop fooling around, or you will never **achieve** anything.
別再無所事事了，你這樣會一事無成的。

❷ If Cliff doesn't study harder, he will never **achieve** his goal of becoming an international lawyer.
克里夫要是不用功一點，那他永遠也無法如願成為一位國際律師。

06 **achievement** [ə`tʃivmənt] 名 C **成就，成績**

- Ms. Barlow was rewarded for her **achievements** in genetic science. 巴洛小姐因遺傳學領域上的成就而獲獎。

補充 a sense of achievement 成就感

- achieve 動 實現
- -ment 名 表「結果」

07 **acquaint** [ə`kwent] 動 ❶ **使認識，介紹**；❷ **使熟悉，使了解**

❶ I am somewhat **acquainted** with your new publication.
我對你的新書大概知道一些。

❷ Reuben has just moved to New Zealand; he needs to get **acquainted** with his new surroundings.
魯賓剛剛搬到紐西蘭，他得先讓自己熟悉一下新環境。

08 **acquire** [ə`kwaɪr] 動 ❶ **獲得，取得**；❷ **學到**　名 acquisition 獲得

❶ In addition to earning some pocket money, you can **acquire** some practical work experience. 除了賺些零用錢，你還可以獲得實際的工作經驗。

❷ Mildred agrees that it is important for children to **acquire** a second language. 蜜德莉同意讓孩子學習第二種語言的重要性。

09 **activity** [æk`tɪvətɪ] 名 C **活動**

- Ms. Flora Pound encourages us to participate in all kinds of extracurricular **activities**.
芙蘿拉・龐得老師鼓勵我們多參加各種課外活動。

- act 動 行動
- -ive 形 表「有⋯⋯特性的」
- -ity 名 表「性質，狀態」

10 **adapt** [ə`dæpt] ❶ 動 **適應**；❷ **使適應**；❸ **改編，改寫**；❹ **改建，改造**

❶ Polar bears **adapt** very well to the artificial environment of the zoo. 北極熊頗能適應動物園的人造環境。

❷ Arabela has just transferred to the school; she is trying hard to **adapt** to the new conditions.
愛勒貝拉剛剛轉學到這所學校，她正努力使自己適應新的環境。

❸ The *Harry Potter* movies and video games have been **adapted** from the books. 小說《哈利波特》已經被改編成電影和電玩遊戲。

❹ All the restrooms in the train station have been **adapted** for use by persons with disabilities. 這座火車站裡的廁所已經全部改成無障礙廁所。

11 **adjust** [ə`dʒʌst] 動 ❶ **調整，調節**；❷ **改變⋯⋯以適應**；❸ **適應**

❶ Max had no problem **adjusting** to the boarding school, but he still prefers the public school.
麥克斯完全可以適應寄宿學校，但他還是比較喜歡公立學校。

❷ If it is too cold in this room, you can **adjust** the air conditioner to make yourself comfortable.
如果房間的冷氣太冷，你可以自行調整至舒適溫度。

❸ After her husband died, Mrs. Jones spent half a year **adjusting** to living alone. 丈夫過世之後，瓊絲太太花了半年左右的時間來適應獨居生活。

12 **adjustment** [əˋdʒʌstmənt] 名 C 調整，調節

・adjust 動 調整
・-ment 名 表「行為」

● The machinist made some **adjustments** to the machine; the small changes helped it to run more smoothly. 機械師稍微調整了機器，小幅調整可以讓機器運轉得更順暢。

13 **adopt** [əˋdɑpt] 動 ❶ 採用，採納；❷ 收養，領養

❶ After careful consideration, the board decided to **adopt** Philip Peterson's plan for expanding the company.
仔細考慮後，董事會決定接受菲利普．彼得森將公司擴大經營的提議。

❷ Last year, Mr. and Mrs. Ruiz **adopted** the orphan; they were thrilled to add a daughter to their family.
去年，魯意茲夫婦收養了一位孤兒。他們很興奮家裡多了個女兒。

相關用法 名 **adoption** 採納，採用

● The adoption of this new technology will greatly improve our ability to diagnose and predict lung cancer.
這項新科技的使用，可以大大地改善我們診斷並預測肺癌的能力。

14 **alert** [əˋlɝt] ❶ 動 向……報警，使警覺 ❷ 形 警覺的 ❸ 名 U 警戒狀態

❶ The highway patrol **alerted** the local police about the robbery and asked for help in solving the crime.
公路巡邏隊向地方員警報備有搶案發生，準備好隨時支援行動。

❷ The soldier remained **alert**; he paid attention to what was happening around him and was ready to act quickly if necessary.
那名士兵保持警戒。他注意四周動靜，做好隨時立即行動的準備。

❸ The government warned the people to be on the **alert** for terrorist attacks. 政府警告人們保持警覺，小心恐怖攻擊。

14

15 **analysis** [əˋnæləsɪs] 名 U 分析　動 analyze 分析　名 analyst 分析者

● Ms. Lynch's **analysis** of current international relations is accurate and reliable. 林屈女士對於當前國際關係的分析，一向可靠又精準。

16 **analyze** [ˋænḷˏaɪz] 動 ❶ 分析；❷ 分解，解析

❶ Stephanie's friend helped her **analyze** the problem in order to better understand it. 史蒂芬妮的朋友幫她分析問題，以便加以釐清。

❷ Albert felt dizzy after he spent the morning **analyzing** chemical compounds in his lab.
今天早上，艾伯特在實驗室分解化學化合物之後就感到頭暈目眩。

17 **application** [ˌæpləˋkeʃən] 名 ❶ Ⓒ 申請表，申請書；❷ Ⓤ 申請；❸ Ⓒ 應用

❶ To whom should I send my **application**?
請問，你知道我的申請表要寄給誰嗎？

・apply 動 申請
・-ation 名 表「動作」

❷ Tyler's **application** to the university has been turned down.
泰勒向那所大學申請入學遭到拒絕。

❸ The **application** of this technology in schools has greatly aroused the students' interest in learning English.
這項科技應用在教學上，已經大大地引起了學生學習英文的興趣。

18 **appoint** [əˋpɔɪnt] 動 ❶ 任命，指派；❷ 約定，安排

❶ Ms. Hess was **appointed** director of the historical society.
何斯小姐被任命為史學協會的會長。

❷ We decided to meet at 1 o'clock in the afternoon, and we both arrived at the **appointed** time.
我們決定在下午一點碰面，而且我們兩個都在約定的時間到達。

19 **appointment** [əˋpɔɪntmənt] 名 ❶ Ⓒ 約定；❷ Ⓤ 任命，委派

❶ May I please reschedule my **appointment** with Mr. Duran for tomorrow?
請問我可以和杜朗先生改約明天嗎？

・appoint 動 任命
・-ment 名 表「行為」

❷ The **appointment** of a new sales manager has been announced; everyone thinks the boss has chosen the right person for the job. 新業務經理的任命已經公告了，大家都認為老闆選對了人來做這份工作。

補充 make an appointment with somebody 和某人約時間見面

20 **arrangement** [əˋrendʒmənt] 名 ❶ Ⓒ 安排，準備工作；❷ Ⓤ 布置，整理

❶ Mr. Davis has made **arrangements** to spend the holidays with his family.
戴維斯先生已經安排了要和家人去渡假。

・arrange 動 安排
・-ment 名 表「行為」

❷ The small rooms in my new house make furniture **arrangement** difficult. 我新房子的那些小房間不太好擺放家具。

21 **assemble** [əˋsɛmbḷ] 動 ❶ 集合，聚集；❷ 裝配，組裝

❶ Let's **assemble** in the conference room to discuss the new product. 我們去會議室討論一下新產品。

❷ Victor likes to build toy robots, although it takes a lot of time to **assemble** all the parts.
維克多喜歡組裝玩具機器人，雖然把零件全部組裝完成會很花時間。

22 **assembly** [əˋsɛmblɪ] 名 U **集會，集合**

• assemble 集合
• -y 名 表「狀態」

• In a democratic society, people have freedom of **assembly**. 在民主社會中，人民享有集會結社的自由。

補充 assembly line 裝配線，生產線

23 **assign** [əˋsaɪn] 動 ❶ **指派**；❷ **分配**　名 assignment 指派

❶ Each class was **assigned** a part of the organic garden to water and weed. 每一個班級都被分配到部分的有機花園，要負責澆水和除草。

❷ Gina was **assigned** to the oldest dorm because she was a freshman. 吉娜被分配到住舊宿舍，因為她是大一新鮮人。

24 **assignment** [əˋsaɪnmənt] 名 C ❶ **作業，功課**；❷ **任務，工作**

• assign 動 指派
• -ment 名 表「行為」

❶ The homework **assignment** is written on the blackboard. 家庭作業寫在黑板上。

❷ The doctor was in Turkey on **assignment** for the United Nations; he was sent to investigate a local epidemic.
那名醫生在土耳其執行一項聯合國任務，他被派去調查當地的一種流行疾病。

25 **assist** [əˋsɪst] 動 ❶ **協助，幫助某人**；❷ **給予協助，幫助**

❶ Would you please **assist** me in getting to my seat, as I am unable to read the numbers?
你可以帶我到我的位子上去嗎？因為我看不到座位的編號。

❷ Joseph **assisted** with preparations for the meeting. Without his help, I could not have finished on time.
約瑟夫幫忙做會議的準備工作。要是沒有他的幫忙，我無法準時完成。

26 **assistance** [əˋsɪstəns] 名 U **幫助，援助**

• assist 動 幫助
• -ance 名 表「動作」

• After the earthquake, Casey received financial **assistance** from the government in order to rebuild his house. 地震過後，卡西獲得政府的紓困補助來重建他的房子。

27 **attach** [əˋtætʃ] 動 **附加，繫上，貼上**　反義 detach 使分離

• Please **attach** your resume to the application and turn it in tomorrow. 請將您的申請表附上履歷，於明日傳回。

28 **attempt** [ə`tɛmpt] ❶ 動 試圖，企圖　❷ 名 C 企圖，嘗試

❶ Bruce **attempted** to write the paper in one week. Although many people thought it was an impossible task, he still wanted to try.
布魯斯企圖在一個星期內寫完報告，雖然很多人都認為這是不可能的任務，但他仍想要拚拚看。

❷ Sidney smelled burnt food and knew his wife's latest **attempt** at cooking had failed.
希德尼聞到食物燒焦的味道，他知道妻子最近學做的菜失敗了。

08 Activities
活動 (2)

15

01 **await** [ə`wet] 動 ❶ 等待，等候；❷ 將降臨到⋯⋯身上

・a- 表「在⋯⋯狀態中」
・wait 等待

❶ I am anxiously **awaiting** John's reply regarding the flight confirmation.
我著急地等候約翰跟我回覆班機的確認結果。

❷ If the man had known that danger **awaited**, he would not have jumped into the river. 那名男子要是知道河裡有多危險，他就不會跳進去了。

02 **awaken** [ə`wekən] 動 ❶ 醒，覺醒；❷ 使意識到；❸ 喚醒，使覺醒；❹ 喚起，激起

・a- 表「在⋯⋯狀態中」
・waken 醒來

❶ This morning, Ariel was **awakened** early by a clap of thunder. 今天一早，艾瑞兒被一聲雷響給驚醒了。

❷ The video was made to **awaken** people to the dangers of drug abuse. 製作這部片子是為了讓人們明白到藥物濫用的危險。

❸ Dennis was **awakened** at 2 a.m. by the sound of someone screaming. 丹尼斯在凌晨兩點時被一陣尖叫聲吵醒。

❹ Wayne's passion for music was first **awakened** by a concert he attended as a child. 韋恩小時候第一次聽音樂會時，就對音樂產生了熱愛。

03 **behave** [bɪ`hev] 動 ❶ 表現，行為舉止；❷ 使行為檢點，使守規矩

・be- 表「致使」
・have 擁有（某種行徑）

❶ Ms. Stanley asked her youngest daughter to **behave** like a young lady in front of the guests.
史坦利太太要她的小女兒在客人面前要有女孩子的樣子。

❷ The mother told her son to **behave** or she would punish him.
那個媽媽叫她的兒子規矩點，不然就要處罰他。

04 **behavior** [bɪˋhevjɚ] 名 U 行為，舉止

• behave 表現
• -or 名 表「性質或狀態」

● Barton was on his best **behavior** when his parents visited his school.
巴爾頓在父母來學校參觀時，表現出了他最好的一面。

05 **breed** [brid] 動 ❶ 使繁殖，飼養；❷（動物）生產，繁殖

❶ Gilbert was born and **bred** in a fishing culture, so he knows how to spearfish. 吉伯特在獵漁文化中長大，所以他知道如何使用魚叉捕魚。

❷ Rats **breed** so quickly that we now have too many of them.
老鼠繁殖得非常快，如今鼠滿為患。

06 **campaign** [kæmˋpen] 名 C ❶ 運動，活動 動 ❷ 從事運動

❶ City hall initiated a **campaign** against street violence last week. 市政府上週發起了一項反街頭暴力的活動。

❷ The workers are **campaigning** for a pay raise. They have planned some activities that should help them achieve their goal.
工人們正在進行要求加薪的示威運動，他們已經計畫好一些活動來達成目標。

07 **celebrate** [ˋsɛlə͵bret] 動 ❶ 慶祝（某人、事）；❷ 慶祝，過節

❶ We threw a party last night to **celebrate** Edgar's promotion.
昨晚我們辦了一場派對慶祝艾迪嘉升官。

❷ Next Wednesday is our wedding anniversary; we're going to **celebrate**. 下個星期三是我們的結婚紀念日，我們要慶祝一下。

08 **celebration** [͵sɛləˋbreʃən] 名 ❶ U 慶祝；❷ C 慶祝（活動）

• celebrate 動 慶祝
• -ion 名 表「行為」

❶ The party is planned in **celebration** of my mother's 70th birthday.
這場宴會是為了慶祝我媽媽的七十歲大壽。

❷ Cornell's novel is a **celebration** of the triumph of humanity over depravity. 康奈爾的小說是為慶祝人性戰勝邪惡而寫。

09 **cheer** [tʃɪr] 動 ❶ 為……歡呼、喝采；❷ 使振奮，使高興；❸ 歡呼，喝采
名 C ❹ 歡呼，喝采

❶ We all **cheered** for Howard as he neared the finish line.
當霍華接近終點線時，我們齊聲歡呼。

❷ The good news **cheered** him up, giving him hope and encouragement. 這個好消息令他振奮，給他帶來希望和鼓勵。

❸ The audience **cheered** as the ballerina finished her performance; everyone clapped and shouted "Bravo!"
當芭蕾女伶完成表演時，觀眾齊聲喝采。每個人都拍手大喊「太棒了」。

❹ When the superstar appeared on the stage, a **cheer** went up from the audience. 當那名超級巨星出現在舞台上的時候，觀眾發出了歡呼聲。

相關片語 **cheer up** 振作起來

- Cheer up! Everything will be all right. 振作起來！一切都會沒事的。

10 **chore** [tʃor] 名 C ❶ **日常工作，例行工作；❷ 討厭的工作**

❶ Watering plants in the garden is one of Nathan's daily **chores**.
幫花園的植物澆水，是南森每天都要做的事。

❷ The cook complained that plucking chickens is really a **chore**; she said it is time-consuming and boring.
廚師嚷嚷說給雞拔毛真是麻煩，既花時間又無聊。

11 **classification** [͵klæsəfəˋkeʃən] 名 U **分類，分級**

- class 等級
- -ify 動 表「使……化」
- -ation 名 表「動作」

- The college uses a student **classification** system to determine tuition payments; for example, graduate students pay more than undergraduate students.
學院用分級制度將學生分等，來決定學費。例如，研究生的學費就比大學生貴。

12 **classify** [ˋklæsə͵faɪ] 動 **將……分類，將……分等級**

- class 等級
- -ify 動 表「使……化」

- How should I **classify** these photos, by location or by subject? 我要怎麼把這些照片分類，是要依地點還是主題來分？

13 **combine** [kəmˋbaɪn] 動 ❶ **使結合；❷ 結合**

❶ Virginia has **combined** her previous writings with her drawings in this new publication.
維吉妮雅在她的新書中放進她以前的的文字創作，並結合了她的插畫作品。

❷ The two small hospitals will **combine** to form one large facility.
這兩間小醫院將合併成一間大醫院。

用法 combine A with B 把 A 和 B 結合

16

14 **command** [kəˋmænd] ❶ 動 **命令** 名 ❷ C **命令；**
❸ U **指揮，控制；❹ U 掌握，運用能力**

❶ The teacher **commanded** her students to stand up.
老師命令學生們都站起來。

❷ The troops withdrew when the general gave the **command**.
那位將軍的一聲下令，部隊撤退了。

❸ The lieutenant has 500 men under his **command**.
這名中尉指揮 500 個人。

❹ Miss Lin was assigned as an oral interpreter to the visiting American delegation because of her strong **command** of both Chinese and English.
林老師的中英文能力都很好，所以被指派擔任來訪美國代表團的口譯工作。

15 **conference** [ˋkɑnfərəns] 名 C 會議，討論會

・confer 動 協商
・-ence 名 表「行動」

● Scholars and experts from all over the world have been invited to attend this year's **conference** on drug control.
世界各地的學者和專家都受邀參加今年的年度藥物控制會議。

16 **connect** [kəˋnɛkt] 動 ❶ 連接，連結；❷ 聯想

❶ Do you know how to **connect** a DVD player to your television?
你知道怎麼把 DVD 播放器連到電視上嗎？

❷ Some people **connect** black cats with bad luck.
有些人將黑貓與厄運做聯想。

用法 connect A with B　把 A 和 B 聯想在一起

17 **connection** [kəˋnɛkʃən] 名 ❶ U 連接；聯絡；❷ C 關係，關聯

・connect 動 連接
・-ion 名 表「行為」

❶ There is something wrong with my Internet **connection**. I can't get online.
我的網路連接有問題，我不能上網。

❷ Cynthia believes there is a **connection** between her skin disease and the stress she's been under. 辛希雅認為，她的皮膚疾病和心理壓力有關。

18 **consult** [kənˋsʌlt] 動 ❶ 與……商議，請教；❷ 查閱（詞典等）

❶ The man **consulted** his lawyer because he needed advice.
那名男子向他的律師請益，尋求建議。

❷ The student kept **consulting** the reference book as he read the textbook. 那個學生在讀課本時，會不斷地查閱參考書。

19 **cooperate** [koˋɑpəˏret] 動 合作，協力

・co- 表「一起」
・operate 工作；運作

● They **cooperated** and got the job done on time. If they hadn't worked together, they wouldn't have made the deadline.
他們同心協力將工作準時完成。如果他們沒有分工合作，就無法在期限內完成。

20 **cooperation** [koˏɑpəˋreʃən] 名 U 合作，協力

・cooperate 合作
・-ation 名 表「狀態」

● The police asked for the community's **cooperation** in catching the robbers as quickly as possible.
警方要求社區與警方合作，以便盡快抓出搶匪。

21 **cooperative** [koˋɑpəˏretɪv] 形 ❶ 合作的；❷ 樂意合作的

> ‧cooperate 合作
> ‧-ative 形 表「有……性質的」

❶ This **cooperative** activity will help the students learn to work together toward a shared goal.
團隊合作可以幫助學生學習如何齊心合作，與他人一同完成共同目標。

❷ According to the police, the suspect is being very **cooperative**. He let them search his home and has given them all the information they wanted. 根據警方的說法，這名嫌疑犯非常合作，他讓警方搜索他的住家，並且供出所有警方想知道的細節。

22 **cope** [kop] 動 對付，妥善處理　同義 manage 處理

● To **cope** with the stress of spending long hours in heavy traffic, Mr. Oreal drinks a lot of coffee.
為了應付交通巔峰時的長程開車，歐瑞爾先生喝了很多咖啡。

23 **council** [ˋkaʊnsḷ] 名 C 會議，議會

● The student **council** meets every Thursday evening.
學生會議於每週四晚上召開。

24 **creation** [krɪˋeʃən] 名 ❶ C 創作品；❷ U 創造，創立

> ‧create 動 創造
> ‧-ion 名 表「行為的結果」

❶ According to the Bible, the **creation** of the world took exactly seven days.
根據《聖經》的記載，七天創造了世界。

❷ Are you familiar with the latest **creations** of the top fashion designers in Paris? 你熟悉巴黎頂尖設計師最新的時裝作品嗎？

25 **deed** [did] 名 C ❶ 行為；❷ 功業，功績　同義 act 行為

❶ Eli did a good **deed** by helping his mother carry the groceries into the house. 伊萊表現良好，他幫媽媽把採購回來的東西搬進屋裡。

❷ The young man rushed into the burning house to save the little girl. What a brave **deed**!
這名年輕男子衝進起火的房子裡，搶救一個小女孩。好英勇啊！

26 **devote** [dɪˋvot] 動 把……奉獻於，致力於

● Gloria has **devoted** much effort to the study of African history.
葛蘿麗亞致力於研究非洲歷史。

用法 devot to something/devote to V-ing 把……奉獻給

27 **discipline** [ˋdɪsəplɪn] 名 ❶ U 紀律；❷ C 學科 動 ❸ 訓練，訓導

- disciple 信徒
- -ine 名 表「具有……屬性的」

❶ Soldiers generally have good **discipline**; they are trained to obey rules and orders.
這些士兵紀律良好，他們被訓練要服從規定和命令。

❷ The **discipline** of anthropology involves the study of human cultures. 人類學這門學科研究人類的文化。

❸ Parents should **discipline** their children by establishing rules and punishing them when they misbehave.
父母應該訂立一些規範來教育孩子，並且懲罰孩子的不當行為。

09 Activities
活動 (3)

17

01 **disconnect** [ˏdɪskəˋnɛkt] 動 切斷（電話、電源）

- dis- 不
- connect 連接

- John had failed to pay his phone bills for months, so his telephone was **disconnected** last week.
約翰好幾個月沒有繳電話費了，所以他的電話上個星期被切斷了。

02 **discovery** [dɪsˋkʌvərɪ] 名 ❶ U 發現；❷ C 被發現的事物

- dis- 除去
- cover 遮蓋
- -y 名 表「狀態」

❶ An infant was found dead in the bushes. The **discovery** of the body shocked the whole neighborhood. 樹叢裡發現了一名死嬰。這個發現震驚了整個社區。

❷ Throughout history, new scientific **discoveries** have changed people's beliefs. 綜觀整個歷史，科學上的新發現改變了人們的信仰。

03 **disguise** [dɪsˋgaɪz] 動 ❶ 掩飾，隱瞞；❷ 把……假扮起來
名 ❸ U 假裝，掩飾；❹ U 假扮，偽裝

- dis- 除去
- guise 裝束

❶ The widow tried not to cry in public; she wanted to **disguise** her sorrow so her relatives wouldn't worry about her.
那名遺孀不想當眾哭泣，她想掩飾自己的悲傷，以免親人擔心。

❷ The spy **disguised** himself as a woman; he changed his appearance so he could slip by the guards unnoticed.
間諜把自己喬裝成女人，他改變了外型以躲過警衛的注意。

❸ Angeline met her future husband after being stranded at the airport; she realized later that the cancelled flight had been a blessing in **disguise**. 安裘琳被困在機場時，認識了她未來的丈夫。她後來明白當時班機的取消，實則是一種賜福。

❹ The rock star left the hotel in **disguise** so that none of the fans gathering at the entrance would recognize him.
搖滾巨星喬裝離開飯店，所以聚集在門口的粉絲都沒認出他來。

04 **dismiss** [dɪsˋmɪs] 動 ❶ 解散；❷ 解雇，開除；❸ 去除或打消（念頭）

❶ The teacher always **dismisses** the class on time so that she can pick up her child. 那位老師一向準時下課，以便她去接自己的小孩。

❷ Two days after Edmund was **dismissed** from his job, he found another position. 艾德蒙被開除兩天之後，找到了另一份工作。

❸ We **dismissed** the idea of buying a new car, as we simply couldn't afford it. 我們打消了買新車的念頭，因為我們就是買不起。

05 **distribute** [dɪˋstrɪbjʊt] 動 ❶ 分配，分發；❷ 散布，分布

- dis- 分開
- trubute 貢物，貢金

❶ During the war, food and resources were **distributed** by the military. 在戰爭期間，食物和資源都由軍方配給。

❷ Cases of H1N1 flu were widely **distributed** throughout Mexico; before long, the disease had spread all over the world.
H1N1 流感案例在墨西哥分布很廣。這個疾病很快也傳到全世界。

06 **distribution** [ˌdɪstrəˋbjuʃən] 名 U ❶ 分發，分配；❷ 分布（區域）；❸ 銷售（量）

- distrubute 分配
- -ion 名 表「行為」

❶ Many volunteers helped with the **distribution** of supplies; soon, every quake victim had something to eat.
許多志工來幫忙分配救援物資。很快地每一位地震災民都拿到食物了。

❷ The scholar is studying population **distribution** in India; she is hoping to find a pattern in the population clusters.
這位學者正在研究印度的人口分布，她想找出印度人口的聚集模式。

❸ Gregory is quite satisfied with the **distribution** of his new book.
葛列格里對自己的新書銷量很滿意。

07 **disturb** [dɪsˋtɝb] 動 ❶ 打擾，妨礙；❷ 使心神不寧，使不安

❶ The loud bursts of thunder **disturbed** Alyson as she tried to fall asleep on the sofa. 愛莉森躺在沙發上快睡著時，一陣轟轟的打雷聲驚醒了她。

❷ The mother was **disturbed** to hear that her son had skipped the tutoring session; she worried that he was going to fail the exam.
母親聽到兒子沒參加課輔班的消息很擔心，她很怕他考試會考不過。

08 **dominate** [ˋdɑməˌnet] 動 ❶ 支配，主導；❷ 在…… 占主要地位

❶ Marshall thinks he is a leader because he usually **dominates** the conversation. 馬歇爾以為自己是領導者，因為他老愛主導談話內容。

❷ Computer games have **dominated** the teenager's life; he seems to think there is nothing more important than role-playing online.
電玩主宰了這名年輕人的生活，他認為似乎沒有什麼事會比線上遊戲來得更重要。

09 **doze** [doz] ❶ 名 C **瞌睡** ❷ 動 **打瞌睡**

❶ Henry likes to have a **doze** in the afternoon.
亨利喜歡在下午小憩一下。

❷ The student was so sleepy that he **dozed** off during class.
那名學生很睏，所以就在課堂上打起瞌睡了。

10 **dye** [daɪ] ❶ 動 **把⋯⋯染上顏色** ❷ 名 U **染料**

❶ Although my mother's hair is silvery now, she is going to **dye** it black. 我媽的頭髮現在變白了，所以她要去把頭髮染黑。

❷ Claudia used fabric **dye** to change the color of her tablecloth from white to blue and orange.
克勞蒂雅用染布顏料，把白色桌布染成藍橘相間的顏色。

11 **eliminate** [ɪˋlɪməˏnet] 動 ❶ **棄置，消除；**❷ **消除，消滅**

❶ Pamela is determined to **eliminate** all the contaminants in her house before summer arrives.
潘蜜拉下定決心，要在夏天來臨之前，把家中所有的汙染物都清掉。

❷ Their goal is to **eliminate** war, famine, and disease and bring happiness to all human beings.
他們的目標是消除戰爭、飢荒和疾病，並為全人類帶來幸福。

相關用法 名 **elimination** 消除

- The drug has contributed to the prevention of the epidemic as well as the elimination of the disease. 這種藥物幫助了流行病的防疫，也幫助了疾病的消除。

12 **encounter** [ɪnˋkaʊntɚ] 動 ❶ **遇到（困難等）；**❷ **意外遇見** ❸ 名 C **偶遇**

❶ After **encountering** and overcoming many obstacles, Ms. Orman finally launched her career as a professional dog trainer.
沃曼小姐在遭遇並克服許多障礙後，終於成為職業訓犬師。

❷ In the hospital, Claire **encountered** an old friend; she hadn't expected to see him there.
克萊兒在醫院裡碰到一位老朋友，她沒想到會在那裡看到他。

❸ The movie documents a man's extraordinary **encounters** with Alaskan brown bears. He lives among the bears for many years while studying their habits. 電影記錄了一名男子與阿拉斯加棕熊的奇異邂逅，男子與棕熊共處了好幾年，研究牠們的習性。

13 **engage** [ɪnˋgedʒ] 動 ❶ 從事；❷ 使訂婚

・en- 表「使」
・gage 擔保品

❶ Della is **engaged** in the study of international folk music. 黛拉從事世界民俗音樂的研究。

❷ Beatrice is **engaged** to Cary; they plan to get married next month. 碧翠斯與開瑞訂婚了；他們計畫下個月結婚。

用法 engage oneself in = be engaged in 從事於

18

14 **engagement** [ɪnˋgedʒmənt] 名 C 訂婚，婚約

・engage 使訂婚
・-ment 名 表「行為」

● Soon after the young couple decided to get married, they announced their **engagement** to their families.
這對年輕人決定結婚後，很快就向家人宣布他們的婚約。

15 **entry** [ˋɛntrɪ] 名 ❶ U 進入，參加；❷ C 入口

❶ Many countries supported Taiwan's **entry** into the World Health Organization and welcomed the Taiwanese as members of the international agency.
許多國家支持台灣加入世界衛生組織，成為這個國際組織的一員。

❷ The **entry** to Rose's castle was hidden by trees and huge rocks.
蘿絲的城堡大門隱藏在樹林和巨石堆中。

16 **errand** [ˋɛrənd] 名 C 差事，任務

● Wilbert has to run a couple of **errands** before picking up his daughter from school. 韋柏特在去接女兒放學前，還有幾件事要先去處理。

17 **establish** [əˋstæblɪʃ] 動 建立，創辦　名 establishment 建立，創立

● Using only donations, Ms. Hughes **established** the first hospital in this remote area. 休斯小姐單靠慈善捐款，就在這個偏遠地區建了第一間醫院。

18 **establishment** [ɪˋstæblɪʃmənt] 名 ❶ U 建立，創辦；❷ C 公司，機關，企業

・establish 動 建立
・-ment 名 表「行為」

❶ Two years ago, Aldrich set up a computer company; he spent most of his savings on the **establishment** of the business. 奧地奇兩年前開了電腦公司，把他大部分的積蓄都投資在這項事業上面。

❷ For more than 100 years, this **establishment** has offered the finest stinky tofu in all of Asia. 一百多年來，這家公司提供全亞洲最好的臭豆腐。

19 **expand** [ɪkˋspænd] 動 ❶ 膨脹；❷ 擴張，發展；❸ 擴大，擴展

❶ Raymond blew air into the balloon, and it **expanded** until it popped. 雷蒙吹氣球，將氣球吹到脹破。

❷ Ms. Li's business **expanded** very quickly. She opened her first store two years ago; now she has 50 stores all over the country. 李女士的事業迅速擴展，她在兩年前開了第一家店，現在她在全國各地已經擁有 50 家分店了。

❸ They are considering **expanding** their business by opening 10 more stores in Taipei. 他們正考慮在台北多開十家分店，以擴大營業。

20 **expansion** [ɪkˋspænʃən] 名 U 擴張，擴展

- expanse 廣闊區域
- -ion 名 表「行為」

● Lee proposed a city regulation that would limit further industrial **expansion**.
李提議制訂都市法規來限制工業區的進一步擴張。

21 **explore** [ɪkˋsplor] 動 ❶ 探勘，在……探險；❷ 探索，探究

❶ A group of scientists are **exploring** the jungle in order to learn more about its inhabitants.
一群科學家正在叢林中探險，期待能更深入了解棲地動物。

❷ Mr. Pierson, an astronomer, loves to **explore** new galaxies in the universe. 皮爾森先生是一位天文學家，喜愛探索宇宙間的新銀河。

22 **found** [faʊnd] 動 ❶ 建立，創立，創辦；❷ 將……建立在

❶ The group **founded** a college in 2009 and established a hospital the following year.
這個集團在 2009 年創辦了一間大學，在隔年又興建了一家醫院。

❷ Martin's theory of love is **founded** on the idea that the more we give, the more we receive.
馬汀對愛的看法，是建立在「給予的愈多，得到的就愈多」這種想法基礎上。

23 **fulfill** [fʊlˋfɪl] 動 履行（諾言等），實現

- full 充分
- fill 裝滿

● Yesterday Herbert's father **fulfilled** his promise to take the boy to the amusement park.
小男孩赫伯特的父親，昨天依約帶他去遊樂園玩。

24 **fulfillment** [fʊlˋfɪlmənt] 名 U ❶ 履行，實現；❷ 成就（感），滿足（感）

- fulfill 履行
- -ment 名 表「行為」

❶ After 10 years of effort, Harriet finally achieved the **fulfillment** of her dream.
經過十年的努力，荷莉特終於實現了她的夢想。

❷ Men tend to look for **fulfillment** and satisfaction in their work.
人傾向在工作中尋找成就感和滿足感。

25 **funeral** [ˋfjunərəl] 名 C **喪葬，葬禮**

- Thousands of people attended the popular singer's **funeral**.
  數千人參加了那位流行歌手的葬禮。

26 **grind** [graɪnd] 動 **磨（碎），碾（碎）**

- Where can I go to **grind** these coffee beans?
  我可以去哪裡磨這些咖啡豆？

27 **habitual** [həˋbɪtʃʊəl] 形 **習慣的，習以為常的**

- Catherine's **habitual** thoroughness is often praised by her friends. 凱瑟琳一向很細心，朋友們常常誇讚她這一點。

・habit 習慣
・-al 形 表「……的」

10 Activities 活動 (4)

19

01 **housework** [ˋhaʊsˏwɝk] 名 U **家事**

- Brandon's mother takes care of the **housework**, while his father works for a non-profit foundation.
  布蘭登的母親在家料理家務，父親則在一家非營利基金會上班。

・house 房子
・work 工作

02 **identify** [aɪˋdɛntəˏfaɪ] 動 ❶ **視……（與……）為同一事物**；❷ **確認，識別**

❶ Lamar began to **identify** with the main character in the novel, who also suffered from depression and anxiety.
拉馬開始能認同小說中的主角，那名主角也為憂鬱症和焦慮症所苦。

・identity 身分
・-fy 動 表「形成；使……化」

❷ The witnesses **identified** the man as the killer. They recognized him right away when the police showed them the photos.
目擊證人指認那名男子就是殺人犯。證人們在警方拿出照片時，立即就認出了兇手。

03 **imitate** [ˋɪməˏtet] 動 **模仿**

- Stephanie's classmates love it when she **imitates** their teachers.
  史蒂芬妮的同學都很喜歡看她模仿老師們的樣子。

04 **imitation** [ˏɪməˋteʃən] 名 ❶ U **模仿**；❷ C **仿製品，贗品**

❶ Children learn by **imitation**; they usually copy their parents' actions. 小孩子藉由模仿學習走路。他們通常會模仿父母的動作。

・imitate 模仿
・-ion 名 表「行為」

❷ When **imitations** of brand-name products look close to the real thing, consumers are often confused.
名牌的仿冒品看起來很像真品，讓消費者分不太出來。

05 **immigrate** [ˋɪmə͵gret] 動 遷移，遷入

- im- 表「向……內」
- migrate 移居

● In 1949, my parents **immigrated** to Taiwan from mainland China because of the war; they eventually settled in Taipei. 因為戰爭，我的父母在 1949 年從中國大陸遷到台灣，並定居於台北。

06 **immigration** [͵ɪməˋgreʃən] 名 U 移居

- immigrate 遷移
- -ion 名 表「行為」

● Increased **immigration** has strengthened the vitality of our society. 移民人口增加，讓我們的社會更具活力。

07 **incident** [ˋɪnsədn̩t] 名 C 事件，事故

- in- 表「在內」
- cid 表「落」
- -ent 名 表「做……動作的物」

● Deanna didn't tell anyone about the **incident** in which she lost her diary.
笛安娜沒有跟任何人說她昨天掉了日記本的事情。

08 **input** [ˋɪnpʊt] 名 U 投入

- in- 表「入」
- put 放

● Johnny appreciated his fans' valuable **input** on his latest novel. 強尼感謝粉絲對他最新小說的熱情投入。

09 **inspect** [ɪnˋspɛkt] 動 ❶ 檢查，審查；❷ 視察

❶ The engineer is **inspecting** the machine; he is examining it carefully to find out what's wrong with it.
技師正在檢查機器。他仔細地檢查，以找出問題到底出在哪裡。

❷ As an officer in the Department of Health, Ms. Preston regularly **inspects** local restaurants.
普斯頓小姐是衛生局的官員，必須定期視察當地的餐廳。

10 **inspection** [ɪnˋspɛkʃən] 名 C 檢查，檢驗

- inspect 檢查
- -ion 名 表「行為」

● In preparation for the factory's annual **inspection**, all employees were ordered to clean their workspaces. 在工廠年度審查之前，所有員工必須清理工作空間。

11 **install** [ɪnˋstɔl] 動 安裝，設置　名 installation 安裝

- in- 表「入；裡面」
- stall 欄，廄

● Tami is going to **install** an air conditioner in her bedroom before summer. 在夏天之前，妲咪要在自己的臥室裡裝一台冷氣機。

12 **interact** [ˌɪntəˋrækt] 動 ❶ 互動；❷ 互相作用，互相影響

・inter- 表「互相」
・act 動作；作用

❶ Kaitlin enjoys **interacting** with children and observing their growth. 凱琳喜歡與孩子互動，並且觀察孩子們的成長情形。

❷ The scientist is observing how the two chemicals **interact**. 這名科學家正在觀察這兩種化學物質如何交互作用。

13 **interaction** [ˌɪntəˋrækʃən] 名 U ❶ 互相影響；❷ 互動

・interact 互動
・-ion 名 表「行為」

❶ The study suggests that close **interaction** between teachers and students can improve the quality of education. 這份研究顯示師生之間的緊密互動，可以幫助改善教學品質。

❷ The researchers are studying the **interaction** of the chemicals with the environment and the effects on human health. 研究人員正在研究這些化學物質與環境的相互影響，以及對人類健康的影響。

14 **interfere** [ˌɪntɚˋfɪr] 動 ❶ 妨礙，干擾；❷ 介入，干涉

❶ In Taiwan, use of electronic devices is prohibited on domestic flights because it **interferes** with communications between the pilots and the control tower. 在台灣，國內線班機上禁止使用電子儀器，因為會干擾機師與塔台之間的通訊。

❷ Stop **interfering**; do not try to influence something that does not concern you! 不要再涉入了，不要想去影響和你無關的事情。

15 **introduction** [ˌɪntrəˋdʌkʃən] 名 ❶ U 引進，傳入；❷ C 介紹，正式引見；❸ C 引言，序言

・introduce 引進
・-tion 名 表「行為」

❶ Until the **introduction** of horses and guns, Native Americans hunted with spears, clubs, and bows. 在馬匹和槍枝的引進之前，北美原住民的打獵工具是矛、棍棒和弓箭。

❷ The lecturer needs no **introduction**; he is already well-known to the students. 這位演講者不需要介紹，所有的學生都認識他。

❸ The essay's **introduction** gives a general idea of what is to follow. 這篇論文的序言大略說明接下來要談論的東西。

補充 self-introduction 自我介紹

20

16 **investigate** [ɪnˋvɛstəˌget] 動 調查，研究

・in- 表「向內」
・vestige 痕跡
・-ate 動 表「使成為」

● Dr. Anna Brown and her colleagues have been **investigating** the causes of cancer for many years. 安娜．布朗博士和同僚已經研究致癌原因很多年了。

17 **investigation** [ɪnˌvɛstəˋgeʃən] 名 ❶ C 研究，調查；❷ U 研究，調查

❶ The police captain ordered an **investigation** of the accident to determine its cause.
警長下令對這起意外事件展開調查，要找出肇事原因。

· investigate 調查
· -ion 名 表「行為」

❷ The murder case is under **investigation**; the police have not found the murder weapon. 這起凶殺案還在調查中；警方尚未找到兇器。

18 **manners** [ˋmænɚz] 名（複）❶ 禮貌，規矩；❷ 風俗，習慣

· manus 手
· -er 名 表「物」
· -s（複數）

❶ It is considered bad **manners** to talk with your mouth full. 嘴巴塞滿食物講話是很失禮的。

❷ To learn more about a country, you should study the people's customs and **manners**. 為了深入了解一個國家，你應該要研究人民的風俗習慣。

19 **mischief** [ˋmɪstʃɪf] 名 U ❶ 頑皮，淘氣，惡作劇；❷ 傷害，損害

❶ These schoolchildren are full of **mischief**; they often play tricks on their teacher. 這些學童很喜歡惡作劇，他們常常捉弄老師。

· mis- 表「壞，不當」
· chief 表「頭腦」

❷ The **mischief** caused by the teens included a broken mailbox, a damaged lawn, and overturned garbage cans. 那些青少年破壞的東西包括打壞一個郵筒、破壞一塊草地，以及推倒了幾個垃圾桶。

20 **mow** [mo] 動 刈，刈草；割（草）　名 mower 刈草者

● Francis earns money by **mowing** his neighbors' lawns on the weekends. 法蘭西斯靠週末時幫鄰居割草來賺外快。

21 **nap** [næp] ❶ 名 C 打盹兒，午睡　❷ 動 打盹，小睡

❶ In Latin countries, people take a **nap**, called "a siesta," in the early afternoon. 在拉丁語系國家，人們會在午後打個盹，這叫做「希耶斯塔」。

❷ After lunch, my dad **napped** on the sofa. 午餐過後，我爸爸在沙發上打盹。

22 **neglect** [nɪgˋlɛkt] 動 ❶ 忽略，忽視；❷ 疏忽；❸ 忘了做
名 U ❹ 忽略，疏忽

❶ The old house has been **neglected** for a long time. Its window frames and wooden doors are decaying.
這間老房子被遺棄已久，窗框和木門都快腐朽了。

❷ Although Jeffrey had to work two part-time jobs to support his family, he never **neglected** his studies. In fact, he graduated with honors.
雖然傑佛瑞要打兩份工養家，但他沒荒廢學業。事實上，他以優等成績畢業。

❸ Alfredo has **neglected** to weed his garden for several weeks.
奧弗瑞多已經好幾個星期忘記幫花園除草了。

❹ After 10 years of **neglect**, the hut collapsed.
小屋被棄置十年之後倒塌了。

23 **negotiate** [nɪˋgoʃɪˏet] 動 ❶ 通過談判達成，談成；❷ 談判，協商，洽談

❶ Allen **negotiated** his compensation for the job over the phone. 艾倫透過電話商談他的工作薪資。

❷ To put an end to the strike, the management will **negotiate** with the laborers; they hope to reach an agreement quickly.
為了要讓罷工趕快落幕，資方將與勞方談判；雙方希望可以盡快達成協議。

24 **observation** [ˏɑbzɝˋveʃən] 名 C ❶ 觀察；❷ 言論，意見，看法

❶ Dr. Liu's new book contains his **observations** of daily life among tribal societies in Africa.
劉博士的新書，是他對非洲部落人民日常生活的觀察集結。

- observe 觀察
- -ation 名 表「動作」

❷ Mr. Rainey frequently publishes his **observations** on the global economy. 雷尼先生頻頻對全球經濟發表看法。

25 **observe** [əbˋzɝv] 動 ❶ 看到，注意到；❷ 觀察，觀測；❸ 遵守，奉行；❹ 慶祝（節日等）

❶ Emily **observed** that her parents' relationship was improving.
愛蜜莉注意到爸媽的關係正在改善當中。

❷ Before writing a report on the stars, we decided to **observe** the sky every night for a week.
為了寫星星的報告，我們決定每天晚上都觀察夜空，並持續一星期。

❸ Every citizen must **observe** the laws; anyone who breaks them will be punished.
每一位公民都應該遵守法律，任何違反法律的人都會受到懲處。

❹ Most people in the United States **observe** Christmas; some of them celebrate the holiday by having a party.
在美國，大部分的人都過耶誕節，有些人還會舉辦派對來慶祝。

26 **obtain** [əbˋten] 動 得到，獲得

● Nelly **obtained** several research grants during her years as an academic. 乃麗在大學時，曾經獲得過幾個研究補助金。

27 **overcome** [ˌovɚˋkʌm] 動 ❶ 戰勝，克服；❷ 壓倒，使受不了

❶ Selina had to **overcome** her shyness in order to speak in front of the whole school.
瑟琳娜必須要克服怯場，才能在全校面前演講。

❷ At the funeral, the widow was **overcome** with grief; she couldn't stop crying. 遺孀在喪禮上悲痛不已，淚水潰堤。

- over- 表「超越，越過」
- come 到達

28 **overlook** [ˌovɚˋlʊk] 動 ❶ 看漏，忽略；❷ 眺望，俯瞰

- over- 表「在上」
- look 看

❶ After Violet **overlooked** a major problem in her company, she suffered a great loss.
薇兒莉因為忽略了公司的一個大問題，因而遭受重大損失。

❷ There used to be a castle on the hill **overlooking** the city.
過去這座山丘上有一座城堡，俯瞰著整個城市。

29 **parade** [pəˋred] 名 C ❶ 遊行；❷ 閱兵（典禮） ❸ 動 遊行，列隊行進

❶ Cecilia made her own costume to wear in the Halloween **parade**.
賽西莉亞穿著自己設計的服裝參加萬聖節遊行。

❷ On National Day, the president inspected the military **parade**.
國慶日當天，總統檢閱了閱兵。

❸ As the soldiers **paraded** past, the president applauded.
當士兵列隊行進通過，總統拍手鼓掌。

30 **participate** [pɑrˋtɪsəˌpet] 動 參加，參與

- part 部分
- cipate 表「拿，取」

● Ruth **participated** in a scientific study of herbal medicines. 露絲參與了草藥的科學研究。

31 **participation** [pɑrˌtɪsəˋpeʃən] 名 U 參加，參與

- participate 參加
- -ion 名 表「行為」

● Your **participation** in the discussion was much appreciated, and we hope you'll join us again next year.
我們很感激你們這次前來參與討論，希望你們明年能再來參加。

11 Activities 活動 (5)

21

01 **preparation** [ˌprɛpəˋreʃən] 名 ❶ C 準備工作；❷ U 準備，預備

- prepare 動 準備
- -ation 名 表「動作」

❶ All of the **preparations** for Annie's wedding must be done by tomorrow.
安妮的婚禮務必在明天做好所有的準備工作。

❷ The cook sharpens her knife in **preparation** for cutting the fish. She also greases the pans so they are ready for baking.
廚師把刀磨利，準備切魚。她也把鍋底塗上油做好烘烤的準備。

02 **presentation** [ˌprɛznˋteʃən] 名 ❶ U 提出，遞交；❷ U 贈送，授予；❸ C 報告

- present 動 提出
- -ation 名 表「動作」

❶ The **presentation** of new evidence changed the court's decision. 新證據的提出，改變了法庭的判決。

❷ The **presentation** of prizes began right after the contest; Phil was awarded first prize. 比賽結束後直接進行頒獎；由菲爾摘冠。

❸ During the meeting, the manager gave a **presentation** on the new cell phone and demonstrated its functions.
在會議上，經理針對新款手機做了簡報，並且示範了手機的功能。

03 **preservation** [ˌprɛzɚˋveʃən] 名 U 保持，維護，維持

- preserve 動 保存
- -ation 名 表「動作」

● The local government has spent a lot of money on the **preservation** of the old church, so it is still in good condition. 地方政府已經花了很多錢維護這座老教堂，所以教堂的狀態仍維持良好。

04 **pretend** [prɪˋtɛnd] 動 ❶ 假裝，佯稱；❷（在遊戲中）假扮，裝作；❸ 假裝，裝模作樣

- pre- 表「預先」
- tend 傾向

❶ Hector **pretended** he was innocent, but he actually planned the whole robbery. 赫克特裝無辜，但事實上整起搶案都是他策劃的。

❷ Let's **pretend** that we are in the forest and there are many beasts around. 我們就假裝是在森林裡面，周圍有很多野獸。

❸ The boy isn't really sick; he is just **pretending**.
那個男孩並不是真的病了，他只是在裝病而已。

05 **prevent** [prɪˋvɛnt] 動 ❶ 防止，預防；❷ 阻止，制止　名 prevention 防止

❶ Ms. Mills believes the surest way to **prevent** war is to increase cultural exchanges. 密斯小姐相信要防止戰爭最可靠的方法，是增進文化交流。

❷ The bad weather **prevented** the friends from going on a picnic.
壞天氣讓幾個朋友無法去野餐。

用法 prevent something from V-ing/being p.p. 阻止，預防（某事發生）

06 **prevention** [prɪˋvɛnʃən] 名 U 預防，防止

- prevent 預防
- -ion 名 表「行為」

● Paris has done extensive research on the **prevention** of seasonal wildfires.
派里斯已經做完預防季節性野火的大規模研究。

07 **procedure** [prəˋsidʒɚ] 名 U 程序，手續，步驟

- pro- 表「先，前」
- cede 讓與
- -ure 名 表「動作」

● Benjamin is familiar with the **procedures** involved in opening a new restaurant.
班傑明熟悉開新餐廳所需的流程。

08 **process** [ˋprɑsɛs] 名 C ❶ 過程；❷ 步驟 動 ❸ 處理 名 procession 過程

❶ Repetition plays an important role in the learning **process**.
在學習的過程中，「重複」扮演重要的角色。

❷ They are using a new **process** to make wine.
他們正在用一種新的步驟製造葡萄酒。

❸ The data are being **processed** by the computer. 數據正在經電腦處理中。

補充 processed food 加工食品

09 **protection** [prəˋtɛkʃən] 名 U 保護

- protect 保護
- -ion 名 表「行為」

● These thick waterproof coats offer complete **protection** against the cold and rain.
這些厚實又防水的大衣能隔絕寒冷和雨水，提供完全的保護。

10 **protective** [prəˋtɛktɪv] 形 ❶ 保護的，防護的；❷（對人）關切保護的

- protect 保護
- -ive 形 表「……的」

❶ All the factory workers have to wear **protective** gloves to prevent injuries from the chemicals.
在這間工廠裡，所有的工人都要帶防護手套，以避免雙手被化學藥品弄傷。

❷ Chinese parents are usually very **protective** of their children. They want to make sure their children are safe and well cared for at all times. 華人父母通常很保護小孩。他們想要確保小孩安全無虞且受到良好照顧。

11 **pursue** [pɚˋsu] 動 ❶ 從事，繼續；❷ 追求（目標等）；❸ 追蹤，追捕；❹ 向……求愛

❶ After Paul graduated from college, he decided to **pursue** his studies abroad. 保羅在大學畢業後，決定到國外留學。

❷ The dancer has spent years **pursuing** his goal—achieving perfection. 這名舞者幾年以來都在追求他的目標——臻至完美。

❸ The police **pursued** the killer on foot; they followed him into the forest before catching him.
警方正徒步追捕那名殺人犯。為了逮捕他，警方尾隨進入了森林。

❹ Willard has been **pursuing** Sue for months, but he has never gotten a date with her. 威勒德追蘇追了好幾個月，但都沒能成功約他出來。

12 **pursuit** [pɚˋsut] 名 U ❶ 追求；❷ 追蹤 動 pursue 追求

❶ Daryl has wasted her life in the meaningless **pursuit** of short-term pleasure. 達麗兒浪費生命去追求無意義的短暫歡樂。

❷ The two robbers took off with three policemen in **pursuit**; they were finally arrested several hours into the chase.
兩名搶犯逃逸，三名警察追捕在後。在數小時的追逐之後，終於將搶犯逮捕歸案。

22

13 **react** [rɪˋækt] 動 ❶ 作出反應；❷ 影響，起作用

- re- 表「互相」
- act 行動

❶ Ashley **reacted** calmly to the crisis and avoided a major conflict. 艾許莉冷靜面對危機，避免發生重大衝突。

❷ Nails get rusty because the iron **reacts** with oxygen in the air, creating rust. 因為鐵會在空氣中氧化，所以鐵釘會生鏽。

14 **reaction** [rɪˋækʃən] 名 C ❶ 反應；❷ 反作用

- react 作出反應
- -ion 名 表「行為」

❶ Jan yelled at me when I told him the news; I didn't expect such an angry **reaction**.
當我把消息告訴彥時，他對我大吼大叫；我沒想到他的反應會這麼大。

❷ Neta claims that every action has an equal and opposite **reaction**. 妮妲表示，每一個動作都會產生一個同樣大小的反作用力。

15 **reception** [rɪˋsɛpʃən] 名 C ❶ 接待會，歡迎會，宴會；❷（單數）接待，歡迎

❶ Stephen met his wife, Joyce, five years ago at his best friend's wedding **reception**. 史蒂芬五年前在死黨的婚宴上認識了妻子喬伊絲。

❷ The visitors had a warm **reception** when they reached the village. All the villagers sang and danced to welcome them.
參訪者抵達村莊時，受到了熱情的接待。所有的村民都以唱歌跳舞的方式來歡迎他們。

16 **recycle** [riˋsaɪkḷ] 動 使再循環，再利用

- re- 表「再；重新」
- cycle 循環

● Irene does not throw away used envelopes. She **recycles** them by writing telephone messages on the backs.
艾琳不把用過的信封丟掉。她將信封回收，用信封的背面來記錄電話留言。

17 **reform** [rɪˋfɔrm] ❶ 名 U 改革 ❷ 動 改革，革新

❶ The education **reform** that Florine proposed proved to be too radical; therefore, it failed. 芙洛琳提議的教改案顯然過於急進，終告失敗。

❷ After the terrorist attack, efforts were made to **reform** security measures in all airports. 在恐怖攻擊過後，所有機場都改革了安檢措施。

18 **refresh** [rɪˋfrɛʃ] 動 ❶ 消除疲勞，使重新提起精神；❷ 回復，喚起（記憶）

- re- 表「再」
- fresh 精力充沛的

❶ A cool shower always **refreshes** Dale after he works in the hot sun.
在大太陽底下工作幾個小時後，沖個冷水澡就能讓戴爾消除疲勞。

❷ Taking notes is a good habit, as it can help you **refresh** your memory. 作筆記是很好的習慣，可以幫助喚起記憶。

19 **register** [ˋrɛdʒɪstɚ] ❶ 動 註冊，登記❷ 名 C 登記，註冊 名 registration 登記

❶ Ferdinand is going to **register** the birth of his twin daughters today. 斐迪南今天要去辦理雙胞胎女兒的出生登記。

❷ Since you are not on the electoral **register**, you cannot vote in the election. 因為你不在選民名冊上，所以不能投票選舉。

20 **registration** [ˌrɛdʒɪˋstreʃən] 名 U 登記，註冊

- register 動 註冊
- -ation 名 表「動作」

● **Registration** for next semester will begin this Thursday. 下學期的註冊將從這星期四開始。

21 **renew** [rɪˋnju] 動 ❶ 更換（執照等）；❷ 重新開始，繼續；❸ 換新

- re- 表「再」
- new 新的

❶ Justina's passport is about to expire, so she should **renew** it as soon as possible.
賈絲汀娜的護照快過期了，她應該要盡快申請換發。

❷ After a 10-minute break, they **renewed** their efforts to finish the job before noon.
在十分鐘的短暫休息之後，他們繼續努力要在中午以前完成工作。

❸ Joaquin **renewed** the finish on the desk by applying a fresh coat of wax and polishing it until it gleamed.
沃昆用一層新的蠟來修補書桌的油漆，並將桌子磨到發亮。

22 **repair** [rɪˋpɛr] 動 ❶ 修理，修補；❷ 補救，糾正
名 ❸ U 修理，修補；❹ C 修理工作，修補工作

❶ Ken's roof needs to be **repaired** because it is leaking.
肯住的屋頂該修一修了，一直在漏水。

❷ Winston made a stupid mistake; now he is trying to **repair** the damage he caused.
溫士頓犯了一個愚蠢的錯誤，現在他在想辦法彌補他所造成的傷害。

❸ The earthquake damaged the bridge; it will need to be **repaired** before it can be used again.
地震對那座橋造成損害，需要修復後才能再度通行。

❹ Rain is dripping from a leak in the roof; **repairs** must be made before another typhoon hits.
雨水正從屋頂的裂縫滴下來，在下一個颱風來襲之前，一定要把屋頂修好。

23 **replace** [rɪˋples] 動 **取代，以……代替**

- re- 表「重新」
- place 地方

● After the recent rise in oil prices, scientists began searching for new energy resources to **replace** the fuel.
最近油價的上漲，使得科學家開始尋找替代石油的新能源。

用法 replace A with B　用 A 取代 B

24 **replacement** [rɪˋplesmənt] 名 ❶ Ⓤ **代替，更換**；❷ Ⓒ **代替者，代替物**

- replace 取代
- -ment 名 表「方法」

❶ Steward's car broke down several times on his way to the office; it is in need of **replacement**.
史都華德的車在他上班途中熄火好幾次，車子得換（引擎）了。

❷ Since the secretary quit unexpectedly, they had to rush to find a **replacement** for her. 因為祕書無預警地辭職，他們得趕緊找個人來補這個缺。

25 **represent** [ˏrɛprɪˋzɛnt] 動 ❶ **象徵**；❷ **代表**；❸ **意味著，相當於**

- re- 表「重新」
- present 呈現

❶ Ramon often wonders why the bald eagle **represents** the United States. 拉蒙常感到納悶：為什麼禿鷹會象徵美國？

❷ There are 154 foreign students at the university, **representing** 13 different countries.
這所大學裡一共有 154 位外國學生，代表 13 個不同的國家。

❸ The new discovery **represents** a major breakthrough in the field of cancer research. 這項新發現是癌症研究領域中的重大突破。

26 **representation** [ˏrɛprɪzɛnˋteʃən] 名 ❶ Ⓤ **代表，代表權**；❷ Ⓒ **表現，表示**

- represent 代表
- -ation 名 表「狀態」

❶ Environmental groups say they need more effective **representation** to speak and vote for them in parliament.
環保團體表示，他們需要更有力的代表能在國會上為他們發聲和投票。

❷ In the poem, red roses are a symbolic **representation** of passion and love. 在詩中，紅玫瑰是激情與愛情的象徵。

27 **rescue** [ˋrɛskjʊ] ❶ 名 U 援救，營救　❷ 動 援救，營救

❶ What is the latest news on the **rescue** of thousands of flood victims? 搶救數千名水患災民的行動有何最新進展？

❷ The firefighter successfully **rescued** the little girl from the burning house, but he regretted that he failed to save her mother. 消防隊員從失火的房子裡成功救出小女孩，但很遺憾沒能來得及救出女孩的媽媽。

12 Activities 活動 (6)

23

01 **research** [rɪˋsɝtʃ] ❶ 名 C 研究，調查　❷ 動 研究，調查

・re- 表「再」
・search 尋找

❶ More **research** is needed on the ancient artifacts discovered by Ms. Fuller in order to understand their importance. 富勒小姐所發現的古代手工藝品需要投入更多的研究，才能一探這些工藝品的重要性。

❷ Scientists are **researching** H1N1 cases, trying to uncover new facts about the disease. 科學家正在研究 H1N1 的病例，想對這個疾病有更多的了解。

02 **reservation** [͵rɛzɚˋveʃən] 名 C ❶ 預訂；❷（印第安）保留區

・re- 表「事先」
・serve 服務
・-ation 名 表「動作」

❶ Teresa made a **reservation** at an Italian restaurant for a special dinner tonight. 泰瑞莎在一家義式餐廳預訂了今晚的特別晚宴。

❷ Native American cultures and traditions can be experienced on the Indian **reservations**. 在印第安保留區裡，人們可以體驗印第安人的文化和傳統。

03 **reserve** [rɪˋzɝv] 名 C ❶ 保護區，禁獵區；❷ 儲藏量，儲備（物）
動 ❸ 儲備，保存；❹ 預約，預訂

・re- 表「事先」
・serve 服務

❶ No one can hunt in the wildlife **reserve**; all the wild animals here are protected. 沒有人可以在這個野生保護區打獵，這裡所有的野生動物都受到保護。

❷ Larry has a large **reserve** of food to make it through the winter. 賴瑞儲備大量食物，以便過冬。

❸ During the drought, people **reserved** as much water as possible for later use; they also stored food. 久旱無雨期間，人們盡可能把水儲存起來，以供日後使用；他們也會儲存食物。

❹ I have booked two tickets to New York and **reserved** a double room at the hotel. 我訂了兩張去紐約的機票，並在飯店訂了一間雙人房。

相關片語 **in reserve** 備用的

- Before the typhoon hit, my mother put some water in reserve in case we need it later. 在颱風來之前，我媽媽儲存了一些水來備用。

04 **resign** [rɪˋzaɪn] 動 ❶ 辭去；❷ 辭職　名 resignation 辭職

❶ Ms. Luther **resigned** from the board of directors yesterday.
昨天，路德小姐辭去了董事會的席位。

❷ The manager **resigned** without hesitation after he was offered a better job in a another company.
經理得到別家公司開出的更好工作條件之後，他就毫不猶豫地辭職了。

05 **resignation** [ˏrɛzɪgˋneʃən] 名 ❶ C 辭呈；❷ U 辭職

- resign 辭職
- -ation 名 表「動作」

❶ Francis has submitted his **resignation**, effective on the first of the month. 法蘭西斯遞出了辭呈，下個月一號離職生效。

❷ The president announced the **resignation** of the minister of foreign affairs. The deputy foreign minister is expected to succeed him. 總統宣布外交部長的請辭，據說將由外交部次長來接任。

06 **respond** [rɪˋspɑnd] 動 ❶ 作出反應；❷ 回覆，回答；❸ 以……回答

❶ Ian has **responded** to his professor's criticism by revising the project. 伊恩已經應教授的要求，修改了提案。

❷ I wrote a letter to Donald three days ago, but he has not **responded**. 我三天前寫了一封信給唐納德，但他還沒有回覆。

❸ When asked for his opinion of the incident, the politician **responded** that he had no comment.
當被問到對該事件的看法時，那名政治人物回答說他不予置評。

用法 respone to 回覆，回應

07 **response** [rɪˋspɑns] 名 C ❶ 回答，回覆；❷ 反應，回應

❶ Nicole offered no **response** to my inquiry. 妮可沒有回覆我的詢問。

❷ The speaker's words provoked an angry **response** from the audience; some of the people waved their fists in his face.
演講者的言論引起聽眾的憤怒反應，當中有一些人在他面前揮舞拳頭。

相關片語 **in response to** 對……的反應、回應

- The company keeps improving its products in response to customer demands. 這家公司持續改良產品，來回應消費者的需求。

08 **restore** [rɪˋstor] 動 ❶ 修復，修補；❷ 恢復

- re- 表「再，重新」
- store 貯存

❶ Anthony has **restored** his father's paintings to their original condition. 安東尼已經將父親的畫作都修復好了。

❷ Since the power has been **restored**, all employees should return to their desks. 因為又重新掌握了權力，所有員工都應該重回工作崗位。

09 **retire** [rɪˋtaɪr] 動 退休　名 retirement 退休

● Before Victor can **retire**, he must save enough money to support himself until he dies. 維克多在退休之前，必須存夠自己的養老金。

10 **retirement** [rɪˋtaɪrmənt] 名 U 退休

● Keith wants to take early **retirement**, so he has been saving as much money as he can.
基斯因為想盡早退休，所以一直盡可能地努力存錢。

- retire 退休
- -ment 名 表「狀態」

11 **reunion** [riˋjunjən] 名 C 團聚，重聚

● For our 50th college **reunion**, we gathered for a banquet. 我們為第 50 次的大學同學會，舉辦了一場宴會。

- re- 表「再」
- union 聯合

12 **reveal** [rɪˋvil] 動 ❶ 揭露，洩露；❷ 展現，顯露出　名 revelation 揭露

❶ Mrs. Leonard published a book **revealing** the president's secret operation. 李奧納多夫人出了一本書，揭露總統的祕辛。

❷ A crack between the door and the frame **revealed** a cozy bedroom. 從門縫中可見那是一間舒適的臥房。

13 **revenge** [rɪˋvɛndʒ] ❶ 名 U 報仇，報復　❷ 動 替……報仇

❶ Adolph took **revenge** on the gangster who had destroyed his fruit stand. 阿道夫對那名打爛他水果攤的流氓還以顏色。

❷ By killing his uncle, Hamlet **revenged** the death of his father.
哈姆雷特殺了叔父，報了殺父之仇。

24

14 **reward** [rɪˋwɔrd] 名 C ❶ 報答，報償，獎賞；❷ 酬金，獎品
動 ❸ 報答，報償，酬謝，獎勵

❶ Calvin's **reward** for his hard work was a weekend trip to his favorite spa for some rest and relaxation.
卡爾文週末要去泡他最喜愛的溫泉，好好休息放鬆，以犒賞自己的賣力工作。

❷ A $50,000 **reward** had been offered for information leading to the capture of the bank robbers.
警方宣布，凡提供消息協助逮捕銀行搶犯者，提供美金五萬元酬金。

❸ The winner of the talent show was **rewarded** with $1 million and a recording contract.
那個選秀節目的優勝者獲得了 100 萬元和一紙唱片合約的獎賞。

15 **routine** [ru`tin] ❶ 名 C 例行公事，日常工作 ❷ 形 日常的，例行的

❶ One of Dad's **routines** is to walk the dog after dinner.
父親每天一定要做的事，就是在晚餐後去遛狗。

❷ The worker is making a **routine** check of the machine; he has to do this twice a day. 工人正在對機器做例行檢查，他每天都得檢查兩次。

16 **sack** [sæk] 動 ❶ 裝……入袋；❷ 開除，解雇 ❸ 名 C 一袋（的量）

❶ Eleanor **sacked** up two bags of potatoes this morning and took them to the market to sell. 艾琳諾今早裝了兩袋馬鈴薯，運到市場去賣。

❷ The man was **sacked** last month, and he has not found a new job yet. 這名男子上個月被解雇了，他還沒有找到新工作。

❸ The farmer put four **sacks** of potatoes on the horse's back and left for the market. 農夫在馬背上放了四袋馬鈴薯，然後前往市場。

17 **seek** [sik] 動 ❶ 尋找，探索；❷ 企圖，試圖 同義 attempt 企圖

❶ Lynn **sought** shelter from the heavy rain on her way home.
琳恩在回家途中找了個地方躲大雨。

❷ Franklin **sought** to improve his grades by asking his teachers for extra homework. 法蘭克林跟老師要求額外的作業，以加強自己的學業成績。

18 **strategy** [`strætədʒɪ] 名 C 策略，計謀 形 strategic 策略的

● By adopting a flexible **strategy**, Ms. Oakley has become a successful mediator of political conflicts.
歐克利女士採用彈性策略，這讓她在政治衝突中得以成為一位成功的斡旋者。

19 **survey** [sɚ`ve] ❶ 名 C 調查 ❷ 動 調查

❶ A new **survey** shows the percentage of single-parent families has increased recently. 一項新調查顯示，單親家庭的比例最近上升了。

❷ Most of the students who were **surveyed** said they have been under great pressure from schoolwork.
接受調查的大部分學生，都表示他們的學業壓力一直很大。

補充 a market survey 市場調查

20 **unite** [ju`naɪt] 動 ❶ 使統一，使聯合；❷ 兼備（各種特性） 名 unity 統一

❶ The company is going to **unite** the two departments into one.
這家公司將會把兩個部門合併為一。

❷ Carrie's novel **unites** her sense of humor with her great compassion. 凱莉的小說兼具幽默感與悲天憫人的情懷。

補充 the United States 美國；United Nations 聯合國

21 **upset** [ʌpˋsɛt] 動 ❶ 打亂，攪亂；❷ 使心煩意亂；❸ 使（腸胃）不適
形 ❹ 心煩的，苦惱的

・up- 表「向上」
・set 放

❶ The typhoon **upset** the friends' plan to spend a day on the beach; they have postponed the trip until next month.
颱風破壞了那群朋友到海邊消磨一整天的計畫，他們把計畫延到下個月了。

❷ Her inability to contact Franklin really **upset** Bridget; she was anxious about his safety.
聯絡不上法蘭克林，讓布麗姬特很擔心，她怕他會出事。

❸ The stinky tofu **upset** Giselle's stomach; she still feels sick today.
吉賽兒吃了臭豆腐之後腸胃不適，一直到今天都還感到不舒服。

❹ They are very **upset** that their father has cancer; they are worried that it is incurable. 父親得了癌症，讓他們很憂心；他們擔心病治不好。

22 **waken** [ˋwekn̩] 動 ❶ 喚醒；❷ 醒來，睡醒

・wake 醒的
・-en 動 表「變為……」

❶ Roy prefers to wake up naturally rather than being **wakened** by his alarm clock.
羅伊喜歡睡到自然醒，不喜歡被鬧鐘叫醒。

❷ Once the boy **wakened** from sleep, he got out of bed.
男孩睡覺一醒來，就會立刻下床。

23 **whistle** [ˋhwɪsl̩] ❶ 動 吹哨，鳴笛 ❷ 名 C 哨子，汽笛

❶ Cathy is very forgetful, so she bought a kettle that **whistles** when the water boils. 凱絲很健忘，所以買了一只水燒開會鳴笛的水壺。

❷ The policeman blew his **whistle** and raised his hand, causing all of the cars to stop. 警察吹哨子、舉起手，讓所有的車子都停了下來。

24 **sacrifice** [ˋsækrəˏfaɪs] ❶ 動 犧牲，獻出 ❷ 名 C 犧牲

❶ Jack came from a poor family, and his parents had to **sacrifice** much to pay for his education.
傑克來自一個貧窮的家庭。為了供他受教育，他的父母必須犧牲很多東西。

❷ The architects and workers made many **sacrifices** so that the tunnel could be completed on time.
建築師和工人都做了許多犧牲，那條隧道的興建才能如期完成。

25 **strive** [straɪv] 動 努力，奮鬥

● Letitia is **striving** to make her customers happy by expanding her services while keeping her prices low.
蕾蒂希擴大服務項目，卻未抬高價格，努力讓客戶滿意。

26 **transform** [træns`fɔrm] 動 ❶ 使改變，將……改成；❷ 改變

❶ Arnold **transformed** his plain, older house into a pleasant retreat last summer.
去年夏天，阿諾德把他儉樸的老房子改建成一間舒適的別墅。

- trans- 表「超越」
- form 形式

❷ For a month, the schoolchildren have been observing caterpillars as they **transform** into butterflies.
這一個月以來，學童們都在觀察毛毛蟲如何變成蝴蝶。

27 **usage** [`jusɪdʒ] 名 U ❶ 使用，用法；❷ 慣用法

- use 用
- -age 名 表「動作」

❶ We should be careful about water **usage** and never waste it. 我們應該小心使用水，不可浪費。

❷ Are you aware that the English word **usage** can differ between American and British speakers?
你有注意到美式英語和英式英語的用字不一樣嗎？

13 Movements 動作 (1)

25

01 **approach** [ə`protʃ] 動 ❶ 接近，靠近；❷ 找……商量；❸ 著手處理，開始對付；❹（時間）接近，靠近
名 ❺ U 接近，靠近；❻ C 方法，態度

❶ As the stranger **approached** the house, the dog started to bark.
陌生人靠近房子時，狗開始對他吠叫。

❷ Last evening, Frank **approached** the manager about taking a week off. 昨天下午，法蘭克找經理商量要請假一個星期的事。

❸ Scientists are trying to determine the best way of **approaching** the pollution problem. 科學家們一直想找出處理汙染問題的最佳方法。

❹ As the end of the semester **approaches**, all of the students are busy studying. 期末考的時間越來越近，所有的學生都在 K 書。

❺ Cuckoos announce the **approach** of spring.
布穀鳥宣告了春天的腳步越來越近。

❻ Bruce's **approach** to every problem is to analyze all the relevant facts before making a decision.
對於每個問題，布魯斯都會先分析所有的相關因素，然後再作出決定。

用法 an approach to something 針對某事的方法
an approach to V-ing 針對……如何做的方法

02 **arise** [əˋraɪz] 動 產生，出現　同義 occur 發生

・a- 表「在……之中」
・rise 升起

● Work on the project went smoothly for months before an unexpected problem **arose**.
該計畫順利進行了幾個月之後，才出現一個意料之外的問題。

03 **balance** [ˋbæləns] 名 ❶ U 平衡，均衡；❷ C 協調，和諧；❸ C 結餘
動 ❹ 使平衡，保持……的平衡

❶ Little Charles lost his **balance** and fell backward.
小查爾斯一個重心不穩便往後跌倒了。

❷ As a successful career woman, Mrs. Walker manages to find a **balance** between her work and her family.
身為一位成功的職業婦女，韋克太太努力在工作與家庭之間保持平衡。

❸ The man is very poor. The **balance** on his account is only NT$200. 這名男子很窮，他的帳戶上結餘只剩兩百塊台幣。

❹ I had the wheels on my car **balanced** this morning.
今天早上我將車輪的平衡調節好了。

04 **blink** [blɪŋk] 動 ❶ 眨眼睛擠出（眼淚等）；❷ 眨眼　❸ 名 C 一瞬間

❶ Amy **blinked** away her tears and went on cutting the onion.
艾咪眨著眼、流著淚，繼續切洋蔥。

❷ I could hardly open my eyes in the bright sunlight; all I could do was **blink**. 在耀眼的陽光下，我眼睛張不開，只好猛眨眼。

❸ The car crashed into the tree in the **blink** of an eye; it happened so quickly that people in the area were shocked.
車子瞬間撞上了樹。事情發生得很快，周圍的人們都嚇了一跳。

05 **bounce** [baʊns] 動 ❶ 蹦蹦跳跳；❷（球）彈起

❶ Robin and his brothers enjoy **bouncing** on the bed, but their parents say it is dangerous.
羅賓和兄弟們喜歡在床上跳來跳去，他們的父母警告他們那樣很危險。

❷ The ball hit the wall and then **bounced** several times on the ground. 那顆球打到牆壁，然後在地上彈了幾下。

06 **bump** [bʌmp] 動 ❶ 碰，撞；❷ 使碰撞

❶ The police officer ran after the pickpocket, **bumping** into some shoppers on the way. 那名警員追趕扒手，一路上撞上了一些顧客。

❷ All of sudden, the lights went out; I **bumped** my head against the door as I tried to leave the dark room.
突然間，燈熄滅了。我摸黑想走出房間時，頭撞到了門。

相關片語 **bump into** 偶遇

- Susan bumped into her old friend Martha as she walked to work today.
蘇珊今天在走路上班的途中，巧遇了老友瑪爾莎。

07 **bury** [ˋbɛrɪ] 動 ❶ **埋葬；**❷ **掩藏**　名 burial 埋葬

❶ After the funeral, the dead man was **buried** in the cemetery.
喪禮過後，死者被葬在墓園裡。

❷ Claudia's dog found a bone and **buried** it under an oak tree in her garden. 柯蘿蒂亞的狗找到了一根骨頭，並把骨頭藏在她花園的一顆橡樹底下。

08 **cast** [kæst] 動 ❶ **投，擲，拋，扔；**❷ **投射（光線、視線）**
名 C ❸ **班底，演員陣容**

❶ The boy **cast** a pebble into the pond. 男孩往池塘裡扔了一顆鵝卵石。

❷ The full moon **cast** sharp shadows on the walls of the buildings.
滿月的狹長影子投射到房子的牆上。

❸ Many people want to see the play because the **cast** is very strong. 很多人想看這齣戲，因為演員陣容非常堅強。

09 **chew** [tʃu] 動 ❶ **咀嚼，嚼碎；**❷ **深思，細想**

❶ The pills that the doctor gave Edgar should be **chewed** first and then swallowed with warm water.
醫生開給愛德格的藥丸要先嚼碎，再以溫水吞服。

❷ Wendy **chewed** over the problem for five hours before making her decision. 溫蒂琢磨這個問題五個小時之後才做出決定。

補充 chewing gum 口香糖

10 **choke** [tʃok] 動 ❶ **使窒息，哽住；**❷ **窒息，噎住，說不出話來**

❶ The passerby thought about running into the burning building to save the dog, but when the roof caved in, he **choked** and didn't move.
那名路人想闖進失火的屋子去搶救那隻狗，結果屋頂塌落，他被嗆得無法行動。

❷ When you are **choking** on a fish bone, you should not swallow rice. 哽到魚骨時，不可以吞飯。

相關片語 ❶ **choke back** 抑制，忍住；❷ **choke up**（因激動）說不出話來

❶ The girl choked back her tears, as she didn't want others to see her cry. 女孩忍住淚水，因為她不想讓別人看到她在哭。

❷ Daphne choked up when we mentioned her ex-boyfriend. She was so upset that she couldn't talk.
當我們提到黛芬妮的前男友時，黛芬妮整個人楞住，激動得說不出話來。

11 **chop** [tʃɑp] 動 ❶ 砍，劈；❷ 砍成，劈出；❸ 切細，剁碎
名 C ❹（豬、羊的）肋骨肉，排骨

❶ Sylvia enjoys **chopping** wood because it gives her a workout.
希維雅喜歡劈材，因為這可以幫助她健身。

❷ To save the people inside the burning house, the firefighter **chopped** a hole in the door with an axe.
為了搶救身陷房屋火海的人，消防隊員用斧頭將門劈出一個洞。

❸ When Mom was done slicing the onion, I helped her **chop** up the cabbage. 當媽媽在把洋蔥切成薄片時，我幫她把甘藍菜剁碎。

❹ When I arrived home, Mom said we were having lamb **chops** for dinner. 當我回到家時，媽媽說我們晚餐要吃羊排。

26

12 **click** [klɪk] ❶ 動（在電腦上）使用滑鼠點選 ❷ 名 C 卡嗒聲，喀嚓聲

❶ Maria **clicked** on the icon to open the computer program.
瑪麗亞點選圖示，開啟電腦程式。

❷ With a **click**, the e-mail was sent. 卡嗒一聲，電子郵件就被寄出了。

13 **crawl** [krɔl] 動 ❶ 爬行，蠕動；❷ 緩慢移動

❶ After baby turtles hatch, they **crawl** to the ocean and swim away.
幼龜孵化出生後，會爬行進海中游走。

❷ The traffic is **crawling** along the road because of a car accident ahead. 前方出了車禍，行車只能一路上緩緩推進。

14 **creep** [krip] 動 ❶ 爬行，匍匐而行；❷ 躡手躡足地走；❸ 蔓延
名 C ❹ 毛骨悚然的感覺

❶ Charlene's cat **crept** toward the remote-control toy car and attacked it. 查琳的貓向遙控玩具車匍匐前進，然後進行攻擊。

❷ To avoid waking up the sleeping baby, the mother **crept** out of the room. 因為怕吵醒正在睡覺的寶寶，媽媽躡手躡腳地走出房間。

❸ Ivy **crept** up the wall of the house. 常春藤攀著房子的牆壁生長。

❹ The ghost story was so scary that it gave us the **creeps**.
那個鬼故事嚇死人了，令我們毛骨悚然。

補充 形 creepy 令人毛骨悚然的，不寒而慄的

- The sound of the cat crying at midnight was **creepy**, causing the man to look around nervously. 半夜裡，貓叫聲聽起來很淒厲，男子緊張地四處張望。

15 **crush** [krʌʃ] ❶ 動 壓碎，壓壞 ❷ 名 C 迷戀

❶ Genaro always **crushes** aluminum cans before tossing them into the recycling bin. 加納洛都會把鋁罐壓扁之後才丟入回收桶。

❷ Troy has a huge **crush** on the pretty girl in his class; he wants to ask her out. 特洛伊很迷班上那個正妹，他很想約她出去。

16 **dash** [dæʃ] 動 ❶ 急奔；猛衝；❷ 猛撞，擊碎 名 C ❸ 急衝；❹ 短跑

❶ Shortly after the class was dismissed, Charlotte **dashed** off to meet her boyfriend. 夏洛特一下課，就衝去找男友。

❷ As the typhoon hit, the waves **dashed** against the wall, sending water onto the road above.
颱風來襲時，海浪打上了牆，把海水送到了上方的馬路上。

❸ The student made a **dash** for the school bus. Once inside, he took a minute to catch his breath.
學生衝去搭校車。坐上車之後，他氣喘吁吁了好一會兒。

❹ The fastest runner won the 100-meter **dash**.
那個跑得最快的人贏得了一百公尺短跑。

相關片語 **dash off** 匆忙完成

● The woman dashed off a note to her husband and rushed out of the house. 婦女匆匆忙忙留給丈夫一張字條，然後就直奔出門了。

17 **depart** [dɪˋpɑrt] 動 出發，離開 名 departure 離開

‧de- 表「離去」
‧part 分開

● Do you know when the next train **departs**?
你知道下班列車什麼時候開嗎？

18 **departure** [dɪˋpɑrtʃɚ] 名 U 出發，起程 反義 arrival 到來

‧depart 離開
‧-ure 名 表「動作」

● Our plane's **departure** is delayed for three hours.
我們的班機晚三個小時起飛。

19 **dodge** [dɑdʒ] 動 ❶ 閃開，閃身躲開；❷ 躲避，巧妙地迴避
名 ❸ C 託詞，(推託的)妙計

❶ On the battlefield, soldiers ran fast to **dodge** bullets.
在戰場上，士兵們快跑閃避子彈。

❷ The pop singer skillfully **dodged** the reporter's question; he didn't want to talk about his private life.
那名流行歌手有技巧地迴避記者的問題，他不想談私生活。

❸ Many companies donate money to charities as a tax **dodge**.
許多公司會捐錢給慈善團體來避稅。

補充 dodge ball 躲避球

20 **erase** [ɪˋres] 動 ❶ 擦掉，抹去；❷ 清除，忘卻 名 eraser 橡皮擦

❶ The teacher **erases** the blackboard every day before leaving the classroom. 那位老師每天在離開教室之前都會把黑板擦乾淨。

❷ Christine witnessed the terrible accident; she tried to **erase** the image from her mind, but she just couldn't forget it.
克莉絲汀目睹了那場可怕的意外。她想把那個畫面從記憶中抹去，但就是忘不了。

21 **escape** [əˋskep] 動 ❶ 逃跑，逃脫；❷ 漏出，流出；❸ 避免，逃脫
名 C ❹ 逃跑，逃脫；❺ 逃避（現實），解悶

❶ The rabbit **escaped** from the trap and ran away.
兔子從陷阱裡逃了出來，跑走了。

❷ Let's open all the windows because it smells like some gas has **escaped** from the tank. 好像有瓦斯外洩的味道，我們把所有窗戶都打開吧。

❸ The little boy was lucky to **escape** being killed in the car accident. 那個小男孩在那場車禍中倖存。

❹ The spy made her **escape** after putting on a disguise; her enemies never caught her. 那名間諜扮裝後逃走了，敵方並沒有抓到她。

❺ After work, Elliott plays online games as an **escape**; it allows him to forget about his job for a short time.
下班後，艾略特會玩線上遊戲來解悶，這能讓他暫時忘卻工作。

補充 a narrow escape 死裡逃生

22 **fasten** [ˋfæsn̩] 動 繫緊，閂住

• Emily **fastened** the lock on the door before she left the house. 艾蜜莉把門鎖好之後才出門。

• fast 牢固
• -en 動 表「變為……」

23 **fetch** [fɛtʃ] 動 拿來

• Walter's dog **fetches** the newspaper for him every morning.
華特的狗每天早上都會把報紙叼來給他。

24 **flee** [fli] 動 逃走，逃離

• Amanda will never forget the time everyone **fled** her village as a herd of angry elephants ran through it .
阿曼達永遠忘不了，當時有一群抓狂的大象在村子裡東奔西跑，嚇得大家抱頭鼠竄。

14 Movements 動作 (2)

27

01 **fold** [fold] 動 ❶ 摺疊；❷ 交疊，交叉

❶ Alice **folded** all the laundry and put it back neatly in her drawers.
艾莉絲把所有洗好的衣服都摺好，整齊地放進抽屜裡。

❷ When people feel uncomfortable or nervous, they may **fold** their arms across their chest as if to protect themselves.
人們感到不舒服或緊張時，會在胸前交叉雙臂，像是要保護自己。

02 **frown** [fraʊn] ❶ 動 皺眉，表示不滿 ❷ 名 C 蹙額，皺眉

❶ Gerard **frowned** with disapproval when he read his son's report card. 吉羅德看著兒子的學校成績單，不悅地皺著眉。

❷ The coach had a **frown** on his face after watching the players' performance during the game.
教練對球員在比賽中的表現感到不滿意，他皺著眉頭看著球員們。

03 **gaze** [gez] ❶ 動 凝視，注視 ❷ 名 C 凝視，注視 同義 stare 凝視

❶ Megan **gazed** up at the stars and wondered how big the universe really is. 梅根凝望著星空，想著宇宙到底有多廣大啊。

❷ Juliet turned her **gaze** to the handsome man as he walked into the hall. 當那個帥哥走進大廳時，茱麗葉的視線轉而對他凝視。

04 **gesture** [ˋdʒɛstʃɚ] 名 C ❶ 姿勢，手勢；❷ 姿態，表示
動 ❸ 用手勢（或動作）表示

❶ The police officer made a **gesture** at the driver, indicating that he should stop his car. 警察向駕駛做了一個手勢，要求他停車。

❷ Richard invited his new colleague to dinner as a **gesture** of friendship. 李察邀請新同事一起吃晚餐，以示善意。

❸ The customer raised her hand and **gestured** for the waiter to come over. 那位顧客舉起手，打手勢叫服務生過來。

05 **glance** [glæns] ❶ 動（粗略地）看一下，一瞥，掃視 ❷ 名 C 一瞥，掃視

❶ Carlos **glanced** at the newspaper and was surprised to see his name in the headlines.
卡勒斯瞄了一下報紙，很驚訝地看到自己的名字出現在頭條新聞中。

❷ Three minutes before the meeting, the manager took a quick **glance** at the document and rushed into the conference room.
會議前三分鐘，經理迅速地瀏覽過文件，然後衝進會議室。

06 **glide** [glaɪd] 動 ❶ 滑翔；❷ 滑動，滑行

❶ An eagle **glides** effortlessly over the forest.
一隻老鷹悠悠地從森林上空飛過。

❷ Yesterday afternoon, I saw a snake **gliding** over the lawn; it was moving quietly and smoothly.
昨天下午，我看到草坪上有一條蛇溜過；它安靜又平穩的滑動。

07 **glimpse** [glɪmps] ❶ 動 瞥見，看一眼 ❷ 名 C 瞥見，一瞥 同義 spot 瞄到

❶ Marsha **glimpsed** at her watch and decided it was time to go.
瑪爾莎看了一眼手錶，決定是時候該離開了。

❷ Candice caught a **glimpse** of the man; she saw him for only a very short time and did not get a good look at him.
坎蒂絲瞄了男子一眼。她只是瞄了一下，並沒有看得很清楚。

08 **grab** [græb] 動 ❶ 攫取，抓取；❷ 匆忙地做 名 ❸ C 抓住，攫取

❶ Edna carefully **grabbed** the stranded kitten from the branch of the pine tree. 葉德娜小心翼翼地從松樹枝上抓下受困的小貓。

❷ After getting up late, Monica **grabbed** some breakfast and rushed to the bus stop. 因為起床起晚了，莫妮卡抓了些早餐就衝向公車站。

❸ The goalie made a **grab** for the ball; although he didn't catch it, he tipped it over the net.
守門員碰到了球。雖然他沒有逮住球，但把球撥出了網外。

09 **grasp** [græsp] 動 ❶ 抓牢，緊握；❷ 領會，理解
名 C ❸ 抓，控制；❹ 理解，領會

❶ Sean **grasped** the rope cast down by his friends and climbed out of the ditch. 西恩緊握朋友丟下來的繩子，從溝裡面爬出來。

❷ The students didn't **grasp** the teacher's meaning, so she had to explain it again. 學生們不懂女老師的意思，所以她得再解釋一次。

❸ The robber grabbed the woman, but luckily she slipped from his **grasp** and ran away. 搶匪抓住女子，幸虧女子掙脫逃出來了。

❹ This complicated math problem is beyond my **grasp**; I don't understand it at all. 這題複雜的數學題超出我的理解，我完全看不懂。

10 **grin** [grɪn] ❶ 動 露齒而笑 ❷ 名 C 露齒的笑

❶ When Guadalupe asked if she could sit next to me, I **grinned** with approval. 關德露普問我是否可以坐我旁邊，我微笑應允。

❷ A **grin** broke out on the boy's face when his father handed him the gift. 爸爸把禮物交到小男孩手上時，男孩露齒笑了出來。

11 **hug** [hʌg] ❶ 動 緊抱，擁抱　❷ 名 C 緊抱，擁抱　同義 embrace# 擁抱

❶ The first thing Larry does when he comes home is **hug** his wife and children. 賴瑞回家的第一件事，就是擁抱妻子和孩子。

❷ The grandmother gave her grandson a big **hug**; the boy smiled broadly in her arms. 祖母給孫子一個大擁抱，男孩在她的臂彎裡笑得很開心。

12 **insert** [ɪnˋsɝt] 動 插入，嵌入

• Antonio **inserted** a photo in his resume before sending it out.
安東尼歐在履歷中挾帶了一張照片後才寄出去。

28

13 **kneel** [nil] 動 跪下，跪著

・knee 膝

• Ryan **knelt** down to weed the flower bed and found a colorful caterpillar. 雷恩跪在花圃除草時，發現了一隻鮮豔的毛毛蟲。

14 **lean** [lin] 動 ❶ 倚，靠；❷ 依賴

❶ Morris **leaned** against the wall while he waited for Celia to arrive.
莫里斯靠著牆，等待西莉雅到來。

❷ As a young child, I always **leaned** on my parents when I got into trouble. 在我小時候，每當闖禍時，我就會去我爸媽來幫忙解決。

15 **leap** [lip] ❶ 動 跳，跳躍　❷ 名 C 跳躍

❶ Kirk's horse **leaped** over all the obstacles and reached the finish line first. 寇克的馬跳過所有障礙，首先抵達終點。

❷ As the fire broke out, the room filled with smoke; the frightened man took a **leap** from the window.
火災發生時，房間裡煙霧瀰漫，受到驚嚇的男子從窗戶跳了出去。

16 **march** [mɑrtʃ] ❶ 動（齊步）前進，行軍　❷ 名 C 遊行抗議，遊行示威

❶ On Double Tenth Day, groups of soldiers **marched** by the presidential palace; their steps were stiff and regular.
雙十節時，一批批士兵從總統府前面行進而過，步伐整齊劃一。

❷ Tomorrow, some people will go on a **march**; they will walk from the square to city hall to protest the new policy.
明天有一些人會去遊行示威，他們會從廣場走到市政府來抗議新政策。

17 **peel** [pil] ❶ 名 C（水果等的）皮　❷ 動 削……的皮，剝……的殼

❶ Beth likes to add dried orange **peels** as flavoring in her cooking.
貝絲喜歡在煮菜時加點陳皮提味。

❷ In the kitchen, the cook **peeled** the potatoes and then cut them into chunks. 在廚房裡，廚師先把馬鈴薯削皮，再把它們切成塊狀。

相關片語 **peel off** 去掉，扯掉

- When the little boy got the present, he peeled off the wrapper to see what was inside. 小男孩收到禮物後立刻扯掉包裝紙，想看裡面是什麼東西。

18 **peep** [pip] 動 ❶ **竊，偷看；** ❷ **隱約顯現，緩緩出現** 名 ❸ Ⓒ **窺視，偷看**

❶ The boy wanted to know what was happening inside the house, so he **peeped** through a window.
小男孩很好奇房子裡發生了什麼事情，所以他在窗戶旁窺視。

❷ Shortly after the rain stopped, the sun **peeped** through the clouds. 雨停後不久，太陽緩緩地在雲端中露出臉來。

❸ The mother took a **peep** at her son's diary before putting it back in the drawer. 媽媽在把兒子的日記放進抽屜之前，偷偷翻了一下。

19 **peer** [pɪr] ❶ 動 **凝視，盯著看**
❷ 名 Ⓒ **（常作複數）（地位等）同等的人，同輩，同儕**

❶ Ms. Lindel was late getting to the office, and she **peered** around the corner to see if her boss was there yet.
琳黛小姐上班遲到了，所以在轉角處察看老闆有沒有在附近。

❷ Teenagers spend much more time with their **peers** than with their parents. 青少年跟同儕在一起的時間，要比跟和父母在一起的時間來得多。

補充 peer pressure 同儕壓力

20 **polish** [ˋpɑlɪʃ] ❶ 名 Ⓤ **磨光粉，擦亮劑；** ❷ **（單數）磨光，擦亮**
❸ 動 **磨光，擦亮**

❶ Chuck rubbed black shoe **polish** all over his painting to create a feeling of night. 恰克拿黑鞋油塗滿他的畫，以呈現出黑夜的感覺。

❷ Your shoes are covered with dirt; you should give them a **polish**.
你整個鞋子都是泥土，你應該把它們擦一擦。

❸ After the renovation, the hotel staff washed and **polished** the floor in the lobby until it was smooth and glossy.
飯店整修完畢後，員工們清洗大廳的地板，並把地板擦得亮晶晶的。

補充 nail polish 指甲油

21 **punch** [pʌntʃ] ❶ 名 Ⓒ **拳打** ❷ 動 **用拳猛擊**

❶ Marjorie was furious enough to throw a **punch** at the robber.
瑪裘莉很火大，就揍了搶匪一拳。

❷ Insulted by the man, Kent clenched his fist and **punched** him in the face. 肯特被男子一侮辱，拳頭一握就往他的臉上揍去。

22 **quake** [kwek] ❶ 名 C 地震 ❷ 動 顫抖，哆嗦

❶ For months after the **quake**, Haruki had nightmares about his house falling down. 地震過後，春樹做了幾個月房子倒塌的惡夢。

❷ Seeing the bear, the hunter **quaked** with fright; his hands were shaking so violently that he could hardly hold his rifle.
獵人看到那隻熊，嚇得直打哆嗦。他的手抖個不停，簡直無法握住來福槍。

23 **remove** [rɪˋmuv] 動 ❶ 移動，搬開；❷ 脫掉，去掉；❸ 把…… 免職

❶ Your desk is cluttered with too many unnecessary items. You should **remove** some of them.
你的桌子上堆了太多不必要的東西，你得移走一些。

- re- 表「再」
- move 移動

❷ The woman **removed** her gloves so she could feel the quality of the cloth. 女子脫掉手套，這樣才能摸出布料的品質。

❸ The clerk was **removed** from the post because of his poor performance. 那位職員因為表現不佳，被解雇了。

24 **rid** [rɪd] 動 使擺脫，使免除

- The leaders of several different countries have signed an agreement to **rid** the world of nuclear weapons.
幾個不同國家的領導人已經簽署協定，要讓世界擺脫核子武器。

相關片語 **get rid of** 擺脫

- They got rid of the old sofa after they bought a new one.
他們買了新沙發之後，就把舊沙發丟掉了。

25 **scatter** [ˋskætɚ] 動 ❶ 撒在…… 上面，散布；❷ 使消散，使分散；❸ 散落，分散

❶ Darren **scattered** wildflower seeds in his yard last year, and now they are all blossoming.
達仁去年在院子裡撒下的野花種子，如今都開花了。

❷ The shot **scattered** the birds; they flew from the trees in many different directions. 槍聲驅散了樹上的小鳥。小鳥四處飛竄。

❸ The mirror slipped out of the little girl's hand, and the broken pieces of glass **scattered** all over the floor.
鏡子從小女孩的手上滑落，碎片散落一地。

26 **scoop** [skup] 動 ❶ 挖出；❷ 用勺舀，用鏟子鏟 名 ❸ Ⓒ（一）勺，（一）鏟

❶ Crystal used her fingers to **scoop** the rest of the honey from the jar. 克莉絲朵用手指把罐子裡剩下的蜂蜜挖出來。

❷ The vendor **scooped** some ice cream and put it on the cone.
小販用勺舀出冰淇淋，然後放在蛋捲筒上。

❸ Mom put two **scoops** of mashed potatoes on my dish.
媽媽放了兩勺馬鈴薯泥在我的盤子上。

15 Movements
動作 (3)

29

01 **seal** [sil] ❶ 動 封，密封 ❷ 名 Ⓒ 印章，圖章

❶ The girl put her magazines in the box and **sealed** it with sticky tape. 女孩把她的雜誌放進箱子裡，然後用膠帶把箱子封起來。

❷ After the president read the document, she affixed her **seal** to it.
在董事長看過文件之後，她在上面蓋了印章。

相關用法 **sealed** 形 密封的

- Some waste from nuclear power plants is buried in sealed containers.
一些來自核能發電廠的廢料被裝在密封的容器中加以掩埋。〔91 年學測補考〕

02 **seize** [siz] 動 ❶ 抓住，捉住；❷ 奪取，攻占；❸ 抓住（時機等），利用；❹ 理解，了解

❶ The brave soldier **seized** the gun from the enemy and knocked him to the ground.
那名勇敢的阿兵哥一把抓住敵人的槍枝，然後把他擊倒在地。

❷ During the sudden attack, the army **seized** the city.
軍隊進行突襲後，攻占了城市。

❸ While traveling abroad, Jared **seized** the chance to improve his English. 在國外旅遊的時候，傑瑞德會抓住機會來練自己的英文。

❹ A good writer knows how to **seize** an idea and develop it to the fullest extent. 一名好的作家懂得抓住一個想法，然後將之發揮得淋漓盡致。

補充 seize the day 把握今朝

03 **shave** [ʃev] ❶ 動 刮鬍子 ❷ 名 Ⓒ 刮鬍子，修面

❶ Raul doesn't **shave** because he feels more handsome with a full beard. 勞爾覺得滿臉落腮鬍比較帥，所以他不刮鬍子。

❷ Herbert's beard is too long; he needs a **shave**.
赫伯特的鬍子太長了，他需要刮個鬍子。

04 **skip** [skɪp] 動 ❶ 迅速翻閱；❷ 蹦蹦跳跳；❸ 略過，漏掉　同義 miss 漏掉

❶ Yvonne **skipped** through the book of poems until she found a short one. 伊芳迅速翻閱詩集，找到了一首比較短的詩。

❷ A group of children are **skipping** around on the lawn.
一群小孩在草坪上蹦蹦跳跳。

❸ Edwina got up late this morning, so she **skipped** breakfast and left directly for work. 艾德文娜今天早上太晚起床，所以沒吃早餐就去上班了。

05 **snap** [snæp] 動 ❶ 彈（手指）使劈啪作聲；❷ 突然折斷

❶ Whenever Leroy has a great idea, he **snaps** his fingers.
李諾只要想到好點子，就會彈指頭發出聲響。

❷ Feeling very angry, Tyrone **snapped** the pencil in two.
泰倫怒火中燒，便喀嚓一聲把鉛筆折成了兩半。

補充 snapshot 名 快照

06 **spit** [spɪt] ❶ 動 吐（口水等）；❷ 吐口水，吐痰　❸ 名 U 唾液，口水

❶ The baseball player **spat** out a wad of chewing tobacco before stepping up to the plate.
那名棒球球員在步上投手板之前，吐了一團嚼過的菸草。

❷ It is highly unsanitary to **spit** in public places.
在公共場所吐痰是很不衛生的。

❸ When the man yelled at me, his **spit** flew onto my face.
男子在對著我吼叫時，他的口水濺到了我的臉上。

07 **squeeze** [skwiz] 動 ❶ 緊握；❷ 擠，榨；❸ 榨出，擠出；❹ 擠著行進
名 C ❺ 擠，榨；❻ 緊握

❶ Lisa nervously **squeezed** her hands when she got onstage.
莉莎在上場時，緊張地搓揉著自己的手。

❷ Mortimer **squeezed** the tube of toothpaste in the middle even though that drove his brother crazy.
摩帝馬刷牙時都擠牙膏的中段部位，這讓他的老哥很抓狂。

❸ The girl **squeezed** some juice from the oranges.
女孩從柳橙中擠出了一些汁。

❹ Perry **squeezed** through the crowd to meet his girlfriend.
斐瑞擠過人群來和女友碰面。

❺ To get more juice, the cook gave the lemon another **squeeze**.
廚師又擠了一下檸檬，擠出了更多的汁來。

❻ The patient's mother gave the surgeon's hand a firm **squeeze** to show her appreciation. 病人的母親緊緊握住醫師的手，表達她的感激。

相關片語 **squeeze . . . in** 為……挪出時間

- Although the doctor's schedule was full, the nurse still managed to squeeze me in. 雖然醫生已經滿診，護士還是想辦法為我挪出看診時間。

08 **stab** [stæb] ❶ 動 刺，戳，刺傷 ❷ 名 C 刺，刺傷

❶ Louis lightly **stabbed** the baked potato with a fork to see if it was done. 路易斯用叉子稍微戳了一下烤洋芋，看是不是已經熟了。

❷ The man took a knife from his pocket and killed the woman with a **stab** to the heart. 男子從口袋裡面拿出了一把刀，刺進女子的心臟，殺死了她。

09 **stare** [stɛr] ❶ 動 盯，凝視 ❷ 名 C 盯，凝視，瞪眼

❶ Katherine **stared** at her boyfriend in disbelief; he could be so absentminded! 凱瑟琳不敢置信地瞪著男友；因為男友這麼心不在焉！

❷ When the father gave his daughter a hard **stare**, she stopped screaming right away. 爸爸很兇地看著女兒，女兒馬上就停止尖叫了。

10 **strip** [strɪp] ❶ 動 剝去，脫掉 ❷ 名 C 狹長的一條或一片

❶ The boy **stripped** off his clothes before stepping into the hot bath. 男孩在踏進熱水浴缸之前，先脫掉了衣服。

❷ Adriana grows cooking herbs in a **strip** of garden behind her house. 安德莉娜在她家後面的一塊狹長花園裡，種了一些食用香草。

用法 strip A from B = strip B of A 剝掉、取走 B 的 A

11 **switch** [swɪtʃ] 動 ❶ 轉換；❷ 打開（或關掉）……的開關
名 C ❸ 開關；❹ 變更，改變

❶ Why does Brian keep **switching** the television channel?
為什麼布萊恩看電視時老是轉台啊？

❷ The room was dark, so I **switched** on the light.
房間很暗，所以我打開了電燈。

❸ Press the **switch**, and then the machine will start to work.
按一下開關，機器就會開始運轉。

❹ The manager made the **switch** to low-energy light bulbs, but not everyone liked the change. 經理換了省電燈泡，但不是每個人都領情的。

12 **tighten** [ˋtaɪtn̩] 動 使變緊 反義 loosen 鬆開

- tight 緊的
- -en 動 表「變為……」

- Martin must **tighten** all the loose screws on his patio roof before the thunderstorm.
馬汀得在下大雷雨之前，把露台屋頂所有鬆脫的螺絲都鎖緊。

相關片語 ❶ **tighten up** 使更嚴格，使加強
❷ **tighten one's belt** 束緊腰帶度日

❶ Since the terrorist attack, the government has taken steps to tighten up security on foreign flights into the country.
在恐怖攻擊過後，該國政府已經採取措施加強國際航班的安全性。

❷ After being out of work for half a year, the man had to tighten his belt. Every day, he spent as little money as possible.
男子已經失業半年了，只得勒緊褲帶度日。他每天都盡量少花錢。

13 **toss** [tɔs] 動 ❶ 拋，扔；❷ 擲（硬幣）打賭；❸ 顛簸；❹ 翻來覆去

❶ Wayne usually just **tosses** his dirty clothes around his apartment.
韋恩老是把髒衣服扔得滿屋子都是。

❷ They **tossed** a coin to see who would play the game first.
他們擲幣決定誰先開始玩遊戲。

❸ As the storm approached, the boat **tossed** about on the huge waves. 在暴風雨接近之際，船隻在巨浪上顛簸著。

❹ Worried about the upcoming exam, Dolores kept **tossing** and turning in her bed; she didn't sleep all night.
想到即將來臨的考試，多洛莉絲整夜翻來覆去，無法成眠。

14 **tremble** [ˋtrɛmbḷ] 動 ❶ 顫抖，發抖；❷ 焦慮，擔憂；❸ 搖晃

❶ The girl **trembled** with cold because she was not wearing enough clothes. She shook in a way that she couldn't control.
女孩衣服穿得不夠多，冷得直打哆嗦，無法控制。

❷ Mrs. Graham **trembled** at the very thought of her family being in danger. 葛瑞翰太太只要一想到家人可能遭遇危險，就焦慮不堪。

❸ Whenever a truck passes by, the chandelier hanging from the dining room ceiling **trembles**.
只有一有卡車經過，吊在餐廳天花板上的吊燈就會搖晃。

15 **tug** [tʌg] 動 ❶ 用力拉或拖（某物）；❷ 用力拉（或拖）

❶ A passing truck driver offered to **tug** Nell's car out of the mud.
一輛路過的卡車幫奈爾把車拖出泥地。

❷ The little girl **tugged** at her father's sleeve and pulled on his pants to get his attention.
小女孩拉了拉爸爸的袖子，又用力拉他的褲子，以引起爸爸的注意。

30

16 **tumble** [ˋtʌmbḷ] 動 跌倒，滾下

● When Maya was a little girl, she loved to **tumble** down grassy hills. 瑪雅小時候很喜歡從野草遍布的小丘上滾下來。

17 **twist** [twɪst] 動 ❶ 旋轉；❷ 編，織；❸ 扭傷；❹ 歪曲，曲解
名 C ❺ 意外轉折

❶ The man **twisted** the knob, and the door opened.
男子轉動門把，門就開了。

❷ Emma **twisted** some wildflowers into a garland to wear on her head. 艾瑪用一些野花編成花冠戴在頭上。

❸ During the basketball game, the player tumbled and **twisted** his ankle. 在籃球比賽中，那名球員跌倒，扭傷了腳踝。

❹ The actress accused the reporter of **twisting** the facts; she claimed that he deliberately changed the meaning of her words.
女演員指控記者扭曲事實，表示記者故意曲解她的話。

❺ The novel has a **twist** in the last chapter; it is a really unexpected turn of events.
這本小說在最後一章有了意外轉折，那真是一個出乎意料的劇情轉變。

18 **wag** [wæg] 動 搖，搖擺

- When Mr. Wang comes home from work in the evening, his little dog **wags** her tail and runs around in happy circles.
王先生晚上下班回到家後，他的小狗會對他搖尾巴，然後興奮地繞著圈子跑。

19 **wander** [ˋwɑndɚ] 動 漫遊，閒逛

- Herds of horses and cattle always **wander** around the lake.
成群的馬和牛總在湖的四周悠哉地晃著。

20 **whip** [hwɪp] ❶ 動 鞭打　❷ 名 C 鞭子

❶ The little boy was **whipped** as a punishment.
小男孩被鞭打，作為懲罰。

❷ The cowboy used his **whip** to make the horse run faster.
牛仔用鞭子抽打那匹馬，要牠跑快一點。

21 **wink** [wɪŋk] 動 眨眼

- Ervin wasn't sure if Sue **winked** at him or if she had a twitch in her eye. 艾爾文不確定蘇是在對他眨眼睛，還是她眼睛痛在眨眼。

22 **wipe** [waɪp] 動 擦拭

- Lloyd **wipes** the dirt off his leather boots and polishes them every night. 羅伊德每天晚上都會撣去皮靴上的塵土，並且將它們擦拭一番。

23 **wrap** [ræp] 動 ❶ 包，裹；❷ 圍，披

❶ Eudora **wrapped** the present in gold paper before sending it to her friend. 尤朵拉在把禮物寄出給朋友之前，先用金色的紙把禮物包好。

❷ Jerry **wraps** himself up in three blankets to keep warm on freezing winter nights. 在寒冷的冬夜，傑瑞裹了三層毯子取暖。

24 **yawn** [jɔn] ❶ 名 C 哈欠 ❷ 動 打哈欠

❶ Gilbert faked a **yawn** to indicate his boredom as Beverly continued her pointless speech.
吉伯特聽著貝芙麗毫無重點的演講，假裝打個哈欠，以示無聊。

❷ Feeling sleepy, the man **yawned** and went to bed.
男子很睏，打哈欠後就上床睡覺了。

25 **scratch** [skrætʃ] 動 ❶ 搔，抓；❷ 抓破，抓傷；❸ 潦草地塗寫
名 C ❹ 抓痕，擦傷

❶ Some elderly people find it hard to **scratch** their backs. They need help when they have an itch.
老人家抓不太到自己的背，所以背癢的時候需要幫忙。

❷ Jared was upset when his cat **scratched** his expensive furniture.
賈瑞德的貓抓破了他昂貴的家具，讓他很生氣。

❸ Alston **scratched** a note and left it on the dining room table before rushing out of the house.
奧斯頓草草寫了一張字條留在餐桌上，就匆匆出門了。

❹ After walking through the brambles, the climber's arms were covered with **scratches**. 那個登山客通過有刺灌木叢時，手臂都被劃傷了。

26 **shrug** [ʃrʌg] ❶ 動 聳（肩） ❷ 名 C 聳肩

❶ Tim **shrugged** his shoulders when his friend asked how he felt about going to the party.
朋友問提姆對參加派對有無興趣時，提姆聳了聳肩。

❷ Shirley's **shrug** indicated she didn't care what they did next.
雪麗聳了聳肩，表示不在乎他們的後續動作。

27 **split** [splɪt] 動 ❶ 劈開；❷ 分擔 名 C ❸ 裂縫；裂痕

❶ Nathaniel spends one afternoon a week **splitting** wood.
納森尼爾每週都會花一個下午的時間來劈材。

❷ After the meal, they **split** the bill evenly among the six of them.
他們用完餐後，六個人平均分攤了費用。

❸ The roots of the old tree have caused a **split** in the rock.
這棵老樹的樹根已經讓岩石都裂開了。

28 **sway** [swe] 動 ❶ 搖動，搖擺；❷ 使動搖，影響 名 U ❸ 搖動，搖擺

❶ The boat began to **sway** in the choppy water; before long, it capsized. 船隻開始在波浪起伏的海上搖搖晃晃，不久就翻覆了。

❷ The woman was **swayed** by their words and changed her mind. 女子受到他們的話所影響，改變心意了。

❸ The boat moved from side to side on the sea; the **sway** made me feel sick. 船隻在海上搖來搖去，晃得我想吐。

29 **withdraw** [wɪðˋdrɔ] 動 ❶ 抽回，移開；❷ 提取；❸ 撤退，撤離

❶ After touching the girl's hair, Duncan **withdrew** his hand quickly. 鄧肯摸了一下女孩的頭髮，又馬上把手收回去。

- with- 表「向後」
- draw 拉

❷ Matthew stopped at an ATM and **withdrew** some cash before picking up his date. 馬修在約會之前，從自動提款機領了一些錢。

❸ After the war, both countries **withdrew** their troops from the region. 戰爭結束之後，兩個國家都將軍隊撤出了那個區域。

16 Leisure & sport 休閒與運動 (1)

31

01 **adventure** [ədˋvɛntʃɚ] 名 ❶ U 冒險（精神）；❷ C 冒險（活動）

❶ Ron, a man who loves **adventure**, has always wanted to explore the Antarctic. 榮恩，一個熱愛冒險的人，他老想著要去探索南極洲。

❷ Warren made a movie about his **adventures** in Africa. 瓦倫拍了一部有關他在非洲探險的電影。

02 **amuse** [əˋmjuz] 動 ❶ 使歡樂，逗……高興；❷ 娛樂，消遣

❶ The clown **amused** the children by making funny faces. 小丑變換各種滑稽的表情，來逗兒童開心。

❷ As she waited, Tracy **amused** herself by reading a novel. 翠西在等待期間，看小說自娛。

03 **amusement** [əˋmjuzmənt] 名 ❶ U 娛樂；❷ C 消遣，娛樂活動

❶ The members of the Stuart family often sing and dance for their own **amusement**. 史都華家常唱歌跳舞，自我娛樂一番。

- amuse 使歡樂
- -ment 名 表「產物」

❷ My favorite **amusement** is cross-stitching; it gives me a lot of pleasure. 我最喜歡的消遣是十字繡，這給我帶來很大的樂趣。

補充 amusement park 遊樂園

04 **athlete** [ˋæθlit] 名 C **運動員，體育家**　形 athletic 體育的

- Katharine was once a professional **athlete**, and now she is a successful business owner.
凱瑟琳以前是職業運動員，現在則是一位成功的企業家。

05 **athletic** [æθˋlɛtɪk] 形 ❶ **運動的，體育的**；❷ **體格健壯的**

・athlete 運動員
・-ic 形 表「……的」

❶ All the students in our school are getting ready for an **athletic** meeting next week.
我們學校的所有學生，都在為下週的運動會緊鑼密鼓地做準備。

❷ Jack doesn't look **athletic**, but he is excellent at sports, especially baseball. 傑克的體格看起來不是很壯，但事實上他很擅長運動，尤其是棒球。

06 **badminton** [ˋbædmɪntən] 名 U **羽毛球**

- Adam was on the **badminton** team when he was a junior high school student. 亞當念國中的時候曾加入羽球校隊。

07 **bingo** [ˋbɪŋgo] 名 U **賓果遊戲**

- Rae has been playing **bingo** on Friday nights for more than 30 years. 芮伊每週五晚上都會玩賓果遊戲，這個習慣持續三十多年了。

08 **champion** [ˋtʃæmpɪən] 名 C **冠軍**

- Kirsten, the defending **champion**, is under great pressure this year to keep her title. 衛冕者柯絲頓今年面臨冠軍保衛戰的強大壓力。

09 **championship** [ˋtʃæmpɪən͵ʃɪp] 名 C ❶ **冠軍地位，冠軍稱號**；❷ **（常作複數）錦標賽**

・champion 冠軍
・-ship 名 表「身分」

❶ Jose, our most talented tennis player, has won three **championships** in a row.
荷西已連續贏了三次網球賽冠軍，他是一位天才網球選手。

❷ The volleyball team won a gold medal at the world **championships** last year. 那支排球隊贏得了上一屆的世界錦標賽冠軍。

32 10 **circus** [ˋsɝkəs] 名 C **馬戲團，馬戲表演**

- Carmen's father promised to take her to the **circus** on her birthday. 卡門的父親答應在她生日時，帶她去看馬戲團。

11 **collection** [kəˋlɛkʃən] 名 ❶ U 收集；❷ C 收藏品

❶ Andrew has spent his entire life building this **collection** of antiques. 安德魯花了一輩子的時間收集到這些古董。

❷ Mr. and Mrs. Smith have a very good **collection** of ceramics.
史密斯夫婦收藏了不少的陶器。

- collect 收集
- -ion 名 表「行為；行為結果」

12 **compete** [kəmˋpit] 動 ❶ 競爭，比賽；❷ 媲美，比得上

❶ Why are Harold and his brother always **competing** against each other? 哈樂德和他哥哥為什麼老愛爭來爭去？

❷ When it comes to swimming, Helen can't **compete** with her brother. He swims much faster than she does.
說到游泳，海倫比不上她哥哥。她哥游得比她快多了。

13 **competition** [͵kɑmpəˋtɪʃən] 名 ❶ C 競賽，比賽；❷ U 競爭，角逐

❶ Joshua lost the chess **competition** because he was overconfident. 約書亞因為過於自大，輸掉了西洋棋比賽。

❷ **Competition** for the job is intense; all of the candidates are doing their best to get the position.
這些求職應徵者之間的競爭很激烈，他們都盡最大的努力要得到那份工作。

- compete 競爭，比賽
- -ion 名 表「行為」

14 **competitive** [kəmˋpɛtətɪv] 形 ❶ 競爭的；❷ 好競爭的

❶ In this highly **competitive** society, you definitely have to arm yourself with as much knowledge as possible.
在高度競爭的社會裡，人必須盡可能地讓自己擁有豐富的知識。

❷ Lonny is not a **competitive** person; actually, he doesn't care about winning at all. 藍尼並不好勝。事實上，他根本不在乎輸贏。

- compete 競爭，比賽
- -ive 形 表「……特性的」

15 **competitor** [kəmˋpɛtətɚ] 名 C 競爭者，對手，敵手

- Deborah is worried that if she takes a vacation, her **competitors** will steal her customers.
黛博拉擔心，如果她去渡假，競爭對手會趁機搶走她的客戶。

- com- 表「一起」
- petitor 懇求者

16 **contest** [ˋkɑntɛst] 名 C 比賽，競賽　名 contestant 角逐者

- Theodore is too nervous to sleep because of tomorrow's talent **contest**. 希歐多爾明天要參加才藝比賽，緊張得睡不著。

17 **defeat** [dɪˋfit] ❶ 名 U 失敗，戰敗 ❷ 動 戰勝，擊敗

❶ Antonia refused to accept **defeat** and kept trying until she succeeded. 安東妮雅不向失敗低頭。她不斷地嘗試，終於成功了。

❷ The candidate was **defeated** by a vote of 25,000 to 11,000; he was depressed to learn that he had lost the election.
這名候選人以 25000 票對 11000 票落選。得知道自己輸了選舉，他感到很沮喪。

18 **dive** [daɪv] 動 ❶ 跳水；❷ 潛水；❸ 俯衝 名 ❹ C 跳水

❶ Chris prefers to **dive** into the pool rather than walking down the steps in the shallow end.
克里斯比較喜歡直接跳入游泳池，勝過從淺水端走下階。

❷ Those women **dived** for pearls without wearing any breathing equipment! 那些婦人沒有穿戴任何呼吸器材就潛進水裡採集珍珠。

❸ The bombers **dived** down from the sky to attack the enemy's power plant. 轟炸機從天空俯衝下來攻擊敵人的發電廠。

❹ Thousands of spectators cheered and clapped after the athlete performed a spectacular **dive** from the high diving board.
運動員從跳水板上做了一個精彩的高空跳水，數千名的觀眾為之歡呼鼓掌。

相關用語 **diver** 名 跳水選手

- The diver jumped into the water headfirst, with his arms over his head.
跳水選手雙手抱著頭部，由頭部先進入水裡。

補充 diving board 跳水板；scuba diving 戴水肺潛水

19 **entertain** [ˏɛntɚˋten] 動 使娛樂，使歡樂 名 entertainment 娛樂

- We were all **entertained** by Curtis's hilarious jokes.
柯帝士令人捧腹的笑話讓我們都很開心。

17 Leisure & sport 休閒與運動 (2)

33

01 **entertainment** [ˏɛntɚˋtenmənt] 名 U 餘興，娛樂

- entertain 使娛樂
- -ment 名 表「產物」

- Peggy plays the piano in a hotel for the guests' **entertainment**. 佩姬在一家飯店當鋼琴師，為賓客彈琴助興。

02 **hike** [haɪk] ❶ 動 徒步旅行，遠足 ❷ 名 C 徒步旅行，遠足

❶ If the weather is fine tomorrow, Kim Moore and I will go **hiking**.
如果明天天氣不錯，我就會和金・摩爾去健行。

❷ Yesterday, they went on an eight-mile **hike** through the forest to the lake. 昨天，他們步行八英里穿越森林去到了湖邊。

補充 hitchhike 動 搭便車（旅行）

03 **journey** [ˋdʒɝnɪ] ❶ 名 C 旅行 ❷ 動 旅行

❶ Since Kaley loves adventure, she embraces the **journey** of life as a series of interesting surprises.
凱莉熱愛冒險，她視生命的旅程為一連串有趣的驚喜之旅。

❷ The businessman **journeyed** frequently to France and other countries. 那名商人經常往來法國和其他等國家。

04 **leisure** [ˋliʒɚ] ❶ 名 U 閒暇，空暇時間 ❷ 形 空閒的

❶ Matty often replies to e-mails and phone calls at his **leisure**.
麥迪空閒時間常會回覆電子郵件和電話。

❷ In her **leisure** time, Alina usually watches TV.
艾麗娜空閒時通常會看電視。

用法 at one's leisure 在（某人）閒暇時

05 **marathon** [ˋmærə͵θɑn] 名 C ❶ 馬拉松賽跑；❷ 耐力比賽

❶ Adonis ran the **marathon**; he finished the long race of about 26 miles in just three hours. 亞多尼斯參加了馬拉松比賽。他在短短的三個小時之內，就完成了長達約 26 英里的比賽。

❷ People are gathering in this seaside village for a dance **marathon** that will take place tomorrow.
人群正湧進這座海濱村莊，明天村子裡會舉行一場舞蹈耐力賽。

06 **MTV** [ɛm ti vi] 名 C 音樂電視

● **MTV** Networks is an American television company; it broadcasts popular music as well as videos of the singers or groups performing it.
「MTV 電視網」是美國一家電視公司，播放流行音樂，以及歌手或團體表演的錄影帶。

07 **photography** [fəˋtɑgrəfɪ] 名 U 照相，攝影

● The **photography** in Hector's film demonstrates a realist approach. 赫克特的攝影是以寫實手法來拍攝的。

- photo- 表「照相（的）」
- graph 圖

08 **recreation** [͵rɛkrɪˋeʃən] 名 U 消遣，娛樂

● Alexander considers camping to be the best form of **recreation** for people today.
亞歷山大認為露營是對現代人最好的休閒。

- re- 表「重新」
- create 創造
- -ion 名 表「行為的結果」

09 **relax** [rɪˋlæks] 動 ❶ 使輕鬆，使休息；❷ 鬆弛，放鬆

❶ Soaking in a warm bath can **relax** your body and mind. 在浴缸中泡熱水澡，可以放鬆身心。

❷ After a hard day's work, Robert **relaxed** with a hot bath. 在一天繁重的工作之後，羅伯特會泡個熱水澡來放鬆。

- re- 表「再，重新」
- lax 散漫的

10 **relaxation** [ˌrilæksˋeʃən] 名 U 休息，消遣，娛樂

- Eleanor often listens to poetic music for **relaxation**. 艾琳諾常聽詩歌音樂來放鬆自己。

- relax 使輕鬆
- -ation 名 表「狀態」

11 **skate** [sket] 動 溜冰

- Last winter, Johnny had a good time **skating** on an ice-covered lake in Canada. 去年冬天，強尼在加拿大的結冰湖泊上溜冰溜得很開心。

補充 roller-skating 輪式溜冰；in-line skating 溜直排輪；ice-skating 冰上溜冰；figure skating 花式溜冰

34

12 **ski** [ski] 動 滑雪

- Howard goes **skiing** in Canada every winter. 霍華每年冬天都會去加拿大滑雪。

13 **tourism** [ˋtʊrɪzəm] 名 U 旅遊（業），觀光（業）

- To promote **tourism**, the government sponsors monthly events designed to attract visitors. 政府為了推動觀光，每個月都會贊助各種活動來吸引遊客。

- tour 旅遊
- -ism 名 表「……主義」

14 **tourist** [ˋtʊrɪst] ❶ 名 C 觀光客，遊客 ❷ 形 觀光的，旅遊的

❶ Some **tourists** were trapped in the mountain resort last week because of the landslide. 上個星期，一些遊客因為山崩被困在山上的渡假村。

❷ Kenting National Park is a famous **tourist** spot in Taiwan; every year, people come from many different countries to enjoy the scenery. 墾丁國家公園是台灣一個著名的觀光景點，每年都會吸引許多來自不同國家的遊客。

- tour 旅遊
- -ist 名 表「做……的人」

15 **traveler** [ˋtrævlɚ] 名 C 旅行者，旅客，遊客

- Low-budget **travelers** and backpackers must be flexible while on the road. 預算較少的旅客或背包客，必須要規劃比較有彈性的行程。

- travel 旅遊
- -er 名 表「人」

16 **sightseeing** [ˋsaɪt͵siɪŋ] 名 U **觀光，遊覽**

- sight 觀光地
- see 看
- -ing 名 表「動作」

● Leo takes his children for some **sightseeing** in the countryside once a month.
李歐每個月都會帶孩子們去鄉下遊玩一趟。

17 **sled** [slɛd] ❶ 名 C **雪橇** ❷ 動 **滑雪橇** 同義 sledge 雪橇

❶ In the summertime, my sisters and I improvised **sleds** out of flattened pieces of cardboard and slid down the grassy hillsides.
夏天時，我和姐妹們會用壓平的厚紙板，湊合著做出雪橇，在山坡上滑草。

❷ It has been snowing heavily today; I think we may be able to go **sledding** tomorrow morning.
今天一直在下大雪，我想明天早上可能可以去滑雪橇。

18 **sledge** [slɛdʒ] ❶ 名 C **雪橇** ❷ 動 **滑雪橇** 同義 sled 雪橇／乘雪橇

❶ In wintertime, people in Alaska use **sledges** to travel over snow and ice. 冬天時，阿拉斯加的人們會在冰雪上乘雪橇來做交通往返。

❷ Some people are skiing on the snow-covered hill, while others are **sledging**. 在這座白雪皚皚的山上，有人在滑雪，有人在滑雪橇。

19 **sleigh** [sle] ❶ 名 C **輕便雪橇** ❷ 動 **駕雪橇，乘雪橇**

❶ Tim and Jewel held hands under the blanket as two white horses pulled their **sleigh** across the moonlit snow. 提姆和茱兒在毛毯下手拉著手，乘坐在兩匹白馬拖曳的雪橇上，橫越過月光照耀的雪地。

❷ They used to **sleigh** and skate on the frozen lake in winter.
他們以前冬天時常會在結冰的湖面上駕雪橇和滑冰。

20 **sportsman** [ˋsportsmən] 名 C **運動員，運動家**

- sports 運動
- man 人

● The career of a professional **sportsman** is usually very short. 職業運動員的生涯通常很有限。

21 **sportsmanship** [ˋsportsmən͵ʃɪp] 名 U **運動家精神**

- sportsman 運動員
- -ship 名 表「狀態」

● **Sportsmanship** is more important than winning or losing a game. 運動精神比比賽的輸贏更重要。

22 **surf** [sɝf] 動 ❶ **作衝浪運動**；❷ **上網瀏覽** 名 ❸ U **碎浪，浪花**

❶ I saw a dog surfing on a **surfboard**. What an interesting sight!
我看到一隻狗在衝浪板上衝浪，真是個有趣的畫面！

❷ I am **surfing** the Internet to find some information for my report. 我正在上網瀏覽，要找一些和我報告有關的資料。

❸ Sitting on the beach, we heard the sound of **surf** breaking on the rocks. 我們坐在沙灘上，聽著浪花拍打在岩石上的聲音。

23 **tug-of-war** [tʌg·ɑv·wɔr] 名 C **拔河比賽**

- tug 用力拉
- war 競賽

● Students in Grades 3 and 4 challenged each other to a **tug-of-war** on sports day.
三年級和四年級的學生約好在運動日那一天，要互相比賽拔河來一較高下。

24 **voyage** [ˋvɔɪɪdʒ] ❶ 名 C **航海，航行** ❷ 動 **航海，航行**

❶ Alison dreams about making a **voyage** across the Pacific Ocean in her sailboat. 愛麗森夢想駕著她的帆船，遠航橫渡太平洋。

❷ Columbus **voyaged** across the sea and reached the North American continent. 哥倫布航行橫越大海，抵達北美洲大陸。

Part 2 →

Objects
物品

18 Food & drinks
飲食 (1)

35

01 **alcohol** [ˋælkə͵hɔl] 名 U ❶ 酒；❷ 酒精　形 名 alcoholic 含酒精的；嗜酒者

❶ The man drank too much **alcohol** at the bar and got drunk.
男子在酒吧喝了太多酒，喝醉了。

❷ Frankie used **alcohol** to clean the open wound on his arm before he applied the medicine. 法蘭奇在手臂傷口上藥之前，先用酒精消毒傷口。

02 **bacon** [ˋbekən] 名 U 培根，燻豬肉，鹹豬肉

- How many strips of **bacon** would you like on your sandwich?
你想在三明治上放多少條培根？

03 **berry** [ˋbɛrɪ] 名 C 莓果

- Lisa bought some fresh **berries** at the farmer's market and made a birthday cake for her son.
莉莎在農莊市場買了一些新鮮漿果，並用來為兒子做了一個生日蛋糕。

04 **biscuit** [ˋbɪskɪt] 名 C 小麵包，軟餅，餅乾

- Dolly brought some of the **biscuits** her grandmother made to school. 桃麗帶了一些祖母烤的餅乾去學校。

05 **broil** [brɔɪl] 動 烤

- They made a fire and **broiled** fish over it. 他們升了一堆火，在上面烤魚。

06 **buffet** [buˋfe] 名 C 自助餐，快餐

- During the **buffet**, people served themselves from a long counter and then returned to their tables to eat.
在吃自助餐時，人們自己去長桌上拿食物，然後回到自己的座位上用餐。

07 **calorie** [ˋkælərɪ] 名 C（熱量單位）卡，卡路里

- Each of those chocolate cookies contains 50 **calories**.
那些巧克力餅乾每一個的熱量是 50 卡。

08 **cheese** [tʃiz] 名 U 起司，乳酪

- Bavarian **cheese** is one of Bob's favorite foods.
巴伐利亞起司是鮑伯最愛吃的食物。

09 **cherry** [ˋtʃɛrɪ] 名 C **櫻桃**

- Douglas can't wait to buy some **cherries**, which are now in season. 現在是產櫻桃的季節，道格拉斯等不及想買些來吃了。

補充 cherry blossom 櫻花

10 **chip** [tʃɪp] 名 C ❶ **炸馬鈴薯條**；❷ **晶片**

❶ I don't understand how Travis can eat only potato **chips** and nothing else.
我想不透托維斯怎能只靠吃洋芋片過活，他其他東西都不吃。

❷ The worker's job is to add transistors to the **chips**.
這個工人的工作是將電晶體裝配到晶片上。

36

11 **cigar** [sɪˋgɑr] 名 C **雪茄**

- Gary smokes only **cigars**, not cigarettes. 蓋瑞不抽香菸，只抽雪茄。

12 **cigarette** [ˏsɪgəˋrɛt] 名 C **香菸**

- Don't you know that smoking **cigarettes** is harmful to your lungs? 你難道不知道抽菸對肺部有害嗎？

> ‧cigar 雪茄
> ‧-ette 名 表「小的……」

13 **cocktail** [ˋkɑkˏtel] 名 U **雞尾酒**

- Genna had a severe headache this morning because she drank too many **cocktails** last night.
金娜昨晚喝了太多雞尾酒，今天早上頭痛得很厲害。

補充 cocktail party 雞尾酒會

> ‧cock 公雞
> ‧tail 尾

14 **coconut** [ˋkokəˏnət] 名 C **椰子**

- John was hit by a falling **coconut** when he was sunbathing on the beach last week.
約翰上星期在海灘上做日光浴時，被一顆掉落的椰子給打中。

> ‧coco 椰子
> ‧nut 核果

15 **consume** [kənˋsjum] 動 ❶ **消耗，花費**；❷ **吃完，喝光**

❶ Mervin bought this car because its engine **consumes** less fuel than other models. 麥爾文買這款車，是因為它的引擎耗油量比其他款車少。

❷ The guests **consumed** all the food on the dining table and drank three bottles of red wine.
客人把餐桌上的菜餚都吃光，而且也把三瓶紅酒都喝光了。

16 **crisp** [krɪsp] 形 ❶ 脆的，酥的；❷ 新鮮爽口的 ❸ 動 發脆

❶ Nancy baked the bread in the oven until it was golden and **crisp**.
南茜用烤箱烤麵包，把麵包烤到呈金黃色、變得酥脆。

❷ Faye and her colleagues take turns preparing **crisp** carrots and celery sticks to share at work every day. 菲每天都會和同事們輪流準備新鮮爽口的胡蘿蔔和芹菜莖，在上班時和大家一起享用。

❸ Lillian baked the turkey until its skin had **crisped**.
莉莉安把火雞的皮烤到酥脆。

17 **crispy** [krɪspɪ] 形 酥脆的

• crisp 脆酥的
• -y 形 表「……的」

● Be sure to seal the bag tightly so the chips will stay **crispy** for a while.
要把袋口封緊，這樣洋芋片可以保持酥脆一陣子。

18 **cube** [kjub] 名 C 立方體，立方形物體

● Jocelyn took some ice **cubes** out of the fridge and put them in her coke. 賈思琳從冰箱拿了一些冰塊，放進可樂裡。

19 **cucumber** [ˋkjukəmbɚ] 名 C 黃瓜

● In summer, my mom likes to preserve **cucumbers** with salt and put them in the refrigerator.
夏天時，我媽媽喜歡用鹽醃漬小黃瓜，然後放進冰箱冰。

相關片語 **as cool as a cucumber** 鎮定自若

● In an emergency, you should stay as cool as a cucumber.
在危急時刻，你應該要保持鎮定。

20 **dairy** [ˋdɛrɪ] 形 ❶ 牛奶製的；乳品的 名 C ❷ 製酪場，乳牛場；❸ 乳品店

❶ Mara is allergic to **dairy** products, so she can't drink milk or eat cheese. 瑪拉對乳製品過敏，所以不能喝牛奶或吃起司。

❷ The schoolchildren will visit a **dairy** to learn how milk is obtained and converted into butter and cheese.
這些學童將參觀一家製乳場，學習牛奶是如何保存並製作成奶油和起司的。

❸ We ran out of milk, so we bought some at the **dairy** on the corner. 我們的牛奶喝光了，所以我們在街角的乳品店買了一些牛奶。

補充 nondairy 形 不含乳製品的

21 **diet** [ˋdaɪət] 名 C ❶ 飲食；❷ 特種飲食 動 ❸ 進規定的飲食，節食

❶ In Japan, many people's **diets** consist mainly of rice, fish, and vegetables. 日本人的飲食主要是米飯、魚肉和蔬菜。

❷ Cindy is on a **diet**; she doesn't eat fast food or desserts.
辛蒂正在節食，她不吃速食和甜點。

❸ Kelvin is **dieting** to lose 5 pounds this month.
為了要在一個月之內減輕五磅，凱文正在節食。

補充 diet drink 低卡飲料

22 **dine** [daɪn] 動 進餐，用餐

- Mr. and Mrs. Edison often **dine** out with their friends on Friday nights. 愛迪生夫婦每週五晚上常和朋友上館子。

19 Food & drinks 飲食 (2)

37

01 **feast** [fist] 名 C 筵席，盛宴

- Robin prepared a **feast** for his wife's birthday.
羅賓為妻子的生日準備了一場宴會。

02 **flavor** [ˋflevɚ] 名 ❶ U 味，味道；❷ C 香料，調味料 動 ❸ 給……調味

❶ Before the mother bought ice cream for her son, she asked him which **flavor** he wanted— chocolate or vanilla.
媽媽在買冰淇淋給兒子時，問他喜歡巧克力還是香草口味的。

❷ Jonathan is very sensitive to taste, and he doesn't like any artificial **flavors** in his food. 喬納森的味覺很敏感，不喜歡食物裡放進人工香料。

❸ Before putting the fish into the steamer, the cook **flavored** it with soybean sauce and vinegar. 把魚放進蒸鍋之前，廚師加上醬油和醋做調味。

03 **fry** [fraɪ] 動 煎，炸，炒

- Michelle is **frying** chicken wings for us. 蜜雪兒正在幫我們炸雞翅。

04 **garlic** [ˋgɑrlɪk] 名 U 大蒜，蒜頭

- The smell of **garlic** always reminds Dan of his mother's cooking.
大蒜的味道會讓丹想起媽媽做的菜。

05 **ginger** [ˋdʒɪndʒɚ] 名 U 薑

- Helga likes to boil **ginger** and brown sugar to make tea in the winter. 冬天時，荷佳喜歡加入紅糖和薑煮茶來喝。

06 **grain** [gren] 名 C ❶ 穀粒；❷（砂、鹽等的）粒

❶ Ross stores **grains** of rice in glass containers rather than in clay pots. 蘿絲把米粒存放在玻璃罐裡，而不是存放在陶土罐裡。

❷ After walking on the beach for a while, I felt **grains** of sand in my shoes. 我在海灘上走了一會之後，覺得鞋子進沙了。

07 **grapefruit** [ˋgrep͵frut] 名 C 葡萄柚

‧grape 葡萄
‧fruit 水果

● Nicholas claims that his energy comes from eating one **grapefruit** every morning.
尼可拉斯常保精力旺盛的祕訣，是每天早上吃一顆葡萄柚。

08 **greasy** [ˋgrizɪ] 形 油膩的，多脂的

‧grease 油脂
‧-y 形 表「……的」

● Ellie set the **greasy** bacon strips on a paper towel before serving them. 愛莉把油膩的培根條放在紙巾上，然後再盛上盤。

09 **gum** [gʌm] 名 U 口香糖　同義 chewing gum 口香糖

● The boy put a stick of **gum** in his mouth and started to chew it.
男孩把一片口香糖放進嘴巴，開始嚼了起來。

10 **ingredient** [ɪnˋgridɪənt] 名 C ❶（混合物的）組成部分，（烹飪的）原料；❷（構成）要素，因素

❶ The **ingredients** for the cake are as follows: 3 cups of flour, 1 cup of sugar, and 2 teaspoons of baking powder.
製作這個蛋糕的原料如下：三杯麵粉、一杯糖和兩匙發粉。

❷ Timing is the most important **ingredient** of a good stand-up comedy performance. 時間的掌握，是演好單人喜劇最重要的一環。

38

11 **jelly** [ˋdʒɛlɪ] 名 U 果凍，果醬

● Hollie's favorite snack is peanut butter and **jelly** on a piece of toast. 荷莉最喜歡的點心是塗上花生醬和果醬的土司麵包。

12 **liquor** [ˋlɪkɚ] 名 U 酒，含酒精飲料　同義 spirits 烈酒

● What kind of **liquor** goes best with orange juice?
什麼酒最適合加柳橙汁一起喝？

13 **lollipop** [ˋlalɪ͵pap] 名 C 棒棒糖

● The little girl loves all kinds of sweets, including jelly beans and **lollipops**. 這個小女孩愛吃各種糖果，像是豆形軟糖和棒棒糖。

14 **mineral** [ˋmɪnərəl] 名 C 礦物（質）

- If we have a healthy diet, we get all the vitamins and **minerals** we need from our food.
  只要我們飲食健康，從食物中就能攝取到所有所需的維他命和礦物質。

15 **mixture** [ˋmɪkstʃɚ] 名 C ❶ 混合物；❷ 混合，混雜

- mix 混合
- -ure 名 表「狀態」

❶ Ali drank a **mixture** of lemon juice, honey, and warm water to treat his cold.
阿里把檸檬汁、蜂蜜摻著溫水喝來治療感冒。

❷ With its **mixture** of cultures, New York City is considered one of the most interesting places on Earth.
因為多樣不同的文化混合，紐約成為世界上最有趣的地方之一。

16 **mushroom** [ˋmʌʃrum] 名 C 蘑菇，菇

- Elliot was told not to eat wild **mushrooms** because they could be poisonous. 有人告訴艾略特，野生菇類可能有毒，所以不要吃。

17 **pancake** [ˋpænˏkek] 名 C 薄煎餅

- pan 平底鍋
- cake 餅狀食物

- Denise was so hungry after school today that she stopped for a blueberry **pancake** on her way home.
  丹妮絲今天放學時太餓了，回家途中就買了一塊藍莓煎餅吃。

18 **pasta** [ˋpɑstə] 名 U 義式麵糰

- Elfreda learned how to make **pasta** from her grandfather.
  愛芙達從祖父那裡學會怎麼做義式麵糰。

19 **pea** [pi] 名 C 豌豆

- Barbara uses green **peas** and tomatoes in her dishes for both color and flavor. 芭芭拉用豌豆和番茄將每道菜都煮的色香味俱全。

20 **pickle** [ˋpɪkl̩] ❶ 名 C 醃漬食品，泡菜 ❷ 動 醃製，將……做成泡菜

❶ As Jude bit into the fat green **pickle**, juice squirted onto his white trousers. 朱德大口咬下肥美的醃黃瓜，汁液噴到了他的白色長褲上。

❷ Koreans **pickle** vegetables by putting them in vinegar or salt water. 韓國人把蔬菜浸到醋或鹽水裡來做泡菜。

21 **plum** [plʌm] 名 C 梅子，洋李

- These **plums** are not ripe yet, so you should wait a few days before eating them. 這些梅子還沒熟，所以你應該等個幾天再吃。

補充 plum blossom 梅花

22 **portion** [ˋporʃən] 名 C ❶(一)部分；❷(食物等的)一份，一客
動 ❸ 把……分成多份，分配

❶ After reading only a **portion** of the novel, Lovelyn was too fascinated to put the book down.
羅芙琳只讀了一部分的小說，就愛不釋手了。

❷ The man ordered a half **portion** of roast chicken but found it was not enough food for him. 男子點了半隻烤雞，結果還是吃不飽。

❸ The mother **portioned** out the pie so that all her children had a piece. 媽媽將派分成了好幾塊，所以每個孩子都可以得到一塊。

20 Food & drinks 飲食 (3)

39

01 **powder** [ˋpaʊdɚ] ❶ 名 U 粉末 ❷ 動 撲粉

❶ Mrs. Gray put the milk **powder** in the nursing bottle and mixed it with some hot water.
葛雷太太把奶粉放進奶瓶裡，再加入一些熱水攪拌混合。

❷ After **powdering** her face, the girl put on lipstick and eye shadow. 女孩在臉上撲粉之後，擦上口紅和眼影。

02 **protein** [ˋprotiɪn] 名 U 蛋白質

- Beans and eggs contain high quantities of **protein**.
豆類和蛋豐含蛋白質。

03 **raisin** [ˋrezn̩] 名 C 葡萄乾

- Adding **raisins** and nuts to a bowl of cereal is a nutritious way to enrich the taste. 在麥片中加入葡萄乾和堅果，既營養又好吃。

04 **raw** [rɔ] 形 ❶ 生的，未煮過的；❷ 未加工的

❶ When Daniel goes to a Japanese restaurant, he always orders a lot of **raw** fish. 丹尼爾去日本料理店用餐時，都會點很多生魚片。

❷ The country imports **raw** materials from other nations because it lacks natural resources. 這個國家缺乏自然資源，所以從其他國家進口原料。

05 **recipe** [ˋrɛsəpɪ] 名 C 食譜，烹飪法

- Adeline collects **recipes** and then experiments with different ways of cooking to create her own style.
  雅德琳收集食譜，然後嘗試各種烹飪方式，創造出自己的菜色。

06 **refreshment** [rɪˋfrɛʃmənt] 名 ❶ U 飲料；❷ C（常作複數）茶點，便餐

❶ Can I offer you a **refreshment**: beer, wine, orange juice, or water?
你要喝些什麼？啤酒、葡萄酒、柳橙汁還是白開水？

- re- 表「再」
- fresh 精力充沛的
- -ment 名 表「產物」

❷ After the meeting, the press officials offered us some **refreshments**; the drinks and desserts were delicious.
記者會結束後，新聞部的官員提供了一些點心。那些飲料和甜點都很美味。

07 **roast** [rost] ❶ 形 烘烤的 ❷ 動 烘，烤 ❸ 名 C 野外烤肉聚會

❶ The **roast** duck Ricardo made for the banquet was so tender and juicy that all the guests loved it.
瑞卡多在宴會烤的鴨鮮嫩又多汁，所有的客人都讚不絕口。

❷ The camper made a fire near the river and **roasted** some fish for lunch. 露營者在河邊生了一堆火，烤了一些魚當作午餐。

❸ They are going to have a hot dog **roast** in their yard this Sunday, and 10 neighbors will attend.
這個星期天，他們將在院子舉辦一個烤熱狗的野餐會，有十位鄰居會來參加。

08 **sausage** [ˋsɔsɪdʒ] 名 C 香腸，臘腸

- To make **sausage**, the cook mixed the chopped meat with the spices and stuffed the mixture into the pork gut.
  廚師為了做香腸，把剁好的豬肉和香料混合好，再把它們塞進豬腸裡。

09 **spaghetti** [spəˋgɛtɪ] 名 U 義大利麵條

- Sandra usually allows 15 minutes to cook **spaghetti** in boiling water. 珊德拉通常會把義大利麵丟進滾水裡煮上十五分鐘。

10 **spice** [spaɪs] 名 ❶ C 香料，調味品；❷ U 趣味，風味
動 ❸ 加香料於 ❹ 使增添趣味

❶ India has a long history of exporting **spices** by way of merchant ships. 印度商船外銷香料的歷史很悠久了。

❷ To add some **spice** to her boring life, Heather planned an exciting trip to London.
海瑟為了讓自己無聊的生活有趣些，她打算去倫敦好好玩一下。

❸ The steak is **spiced** with rosemary, which will give it more flavor. 這個牛排加上迷迭香，可以增添風味。

❹ The speech was **spiced** with jokes and stories, which made it very interesting. 這篇演講運用笑話和故事來增添趣味，變得更有趣了。

40

11 **spoil** [spɔɪl] 動 ❶（食物等）變壞；❷ 搞糟，糟蹋；❸ 寵壞，溺愛

❶ Let's store all the leftovers in the refrigerator so they won't **spoil**. 我們把剩菜剩飯都放進冰箱，這樣才不會壞掉。

❷ The heavy rain **spoiled** their hiking trip and ruined the day. 這場大雨讓他們的健行泡湯，也讓那一天泡湯了。

❸ The mother **spoils** her children by giving them everything they ask for. 這個媽媽寵壞了孩子，不管他們要什麼她都給。

12 **stale** [stel] 形 不新鮮的　反義 fresh 新鮮的

• Open a new bag of potato chips because these are **stale**. 這些洋芋片都不新鮮了，再開包新的吧。

13 **starve** [stɑrv] 動 餓死，挨餓　名 starvation 飢餓，挨餓

• Even after two months without food, a cockroach will not **starve** to death. 蟑螂即使兩個月不吃東西，也不會餓死。

14 **sticky** [ˋstɪkɪ] 形 黏的

• Serena never had **sticky** rice until she traveled to Taiwan. 瑟瑞娜來臺灣旅遊時，第一次吃到糯米。

- stick 黏住
- -y 形 表「性質，狀態」

15 **tender** [ˋtɛndɚ] 形 ❶ 嫩的，柔軟的；❷ 溫柔的　反義 tough 肉質老的

❶ After being cooked over a low flame for three hours, the meat becomes very **tender**. 肉用小火煮了三個小時之後，變得非常的嫩。

❷ The mother was **tender** toward her injured son; she bandaged his wound carefully and gently. 媽媽對受傷的兒子很溫柔，她輕柔、仔細地用繃帶幫他包紮傷口。

16 **tobacco** [təˋbæko] 名 U 菸草

• Some baseball players chew **tobacco** for minor stimulation while playing the game. 有些棒球選手在打球時會嚼菸草來稍稍提神。

17 **vitamin** [ˋvaɪtəmɪn] 名 C 維他命

• Several years ago, Heather started taking a **vitamin** pill after breakfast every day. 海瑟從幾年前開始，在每天早餐後都會服用維他命。

18 **yolk** [jok] 名 C 蛋黃

- The yolk of a duck egg is larger and more tasty than the **yolk** of a chicken egg. 鴨蛋蛋黃比雞蛋蛋黃要來得大，而且比較好吃。

補充 egg white 蛋白

19 **spicy** [ˋspaɪsɪ] 形 辛辣的

- spice 調味品
- -y 形 表「性質」

- Daren was overwhelmed by the **spicy** dishes prepared by his friends from Thailand.
泰國朋友煮的辣味菜，讓戴倫吃不消。

20 **syrup** [ˋsɪrəp] 名 U 糖漿

- Devin cannot resist maple **syrup**, especially with French toast.
戴文就是抗拒不了楓糖糖漿，尤其是吃法式土司的時候。

21 **vinegar** [ˋvɪnɪgɚ] 名 U 醋

- The salad needs some salt and **vinegar**. 沙拉裡要加點鹽巴和醋。

22 **walnut** [ˋwɔlnət] 名 C 胡桃

- Until he lost his molars, Uncle Pete could crack **walnuts** open with his bare teeth. 皮特叔叔的臼齒掉了之前，他光用牙齒就能咬開胡桃。

23 **yogurt** [ˋjogɚt] 名 U 優格

- Bradley eats frozen **yogurt** as a healthy alternative to ice cream.
布德里為了健康，吃冷凍優格來代替冰淇淋。

21 Clothes & accessories 衣服與配件 (1)

41

01 **blouse** [blaʊz] 名 C （婦女的）短上衣，短衫

- I think this blue **blouse** will match your white skirt.
我覺得這件藍色上衣和你的白色裙子會很配。

02 **boot** [but] 名 C （長筒）靴

- Jay went to a pawn shop and traded his old leather **boots** for a nice suit. 傑拿舊皮靴去當鋪換了一套不錯的西裝回來。

03 **bracelet** [ˋbreslɪt] 名 C 手鐲，臂鐲

- Ben was happy to find the jade **bracelet** his wife wore on their wedding day. 班找到妻子在他們結婚當天戴的那隻玉鐲，感到很高興。

04 **brassiere** [brəˋzɪr] 名 C 胸罩　同義 bra 胸罩

- Around the age of 13, many girls start wearing a **brassiere**.
許多少女到了十三歲左右便開始穿胸罩。

05 **collar** [ˋkɑlɚ] 名 C 衣領，頸圈

- Enraged, Brett grabbed Darren by his **collar** and asked him where all their money had gone.
布列特火大地抓住戴倫的衣領，問說他們的錢都到哪裡去了。

補充 white-collar 白領階級的；blue-collar 藍領階級的

06 **costume** [ˋkɑstjum] 名 C ❶ 服裝；❷ 戲服

❶ After school, Renee went home to put on her **costume** for the party. 芮妮放學後，就回家換衣服去參加派對。

❷ During the play, the actor has to change into five different **costumes**. 演戲的時候，這個演員得換上五套不同的戲服。

07 **diaper** [ˋdaɪəpɚ] 名 C 尿布

- After giving her baby a bath, the mother put a **diaper** around its bottom. 媽媽在幫寶寶洗完澡後，幫寶寶的屁股包上尿布。

42

08 **fancy** [ˋfænsɪ] 形 ❶ 花俏的　名 ❷ C 愛好，迷戀　動 ❸ 想像；❹ 喜愛

❶ Mabel prefers plain clothes to **fancy** ones.
梅寶喜歡素一點的衣服，不喜歡太花俏的。

❷ Justin took a **fancy** to the prettiest girl in the class; he wanted to ask her out. 賈斯汀很喜歡班上最正的正妹，他想約她出去。

❸ The little girl is wearing a beautiful dress and **fancies** herself a princess. 小女孩穿著一件漂亮的洋裝，幻想自己是一名公主。

❹ Linda wants to see a late movie with her friends, but she doesn't **fancy** the idea of walking home alone in the dark.
琳達想跟朋友去看晚場電影，但不想獨自走夜路回家。

09 **fashion** [ˋfæʃən] 名 ❶ U 流行式樣，時尚；❷ C 方式

❶ Carrie doesn't like the current **fashion** of short skirts and high heels. 凱莉不喜歡時下流行的短裙和高跟鞋。

❷ The teacher asked the boys to stop fighting and solve their problem in a civilized **fashion**.
老師要男孩們停止打架，要求他們用文明的方式來解決問題。

補充 in fashion 流行／out of fashion 不流行

10 **fashionable** [ˋfæʃənəbḷ] 形 流行的，時髦的

● Natalie always needs to wear **fashionable** clothing; she has become a slave to the fashion industry.
娜塔莉一定要穿潮服。她已經變成時尚產業的受害者了。

・fashion 流行
・-able 形 表「有……特性的」

11 **gown** [gaʊn] 名 C ❶ 女禮服，長禮服；❷（學生畢業典禮時穿的）長袍

❶ The bride looks stunning in her wedding **gown**.
新娘穿著結婚禮服看起來好美啊。

❷ Clarissa's parents were very proud to see her wearing a cap and **gown** at her college graduation.
父母在克蕾莉莎的大學畢業典禮上，驕傲地看著穿戴學士帽、學士服的她。

補充 evening gown 晚禮服；night-gown 女用長睡袍

12 **jewel** [ˋdʒuəl] 名 C ❶ 寶石；寶石飾物；❷ 珍貴的東西 同義 gem 寶石

❶ A ruby is a dark red precious **jewel**. 紅寶石是一種暗紅色的珍貴寶石。

❷ The tropical islands are **jewels** of nature surrounded by a sea of sparkling blue water. 被閃動湛藍大海環繞的熱帶島嶼，猶如大自然的寶石。

13 **jewelry** [ˋdʒuəlrɪ] 名 U（總稱）珠寶，首飾

● Pamela sold all her **jewelry** for cash to pay her husband's debts.
潘蜜拉變賣她所有的珠寶，來償還丈夫所欠下的債務。

・jewel 寶石
・-ry 名 表「……類的事物」

14 **knit** [nɪt] 動 編織

● Juliet **knitted** sweaters for her family members as birthday gifts.
茱麗葉織毛衣給家人當生日禮物。

15 **lace** [les] 名 U 花邊

● The lady bought a dress trimmed with **lace**.
那位女士買了一件有花邊的洋裝。

16 **laundry** [ˋlɔndrɪ] 名 ❶ U 洗衣；❷ C 洗衣店，洗衣房

❶ Doreen borrowed some clean clothes from her sister because she was too busy to do the **laundry**.
多琳忙得沒空洗衣服，就向妹妹借了一些乾淨的衣服來穿。

・launder 洗滌
・-y 名 表「性質」

❷ It is better to dry-clean the sweater, so I will send it to the **laundry** on the corner. 這件毛衣最好乾洗，所以我要把它拿到街角的洗衣店送洗。

補充 laundromat 名 自助洗衣店

17 **mend** [mɛnd] 動 ❶ 修理，修補；❷ 改善，糾正

❶ Prudence **mended** a hole in her favorite jeans by sewing a patch of blue fabric over it. 普登絲在最愛的牛仔褲上縫了一塊藍色布來補破洞。

❷ Bonnie had behaved very badly toward her sisters; she promised that she would **mend** her ways.
邦妮以前對姊妹們都不好，她答應會改過自新。

相關片語 **on the mend** 在好轉中

- After the operation, the patient was on the mend.
手術後，病人的狀況在好轉。

22 Clothes & accessories 衣服與配件 (2)

43

01 **necktie** [ˋnɛk͵taɪ] 名 C 領帶，領結

- Mr. Dodge didn't like wearing **neckties**, but he owned more than 50 bright and colorful bow ties.
道吉先生不喜歡打領帶，但他有 50 幾個顏色繽紛亮麗的領結。

・neck 頸
・tie 帶子

02 **overcoat** [ˋovɚ͵kot] 名 C 外套，大衣

- Don't forget to bring your **overcoat** because it could be cold at night. 別忘了帶件外套，晚上可能會冷。

・over- 表「在外的」
・coat 外套

03 **pearl** [pɝl] 名 C 珍珠

- Edith's favorite piece of jewelry is a string of **pearls** she received as a birthday gift from her mother.
伊蒂絲最喜歡的珠寶，是母親送給她當生日禮物的那串珍珠。

04 **rag** [ræg] 名 C ❶ 破布，抹布；❷ 破爛衣衫

❶ The farmer recycled his old shirts by ripping them into strips and using them as work **rags**. 農夫將舊襯衫撕成小塊回收當抹布使用。

❷ The homeless man, who is dressed in **rags**, needs clothes as well as food. 這名衣衫襤褸的遊民不僅需要食物，也需要衣物。

相關片語 **from rags to riches** 由貧致富

- The movie tells the story of a young man who went from rags to riches.
  這部電影敘述一個由貧致富的年輕人的故事。

05 **ribbon** [ˋrɪbən] 名 C 緞帶

- Mike tied a yellow **ribbon** on his daughter's ponytail.
  麥克在女兒的馬尾上綁了一條黃緞帶。

06 **robe** [rob] 名 C 長袍，浴衣，睡袍

- The magician took a burning sword out of his **robe** and turned it into a dove; then the dove flew away.
  魔術師從長袍中抽出一把燃燒的劍，然後將劍變成了一隻鴿子飛走了。

07 **scarf** [skɑrf] 名 C 圍巾，披巾

- Sally was equipped with gloves, a **scarf**, and ski boots when she went skiing. 莎莉去滑雪時穿戴著手套、圍巾和雪靴。

08 **sew** [so] 動 縫合，縫上

- Annie's mother **sewed** up all the holes in her old blue jeans.
  安妮的母親替她縫上舊藍色牛仔褲上的所有破洞。

09 **sexy** [ˋsɛksɪ] 形 性感的

- When Desiree goes out dancing, she always wears a **sexy** dress to attract men's attention.
  狄賽莉去參加舞會時，都會做性感裝扮來吸引男人的目光。

> ・sex 性
> ・-y 形 表「狀態」

44 10 **sleeve** [sliv] 名 C 袖子

- After the earthquake, Monty promptly rolled up his **sleeves** and helped with the rescue effort. 曼提在地震後立刻捲起衣袖幫忙救災。

11 **stockings** [ˋstɑkɪŋz] 名（複）長襪

- Loretta loves to wear two different-colored **stockings**. 蘿瑞妲喜歡穿兩隻不同顏色的長襪。

補充 silk stockings 絲襪

> ・stock 貯存
> ・-ing 名 表「產物」
> ・-s（複）

12 **style** [staɪl] 名 ❶ U 流行款式；❷ C（商品等的）類型，式樣

❶ Ms. Morgan has a good sense of fashion; she always wears clothes with **style**. 摩根小姐的流行品味極佳，她穿衣服很有風格。

❷ The store carries shoes in a wide variety of **styles** and sizes.
這家店提供各種式樣和尺寸的鞋子。

13 **tailor** [ˋtelɚ] 名 C（男裝）裁縫師

- The actor had his suit made by an American **tailor**.
那位男演員的禮服出自一位美國裁縫師之手。

補充 tailor-made 形 量身訂做的

14 **thread** [θrɛd] 名 C 線

- Using only needle and **thread**, Erica converted her old blue skirt into a new handbag.
艾莉卡只用針和線，就把她的舊藍裙子改成一個新的手提包了。

相關片語 ❶ **pick up the thread(s)** 重新繼續
❷ **hang by a thread** 岌岌可危

❶ After a 10-minute break, they picked up the threads of their discussion. 在休息十分鐘之後，他們重新繼續他們的討論。

❷ After he was hit by the truck, the old man's life was hanging by a thread. 老人被一輛卡車撞到，性命岌岌可危。

補充 a needle and thread 針線

15 **tight** [taɪt] 形 ❶ 緊身的；❷ 緊的，不鬆動的；❸（行程等）緊湊的，排得滿滿的；❹（比賽等）勢均力敵的

❶ Todd must have gained some weight because his old jeans are too **tight** now. 陶德一定是變胖了，因為他的舊牛仔褲現在變得好緊。

❷ The top of this bottle is too **tight**; I can't unscrew it.
瓶蓋太緊了，我轉不開。

❸ I have a very **tight** schedule today; I am not sure if I can finish everything in the time that is available.
我今天的行程好滿，不確定每件事都可以如期搞定。

❹ In the beginning, the game was very **tight**; it wasn't clear which team would win. 比賽剛開始時勢均力敵，勝負難分。

16 **trend** [trɛnd] 名 C 趨勢，時尚

- This magazine focuses on new dieting **trends** and techniques.
這本雜誌專門介紹新的飲食趨勢和方法。

相關用法 形 **trendy** 時髦的，流行的

- Every month, Annie spends a lot of money on trendy clothes.
安妮每個月都會花很多錢來買潮服。

17 **vest** [vɛst] 名 C 背心

- Raymond is looking for a **vest** to go with his new T-shirt.
雷蒙在找一件能搭配他新 T 恤的背心。

18 **weave** [wiv] 動 編，織

- Josephine used straw and vines to **weave** a basket for carrying fruit. 約瑟芬用稻草和藤蔓編了一個水果籃。

19 **zipper** [ˋzɪpɚ] 名 C 拉鍊

- In the 1980s, Michael Jackson wore a red leather jacket with lots of **zippers**.
在 1980 年代，麥克．傑克森曾穿過一件縫有很多拉鍊的紅色皮外套。

・zip 拉開拉鍊
・-er 名 表「物」

23 Materials & articles 材料與物品 (1)

45

01 **acid** [ˋæsɪd] ❶ 名 C 酸 ❷ 形 酸的，有酸味的 同義 形 sour 酸的

❶ Be careful when handling the **acid**, or it may burn your skin.
拿酸性液體時要小心，因為它們會灼傷皮膚。

❷ My father doesn't like any **acid** fruits such as lemons and grapefruits; he dislikes the sharp, sour taste.
我爸爸不喜歡任何酸的水果，像是檸檬和葡萄柚；他不喜歡刺激的酸味。

02 **aluminum** [əˋlumɪnəm] 名 U 鋁

- Corrine uses utensils made of **aluminum** for camping because they are light. 鋁製品很輕巧，所以可琳用它們作為露營用具。

03 **ash** [æʃ] 名 ❶ U 灰，灰燼；❷ C 廢墟

❶ Volcanic **ash** can become trapped in the clouds and travel a great distance. 火山灰可能會混進雲裡頭，跟著長距離飄行。

❷ After the severe earthquake and resulting fires, the town was ruined. Most of the buildings were left in **ashes**.
在大地震過後引發火災，一座小鎮遭到摧毀，大部分的建築物成了一片廢墟。

04 **attachment** [əˋtætʃmənt] 名 C 附件，配件

- The juice extractor has three **attachments** that can be put on the machine to make it do different jobs.
這台榨汁機有三個配件，可以安裝在機器上，完成不同功能。

・attach 附加
・-ment 名 表「產物」

05 **award** [əˋwɔrd] ❶ 名 C 獎，獎品 ❷ 動 授予

❶ Kimber established a foundation to give financial **awards** to students in need. 金柏設了一個基金會，來獎勵清寒學生。

❷ The student was **awarded** the prize for his excellent performance at school. 這名學生因為在校表現傑出而獲獎。

06 **ax** [æks] ❶ 名 C 斧頭 ❷ 動 削減，撤銷

❶ In the yard, the man was chopping wood with an **ax**.
男子正在院子裡用斧頭劈材。

❷ To save money, the service has been **axed**.
為了節省開銷，這項服務已被取消。

07 **backpack** [ˋbækˏpæk] 名 C（登山、遠足用的）背包

・back 後面；背
・pack 包，背包

● The hikers carried water, maps, and first aid kits in their **backpacks**. 健行者在背包中放入水、地圖和急救箱。

08 **baggage** [ˋbægɪdʒ] 名 U 行李 同義 luggage 行李〔英式〕

● When Candy travels, she keeps her **baggage** light so she can move around easily. 康蒂旅行時的行囊都很輕便，這樣才方便她到處玩。

09 **bait** [bet] 名 C ❶ 餌；❷ 誘餌，引誘物 動 ❸ 置餌於；❹ 挑釁

❶ The fisherman pulled the catfish out of the water after it took the **bait**. 等鯰魚吃下誘餌，漁夫把魚拉出水面。

❷ Stanley took the **bait**—a large chocolate cookie—and stopped crying. 史丹利拿到了一大塊巧克力餅乾，就不哭了。

❸ To catch the mouse, my father **baited** the trap with a slice of cheese. 為了抓住那隻老鼠，我爸爸在陷阱裡放了一塊起司當誘餌。

❹ Although the mob kept **baiting** the police, the officers remained calm. 暴民不斷對警方挑釁，但警方依然保持冷靜。

相關片語 **rise to the bait** 入圈套

● Whenever her classmates deliberately try to make her angry, the girl responds. She rises to the bait every time.
只要同學故意惹她生氣，她就會動怒；她每次都會上鉤。

10 **battery** [ˋbætərɪ] 名 C 電池

● Edward uses rechargeable **batteries** whenever he can.
愛德華盡可能使用充電電池。

11 **blanket** [ˋblæŋkɪt] ❶ 名 C 毛毯，毯子 ❷ 動 覆蓋

❶ The flight attendant offered me a **blanket** when I was aboard.
我登機後，空服員給了我一條毯子。

❷ It snowed heavily last night; this morning, everything outside was **blanketed** with snow.
昨天晚上雪下得很大，今天早上大地覆上一片白雪。

46

12 **brass** [bræs] 名 ❶ U 黃銅；❷ C（交響樂隊的）銅管樂器

❶ The door handle is made of **brass**. 這個門把是黃銅製的。

❷ Theodore considers Miles Davis to be the greatest **brass** player in jazz history. 希歐多爾認為邁爾斯．達維斯是爵士音樂史上最優秀的銅管樂樂手。

13 **broom** [brum] 名 C 掃帚

- The boy swept the floor with a **broom**. 男孩拿掃帚掃地板。

補充 new broom 新上任者

14 **bulb** [bʌlb] 名 C 電燈泡

- Josh always stores extra light **bulbs** in his workshop in case any lights burn out. 喬許的工作室都會放一些電燈泡備用，以防燈泡壞掉。

15 **cane** [ken] 名 C 手杖，拐杖

- Bonnie loves to see Charlie Chaplin walking like a penguin and spinning his **cane** on television.
邦妮很喜歡看卓別林在電視上像企鵝一樣走路、拿著手杖轉來轉去。

16 **cement** [sɪˋmɛnt] 名 U 水泥

- Ruby put colorful tiles on the gray **cement** wall in her front yard.
露比把前院的灰水泥牆鋪上彩色瓷磚。

17 **clip** [klɪp] 名 C ❶ 迴紋針；❷ 剪報

❶ Richard fastened several pieces of paper with a **clip**.
理查用迴紋針將幾張紙夾住。

❷ Jaclyn found a box of old **clips** her grandmother had collected half a century ago. 賈克琳找到了半個世紀前祖母所收集的一箱舊剪報。

18 **combination** [͵kɑmbəˋneʃən] 名 C ❶ 組合，結合；❷ 對號密碼

❶ Rita ordered the lobster and baked potato **combination** for dinner. 芮塔點了龍蝦和烤洋芋套餐當晚餐。

- combine 結合
- -ation 名 表「動作」

❷ The man couldn't open his briefcase after he forgot the **combination** for the lock.
男子忘了公事包的密碼鎖號碼，所以無法打開公事包。

19 **conductor** [kənˋdʌktɚ] 名 C ❶ 導體；❷（合唱團、樂隊等的）指揮

- conduce 導致
- -or 名 表「物」或「行為者」

❶ Since electricity flows easily through metal, it is often used as an electrical **conductor**.
金屬能讓電流快速通過，所以常被用來當作電導體。

❷ The **conductor** stands in front of the orchestra and directs the performance. 這名指揮站在交響樂團前指揮表演。

補充 semi-conductor 半導體

20 **container** [kənˋtenɚ] 名 C 容器

- contain 包含
- -er 名 表「物」

● A wide piece of bamboo can be made into a handy water **container**. 一節大竹筒可以用來製作成一個輕巧的水壺。

21 **contrast** 名 [ˋkɑn͵træst] 名 ❶ C 對比物，對照物；❷ U 對比，對照
動 [kənˋtræst] 動 ❸ 對比，對照；❹ 形成對照

❶ In Carolyn's painting, the bright, sunlit clouds and dark blue ocean form an interesting **contrast**.
在卡洛琳的繪畫作品中，被日光穿透的雲朵和湛藍海洋形成有趣的對比。

❷ Malcolm's chocolate fudge cake is very rich in **contrast** to your fruit tart. 跟你的水果塔比起來，麥爾肯的巧克力岩漿蛋糕看起來十分誘人。

❸ The teacher asked the students to **contrast** this painting with the one in the book by pointing out all the differences.
老師要學生們比較這幅畫和書中那幅畫的不同之處。

❹ These red maple leaves **contrast** nicely with the green water in the lake. 這些紅色的楓葉和綠色的湖水形成極佳的對比。

相關片語 **by contrast** 相比之下

● Mark's sister is stingy; by contrast, he is quite generous.
馬克的姊姊很小氣。相較之下，馬克很大方。

22 **convenience** [kənˋvinjəns] 名 ❶ C 便利設施；❷ U 方便

- convene 集合
- -ence 名 表「性質，狀態」

❶ Tom's mobile home has all the modern **conveniences** of most apartments.
湯姆的活動房屋，現代化的設備一應俱全，和多數公寓一樣。

❷ The cafe provides free Internet access for the **convenience** of its customers. 這家咖啡店為了顧客便利，提供了免費上網服務。

[相關片語] **at one's convenience** 就某人方便

- Please give me a call at your convenience. 請你方便的時候打個電話給我。

[補充] convenience store 便利商店

23 **copper** [ˋkɑpɚ] 名 U **銅**

- **Copper** wire is one of the best conductors of heat and electricity. 銅線是最佳的導熱和導電物之一。

24 **cord** [kɔrd] 名 C ❶ **細繩，粗線**；❷ **絕緣電線**

❶ The **cord** used to bind the package is thick and strong.
用來綁包裹的繩子又粗又強韌。

❷ This telephone **cord** is too short to reach the table where we want to put the phone. 這條電話線太短了，連不到我們想裝電話的桌子上。

24 Materials & articles
材料與物品 (2)

47

01 **cushion** [ˋkʊʃən] ❶ 名 C **墊子，坐墊，靠墊** ❷ 動 **緩和……的衝擊**

❶ Murray put a **cushion** on the seat to make it more comfortable.
莫瑞放了一個坐墊在座位上，坐起來更舒服。

❷ Generous severance allowances will help **cushion** the blow of the layoffs. 一筆好的資遣費有助於緩和臨時解雇所造成的衝擊。

02 **decoration** [ˌdɛkəˋreʃən] 名 C **裝飾品，裝飾物**

- decorate 動 裝飾
- -ion 名 表「行為的結果」

- To make the Christmas tree more attractive, the Wangs put some **decorations**, such as strings of lights and ribbons, on it.
為了讓耶誕樹看起來更漂亮，王家在上面放了一些裝飾品，像燈串和緞帶一類。

03 **dirt** [dɝt] 名 U ❶ **汙物，灰塵**；❷ **泥，土**　形 dirty 髒的

❶ Samantha's mother cannot understand why she always comes home covered in **dirt**.
莎曼莎的母親想不通，她為什麼老是一身髒兮兮地回到家。

❷ The gardener put the plant into the pot and packed the **dirt** around its roots. 園丁把植物放進一個盆子裡，然後在它的根部周圍填上泥土。

04 **disk** [dɪsk] 名 C ❶ 圓盤，盤狀物；❷ 光碟片 同義 disc 圓盤

❶ Look at the full moon; it is like a **disk** in the sky.
看看天空中那輪滿月，它像是一個圓盤。

❷ After the file was saved, Henry removed the **disk** from the computer drive. 把檔案存檔之後，亨利把磁碟片從磁碟機裡拿出來。

補充 CD = compact disk 光碟；VCD = video compact disk 影音光碟；DVD = digital video disk 數碼影音光碟

05 **dust** [dʌst] ❶ 名 U 灰塵，塵土 ❷ 動 撣掉（灰塵）

❶ Lynn always sneezes when there is **dust** in the air.
只要空氣中有灰塵，琳就會打噴嚏。

❷ The books were dusty, so I spent some time **dusting** them.
書上都是灰塵，我花了點時間把灰塵撣掉。

補充 duster 除塵器；vacuum cleaner 吸塵器

06 **earphones** [ˋɪrˏfons] 名（複）耳機

- ear 耳
- phone 聽筒
- -s（複）

● Harlan wore a pair of **earphones** so that he could listen to the radio without the people around him hearing it.
哈倫戴耳機聽廣播，所以旁邊的人不會聽到聲音。

07 **engine** [ˋɛndʒən] 名 C 發動機，引擎

● Peggy took the bus to work today because her car's **engine** wasn't running properly. 蓓姬今天坐公車上班，因為她車子的引擎怪怪的。

08 **file** [faɪl] ❶ 名 C 檔案，卷宗 ❷ 動 把……歸檔

❶ Janice lost all of her important **files** in a fire.
珍妮絲所有的重要檔案，都在火災中付之一炬了。

❷ The manager asked the secretary to **file** the documents in alphabetical order. 經理要祕書按字母順序將文件歸檔。

09 **firecracker** [ˋfaɪrˏkrækɚ] 名 C 鞭炮，爆竹

- fire 火
- crack 使爆裂
- -er 名 表「物」

● The boy set off the **firecrackers**, and they exploded with a loud noise. 男孩點燃鞭炮，鞭炮發出一聲巨響爆開了。

10 **firework** [ˋfaɪrˏwɝk] 名 C 煙火

- fire 火
- work 作品

● Chinese people shoot off **fireworks** at the beginning of the new year. 華人會在大年初一燃放鞭炮。

11 **frame** [frem] 名 C ❶ 架構，骨架；❷ 框架，框子
❸ 動 給……裝框子，把……裱起來

❶ The **frame** of the bed is made of iron. 這個床架是用鐵做的。

❷ I need to buy a new picture **frame** to hold the photo.
我需要買個新相框來放這張照片。

❸ Norbert **framed** some of his old family photographs and set them on top of his fireplace. 諾柏特把家族的一些舊相片裱起來，放在壁爐上方。

48

12 **fuel** [ˋfjʊəl] 名 U 燃料

● Scientists are trying to find a cleaner **fuel** to replace gasoline.
科學家努力想找出汙染較低的燃料來取代汽油。

13 **gear** [gɪr] 名 ❶ U 設備，工具；❷ C（汽車等）排檔

❶ Eugene owns a shop that sells fishing **gear**. 尤金經營一間釣具行。

❷ The bike has 12 **gears**; you can use them to ride comfortably at different speeds. 這輛腳踏車有十二段變速，你可以自由地調整速度騎乘。

14 **grocery** [ˋgrosərɪ] 名 C 雜貨

● Joanna stopped at the supermarket and bought some **groceries** on her way to the office.
喬安娜上班途中去超市買了點東西。

補充 grocery store 雜貨店

- gross 總的
- -ery 名 表「……類的事物」

15 **hardware** [ˋhɑrd͵wɛr] 名 U ❶ 裝備，設備；❷ 五金器具；❸ 硬體

❶ Jayme examined the **hardware** and found a loose screw. 潔玫檢查了設備，發現一根螺絲鬆掉了。

❷ Mr. Wood deals in **hardware**; he sells tools and equipment that are used in the house and yard.
伍德先生開五金行，他販賣住家和庭院使用的各種工具和器具。

❸ The mobile phone company is moving from **hardware** to software development. 這家手機公司從發展硬體轉型為軟體發展。

- hard 硬的
- ware …… 製品

16 **harmonica** [hɑrˋmɑnɪkə] 名 C 口琴

● American folksinger Bob Dylan plays the guitar and the **harmonica**. 美國民歌手鮑伯．迪倫會演奏吉他和口琴。

17 **headphones** [ˋhɛd͵fons] 名（複）頭戴式耳機

● The phone operators have to wear **headphones** when they work. 接線生工作時必須戴上耳機。

- head 頭
- phone 耳機
- -s（複）

18 **hook** [hʊk] ❶ 名 C 掛鉤 ❷ 動 用鉤鉤住或掛起

❶ Rose installed a **hook** on the back of her bathroom door for hanging her towel. 蘿絲在浴室門後釘了一個掛鉤來掛毛巾。

❷ Ten minutes after setting up his fishing pole, the man had **hooked** a trout; he quickly released the fish and threw his line back in the water. 立好魚竿後 10 分鐘，男子就釣到了一條鱒魚。他隨即把魚放了，重新下鉤。

19 **hose** [hoz] 名 C 水管，軟管

- The gardener used a long **hose** to water the plants.
  園丁用一條長水管替植物澆水。

20 **invention** [ɪnˋvɛnʃən] 名 ❶ C 發明物，創作品；❷ U 發明

▪ invent 發明
▪ -ion 名 表「行為的狀態」

❶ Ms. Meyer's greatest **invention** is a machine that can purify and recycle sewer water.
梅爾小姐最偉大的發明，是那台能淨化和回收使用汙水的機器。

❷ The **invention** of the computer has greatly changed the way we communicate. 電腦的發明已經大大地改變了我們的溝通方式。

21 **ivory** [ˋaɪvərɪ] ❶ 名 U 象牙 ❷ 形 象牙製的

❶ Solomon fights illegal trading of **ivory** in order to protect wild elephants. 索羅門打擊非法的象牙交易來保護野生象群。

❷ The **ivory** carving of the elephant is hard, but it feels smooth.
這個用象牙雕刻的大象很堅硬，但摸起來很滑。

22 **jar** [dʒɑr] 名 C 罐，罈

- Ida put clean mulberries in a **jar** and added some sugar to make jelly. 愛達把洗乾淨的桑椹放進罐子裡，並加了一些糖來做果醬。

23 **junk** [dʒʌŋk] 名 U 垃圾 同義 rubbish, trash 垃圾，廢物

- That old tricycle is not **junk**; it was my great-grandfather's, so please don't throw it away.
  那輛舊三輪車不是廢物，那是我曾祖父留下的，請不要丟掉。

補充 junk food 垃圾食物；junk mail 垃圾郵件

24 **kettle** [ˋkɛtḷ] 名 C 水壺

- Harlan found a **kettle** underneath the sink and used it to boil some water. 哈倫在水槽下方找到了一個水壺，他把水壺拿來燒開水。

25 Materials & articles
材料與物品 (3)

49

01 **kit** [kɪt] 名 C ❶ **成套工具；**❷ **工具箱**

❶ Larry took out the repair **kit** and tried to fix his bike.
賴瑞拿出工具箱，想把腳踏車修好。

❷ Every household should have a first aid **kit** handy.
每個家庭都應該備有急救箱。

補充 first-aid kit 急救箱

02 **knob** [nɑb] 名 C **圓形把手**

● Martha painted the kitchen cabinets orange and the **knobs** yellow.
瑪莎把廚房的櫃子漆成橘色，手把漆成黃色。

03 **knot** [nɑt] ❶ 名 C **（繩等的）結** ❷ 動 **打結**

❶ The sailor tied the two ropes together with a **knot**.
水手打個結把兩條繩索繫在一起。

❷ Carl put on his sports shoes and **knotted** the shoelaces.
卡爾穿上運動鞋，繫上鞋帶。

相關片語 **tie in(to) knots** 使緊張，使忐忑不安

● She tied herself into knots worrying about her son's health.
她很擔心兒子的健康。

04 **label** [ˈlebḷ] 名 ❶ C **標籤，貼紙**
動 ❷ **貼標籤於，用籤條標明；**❸ **把……列為，把……歸類為**

❶ If you don't know how to wash the sweater, just look at the instructions on the **label**.
如果你不知道要如何洗這件毛衣，就看看標籤上的說明。

❷ The clerk **labeled** our luggage when we checked in.
我們在辦理登機手續時，工作人員在我們的行李貼上標籤。

❸ The boy often misbehaves, so his classmates have **labeled** him a troublemaker. 那個男孩經常行為不當，同學把他歸類為麻煩製造者。

05 **ladder** [ˋlædɚ] 名 C ❶ **梯子；**❷ **（發跡等的）途徑**

❶ Ashley needs a **ladder** to reach the boxes at the top of her closet.
愛許莉需要一個梯子來拿衣櫥上方的盒子。

❷ Many people believe that hard work is the **ladder** to success, whereas laziness leads to failure.
許多人相信努力是通往成功的階梯，懶惰則會導致失敗。

06 **leather** [ˋlɛðɚ] 名 ❶ C 皮革製品；❷ U 皮革

❶ Since 1969, Elvin has operated a workshop that produces delicate handmade **leather**. 艾爾文從 1969 年起就經營手工皮製精品店到現在。

❷ This pair of **leather** boots is made of lambskin.
這一雙皮靴是用小羊皮製作的。

07 **lens** [lɛnz] 名 C 透鏡，鏡片

● After cleaning the camera **lens**, Esther started taking pictures.
伊斯特把相機鏡頭擦乾淨之後就開始照相了。

補充 contact lens 隱形眼鏡；fish-eye lens 魚眼鏡頭

08 **linen** [ˋlɪnən] 名 U 亞麻布

● Our ancestors often used **linen** for making rope, thread, and cloth. 我們的祖先廣泛使用亞麻來製作繩子、線和布。

09 **lipstick** [ˋlɪp͵stɪk] 名 C 口紅

● Harmonee's skin is so sensitive that she can't wear any makeup except **lipstick**.
哈莫妮的皮膚很敏感，除了口紅以外，不能塗其他的化妝品。

- lip 唇
- stick 棒

10 **litter** [ˋlɪtɚ] ❶ 名 U 廢棄物，零亂之物 ❷ 動 亂扔廢棄物

❶ You'd better clean up all those piles of **litter** around the house before Mom comes home.
你最好在媽回到家之前，把那堆亂七八糟的東西整理好。

❷ The sign says "No **littering**," so let's pick up all the garbage.
這個告示牌寫著「禁止丟垃圾」，所以我們把所有的垃圾都撿起來吧。

11 **lotion** [ˋloʃən] 名 U 乳液

● Kitty applies body **lotion** every day in the winter because her skin gets very dry. 姬蒂的皮膚在冬天時會很乾燥，所以她每天都會擦身體乳液。

12 **loudspeaker** [ˋlaʊdˋspikɚ] 名 C 揚聲器，擴聲器

● When Dawn wants to talk to all the students in the school at once, she uses the **loudspeaker**.
朵恩要是想跟全校學生即時講話時，就會使用擴音器。

- loud 大聲的
- speak 說
- -er 名 表「物」

50

13 **luggage** [ˋlʌgɪdʒ] 名 U 行李 同義 baggage 行李〔美式〕

- Never leave your **luggage** unattended. 請留意您的行李。

‧lug 拖；拉
‧-age 名 表「數量」

14 **makeup** [ˋmek͵ʌp] 名 U 化妝品

- The woman put some **makeup** on her face to make herself look more attractive. 女子在臉上化了點妝，讓自己看起來更迷人。

‧make up 化妝

15 **marble** [ˋmɑrbl̩] 名 U ❶ 大理石；C ❷ 彈珠

❶ A monument made of white **marble** stands in the middle of the hall. 大廳中央豎立著一座白色的大理石紀念碑。

❷ The cat playfully chased the colorful glass **marbles** that Vera and June rolled back and forth across the floor.
薇拉和茱恩在地板上滾著彩色玻璃珠，那隻貓就追著玻璃珠玩。

16 **medal** [ˋmɛdl̩] 名 C 獎章，紀念章，勳章

- In her living room, Ruth displays all the **medals** she has won in speech contests. 露絲在客廳中展示所有她在演講比賽中贏得的獎牌。

補充 gold medal 金牌；silver medal 銀牌；bronze medal 銅牌

17 **microphone** [ˋmaɪkrə͵fon] 名 C 擴音器，麥克風 同義 mike 麥克風

- When addressing the audience, speak into the **microphone**; it will make your voice louder.
在面對觀眾講話的時候，對著麥克風講，聲音會大一點。

‧micro- 表「擴大的」
‧phone 名 表「傳聲裝置」

18 **mop** [mɑp] ❶ 名 C 拖把 動 ❷ 用拖把拖洗；❸ 擦去（汗水等）

❶ The housekeeper wet the **mop** and used it to wash the bathroom floor. 打掃人員把拖把弄濕，用來洗浴室的地板。

❷ After the man swept the floor, he **mopped** it. 男子掃完地之後接著拖地。

❸ The worker **mopped** the sweat from his forehead with a towel and continued working. 工人用毛巾擦去額頭上的汗水，然後繼續工作。

19 **necessity** [nəˋsɛsətɪ] 名 ❶ U 需要，必要性；❷ C 必需品

❶ Fred always says **necessity** is the mother of invention.
弗列得總是說「需求為發明之母。」

❷ No one can live without basic **necessities** such as food and water. 人類要是缺少食物和水這類的必需品，就無法活下去。

20 **nylon** [ˋnaɪlɑn] 名 ❶ U 尼龍；❷ C 尼龍襪

- -on 常見的纖維製品字尾

❶ The fishing line is made of **nylon**, a very strong artificial material. 這個釣魚線是尼龍製的，這是一種很強韌的人造原料。

❷ My mom bought me three pairs of **nylons**. 媽媽幫我買了三雙尼龍襪。

21 **pad** [pæd] 名 C ❶ 便條紙簿；❷ 襯墊，墊

❶ Curtis grabbed a writing **pad** and made a to-do list for next week. 克堤斯拿了一本便條紙簿，列出下週的待辦事項。

❷ During the game, the hockey players wore shoulder **pads** to protect themselves from injuries.
在比賽時，所有的曲棍球球員都會戴上墊肩來防止受傷。

22 **pail** [pel] 名 C 桶，提桶　同義 bucket 水桶

- The housekeeper refilled her **pail** with fresh water and continued mopping the front steps. 管家重新裝了一桶乾淨的水，繼續拖著前面的階梯。

23 **parcel** [ˋpɑrsḷ] 名 C 小包，包裹

- The mailman left a **parcel** at Beverly's front door.
郵差在貝芙麗的大門口留下一個小包裹。

24 **passport** [ˋpæsˏport] 名 C 護照，通行證

- pass 通過
- port 港

- Since Johnetta lost her **passport**, she has to replace it before her next trip. 喬娜妲弄丟了護照，下次出國之前要先補辦。

25 **pebble** [ˋpɛbḷ] 名 C 小卵石

- The garden path is paved with white **pebbles** from the nearby brook. 這條花園步道是以產於鄰近小河的白卵石鋪成的。

26 **perfume** [ˋpɝfjum] ❶ 名 U 香水　❷ 動 以香氣充滿，薰香

- per- 表「完全，徹底」
- fume 煙；(用香)薰

❶ Hertha never wears **perfume** because she thinks it might attract mosquitoes.
何莎覺得香水可能會招來蚊子，所以她從來不噴香水。

❷ The woman put some lilies in the vase; the flowers quickly **perfumed** the air with a sweet scent.
女子在花瓶裡放了一些百合花，很快地房間就充滿了花的香味。

26 Materials & articles 材料與物品 (4)

51

01 **plastic** [ˋplæstɪk] ❶ 名 U 塑膠 ❷ 形 塑膠的

❶ Derrick prefers to drink water from cups made of glass rather than **plastic**. 德瑞克比較喜歡用玻璃杯喝水，不喜歡用塑膠杯喝水。

❷ Some stores don't offer customers **plastic** bags; we should bring a recycled bag with us. 某些商店不提供塑膠袋給顧客，我們應該自己攜帶環保袋。

補充 plastic surgery 整形手術

02 **pole** [pol] 名 C ❶ 柱，竿；❷ 極地 形 polar 極地的

❶ The telephone **pole**, which is made of wood, is used to support the wires high above the ground.
這個用木製的電話線桿把電話線撐高，遠離地面。

❷ Do you think there is a telephone pole at the North **Pole**?
你想在北極會有電話線桿嗎？

03 **quilt** [kwɪlt] 名 C 被子，被褥

- Lisa makes **quilts** with different flower patterns.
麗莎用各種花朵的圖案來做被子。

04 **razor** [ˋrezɚ] 名 C 剃刀

- raze 鏟平，夷平
- -or 名 表「物」

- Every other day, Franklin uses a **razor** to shave off all his hair. 富蘭克林每兩天就會用剃刀刮去所有的頭髮。

補充 razor blade 剃刀刀片

05 **receiver** [rɪˋsivɚ] 名 C 電話聽筒

- receive 接收
- -er 名 表「行為物」

- When the phone rang, Adelaide immediately picked up the **receiver**. 電話一響，愛黛蕾就拿起電話筒。

06 **resource** [rɪˋsors] 名 C 資源

- re- 加強語氣
- source 來源

- The management of natural **resources** has always been controlled by the government. 自然資源的管理向來由政府統籌。

07 **rug** [rʌg] 名 C 小地毯

- May I please take a look at the brown **rug** with the orange flowers? 請問，我可以看一下那塊有橘色花朵圖案的棕色小地毯嗎？

08 **saucer** [ˋsɔsɚ] 名 C 茶托，淺碟

・sauce 調味醬
・-er 名 表「物」

● Yesterday afternoon, I served my best friend black tea in my best cup and **saucer**.
昨天下午，我用我最好的茶杯和茶碟請我最好的朋友喝紅茶。

補充 flying saucer 飛碟

09 **scarecrow** [ˋskɛr͵kro] 名 C 稻草人

・scare 嚇
・crow 烏鴉

● The crows ignored the straw **scarecrow** that was guarding the plot of soybeans. 烏鴉不理會大豆田旁的稻草人。

10 **screw** [skru] ❶ 名 C 螺絲釘 動 ❷ 旋，擰；❸ 使振作，鼓舞

❶ Harold turned the **screw** to the left to loosen it.
哈樂德將螺絲釘向左轉鬆。

❷ Jackson always **screws** the bottle cap back on after pouring out the contents. 傑克森在倒完瓶中物之後，都會把瓶蓋轉回去。

❸ The shy boy finally **screwed** up enough courage to ask the girl to the party. 害羞的男孩終於鼓起勇氣，邀請女孩去參加舞會。

11 **shampoo** [ʃæmˋpu] 名 U 洗髮精

● Grace knows how to make **shampoo** and conditioner from natural ingredients. 葛瑞絲知道如何用天然原料製作洗髮精和潤髮乳。

12 **shovel** [ˋʃʌvḷ] ❶ 名 C 鏟，鐵鍬 ❷ 動 用鏟鏟（起），用鐵鍬挖

❶ Joel spent a year digging out a swimming pool in his backyard with a **shovel**. 約爾花了一年，用一根鐵鍬在後院挖出一座游泳池。

❷ It took the farmer half a day to **shovel** a ditch around the field.
農夫花了半天的時間，在田的四周鏟出一條溝渠。

52

13 **spade** [sped] 名 C 鏟子

● Gerald enjoys digging up carrots with a **spade** on his organic farm. 吉羅德喜歡在自己的有機農場用鏟子挖胡蘿蔔。

14 **stuff** [stʌf] ❶ 名 U 物品，東西 ❷ 動（烹調上）填塞作料於

❶ Winnie likes to travel without a lot of **stuff** because it gives her a sense of freedom. 溫妮喜歡帶著簡便行李去旅遊，這讓她覺得很自由。

❷ The cook **stuffed** the turkey with garlic, onion, sage, thyme, and parsley. 廚師在火雞裡填塞了大蒜、洋蔥、鼠尾草、百里香和荷蘭芹等香料。

15 **substance** [ˋsʌbstəns] 名 C ❶ 物質；❷ 主旨，要義

❶ The desk is covered with a sticky **substance**; it seems to be some kind of liquid. 桌子有一層黏黏的東西，好像是某一種液體。

❷ The **substance** of Chris's lecture was that humanity should be awakened to global peace. 克里斯的演說旨在喚起全人類致力於全球和平。

16 **tack** [tæk] 名 C 圖釘

● When Beverly stepped barefoot on the **tack**, she screamed at the top of her lungs. 貝芙麗赤腳踩到一根圖釘時，痛得哇哇大叫。

17 **timber** [ˋtɪmbɚ] 名 U 木材

● Joe makes furniture out of the highest quality **timber**. 喬使用最高級的木材來製作家具。

18 **trash** [træʃ] 名 U ❶ 垃圾；❷ 廢話

❶ The boy helped his mother take out the bag of **trash** and put it in the garbage can. 男孩幫媽媽把垃圾拿出去，放進垃圾筒裡。

❷ What Ed just said was absolute **trash**! 艾德剛剛說的根本就是廢話！

19 **tray** [tre] 名 C ❶ 盤，托盤；❷ 一盤的量

❶ Ten minutes after we had ordered, the waiter carried the dishes on a **tray** to our table. 在我們點餐後十分鐘，服務生就用托盤把菜端上我們的桌子。

❷ Irvin passed John a **tray** of dirty dishes and asked him to wash them immediately. 艾文遞了一堆髒碗盤給約翰，要他馬上洗。

補充 ashtray 菸灰缸

20 **vase** [ves] 名 C 花瓶

● Cheryl cut a few roses from her garden and put them in a beautiful **vase** on her dining room table. 綺若從花園裡剪下一些玫瑰花，插在餐桌上一個漂亮花瓶裡。

21 **wax** [wæks] ❶ 名 U 蠟，蜂蠟　❷ 動 給⋯⋯上蠟

❶ Abby knows how to melt the honeycombs from beehives to extract the **wax**. 艾比知道溶解蜂巢取蜂蠟的方法。

❷ The car has been **waxed**; now it is shining in the sun. 這輛車已經打過蠟了，它現在在陽光下閃閃發亮。

22 **screwdriver** [ˋskru͵draɪvɚ] 名 C 螺絲起子

• screw 螺絲釘
• drive 把釘子打入
• -er 名 表「物」

● My father taught me how to use a **screwdriver** when I was 10 years old.
我父親在我十歲時就教過我如何使用螺絲起子。

23 **shaver** [ˋʃevɚ] 名 C 刮鬍鬚的用具

• shave 刮鬍子
• -er 名 表「物」

● Chester received an electric **shaver** as a gift from his children on Father's Day. 父親節時，賈斯特收到孩子們送的禮物——一支電動刮鬍刀。

24 **souvenir** [ˋsuvə͵nɪr] 名 C 紀念品，紀念物

● When Kirby goes on business trips, he always brings back **souvenirs** for his children. 柯比出差時，都會帶紀念品回來給孩子們。

25 **spear** [spɪr] ❶ 名 C 矛，魚叉 ❷ 動 用矛（或魚叉等）刺

❶ Janet is very good at using a **spear** to catch fish.
珍妮特很擅長用魚叉捕魚。

❷ The aboriginal stood in the river **spearing** fish.
那個原住民站在河裡叉魚。

27 Furniture & appliances 家具與設備 (1)

53

01 **appliance** [əˋplaɪəns] 名 C 用具，器具，設備

● We decided to buy some **appliances** for our new apartment, including a refrigerator, a vacuum cleaner, and a dishwasher.
我們決定為我們的新公寓買一些新器具，包括電冰箱、吸塵器和洗碗機。

02 **cabinet** [ˋkæbənɪt] 名 C 櫥，櫃

● Tracie keeps her collection of teddy bears in a big glass **cabinet**.
崔西把她收藏的泰迪熊都放進一個大玻璃櫃裡。

03 **comfort** [ˋkʌmfɚt] 名 ❶ C 使人舒服的設備，方便的東西；❷ U 舒適，安逸；❸ U 安慰 動 ❹ 安慰，慰問

❶ After camping for weeks, Allen longed for the **comforts** of home. 艾倫在外露營了幾週後，開始渴望家裡的舒適生活。

❷ The rich man lives in **comfort** with everything he needs.
這名有錢人安逸度日，要什麼有什麼。

❸ Friends and relatives offered words of **comfort** to the widow; however, no words could make her feel better.
親戚朋友慰問了那位遺孀，但都安慰不了她。

❹ The police tried to **comfort** the woman whose son was missing, telling her not to worry because they would find the boy soon.
警方安撫著走失兒子的婦人，要她別擔心，他們很快會找到她的兒子。

04 **couch** [kaʊtʃ] 名 C **長睡椅** 同義 sofa 沙發

● Hugo was lying on the **couch** watching TV when a thief broke into his house. 雨果窩在沙發上看電視時，一個小偷闖進了他家。

補充 couch potato 成天躺在沙發上看電視的人

05 **cradle** [ˋkredḷ] 名 C ❶ **搖籃**；❷ **發源地**

❶ The mother put the baby boy in the **cradle** and rocked him to sleep. 媽媽把小男嬰放進搖籃裡，然後搖他睡覺。

❷ Ancient Greece is considered the **cradle** of Western civilization. 古希臘被認為是西方文明的搖籃。

相關片語 ❶ **in/from the cradle** 從嬰兒時期
❷ **from the cradle to the grave** 從生到死

❶ Ellis has known his best friend since they were both in the cradle.
艾理斯和他最好的朋友自幼便認識了。

❷ The man lived in this town from the cradle to the grave; he never left. 那名男子從生到死都住在這個小鎮裡，從未離開過。

06 **cupboard** [ˋkʌbɚd] 名 C **食櫥，碗櫃**

・cup 杯子
・board 板

● Please put the dishes in the **cupboard** after you've dried them. 盤子擦乾之後請放進碗櫃裡。

07 **equip** [ɪˋkwɪp] 動 ❶ **裝備，配備**；❷ **使有能力，使有資格，賦予**

❶ The new hospital is well **equipped**; all of the latest medical instruments have been installed.
這家新醫院設備良好，安裝有各種最新的醫療儀器。

❷ Our mastery of English **equips** us with a very important tool for acquiring knowledge and information.
精通英文，是獲得知識和資訊一個非常重要的工具。

08 **equipment** [ɪˋkwɪpmənt] 名 U ❶ 裝備，配備；❷ 設備，用具

❶ They are replacing the old machines with new ones; the **equipment** of the factory will take at least a month.
他們的機器正在汰舊換新，工廠的設備更新最少要花上一個月的時間。

❷ Do you have any camping **equipment** I can borrow for a week?
你有沒有露營用具可以借我一星期？

- equip 動 配備
- -ment 名 表「產物」

09 **escalator** [ˋɛskə͵letɚ] 名 C 電扶梯

- Pay attention and watch your step when you get on and off the **escalator**.
搭乘與離開電扶梯時，請留意您的腳步。

- escalate 動 逐步上升
- -or 名 表「物」

10 **facility** [fəˋsɪlətɪ] 名 C（常作複數）設備，設施

- There are no cooking **facilities** in Evelyn's apartment. 伊芙琳的住處沒有廚房設備。

- facile 易使用的
- -ity 名 表「狀態」

11 **faucet** [ˋfɔsɪt] 名 C 水龍頭

- The **faucet** in Ivy's kitchen is out of order. 艾薇廚房裡的水龍頭壞了。

54

12 **fireplace** [ˋfaɪr͵ples] 名 C 壁爐

- The one **fireplace** in Sheila's house is centrally located.
希拉家中的壁爐位於房子的中央。

- fire 火
- place 地方

13 **furnish** [ˋfɝnɪʃ] 動 為（房間）裝置（家具等），裝備

- Tanya **furnished** her room with an electric heater for the coming winter. 冬天即將到來，唐雅在自己的房中放了一台電暖器。

14 **furniture** [ˋfɝnɪtʃɚ] 名 U 家具

- The antique cupboard in Cathy's dining room is a very valuable piece of **furniture**. 凱西家飯廳裡的古董碗櫃是非常值錢的家具。

15 **locker** [ˋlɑkɚ] 名 C（公共場所供個人用的）衣物櫃

- When Norma walked up to her **locker**, she noticed a piece of paper attached to the door.
諾瑪打開她的置物櫃時，發現櫃子的門後貼了一張紙。

- lock 鎖
- -er 名 表「物」

16 **microwave** [ˋmaɪkrə͵wev] 名 C 微波爐

- micro- 表「微」
- wave 波

● You can reheat your food quickly in the **microwave**.
微波爐可以迅速將食物重新加熱。

17 **plug** [plʌg] 名 C ❶ 塞子，栓；❷ 插頭 動 ❸ 把……塞住

❶ Keith can't take a hot bath because the drain **plug** is missing.
浴缸排水口的塞子不見了，基斯沒辦法泡熱水澡。

❷ Philip's computer didn't work because he forgot to put the **plug** in the socket. 菲利浦的電腦無法啟動，因為他忘記插插頭了。

❸ Lena **plugged** her ears with cotton balls because her husband's snoring disturbed her sleep.
蕾娜用棉花球塞住耳朵，因為丈夫的打呼聲吵得她不能睡。

相關片語 **plug away at** 埋頭苦幹

● The woman kept plugging away at her work; she didn't eat anything or take a rest for 8 hours.
女子繼續埋頭苦幹，她有八個小時沒有吃任何東西或休息了。

18 **recorder** [rɪˋkɔrdɚ] 名 C 錄音機 同義 tape recorder 錄音機

- record 記錄
- -er 名 表「物」

● Ethel always uses a voice **recorder** when she interviews people. 艾瑟兒在作訪問時，都會使用錄音機。

19 **stereo** [ˋstɛrɪo] ❶ 形 立體聲的 ❷ 名 C 立體音響

❶ The difference between **stereo** sound and mono sound is very obvious. 立體聲和單音聽起來明顯不同。

❷ While driving, Roderick likes to listen to Michael Jackson CDs on his car **stereo**. 羅得里克開車時喜歡用車上的立體音響來聽麥克．傑克遜的專輯。

20 **stool** [stul] 名 C 凳子

● Ike stood on a **stool** to replace the broken light bulb in the hanging lamp. 艾克站在一張凳子上，更換壞掉的吊燈燈泡。

21 **tap** [tæp] 名 C ❶ 水龍頭；❷ 輕拍，輕敲 動 ❸ 輕拍，輕敲

❶ Shirley never drinks water directly from the **tap**; she always boils it first. 雪麗從來不生飲水龍頭的水，她都會把水燒開再喝。

❷ I felt a **tap** on my shoulder, but when I turned around, no one was there. 我感到有人拍了我的肩膀，我轉過身，卻沒有看到任何人。

❸ The teacher **tapped** the student on the shoulder to wake him up. 老師輕輕地拍拍學生的肩膀，把他叫醒。

22 **tub** [tʌb] 名 C 浴缸

- Would you like your room with a **tub** or with a shower?
請問您是要有浴缸還是淋浴的房間？

23 **typewriter** [ˋtaɪpˏraɪtɚ] 名 C 打字機

- Traditional **typewriters** have been largely replaced by personal computers. 個人電腦已大幅取代了傳統打字機。

· type 打字
· write 寫
· -er 名 表「物」

24 **socket** [ˋsɑkɪt] 名 C 插座，插口

- Children should not play with electrical **sockets**. It is too dangerous. 兒童不可以玩電源插座，那太危險了。

28 Furniture & appliances
家具與設備 (2)

55

01 **anyplace** [ˋɛnɪˏples] 副 任何地方　同義 anywhere 任何地方

- I can't find my key **anyplace**. I think I have lost it.
我到處都找不到我的鑰匙，我想我把它弄丟了。

· any 任何
· place 地方

02 **aquarium** [əˋkwɛrɪəm] 名 C ❶ 魚缸；❷ 水族館

❶ An **aquarium** filled with colorful fish can bring a sense of serenity to any home. 在家中養一缸色彩繽紛的魚，可以帶來一種平靜的感覺。

❷ People can see many kinds of fish and other water creatures and plants in the **aquarium**.
人們在這個水族館可以看到許多種類的魚和各種水生動植物。

03 **arch** [ɑrtʃ] 名 C 拱門，拱形物

- The beautiful natural rock **arch** in the desert has become a popular tourist destination. 沙漠中那座壯觀的天然石拱門，已經變成了熱門的觀光景點。

04 **barn** [bɑrn] 名 C 穀倉，獸棚

- Christopher keeps all the farm animals except the pigs in the red **barn**. 除了豬群，克里斯多夫把所有的農場動物都養在紅色穀倉裡。

05 **basin** [ˋbesn̩] 名 C 盆地

- Taipei **Basin** was once an ancient lake bed.
臺北盆地以前曾經是一片古老的湖床。

06 **bay** [be] 名 C（海或湖泊的）灣

- Coral **Bay** is famous for the dolphins that frequent the area.
  珊瑚灣因海豚時常現身而聞名。

07 **border** [ˋbɔrdɚ] 名 C ❶ 邊緣，邊境，國界
動 ❷ 與……有共同邊界，與……接壤；❸ 毗鄰，接界

❶ This river marks the **border** between the two counties.
這兩個縣以這條河為界。

❷ The driving range **borders** the city on the south.
高爾夫球練習場位於城市南方的邊緣。

❸ Germany **borders** on a number of European countries, including Belgium and the Netherlands.
德國與幾個歐洲國家接壤，像是比利時和荷蘭。

08 **brook** [brʊk] 名 C 小河，小溪　同義 creek, stream 溪流

- By noon, we had arrived at the **brook**. It was such a small stream that we were able to cross it easily.
  我們在中午前抵達那條小河。那條河很小，我們很輕易就渡過河了。

09 **campus** [ˋkæmpəs] 名 C 校園

- Katherine lived on **campus** when she was a freshman.
  凱瑟琳大一時就住在學校裡。

10 **canyon** [ˋkænjən] 名 C 峽谷

- The best time to visit the Grand **Canyon** is in early spring.
  初春之際，是造訪大峽谷的最佳時機。

補充 the Grand Canyon 大峽谷

11 **cape** [kep] 名 C 岬，海角

- Michael goes down to the **cape** every morning to fish.
  麥可每天清晨都會去岬角垂釣。

56 12 **capital** [ˋkæpətl̩] 名 ❶ C 首都；❷ U 資金
形 ❸ 首要的；❹ 大寫字母的；❺ 可處死刑的

❶ Taipei is the **capital** of the Republic of China. 台北是中華民國的首都。

❷ Alberto and Marlys are debating if they have enough **capital** to start a business. 艾伯托和瑪麗絲在討論他們是否有足夠資金開一家公司。

❸ Let's not waste time on these trivial things; let's get to the **capital** point of the discussion. 不要浪費時間在枝末細節上，我們直接討論重點吧。

❹ Proper nouns such as names of people or places should begin with a **capital** letter. 專有名詞，像是人名和地名，第一個字母應該要大寫。

❺ The cold-blooded murderer was sentenced to death; many people thought the **capital** punishment fit the crime.
那名冷血兇手被處以死刑，許多人認為他罪有應得。

13 **chamber** [ˋtʃembɚ] 名 C **會場，會議廳**

- The banquet will be held in the master **chamber** of the hotel.
晚宴將於飯店主廳舉行。

14 **chimney** [ˋtʃɪmnɪ] 名 C **煙囪**

- Many children are told that Santa Claus sneaks into people's houses through the **chimney** on Christmas Eve and leaves gifts.
大人告訴小孩說，聖誕老人會在聖誕夜從煙囪溜進人們的房子裡，留下禮物。

15 **cinema** [ˋsɪnəmə] 名 ❶ C **電影院**；❷ U **(總稱)電影，電影業**

❶ Most films shown in Taiwan **cinemas** are American.
台灣電影院播放的電影，大部分是美國電影。

❷ Marlon devoted his life to the **cinema** and produced many great films. 馬隆一生獻身於電影，拍了許多好片。

16 **cliff** [klɪf] 名 C **懸崖，峭壁**

- A tree stands high on the **cliff** above the sea.
有棵樹座落於高聳的海崖邊。

17 **collapse** [kəˋlæps] 動 ❶ **倒塌**；❷ **(健康等)垮掉，累倒** 名 ❸ U **倒塌**

❶ Fortunately, no one was home when Lydia's house **collapsed** in the earthquake. 莉迪雅的家在地震時倒塌，還好當時無人在家。

❷ After overworking himself for half a year, Mr. Smith's health **collapsed**, and he was hospitalized.
在半年的工作過度之後，史密斯先生累垮住院了。

❸ The roof of the house fell in suddenly; the **collapse** was caused by the weight of the snow. 房子的屋頂突然坍塌，因為積雪太重了。

18 **construct** [kənˋstrʌkt] 動 **建造，構成** 名 construction 建造

- It took Mr. Jenkins two years to **construct** a mobile home that can also be used as a boat.
傑金斯先生花了兩年，建造了一棟可以當船用的移動式房屋。

19 **construction** [kənˋstrʌkʃən] 名 U 建造

・construct 建造
・-ion 名 表「行為的結果」

● Although it was supposed to be completed before classes began, our new campus is still under **construction**. 我們的新校園在開學前就應該要完工，但現在還在施工中。

20 **continent** [ˋkɑntənənt] 名 C 大陸，陸地，洲　形 continental 洲的；大陸的

● The Eurasian **continent** stretches from the Pacific Ocean to the Atlantic Ocean. 歐亞大陸自太平洋橫跨至大西洋。

21 **cottage** [ˋkɑtɪdʒ] 名 C 農舍，小屋

● Rudy recently renovated his old **cottages** and turned them into guest houses. 魯迪最近整修了他的舊農舍，將它們改建成民宿。

22 **counter** [ˋkaʊntɚ] ❶ 名 C 櫃檯　❷ 形 相反的，對立的

❶ If you ask for Lorna at the front **counter**, the receptionist will direct you to her. 你跟櫃檯人員說要找洛娜，接待人員就會帶你進去找她。

❷ Chapman's opinion is always **counter** to that of his father; that is why they argue frequently.
契布曼的意見總是和他爸爸的意見相佐，這也是他們經常爭吵的原因。

相關片語 **under the counter** 私下地，非法地

● At that time, the book was legally banned; however, it was still available under the counter. 在當時，那本書遭到法定禁止；然而，私底下仍然可以買到。

29 Furniture & appliances 家具與設備 (3)

57

01 **dam** [dæm] ❶ 名 C 水壩　❷ 動 築壩於，築壩攔（水）

❶ The government built a **dam** across the river to create a reservoir of drinking water. 政府在河上築了一道水壩，建了一座儲存飲水的水庫。

❷ The river was **dammed** to prevent flooding.
這條河流上蓋了水壩來防範河水氾濫。

02 **district** [ˋdɪstrɪkt] 名 C 地區

● Our office is in the heart of the commercial **district**.
我們的辦公室位於商業區中心。

03 **ditch** [dɪtʃ] ❶ 名 C 水道，渠道 ❷ 動 拋棄，丟棄

❶ After the heavy rain, the field was flooded; the farmer dug a **ditch** along one side to remove the water.
大雨過後，農田淹水了；農夫在田的周圍挖了一條溝渠讓水排走。

❷ The woman no longer needed the plastic bag, so she **ditched** it in a bin. 這個塑膠袋用不到了，所以女子就把它扔進垃圾桶。

04 **domestic** [də`mɛstɪk] 形 ❶ 家庭的；❷ 國家的，國內的

❶ To everyone's surprise, the young man is interested in **domestic** affairs, including cooking meals and cleaning the house.
令大家驚訝的是，這個年輕人對家務事很有興趣，像是做飯和打掃房子都是。

❷ Max prefers **domestic** beer to imported beer.
麥克斯比較喜歡喝國產啤酒，比較不喜歡喝進口啤酒。

補充 domestic violence 家庭暴力

05 **dormitory** [`dɔrmə͵torɪ] 名 C 學生宿舍 同義 dorm 宿舍

● Irving sneaked out of his **dormitory** at midnight for a snack while everyone else was sleeping.
歐文半夜趁宿舍其他人都睡著時，偷偷溜出去吃宵夜。

06 **dump** [dʌmp] ❶ 名 C 垃圾場 ❷ 動 傾倒

❶ Randy opposed the building of a nuclear waste **dump** in his neighborhood. 朗狄反對在他家附近蓋核廢料場。

❷ Some toxic waste was **dumped** into the river, killing many fish.
一些有毒廢料被倒進河裡，許多魚因此死亡。

07 **enclose** [ɪn`kloz] 動 ❶ 圍住，關住；❷（隨函）附寄

- en- 表「使」
- close 關閉

❶ The old abandoned house is **enclosed** by high-rise apartments, creating a great contrast.
這棟廢棄舊屋四周圍繞著高樓大廈，呈現出強烈對比。

❷ Please remember to **enclose** a stamped, self-addressed envelope when writing. 寫信時請記得在信封內附上一個貼好郵票、寫好地址的信封。

08 **environmental** [ɪn͵vaɪrən`mɛntḷ] 形 環境的，有關環保的

- environ 包圍
- -ment 名 表「行為」
- -al 形 表「……的」

● The **environmental** impact of humans is greater than that of any animal.
人類對環境所造成的衝擊，勝過其他所有動物。

09 **global** [ˋglobl̩] 形 全世界的

- globe 地球
- -al 形 表「關於……的」

● Glen is optimistic that the **global** economy will recover this year. 葛倫樂觀看待全球經濟今年會好轉。

補充 global warming 全球暖化

58

10 **globe** [glob] 名 C（單數）地球　形 global 全球的

● All kinds of events are now broadcast live around the **globe** through satellites. 在今天，各種活動都可以透過衛星進行全球實況轉播。

11 **grave** [grev] ❶ 名 C 墓穴　❷ 形 重大的，嚴重的

❶ Since my grandfather's death, my family has visited his **grave** once a year. 祖父過世之後，家裡每年都會去他的墳上祭拜一次。

❷ Global warming poses a **grave** threat to Earth's ecosystems. 全球暖化嚴重威脅著地球的生態。

相關片語 ❶ **dig one's own grave** 自毀生計
❷ **turn in one's grave** 在九泉之下不得安寧

❶ The man's actions will cause serious problems for him in the future; he is digging his own grave.
這名男子的行為日後必導致嚴重的後果，他是在自掘墳墓。

❷ If Anna's father knew of her wrong decision, he would be turning in his grave. 安娜的父親要是知道安娜做了這種錯誤的決定，會無法瞑目。

12 **greenhouse** [ˋgrin͵haʊs] 名 C 溫室

- green 綠
- house 房子

● Gina has built a **greenhouse** to start her indoor farming business. 吉娜蓋了一間溫室，做起了室內農業。

補充 greenhouse effect 溫室效應

13 **gulf** [gʌlf] 名 C 海灣

● As the super hurricane approached the **Gulf** of Mexico, people living in the coastal regions were alerted about possible calamity.
一個超級颶風正接近墨西哥灣，沿海地區居民保持警戒、慎防災難。

14 **gymnasium** [dʒɪmˋnezɪəm] 名 C 體育館，健身房　同義 gym 體育館

● On the night of the big basketball game, the school **gymnasium** was packed with screaming fans.
在那場籃球大賽當晚，學校體育館擠滿瘋狂尖叫的球迷。

15 **hallway** [ˋhɔl͵we] 名 C 玄關，門廳，走廊

- hall 大廳；走廊
- way 通路

● Dean anxiously waited in the **hallway** outside the delivery room as his daughter-in-law gave birth to her first child. 狄恩的媳婦臨盆生第一胎時，他在產房外的走廊上焦慮地等著。

16 **homeland** [ˋhom͵lænd] 名 C（常作單數）祖國，故鄉

- home 家
- land 陸地

● While studying abroad, Josh missed the sights and smells of his **homeland**. 喬許在國外求學時，很懷念家鄉的景物和味道。

17 **hometown** [ˋhomˋtaʊn] 名 C 故鄉，家鄉

- home 家
- town 城鎮

● I love living in Taipei, but I miss my **hometown** and all my relatives and classmates back in New Zealand. 我喜歡住在台北，但我也很想念紐西蘭的家鄉和親友們。

18 **horizon** [həˋraɪzn̩] 名 ❶（單數）地平線；❷ C（常作複數）（知識、經驗等的）眼界，視野

❶ The morning sun is rising above the **horizon**. 旭日正從地平線東升。

❷ Traveling can broaden your **horizons** and help you gain useful knowledge and experience. 旅行可以開闊你的視野，豐富人生的知識和經驗。

相關片語 **on the horizon** ❶ 地平線上；❷ 未來可能會發生

❶ After sailing the Atlantic for days, the sailors saw an isle on the horizon. 在大西洋上航行了幾天之後，水手們終於在海平面上看到了一座小島。

❷ Although the plan is going well now, there are some problems on the horizon. 雖然這項計畫現在進行得很順利，但未來可能會發生一些問題。

19 **hostel** [ˋhɑstl̩] 名 C 旅舍（尤其指青年旅館）

● Rodney didn't have money to pay his rent, so he had to work at the **hostel**. 羅德尼沒有錢付住宿費，只好在旅館打工還錢。

30 Furniture & appliances 家具與設備 (4)

59

01 **hut** [hʌt] 名 C（簡陋的）小屋

● Spending one night at a fancy hotel costs as much as spending a week in a bamboo **hut** on the beach. 在高級旅館住一晚的價格，可以讓我們在海邊的小竹屋住上一星期。

02 **indoor** [ˋɪn͵dor] 形 室內的，戶內的　副 indoors 在室內

- in- 表「在內」
- door 門

● Plenty of **indoor** activities are available in case it rains. 萬一下雨，還有很多室內活動可以做。

03 **indoors** [ˋɪnˋdorz] 副 在室內，在屋裡　反義 outdoors 在戶外

- in- 表「在內」
- door 門
- -s 構成副詞

● The typhoon is approaching, so you should stay **indoors**. 颱風正在接近，你最好不要出門。

04 **inn** [ɪn] 名 C 小旅館，客棧

● Ingrid was exhausted after driving all day, so she stopped and rested at an **inn**.
英格開了一整天的車累壞了，所以中途在一家小旅館休息了一下。

05 **intimate** [ˋɪntəmɪt] 形 親密的，熟悉的　名 intimacy 親密

- intima 內膜
- -ate 形 表「有……性質的」

● After the **intimate** conversation, Seth and Doreen became closer friends.
希斯和多琳在深入交談後，成了更親密的朋友。

06 **landmark** [ˋlænd͵mɑrk] 名 C ❶ 地標；❷ 重大事件，里程碑

- land 土地
- mark 記號

❶ As one of the tallest buildings in the world, Taipei 101 is a new **landmark** for Taipei City.
台北 101 是全世界最高的建築物之一，也是台北市的新地標。

❷ The fall of the Berlin Wall is a major **landmark** in human history.
柏林圍牆的倒下，是人類歷史上的一個重大事件。

07 **landscape** [ˋlænd͵skep] 名 C 風景，景色

- land 土地
- -scape 名 表「景色」

● The unique desert **landscape** attracts tourists from all over the world. 那片獨特的沙漠景觀吸引了世界各地的遊客。

08 **lawn** [lɔn] 名 C 草坪，草地

● Jasper promised his parents that he would mow the **lawn** on Saturday morning. 賈斯柏答應父母會在星期六早上除草。

09 **lighthouse** [ˋlaɪt͵haʊs] 名 C 燈塔

- light 燈
- house 房子

● There is an old **lighthouse** at the southern tip of the island. 在該島南端有座古老的燈塔。

10 **lobby** [ˋlɑbɪ] 名 C（劇場或旅館等的）大廳，門廊

- Crowds have already gathered in the **lobby** and are awaiting the movie star's appearance.
人群已經湧入大廳，等候那位電影明星的現身。

11 **location** [loˋkeʃən] 名 C 位置，場所

- locate 動 座落於
- -ion 名 表「行為的結果」

- Can you tell me the exact **location** of your restaurant?
請告訴我貴餐廳的正確位置。

60

12 **lunar** [ˋlunɚ] 形 ❶ 月的，月球上的；❷ 陰曆的

- luna 月亮
- -ar 形 表「……的」

❶ A **lunar** eclipse occurs when the moon passes through Earth's shadow. 月亮行經地球的陰影就會產生月蝕。

❷ The Chinese New Year falls on the first day of the **lunar** calendar.
中國新年是陰曆正月初一。

13 **mall** [mɔl] 名 C（設在郊區的）大規模購物中心

- All the stores in the new shopping **mall** are having a sale; no wonder it's so crowded there.
購物中心所有商店都在特價中，難怪人潮湧現。

14 **meadow** [ˋmɛdo] 名 U 草地，牧草地

- The nearby **meadow** used to be a lake, but now it's covered with wildflowers. 旁邊那片草地以前是一座湖，現在卻是遍地野花。

15 **memorial** [məˋmorɪəl] ❶ 名 C 紀念碑，紀念館 ❷ 形 紀念的，追悼的

- memory 紀念
- -al 名 表「狀態」

❶ People gathered at the national **memorial** last weekend to protest the war.
上週末，人群在國家紀念館聚集反戰。

❷ The **memorial** hall was built in memory of the first president.
這座紀念館的建造是為了緬懷第一任總統。

16 **mill** [mɪl] 名 C ❶ 磨坊，麵粉廠；❷ 磨臼，磨粉機 ❸ 動 碾碎，研磨

❶ The farmer took his barley to the **mill**, where he could use a large machine to grind it into flour.
農民把大麥拿到磨坊，那裡有一台可以用來磨麵粉的大型機器。

❷ Before the electric **mill** was invented, people relied on cattle to supply the power. 在電動研磨機發明以前，人類依靠牲口來推動磨臼。

❸ The flour was **milled** from barley. 這麵粉是用大麥磨成的。

相關片語 ❶ **go through the mill** 接受磨鍊
❷ **put through the mill** 使接受磨鍊

❶ The man has gone through the mill; however, he believes all the difficulties he has experienced have made him tougher.
男子飽受磨難，但他認為所有的艱苦將他淬鍊得更堅強。

❷ The test put them through the mill. They had to do a lot of difficult tasks within a short period of time.
那項測試讓他們接受磨鍊，他們必須在很短的時間之內完成許多艱難的任務。

17 **monument** [ˋmɑnjəmənt] 名 C ❶ **紀念碑，紀念塔，紀念館；** ❷ **歷史遺跡，遺址；** ❸ **不朽的作品，豐功偉業**

❶ This **monument** was erected in memory of the flood victims.
這座紀念碑是為紀念洪水罹難者所興建的。

❷ The United Nations has funded projects to preserve ancient **monuments**. 聯合國資助了各種保存古蹟的計畫。

❸ This CD is considered a **monument** to Gino's talent as a guitarist.
這張專輯被認為是吉諾的代表作，展現了他身為吉他手的才華。

18 **motel** [moˋtɛl] 名 C 汽車旅館

- mo(tor) 汽車
- (ho)tel 旅館

● Oscar parked his car in front of the **motel** and spent a night there. 奧斯卡把車停在一家汽車旅館的前面，在那裡住了一晚。

19 **mountainous** [ˋmaʊntənəs] 形 多山的，有山的

- mountain 名 山
- -ous 形 表「多……的」

● The **mountainous** area is always colder than the valley floor. 山上一向比山谷地來得冷。

20 **neighborhood** [ˋnebɚˏhʊd] 名 C ❶ 近鄰，整個街坊；❷ 鄰近地區

- neighbor 名 鄰居
- -hood 名 表「狀態」

❶ Melinda has been constructing her house for a year, and the noise has upset the entire **neighborhood**.
梅琳妲的房子已經蓋了一年了，其噪音讓附近的居民不堪其擾。

❷ The Wangs live in the **neighborhood** of the MRT station; it takes them three minutes to get to the station from their house. 王家人住在捷運站附近，從他們家到車站只有三分鐘的路程。

21 **orbit** [ˋɔrbɪt] ❶ 名 U（天體等的）運行軌道 ❷ 動 環繞（天體等）的軌道運行

❶ Next Sunday, NASA will put another satellite into **orbit**.
下週日，美國太空總署將發射另一顆人造衛星進入軌道。

❷ Mercury takes only 88 days to **orbit** the sun.
水星繞著太陽運行一圈只需要 88 天。

22 **palace** [ˋpælɪs] 名 C 皇宮，宮殿

- Solomon's **palace** is a series of separate buildings rather than one large structure.
  索羅門的宮殿是由連續幾棟獨棟樓房所組成，而非一個單一的大型建築。

23 **peak** [pik] 名 C ❶ 山頂，山峰；❷ 高峰，最高點 ❸ 動 達到高峰

❶ The highest **peak** in the Himalayas is Mount Everest.
喜馬拉雅山的最高峰是聖母峰。

❷ When the pop singer won the Grammy Award for Record of the Year, he was at the **peak** of his career.
那位流行歌手贏得葛萊美獎的年度唱片獎，事業達到了顛峰。

❸ During the financial crisis, unemployment in the United States **peaked** at 10%. 在金融危機期間，美國的失業率攀到了百分之十。

補充 reach one's peak 到達……巔峰狀態

24 **pub** [pʌb] 名 C 酒吧

- After work, Hank likes to meet friends in the local **pub** near his company for a beer.
  下班後，漢克喜歡在公司附近的一家酒吧和朋友聚聚喝個兩杯。

31 Places & buildings 地方與建築

61

01 **pit** [pɪt] 名 C 窪坑，凹處

- The gardener has dug several **pits** in the lawn for planting palm trees. 園丁在草地上挖了幾個洞來種植棕櫚樹。

02 **regional** [ˋridʒənl̩] 形 地區的

- The plan for the development of regional tourism has been approved. 發展地方觀光的計畫已經批准。

· region 名 地區
· -al 形 表「……的」

03 **rural** [ˋrʊrəl] 形 農村的，田園的，有鄉村風味的

- The train passed through breathtaking **rural** landscapes before arriving at a small fishing village in southern Thailand.
  火車行經令人嘆為觀止的鄉間美景，最後抵達泰國南部的一座小漁村。

04 **skyscraper** [ˋskaɪˏskrepɚ] 名 C 摩天大樓

- Whenever it's cloudy, the tops of the **skyscrapers** are hidden from view.
  只要是多雲的天氣，就看不見摩天大樓的頂端。

・sky 天
・scrap 刮；擦
・-er 名 表「物」

05 **slope** [slop] 名 C 斜坡

- Climbing up the steep **slope** tired me out.
  爬上那麼陡的斜坡，把我累壞啦。

06 **stadium** [ˋstedɪəm] 名 C 體育館，運動場

- The **stadium** is at full capacity tonight because this is the final game of the season. 今晚舉行季決賽，運動場上座無虛席。

07 **steep** [stip] 形 ❶ 陡峭的；❷ 急劇升降的，大起大落的

❶ For safety, Robert always shifts into low gear when driving down **steep** hills. 羅伯特為了安全起見，開車下陡坡時都會換成低速檔。

❷ People are complaining about the **steep** rise in oil prices; now they have to pay much more money for the fuel.
人民抱怨油價飛漲，現在汽油的支出高了很多。

補充 steep slope 陡坡

08 **structure** [ˋstrʌktʃɚ] 名 ❶ U 結構，構造；❷ C 構造體，建築物

❶ The students are studying the **structure** of atoms, starting with hydrogen, which contains one proton and one electron.
學生們正在學原子的結構。首先是氫原子：含有一個質子和一個電子。

❷ The new terminal is a steel and glass **structure**.
這座新航站是由鋼和玻璃所蓋成的建築物。

09 **studio** [ˋstjudɪˏo] 名 C 工作室；錄音室

- The Music Department provides professional **studios** for the students. 音樂系為學生提供了專業的錄音室。

10 **suburb** [ˋsʌbɝb] 名 C 郊區　形 suburban 郊區的

- The price of real estate in the **suburbs** can be much lower than prices in the center of the city. 郊區的不動產價格比市中心低很多。

62

11 **summit** [ˋsʌmɪt] 名 C ❶（山等的）尖峰，峰頂；❷ 最高級會議，高峰會

❶ The climbers finally reached the **summit**. Standing on the highest point of the mountain, they enjoyed a fine view of the city.
登山者終於攻頂；他們站在山的至高點上，欣賞美麗的市景。

❷ Presidents from 25 countries attended the **summit** in New York City; after the meeting, they issued a declaration.
來自不同國家的 25 位總統參加了紐約高峰會。會議結束後，他們發表了一個宣言。

12 **surround** [sə`raʊnd] 動 ❶ 圍繞；❷ 包圍，圍困

・sur- 表「在上」
・round 環繞

❶ Many ancient cities were once **surrounded** by walls.
許多古老的城市以前都是城牆環立的。

❷ The police have **surrounded** the building; the killer has nowhere to run. 警方已經包圍了這棟建築，兇手無可遁逃。

13 **universe** [`junə͵vɝs] 名 (單數) 宇宙，全世界

● Beryl thinks that the Great Barrier Reef in Australia is the most beautiful place in the **universe**.
貝麗兒覺得澳洲的大堡礁是世界上最美的地方。

14 **scenery** [`sinərɪ] 名 U 風景，景色

・scene 名 景色
・-ery 名 表「地方」

● Ora traded her apartment for a mountain cabin so she could enjoy the natural **scenery**.
歐拉賣掉公寓住處，買了一間山中小屋，好享受自然美景。

15 **shelter** [`ʃɛltɚ] 名 ❶ C 躲避處，避難所；❷ U 掩蔽，庇護
動 ❸ 掩蔽，庇護；❹ 躲避，避難

❶ Adam made his mansion into a **shelter** for people who have lost their homes. 亞當把自己的宅邸改成避難所，供無家可歸的人們居住。

❷ Those flood victims have lost everything, including their homes, overnight; what they need most is food and **shelter**.
那些水災災民一夜間頓失一切，無家可歸。現在他們最需要的是食物和住所。

❸ The little wooden hut **sheltered** the hunters from the storm and kept them safe. 那間小木屋在暴風雨中庇護了獵人們，讓他們安然無恙。

❹ Some people **sheltered** from the thundershower under the tall tree, which can be very dangerous.
有些人在高樹下躲避雷陣雨，其實是很危險的。

16 **site** [saɪt] 名 C 地點，場所

● There are several picnic **sites** in the park. 公園裡有好幾個野餐區。

17 **solar** [`solɚ] 形 太陽的，日光的

● This small **solar** panel generates enough energy to run the water heater. 這塊小太陽能板所產生的能量，足以讓熱水器運作。

18 **surroundings** [sə`raʊndɪŋz] 名（複）環境，周圍的事物，周圍的情況

- The students study in pleasant **surroundings**; the classrooms are air-conditioned, and the facilities are new. 這些學生在舒適的環境中學習；所有的教室都有空調，而且設備都是新的。

▪ sur- 表「在上」
▪ round 圍繞
▪ -ing 名 表「產物」
▪ -s（複）

19 **tomb** [tum] 名 C 墳墓，墳地

- Ricardo's job is to clean the **tombs** in the graveyard.
瑞卡多的工作是在墓園打掃。

20 **urban** [`ɝbən] 形 城市的，居住在城市的

- Some **urban** property owners rent out their houses because they prefer to live in the countryside.
有些在城市置產的人因為更喜歡住在鄉下，就把城裡的房子租出去。

21 **volcano** [vɑl`keno] 名 C 火山

- **Volcanoes** that erupt without warning can cause great danger.
毫無預警的火山爆發，可能會造成重大死傷。

補充 an active volcano 活火山；
a dormant volcano 休火山；
an extinct volcano 死火山

Part 3 →

Society

社會

32 Social relationship & organizations
社會關係與組織 (1)

63

01 **background** [ˋbækˏgraʊnd] 名 C ❶ 背景；❷（事件等的）背景；❸ 出身背景，經歷

・back 後面的
・ground 地；基底

❶ Angel used darker colors in the **background** of her painting to emphasize the foreground.
安潔在畫中使用較深的背景色來凸顯前景。

❷ This article gives mainly the **background** of the French Revolution; it explains how and when the revolution took place.
這篇文章主要敘述了法國大革命的背景，說明其發生時間與來龍去脈。

❸ I know just a bit about Andy's **background**; he was supposedly born into a very musical family.
安迪的出身背景我只知曉一二，他似乎出身於一個音樂世家。

補充 background information 背景資料

02 **bond** [bɑnd] 名 C 聯結，聯繫 名 bondage 奴役；束縛

- Is Romeo and Juliet's **bond** of love everlasting?
羅密歐與茱麗葉的愛情會天長地久嗎？

03 **charity** [ˋtʃærətɪ] 名 C 慈善團體，慈善事業 形 charitable 慈善的

- The profits from Prince Charles' organic farm are given to **charities** to help the poor and the sick.
查理斯王子將有機農場的收益捐給了慈善團體，用來幫助窮人和病人。

04 **civil** [ˋsɪvḷ] 形 ❶ 公民的；❷ 民事的；❸ 國內的

❶ In a democratic country, every citizen enjoys the same **civil** rights. 在這個民主國家，每一個公民享有同樣的公民權。

❷ Juan is a lawyer who specializes in **civil** law. 璜是民法的專業律師。

❸ During the **civil** war, the government army bravely fought the rebels. 內戰期間，政府軍奮勇與叛軍交戰。

補充 civil rights 公民權；civil law 民法；civil war 內戰；civil servant 公務員

05 **committee** [kəˋmɪtɪ] 名（集合名詞）委員會

・commit 託給
・-ee 名 表「受者」

- Doris has organized a special **committee** that monitors air pollution.
多莉絲組了一個監督空氣汙染的特別委員會。

06 **community** [kəˋmjunətɪ] 名 C 社區

- Mrs. Ricci is the leader of the Italian **community** in San Francisco. 利西夫人是舊金山義大利人社區的總幹事。

07 **divorce** [dəˋvors] ❶ 名 C 離婚 ❷ 動 與……離婚

- di(s)- 表「分開」
- vorce 轉

❶ Candace believes it is easier to get married than it is to get a **divorce**. 康蝶絲相信，結婚比離婚容易多了。

❷ Three years after Fabian **divorced** his wife, he remarried. 富賓恩和妻子離婚三年後再婚了。

08 **foundation** [faʊnˋdeʃən] 名 ❶ C 基金會；❷ C 基礎，根據；❸ U 建立，創辦

- found 建立，創立
- -ation 名 表「動作，狀態」

❶ Andrea used her inheritance to establish an educational **foundation** that serves society. 安德莉亞以繼承得來的遺產，創立了一個教育基金會來回饋社會。

❷ This course will provide students with a solid **foundation** for research. It is highly recommended for those who plan to go to graduate school. 這個課程可以幫學生打下一個紮實的研究基礎，強力推薦給打算要讀研究所的人。

❸ The company has expanded quickly since its **foundation** in 1973. 這家公司自從 1973 年創辦後就迅速地擴展。

09 **friendship** [ˋfrɛndʃɪp] 名 U 友情，友好

- friend 朋友
- -ship 名 表「狀態」

- Although Emma and I have been able to visit each other only in Internet chat rooms the last few years, our **friendship** is as close as ever. 雖然我和艾瑪多年來只能在網路聊天室交談，但我們的友誼依然像過去一樣親密。

10 **generation** [ˌdʒɛnəˋreʃən] 名 C 世代，一代

- generate 產生
- -ion 名 表「行為的結果」

- People born in this century have suffered from the adverse effects of global warming; we wonder what will happen to future **generations**. 出生在這個世紀的人們已經嚐到了全球暖化的惡果，很難想像我們的後代子孫會面臨什麼樣的際遇。

補充 generation gap 代溝

11 **headquarters** [ˋhɛdˋkwɔrtɚz] 名 C 總部，總公司，總局

- head 頭
- quarter 住處

- The board meeting will be held in the company's **headquarters** next Monday. 公司的董事會議將於下週一在總部舉行。

12 **household** [ˋhaʊs͵hold] 名 C 一家人，家庭

- How many **households** are there in your community? 你住的社區有多少戶人家？

補充 a household name 家喻戶曉的名字

・house 房子
・hold 占據；擁有

13 **isolate** [ˋaɪsl̩͵et] 動 ❶ 使孤立，使脫離；❷ 把（傳染病患者等）隔離

❶ Harold never talked to other students and was pretty **isolated** at school. 哈洛德在學校從不和同學說話，非常的孤僻。

❷ All patients with SARS were **isolated** in hospitals, and their families were kept under surveillance at home.
所有的 SARS 患者在醫院裡都被隔離，而他們的家人則在家受監管。

14 **isolation** [͵aɪsl̩ˋeʃən] 名 U 隔離，孤立

- Gordon's classmates treat him coldly; he has a feeling of **isolation**.
戈登的同學對他很冷淡，他有一種被孤立的感覺。

補充 in isolation 隔絕的

・isolate 動 使孤立
・-ion 名 表「行為的狀態」

64

15 **membership** [ˋmɛmbɚ͵ʃɪp] 名 U 會員身分，會員資格

- Does your club have any special requirements for those applying for **membership**?
要加入你的俱樂部，有什麼特殊的條件限制嗎？

・member 名 會員
・-ship 名 表「身分」

16 **mutual** [ˋmjutʃʊəl] 形 ❶ 相互的，彼此的；❷ 共有的，共同的

❶ **Mutual** respect is essential in successful long-term relationships.
互相尊重是維持長期良好關係的必要條件。

❷ Chase and his girlfriend discovered a **mutual** interest in art; also, they both love music.
夏佐和他女朋友發現，他們彼此都對藝術有興趣，而且也都愛好音樂。

17 **nationality** [͵næʃənˋælətɪ] 名 U 國籍

- Rudolph, a man of Swiss **nationality**, has relocated to Thailand and opened a guesthouse.
一名瑞士籍男子魯道夫在泰國落腳，開了一間家庭式旅社。

補充 dual nationality 雙重國籍

・nation 國家
・-al 形 表「……的」
・-ity 名 表「狀態」

18 **ownership** [ˋonɚ͵ʃɪp] 名 U 所有權　動 own 擁有

- The court will reach a conclusion today regarding the **ownership** of Ms. Wood's book.
法院今天會就伍德小姐書籍的著作權爭議做出判決。

・own 擁有
・-er 名 表「人」
・-ship 名 表「狀態」

19 **panel** [ˋpænl̩] 名 C ❶ **專門小組，專題討論小組**；❷ **配電盤，控電板**

❶ Frances asked to join our discussion **panel** and was accepted.
法蘭希絲請求加入我們的專題討論小組，大家同意了。

❷ The printer has a separate button on the control **panel** for scanning. 這部印表機在控制面板上有一個個別的按鈕，是用來掃描的。

20 **partnership** [ˋpɑrtnɚ͵ʃɪp] 名 ❶ U 合夥關係；❷ C 合夥公司

❶ The women have been in a **partnership** for 10 years, and they seem to have run the company with skill.
她們的合夥關係已經有十年了，而且公司好像也經營得很好。

- partner 名 合夥人
- -ship 名 表「狀態」

❷ The computer company is the biggest **partnership** in the country; it is owned by its 15,000 employees, all of whom have a stake in the business. 這家電腦公司是該國最大的一家合夥公司，為其 15000 名的職員所擁有，所有的職員都擁有公司股份。

21 **privilege** [ˋprɪvl̩ɪdʒ] ❶ 名 U 特權，優待　❷ 動 給予……特權或優待

❶ Jack was given the rare **privilege** of using the president's office, which made the others quite jealous.
傑克被賦予使用董事長辦公室的特權，這讓其他人很吃味。

❷ The school should not have **privileged** the students of wealthy parents; they should have treated every student equally. 這所學校不應該給予家庭富裕的學生特權，他們應該公平、平等地對待每一個學生。

22 **racial** [ˋreʃəl] 形 人種的，種族的　名 racism 種族主義

- race 種族
- -ial 形 表「屬於……的」

● Martin Luther King, Jr., devoted his life to abolishing **racial** discrimination.
小馬丁．路德．金終身致力於消弭種族歧視。

23 **rank** [ræŋk] ❶ 名 U 等級，地位，身分　❷ 動 把……分等，把……評級

❶ In Maxine's company, workers' salaries are determined by **rank** and seniority. 在梅可馨的公司裡，員工的薪水是以職務和服務的年資來決定的。

❷ To arrange the seats, the teacher first **ranked** the students according to height. 為了安排座位，老師先把學生們按身高排列。

24 **relative** [ˋrɛlətɪv] ❶ 名 C 親戚，親屬　❷ 形 與……有關係的，相關的

❶ Lawrence is one of my **relatives**; he is my cousin. 勞倫斯是我的一個親戚，他是我的表哥。

- relate 有關
- -ive 名 形 表「與……有關」

❷ The celebrity refused to answer any questions **relative** to his private life. 那位名人拒絕回答有關他私生活的問題。

25 **responsibility** [rɪˏspɑnsəˋbɪlətɪ] 名 U ❶ 責任；❷ 責任感

- response 回應
- -ible 形 表「可……的」
- -ity 名 表「狀態」

❶ The police have **responsibility** for maintaining public order and peace; it is also their duty to ensure the law is respected.
警方有責任維護公共治安，確保法律被遵守也是他們的職責所在。

❷ Donnie is completely lacking in personal and social **responsibility**. 唐尼毫無個人與社會責任感。

用法 take responsibility (for) 為……負起責任

26 **romance** [roˋmæns] 名 ❶ C 戀情，緋聞；❷ U 羅曼蒂克氣氛，浪漫情調

❶ Celebrity **romances** have always been the focus of public attention. 名人的緋聞向來是大眾注目的焦點。

❷ On Valentine's Day, an air of **romance** enveloped the restaurant, as many lovers were dining there.
情人節那一天，那家餐廳瀰漫著浪漫的氣氛，因為有很多情侶在那裡用餐。

27 **tribe** [traɪb] 名 C 部落，族群　形 tribal 部落的

- A **tribe** is a social and political group that shares a common ancestry and culture.
族群是一種社會性和政治性的團體，人們擁有共同的祖先與文化。

28 **union** [ˋjunjən] 名 C 工會，協會

- Preston has to join the **union** in order to get a job at the factory.
普勒斯頓為了在那家工廠謀得一份工作，只好加入工會。

29 **tribal** [traɪbl̩] 形 部落的，種族的

- tribe 名 部落
- -al 形 表「……的」

- For years, the government has been helping the Navajo to preserve their **tribal** culture.
幾年來，政府一直在幫助納瓦霍族維護他們的部落文化。

33 Social relationship & organizations
社會關係與組織 (2)

65

01 **article** [ˋɑrtɪkḷ] 名 C ❶ 文章；❷（物品的）一件 同義 item 品目

❶ The **article** about healthy living that was published in today's newspaper is definitely worth reading.
今天報上一篇有關健康生活的文章絕對值得一讀。

❷ Spencer packed a few **articles** of clothing in his bag and went on a business trip. 史賓賽打包了幾件衣服到他的袋子裡，就去出差了。

02 **artistic** [ɑrˋtɪstɪk] 形 藝術的 名 art 藝術

- **Artistic** value should not be calculated by economic interests. 藝術價值不應該以經濟利益來衡量。

> ‧art 藝術
> ‧-ist 名 表「做……的人」
> ‧-ic 形 表「具有……特性的」

03 **autobiography** [ˌɔtəbaɪˋɑgrəfɪ] 名 C 自傳

- Has anyone contacted you about publishing your **autobiography**? 有人和你聯絡過要出版你的自傳嗎？

> ‧auto- 表「自己的」
> ‧biography 傳記

04 **ballet** [ˋbæle] 名 U 芭蕾舞

- Tracy had practiced **ballet** for five years before she became a stage dancer. 翠西之前苦練了五年芭蕾，才得以登台當舞者。

05 **biography** [baɪˋɑgrəfɪ] 名 C 傳記

- Julia is reading a **biography** of a rock and roll icon. 茱麗亞正在讀一位搖滾樂偶像的傳記。

> ‧bio- 表「生命」
> ‧-graphy 寫（或畫、描繪、記錄）的東西

06 **carve** [kɑrv] 動 刻，雕刻

- Derrick **carved** this statue of a pregnant woman out of wood in three days. 德瑞克在三天內刻好了這座孕婦木雕。

相關用法 **carving** 名 雕刻

- The wooden table is covered with carvings. 這張木桌的表面刻了許多雕刻。

07 **catalogue** [ˋkætəlɔg] 名 C 目錄 同義 catalog 目錄

- You should check the mail-order **catalogue**; it shows all the goods that can be bought and sent to your home.
你可以看看這本郵購目錄，上面列有可以送貨到府的的待售商品。

08 **CD** [si di] 名 C 雷射唱片 (= compact disc)

- In the record store, the student spent NT$250 on a **CD**.
  那名學生在唱片行花了新台幣 250 元買了一張 CD。

09 **ceramic** [sə`ræmɪk] ❶ 形 陶製的；❷ 名 C（常作複數）陶製品

❶ The nurses washed their hands in the **ceramic** water basin.
護士們在陶製洗手台上洗手。

❷ The museum will hold a **ceramic** exhibition for the famous artist.
博物館將展出知名藝術家的陶藝作品。

10 **chain** [tʃen] 名 C ❶ 鏈條，項圈；❷ 一連串，一系列；❸ 連鎖店
動 ❹ 用鎖鏈拴住，拘禁

❶ Before walking into the store, the man tied his dog to a tree with a **chain**. 男子在進入商店之前用鏈條把他的狗拴在樹旁。

❷ The abnormal weather patterns have set off a **chain** reaction in our ecosystem. 異常的氣候型態已經讓我們的生態產生了連鎖反應。

❸ Several supermarket **chains** that are owned by the same company will open in the city. 同公司幾家連鎖超市將在這個城市開業。

❹ Andy **chained** his bicycle to the post and walked into the library.
安迪把他的腳踏車用鏈子拴在柱子上，然後走進圖書館。

補充 food chain 食物鏈；chain store 連鎖店

11 **chapter** [`tʃæptɚ] 名 C 章，回　同義 section, part, division 部，篇，部分

- The topic you are looking for in this book is in **Chapter** 3.
  你找的主題在書裡的第三章。

12 **china** [`tʃaɪnə] 名 U 瓷器，陶瓷器

- Evelyn felt terrible because she broke a piece of her mother's favorite **china** yesterday. 伊芙琳昨天摔破了媽媽最愛的瓷花瓶，覺得很害怕。

66

13 **chorus** [korəs] 名 C 合唱隊　同義 choir 合唱團

- Caroline wants to join the school **chorus** next semester.
  凱洛琳下學期想加入學校的合唱團。

相關片語 **in chorus** 一齊

- The teacher asked a question, and all the students answered in chorus.
  老師問了一個問題，結果所有學生不約而同地齊聲回答。

14 **civilization** [ˌsɪvl̩əˋzeʃən] 名 ❶ C 文化；❷ U 文明

- civil 文明的
- -ize 動 表「使形成」
- -ation 名 表「狀態」

❶ Everyone agrees that the Hindu **civilization** is one of the oldest in the world. 大家都同意印度文化是世界上最古老的文明之一。

❷ The Industrial Revolution, which began in the 18th century, is credited with bringing progress and **civilization** to the world.
一般認為，十八世紀開始的工業革命為世界帶來了進步與文明。

15 **classical** [ˋklæsɪkl̩] 形 ❶ 古典的；❷ 正統的，傳統的

- class 等級
- -ic 名 表「藝術」
- -al 形 表「……的」

❶ When Dolly is stressed, she listens to **classical** music until the tension is gone.
桃莉覺得壓力很大時，就會聽古典音樂來放鬆心情。

❷ **Classical** ballet is quite different from modern ballet; the former is more traditional in style and idea.
古典芭蕾和現代芭蕾有很大的不同，前者在風格和觀念上比較傳統。

16 **column** [ˋkɑləm] 名 C ❶ **專欄**；❷ **圓柱** 名 columnist 專欄作家

❶ Mona reads the sports **column** in the newspaper every day.
蒙娜每天都會看報紙的體育版。

❷ The dome of the church is supported by eight marble **columns**.
這座教堂的圓頂由八根大理石柱子支撐。

17 **comedy** [ˋkɑmədɪ] 名 C **喜劇** 名 comedian 喜劇演員

- Kimberly's favorite movie genre is **comedy** because funny films usually cheer her up.
金柏莉最喜歡的電影類型是喜劇片，因為好笑的電影能讓她心情變好。

18 **comic** [ˋkɑmɪk] ❶ 名 C **連環漫畫** ❷ 形 **喜劇的**

❶ When Dave picks up a newspaper, he prefers to read the **comics** rather than the news.
大衛拿起報紙時，通常是看報紙上的漫畫，而不太看新聞。

❷ The clown wears funny clothes and a large red nose for **comic** effect. 這個小丑穿著滑稽可笑的衣服、戴著一個大大的紅鼻子來製造笑果。

19 **compose** [kəmˋpoz] 動 ❶ 作（詩或曲）；❷ 組成，構成

- com- 在一起
- pose 假裝，冒充

❶ Gladys has **composed** many popular songs throughout her career. 葛萊蒂絲一生中作出許多膾炙人口的歌曲。

❷ The team is **composed** of 10 players. 這個隊伍是由十個球員組成的。

20 **composition** [ˌkɑmpəˋzɪʃən] 名 ❶ Ⓒ 作文；❷ Ⓤ 構成，成分；❸ Ⓤ 創作，寫作

❶ The teacher corrected some grammatical mistakes in the student's **composition**.
老師糾正了學生作文裡的一些文法錯誤。

- com- 表「一起」
- pose 假裝，冒充
- -ion 名 表「行為的結果」

❷ Dr. Bray analyzed the meteorite to determine its **composition**.
布雷博士分析了流星，以找出其成分。

❸ The musician has written a new song. The **composition** took only two weeks, but she still has to write the lyrics.
那位音樂家作了一首新歌。她的在編曲只花了兩個星期，但還沒有填上歌詞。

21 **concert** [ˋkɑnsɚt] 名 Ⓒ 音樂會

- Peggy loves music so much that she will spend lots of money to go to a **concert**. 佩姬熱愛音樂，願意花大錢去聽音樂會。

22 **contribute** [kənˋtrɪbjut] 動 ❶ 投（稿）；❷ 捐獻，捐助；❸ 促成

❶ Doris has been **contributing** articles to travel magazines for years.
多莉絲多年來在旅遊雜誌上寫了許多文章。

- con- 表「一起」
- tribute 貢物，貢金

❷ The rich man **contributed** $2 million to several charities that help the poor. 這名有錢人捐了 200 萬美金給幾個濟貧的慈善機構。

❸ People become addicted to the Internet for many reasons. One factor **contributing** to this phenomenon is easy access to the Net. 有諸多因素可以解釋人們為何會沉迷於網路。促成這個現象的因素之一，是因為上網十分便利。

23 **convention** [kənˋvɛnʃən] 名 ❶ Ⓤ 慣例，習俗；❷ Ⓒ 大會，會議

❶ By American **convention**, a bride is supposed to wear something borrowed and something blue at her wedding.
美國傳統中，新娘在婚禮上要戴借來的東西和藍色的東西。

- convene 集合
- -ion 名 表「行為」

❷ The police were informed of a bomb threat at the upcoming political **convention**. 警方獲報，即將舉行的政治會議受到了炸彈攻擊的威脅。

24 **conventional** [kənˋvɛnʃənḷ] 形 ❶ 傳統式的；❷ 習慣的，慣例的

❶ This new type of surgery is popular because the recovery time is much shorter than that required in **conventional** surgeries. 這種新手術很受歡迎，因為它的復原時間比傳統手術所需要的時間短很多。〔93 年指測補考〕

- convention 慣例
- -al 形 表「……的」

❷ Thumbs-up is a **conventional** gesture that means "good job."
比起大拇指，習慣上是用來表示「做得好」。

25 **creative** [krɪˋetɪv] 形 ❶ 創造性的，有創造力的；❷ 啟發想像力的

❶ Rollins is a **creative** writer; her works are always filled with new ideas.
羅琳絲是個有創造力的作者，她的作品總是充滿新的想法。

- create 動 創造
- -ive 形 表「與……有關的」

❷ Bernard has made some very **creative** toys for his children.
柏納做了一些益智性玩具給自己的孩子玩。

34 Social relationship & organizations 社會關係與組織 (3)

67

01 **cultural** [ˋkʌltʃərəl] 形 文化的，人文的

- culture 名 文化
- -al 形 表「……的」

● Myron is studying to become a **cultural** anthropologist. 麥榮在用功讀書，因為他想成為文化人類學家。

02 **disco** [ˋdɪsko] 名 ❶ U 迪斯可音樂；❷ C 小舞廳，迪斯可舞廳

❶ **Disco**, which is characterized by strong repetitive bass rhythms, was first popular in the 1970s.
以低重音固定節拍聞名的迪斯可音樂，於 1970 年代首度流行起來。

❷ My sister used to go to a **disco** at night, where she and her friends danced to pop music. 我姊姊以前晚上常去迪斯可舞廳和朋友跳流行音樂。

03 **draft** [dræft] ❶ 名 C 草稿　❷ 動 起草

❶ Clyde spent three months completing the first **draft** of his book.
克萊德花了三個月寫完書本的初稿。

❷ The secretary is **drafting** a letter for the manager, who will likely rewrite this rough first version.
祕書正在為經理起草一封信，然後經理本人會再改寫這份粗略的初稿。

04 **dramatic** [drəˋmætɪk] 形 ❶ 戲劇的，劇本的；❷ 戲劇般的，戲劇性的

❶ The singer gives a **dramatic** performance, so she will play Juliet. 這位歌星將有一場戲劇演出，她將扮演茱麗葉。

- drama 名 戲劇
- -(t)ic 形 表「……的」

❷ Ricardo's **dramatic** entrance surprised everyone and was the highlight of the show.
里卡杜戲劇化性的進場方式讓大家驚嘆連連，這是整場表演的高潮。

05 **edit** [ˋɛdɪt] 動 ❶ 編輯，校訂；❷ 主編（報紙、雜誌等），擔任（出版物等）的編輯；❸ 剪輯，剪接（影片等）

❶ As the teacher helped me **edit** my essay, she corrected the errors in spelling and grammar.
老師幫我校訂了我的文章，改正了拼字和文法的錯誤。

❷ Mr. Smith used to **edit** a daily paper; he was responsible for preparing the newspaper for publication.
史密斯先生過去曾擔任過報紙主編，當時他負責統籌該份報紙的出版。

❸ How many days do you need in order to **edit** this footage?
你可以在幾天內剪接完這捲影片？

06 **edition** [ɪˋdɪʃən] 名 C ❶ 版本；❷（發行物的）版，（某版的）發行數

❶ Barry translates Chinese literature into German **editions** for publishers.
巴里為多家出版社翻譯，把中國文學作品翻譯成德文版。

- edit 編輯
- -ion 名 表「行為的結果」

❷ The novel has been very popular; this is the seventh **edition**.
這一本小說非常受歡迎，現在已經是第七版了。

07 **essay** [ˋɛse] 名 C 論說文，散文

- Travis wrote an **essay** about the supernatural powers of animals.
特拉維斯寫了一篇有關動物神奇力量的論文。

08 **exhibit** [ɪgˋzɪbɪt] 動 ❶ 展示，陳列　名 C ❷ 展示品；❸ 展示會

❶ Rick has never publicly **exhibited** his artwork because of his lack of confidence.
瑞克還沒有公開展覽過自己的藝術作品，這是因為他缺乏信心。

- ex- 表「出」
- hib 表「舉辦」

❷ Visitors should not touch any **exhibits** in the museum, as these works of art are very precious.
參觀者不應該觸碰博物館裡的任何展覽品，因為這些藝術品都很珍貴。

❸ Next month, there will be an **exhibit** of impressionistic paintings at the art museum. 下個月，藝術博物館將舉辦一場印象派畫展。

09 **exhibition** [ˌɛksəˋbɪʃən] 名 C 展覽，展示會

- exhibit 展出
- -ion 名 表「行為的結果」

- At the opening of the **exhibition**, complimentary wine and cheese will be served.
在展覽的開幕上，葡萄酒和起司都準備好了。

相關片語 **make an exhibition of oneself** 出洋相

- After getting drunk, the man yelled and sang loudly in the bar, making an exhibition of himself. 男子喝醉了，在酒吧裡又吼又唱，出盡洋相。

10 **fable** [ˋfebḷ] 名 C **寓言故事**

- Clifford likes the way his mother tells the **fable** of the *Three Little Pigs*. 柯利弗德喜歡媽媽說三隻小豬故事的方式。

補充 Aesop's Fables 伊索寓言

11 **fiction** [ˋfɪkʃən] 名 U **(總稱)小說**

- Tom prefers reading **fiction** because stories of imaginary people and events help him to escape from the stress of his own life. 湯姆喜歡看小說，因為奇異的人物情節能讓他逃離現實生活的壓力。

12 **gallery** [ˋgælərɪ] 名 C **畫廊，美術館，藝廊**

- As an art agent, Shane works with **galleries** around the world.
尚恩是藝術品代理商，他和世界各地的藝廊都有往來。

68

13 **instruction** [ɪnˋstrʌkʃən] 名 C ❶ 用法說明，操作指南；❷ 命令，指示

・instruct 教授；指示
・-ion 名 表「行為」

❶ Sharlene read the **instructions** and figured out how to use her new telephone answering machine.
莎蓮看了新電話答錄機的說明書，研究出了使用方法。

❷ If you want to have a quick recovery from the illness, be sure to follow the doctor's **instructions**.
如果你想要病盡快痊癒，就務必要遵守醫師的叮嚀。

14 **journal** [ˋdʒɝnḷ] 名 C **雜誌，期刊**　名 journalism 新聞業

- Ernestine wrote many interesting stories for the travel **journal**.
愛妮絲汀為一本旅遊雜誌寫了許多有趣的經歷。

15 **legend** [ˋlɛdʒənd] 名 C ❶ **傳說，傳奇故事，傳奇文學；** ❷ **傳說中的人或事，傳奇人物**

❶ The story of *King Arthur and the Knights of the Round Table* is perhaps the most well-known of all the Cornish **legends**.
亞瑟王和圓桌武士的故事，大概是康瓦耳傳說中最為人所知的故事。

❷ After winning the championship six consecutive times, Miguel is no doubt a **legend**. 米格爾連續衛冕六次，無疑是個傳奇人物。

16 **literary** [ˋlɪtə͵rɛrɪ] 形 **文學的，文藝的**　名 literature 文學

- Ms. Carver, an authority on American literature, has published several **literary** critiques in journals.
美國文學權威卡爾維女士，已經在多家期刊上發表了數篇文學評論。

17 **literature** [ˋlɪtərətʃɚ] 名 U 文學

- Bonnie was interested in all forms of **literature** and later became a writer.
邦妮對所有類型的文學作品都感興趣，她自己後來也當了作家。

> ・literate 能讀寫的；有文化修養
> ・-ure 名 表「動作」

18 **lullaby** [ˋlʌlə͵baɪ] 名 C 搖籃曲

- Do you remember any **lullabies** your mother used to sing to you? 你還記得你母親以前唱給你聽的搖籃曲嗎？

19 **manual** [ˋmænjʊəl] ❶ 名 C 手冊，簡介 ❷ 形 用手操作的

❶ Almost every electronic device comes with an instruction **manual**, sometimes written in more than one language.
幾乎每一個電器都附有使用手冊，而且有時還是多語解說的。

❷ The tap has **manual** and automatic functions.
這個水龍頭有手動和自動的功能。

20 **musical** [ˋmjuzɪkḷ] ❶ 形 音樂的 ❷ 名 C 歌舞劇，音樂片

❶ Have you ever learned to play a **musical** instrument? 你有沒有學過什麼樂器呢？

❷ The Phantom of the Opera is one of the most successful **musicals** in the world.
《歌劇魅影》是世界上最成功的音樂劇之一。

> ・muse 司掌文藝、音樂與藝術的希臘女神繆斯
> ・-ic 名 表「藝術」
> ・-al 形 表「……的」

21 **opera** [ˋɑpərə] 名 U 歌劇

- Lloyd enjoys all forms of music, from folk to classical **opera**.
羅伊德什麼類型的音樂都喜歡，從民歌到傳統歌劇他都愛。

22 **orchestra** [ˋɔrkɪstrə] 名 C 管弦樂隊

- Wesley plays percussion and brass in the national **orchestra**.
衛斯理在國家管弦樂團裡彈奏敲擊樂器和銅管樂器。

23 **paragraph** [ˋpærə͵græf] 名 C（文章的）段，節

- After reading the first **paragraph** of this mystery novel, Marty was hooked. 馬帝讀了這本推理小說的第一段，就迷上了。

> ・para- 旁；並列
> ・graph 圖表

24 **passage** [ˋpæsɪdʒ] 名 ❶ C（文章的）一段；❷ 走廊，過道；❸（時間的）推移，進行

❶ The teacher told the students to read the **passage** first; then he asked them several questions.
老師叫學生先讀那個段落，然後問他們一些問題。

> ・pass 通過
> ・-age 名 表「場所、動作」

❷ The **passage** leads to the kitchen. 這個走廊通往廚房。

❸ For Floyd, the **passage** from childhood to adulthood was too traumatic to talk about.
對佛洛德而言，他從小到大的成長過程太坎坷，難以向外人說明。

25 **perform** [pɚˋfɔrm] 動 ❶ 演出，表演；❷（人）表現；❸ 執行，做；❹ 演出……以

❶ Sheu Fang-yi, a young Taiwanese dancer, recently **performed** at Lincoln Center for the Performing Arts in New York City and earned a great deal of praise.
許芳宜，一位年輕的台灣舞蹈家，她最近在紐約林肯中心的表演備受讚賞。

❷ Last night, the soccer team won the important match; all the players **performed** well.
昨天晚上，足球隊贏得了重要比賽，所有的球員表現得都很出色。

❸ As a surgeon, Dr. Westlyn has to **perform** operations every day.
威斯林是外科醫生，每天都得操刀動手術。

❹ The magician **performed** a lot of tricks to entertain the audience. 那位魔術師表演了很多把戲來娛樂觀眾。

26 **performance** [pɚˋfɔrməns] 名 ❶ C 演出，表演；❷（人）表現；❸（機器等的）性能，效能

・perform 表演
・-ance 名 表「動」

❶ The violinist will play at The National Theatre tonight; the **performance** begins at 7 o'clock.
今天晚上，這位小提琴家將在國家劇院演出，表演七點開始。

❷ The worker was laid off because of his poor **performance**.
由於工作表現不佳，那名工人被解雇了。

❸ Lester regularly optimizes the **performance** of his computer.
里斯特定期把自己電腦的效能最佳化。

35 Social relationship & organizations
社會關係與組織 (4)

69

01 **flea** [fli] 名 C 跳蚤

● James hiked in an area infested with **fleas** and came home with dozens of bites on his legs. 詹姆斯健行回來，他兩腿被跳蚤咬了幾十個包。

補充 flea market 跳蚤市場

02 **flock** [flɑk] ❶ 名 C 畜群，人群 ❷ 動 聚集

❶ Early every evening, a **flock** of crows noisily congregates in the old tree in Clyde's backyard.
每天傍晚，一群吵雜的烏鴉都會聚集在克萊德後院的老樹上。

❷ Birds of a feather **flock** together. 物以類聚。

03 **porcelain** [ˋpɔrslɪn] 名 U 瓷，（總稱）瓷器

- The hotel replaced the old cracked sinks in all the guest rooms with new fixtures made of **porcelain**.
飯店將客房中壞掉的水槽全部汰舊換新，換成瓷製的設備。

04 **portrait** [ˋportret] 名 C ❶ 肖像；❷ 描繪 同義 depiction 描寫

❶ Pedro loves painting natural landscapes as well as **portraits** of people. 裴卓喜愛畫自然風景畫，也喜愛畫人物肖像。

❷ The play is a tragedy, with realistic **portraits** of women who are trapped in lives of poverty.
這部戲是一個悲劇，寫實地描繪出貧困婦女的生活。

05 **pottery** [ˋpɑtərɪ] 名 U 陶器

- Claudia collects Native American **pottery** from the Southwest and displays it in her gallery.
克勞蒂雅收集美國西南部原住民的陶器，並且在她的藝廊中展示。

- pot 罐，壺
- -er 名 表「人」
- -y 名 表「狀態」

06 **publication** [ˌpʌblɪˋkeʃən] 名 ❶ U 出版，發行；❷ C 出版物，刊物

❶ Many people are looking forward to the **publication** of the writer's next novel; it should be available to the public next month.
人們殷盼著這位作家下一本小說的發行，據說下個月就會上市了。

- public 公眾的
- -ation 名 表「狀態；結果」

❷ Estelle wrote a wide range of **publications** during her academic career. 愛瑟蕾在整個學術生涯中，著作可說是包羅萬象。

07 **publish** [ˋpʌblɪʃ] 動 ❶ 出版，發行；❷ 刊載，刊登

❶ When will the book that Louise translated be **published**? 露薏絲翻譯的書什麼時候會出版？

❷ The newspaper **published** an article written by a cancer patient who shares his personal experience with the disease.
這家報紙刊登了一個想和大眾分享抗癌經驗的癌症病患所寫的文章。

08 **quotation** [kwo`teʃən] 名 C 引文

- quote 動 引用
- -ation 名 表「動作」

● The article begins with a **quotation** from A Tale of Two Cities: "It was the best of times, it was the worst of times . . . ." 這篇文章以一句出自《雙城記》的引文開始：「這是一個最輝煌的時代，也是一個最不堪的時代。」

09 **quote** [kwot] ❶ 動 引用，引述 ❷ 名 C 引文 名 quotation 引文

❶ Candice **quoted** from her favorite poem in the introduction of her speech. 康蒂絲在演說的開場白中引用了她最喜愛的詩。

❷ Some people have claimed that the **quote** "All men are created equal" comes from the Bible. 這句引文「人人生而平等」出自《聖經》。

10 **revise** [rɪ`vaɪz] 動 修改，修正

● Students were asked to **revise** or rewrite their compositions on the basis of the teacher's comments.
學生們被要求根據老師的評語修改他們的作文。

11 **revision** [rɪ`vɪʒən] 名 U 修改，修正

- revise 修正
- -ion 名 表「行為」

● As a writing consultant, Penney helped students with the **revision** of their essays.
潘妮是一位寫作顧問，專門幫學生修訂文章。

12 **rhyme** [raɪm] 動 ❶ 使成韻 名 ❷ C 同韻語，押韻詞；❸ U 押韻

❶ Can you think of a word that **rhymes** with cat?
你可以想到什麼字是與 cat 押韻的嗎？

❷ Row is a **rhyme** for flow. 「row」是「flow」的同韻字。

❸ A lot of modern poetry does not use **rhyme**. 很多現代詩是不押韻的。

相關片語 **no rhyme or reason** 毫無道理，沒頭沒腦

● There was no rhyme or reason for Tom to quit his job; no one understood why he made such a decision.
湯姆沒來由地辭掉了工作，沒有人知道他為何會做出這樣的決定。

13 **rhythm** [`rɪðəm] 名 U 節奏，韻律 形 rhythmic 有韻律的

● Crystal slowed down the **rhythm** of her speech to deliver a powerful conclusion. 克萊絲朵放慢演說的節奏，以營造強而有力的結論。

70 14 **statue** [`stætʃu] 名 C 雕像

● The **Statue** of Liberty in New York Harbor is a symbol of freedom that represents the United States.
紐約的自由女神像，是美國一個代表自由的象徵。

15 **summary** [ˋsʌmərɪ] 名 C 總結，摘要

- sum 概要
- -ary 名 表「與……有關之物」

● After Ms. Murphy gave a short **summary** of her conclusions, the students started asking her questions. 墨非女士對她的結論做出簡要總結後，學生開始發問問題。

16 **text** [tɛkst] 名 ❶ U 原文，文本；❷ 正文

❶ The **text** of Daphne's original manuscript contains more than 10,000 words. 黛芬妮原先的手寫稿超過了十萬字。

❷ The children's book does not have much **text**, but it is filled with pictures. 這本童書裡的文字不多，都是圖畫。

17 **tune** [tjun] ❶ 名 C 曲調，旋律 ❷ 動 調（收音機的）頻道

❶ The singer wrote the **tune** and the lyrics to the song.
這個歌手自己對這首歌譜曲寫詞。

❷ I always **tune** in to FM 103.1 to listen to music while I study.
我讀書的時候都會把收音機調到 FM 103.1 聽音樂。

相關片語 ❶ **out of tune** 與……格格不入或不一致
❷ **in tune with** 與……一致

❶ Derek feels out of tune with his surroundings all the time, but he doesn't care. 德里克覺得自己和周遭的環境格格不入，但他並不在乎。

❷ Their ideas are in tune with ours, so we agreed to work with them. 他們的想法與我們一致，所以我們同意和他們合作。

18 **verse** [vɝs] 名 ❶ C 詩句，詩行，詩節；❷ U 詩，韻文

❶ During the class, the professor quoted some **verses** from William Blake's poem. 教授在課堂上引用了威廉 · 布萊克的幾句詩。

❷ William Shakespeare wrote his plays in **verse**; sometimes he used blank verse, and sometimes he used rhyme.
威廉 · 莎士比亞用詩撰寫劇本；有時是無韻詩，有時是押韻的。

19 **volume** [ˋvɑljəm] 名 ❶ C 卷，冊；❷ U 音量；
❸ U（生產、交易等的）量，額

❶ Ann has collected a set of Hans De Beer's works in 12 **volumes**.
安收藏了漢斯 · 比爾一套十二冊的作品。

❷ Turn the **volume** up; I can't hear the music.
把音量開大聲點，我聽不到音樂。

❸ The increasing traffic **volume** caused congestion.
交通流量漸大造成了塞車。

20 **sculpture** [ˋskʌlptʃɚ] ❶ 名 C 雕刻品，雕像 ❷ 動 雕刻 同義 carve 雕刻

❶ Dan accidentally broke his father's favorite **sculpture**.
丹不小心打破了父親最喜愛的雕像。

❷ In front of the temple, there are two lions **sculptured** in stone.
在這座寺廟前面，有兩隻用石頭雕成的獅子。

21 **sketch** [skɛtʃ] 名 C ❶ 素描，草圖 ❷ 動 為……素描

❶ Rosa made a **sketch** of the ballet dancers before starting her painting. 蘿莎在畫那群芭蕾舞者之前，先畫了一張素描。

❷ The artist **sketched** the magnificent cathedral in only a few minutes. 那位藝術家幾分鐘之內，就畫出了那座莊嚴大教堂的素描。

22 **summarize** [ˋsʌmə͵raɪz] 動 總結，概述，概括

- summary 總結
- -ize 動 表「按……處理」

● Robin **summarizes** her monthly expenses with an accounting software program.
羅賓用一個會計軟體來結算自己每月的花費。

23 **symphony** [ˋsɪmfənɪ] 名 C 交響樂團

- sym- 表「同時」
- -phone 名 表「聲音」
- -y 名 表「狀態」

● Gordon already bought me a ticket to the Vienna **Symphony**. 戈登已經幫我買了一張維也納交響樂團的票。

24 **theme** [θim] 名 C 題目，主題

● The **theme** of respect for different cultures is clearly presented in Mollie's story.「尊重各種不同文化」的主題，在莫莉的故事裡清楚地呈現出來。

25 **tragedy** [ˋtrædʒədɪ] 名 C ❶ 悲劇；❷ 悲劇性事件，慘案 形 tragic 悲劇的

❶ Which kind of story do you prefer to read, a **tragedy** or a comedy? 你比較喜歡讀悲劇還是喜劇？

❷ The airplane crash is really a **tragedy**; more than 250 people were killed. 那場空難真是個慘劇，超過 250 人死亡。

26 **tragic** [ˋtrædʒɪk] 形 ❶ 悲劇的；❷ 悲劇性的，悲慘的 名 tragedy 悲劇

❶ Othello is a **tragic** hero; he killed his wife out of jealousy.
奧塞羅是一個悲劇英雄，他因為忌妒而殺死了妻子。

❷ **Tragic** events are a powerful influence in shaping our personalities. 悲劇事件有很大的影響力，足以塑造人們的人格。

27 **translate** [trænsˋlet] 動 翻譯　名 translation 翻譯

- Oscar spent two years **translating** his favorite French novel into Chinese. 奧斯卡花了兩年把他最喜歡的法文小說翻譯成中文。

用法 translate A into B　將 A 翻譯成 B

28 **translation** [trænsˋleʃən] 名 U 翻譯

- In your opinion, which version of the **translation** is better? 你認為這兩種翻譯版本，哪一個比較好？

· translate 翻譯
· -ion 名 表「行為（的結果）」

36 Money & business 金錢與商業 (1)

71

01 **account** [əˋkaʊnt] 名 C ❶（銀行）帳戶；❷ 解釋，說明；❸ 記述，描述

❶ Mr. Wright opened a new bank **account** for his business transactions. 瑞特先生開了一個銀行帳戶，供業務往來使用。

❷ Would you please give us a detailed **account** of your plan?
可否請你就你的計畫給我們作一個詳盡的說明？

❸ The witness has given an **account** of the accident, but his description was not very clear.
目擊證人已經描述了意外發生的經過，但他的描述不是很清楚。

相關片語 ❶ **account for** 解釋，說明；❷ **on any account** 無論如何

❶ The teacher asked Norman to explain why he was late again, but he couldn't account for his tardiness.
老師要諾曼解釋他為何又遲到了，但諾無法為自己的懶散辯白。

❷ A father should not, on any account, slap his child in public.
一個父親無論如何，都不應該在公共場合對小孩子摑掌。

02 **advertise** [ˋædvɚˏtaɪz] 動 ❶ 為……做廣告，為……宣傳；❷ 登廣告，作宣傳

❶ Milo wonders why banks **advertise** their credit card services so forcefully. 米羅想知道，各家銀行為什麼會如此強力宣傳信用卡服務。

❷ Last month, the company **advertised** in the newspapers for a sales manager. 那間公司上個月在報紙上刊登徵求業務經理的廣告。

03 **advertisement** [ˌædvɚˋtaɪzmənt] 名 ❶ U 廣告，宣傳；❷ C（一則）廣告

❶ Her photos are a good **advertisement** for the beauty product.
她的照片能為美容產品達到很好的廣告效果。

❷ The magazine is full of **advertisements** for cosmetics, making female readers want to buy them.
這本雜誌充滿化妝品的廣告，讓女性讀者蠢蠢欲動。

- advertise 為……做廣告
- -ment 名 表「方法」

04 **afford** [əˋford] 動 ❶ 供得起，買得起；❷ 供給，給予

❶ Ian's parents couldn't **afford** to send him to college, so he took out a student loan. 伊恩的父母負擔不起他上大學的費用，所以他辦了助學貸款。

❷ Reading gives me pleasure; it also **affords** me the opportunity to escape from life's stresses.
閱讀能帶給我快樂，也讓我有機會逃離現實生活的壓力。

05 **agency** [ˋedʒənsɪ] 名 C 代辦處，經銷處

● An employment **agency** contacted Jose about a job opportunity a while ago. 一家就業服務中心不久前通知了荷西一個工作機會。

06 **agent** [ˋedʒənt] 名 C 代理人，代理商，仲介人

● Ms. Upwood is the real estate **agent** who helped us find this affordable house.
阿普伍德小姐是房屋仲介商，她幫我們找到這間不是很貴的房子。

07 **allowance** [əˋlaʊəns] 名 C 津貼，零用錢

● Kelly's travel **allowance** does not cover personal expenses such as recreation.
凱利的旅遊津貼不包括像是娛樂的這種個人費用。

- allow 允許
- -ance 名 表「狀況」

08 **ATM** [e ti ɛm] 名 C 自動存提款機 (= **automated teller machine**)

● Six people were lined up at the **ATM** outside the restaurant.
餐廳外面的自動提款機有六個人在排隊等待。

09 **available** [əˋveləbḷ] 形 ❶ 可得到的，可買到的；❷ 有空的

❶ In this store, the product has been sold out; according to a clerk, it may be **available** in a branch store. 這項產品在這家店已經售完。根據店員的說法，別家分店可能還能夠買得到。

❷ I wonder if you will be **available** tomorrow night.
我想知道你明天晚上有沒有空。

- avail 有用，有益
- -able 形 表「可……的」

10 **bankrupt** [ˋbæŋkrʌpt] 形 ❶ 破產的；❷ 徹底缺乏的，喪失……的

❶ The company didn't have enough money to pay its bills and went **bankrupt**. 那家公司沒有足夠的錢來週轉，後來就破產了。

❷ Patrick believes that society is poisoned by politicians who are morally and ethically **bankrupt**.
派屈克認為，喪失道德和誠信的政客，是社會的毒瘤。

相關用法 **bankruptcy** 名 破產，倒閉

● Without enough money to pay its bills, the company declared bankruptcy. 那家公司沒有足夠的錢來週轉，於是宣告破產。

11 **bargain** [ˋbargɪn] 名 C ❶ 交易，買賣；❷ 特價商品，便宜貨
❸ 動 討價還價

❶ Nelda spent 30 minutes in an antique shop and finally struck a **bargain** with the saleswoman.
妮兒妲在一間古董店駐足了半個鐘頭，總算與女店員達成交易。

❷ I bought the leather boots for a low price; they were a real **bargain**. 我用很低的價錢買了這雙皮靴，真的很划算。

❸ My mother always **bargains** with the vendors at the traditional market over the prices of fruit and vegetables.
我媽媽在傳統市場買水果或蔬菜時，都會和小販討價還價。

相關片語 **bargain for/on** 預料到

● I had not bargained on a sudden change in plans.
我沒預料到計畫會突然改變。

12 **broke** [brok] 形（口）一文不名的，破了產的

● The man was flat **broke**; he had no money for food.
那名男子身無分文，沒有錢買東西吃。

72

13 **budget** [ˋbʌdʒɪt] ❶ 名 C 預算，生活費 ❷ 動 編列預算 ❸ 形 低廉的

❶ Peter is now living on a **budget** of NT$100 per day. He cannot afford any recreational activities.
彼得現在每天的生活費是新台幣 100 元，他無法多花任何娛樂活動的花費。

❷ The government has **budgeted** $1 billion for education reform.
政府編列了十億元的教育改革預算。

❸ You can book cheap flights from **budget** travel agency.
你可以向便宜的旅行社訂購低價機票。

14 **capitalism** [ˋkæpətḷˏɪzəm] 名 U 資本主義

• capital 資本
• -ism 名 表「……主義」

• Karl Marx believed that after the end of **capitalism**, communism would dominate the world's economic systems.
卡爾·馬克思相信，在資本主義時代結束後，共產主義會主宰世界的經濟體系。

15 **career** [kəˋrɪr] 名 C 職業

• Josephine has started a new **career** as an international lawyer.
約瑟芬的新工作是國際法的執業律師。

補充 career woman 職業婦女

16 **commerce** [ˋkɑmɝs] 名 U 商業，貿易，交易　形 commercial 商業的

• The annual international **commerce** fair is sponsored by The World Bank. 這場年度國際貿易博覽會，是由世界銀行主辦的。

17 **commercial** [kəˋmɝʃəl] ❶ 形 商業性的，商務的
❷ 名 C（電視廣播中的）商業廣告

• commerce 名 商業
• -ial 形 表「具……特性的」

❶ Most businessmen are more interested in the **commercial** success of their products than in their educational value.
大部分的商人比較關心他們的產品能否大賣，而不關心產品的教育性意義。

❷ Many TV viewers complained that the show was constantly interrupted by **commercials**. 許多電視觀眾不滿那個節目老是被廣告中斷。

18 **contract** 名 [ˋkɑntrækt] 名 C ❶ 契約，合同　動 ❷ 簽（約）；
動 [kənˋtrækt] ❸ 得（病），沾染（習慣）；❹ 收縮，縮小

❶ Frank read the **contract** carefully and then signed it.
法蘭克仔細看完合約之後才簽名。

❷ The foreign company has been **contracted** to build a tunnel through the mountain. 這家外國公司已經簽約要建造一條穿越山脈的隧道。

❸ Nelson didn't go to school yesterday because he **contracted** a bad cold. 奈爾森昨天沒有去上學，因為他得了重感冒。

❹ Metal **contracts** as it cools and expands as it is heated.
金屬熱脹冷縮。

19 **contribution** [ˏkɑntrəˋbjuʃən] 名 ❶ U 貢獻；❷ C 捐獻的物品（或錢）

❶ Although the woman was not wealthy, she made a **contribution** of NT$10,000 to the earthquake fund. 那名婦人雖然不富有，但她向地震賑災基金會捐獻了一萬塊台幣。

• con- 表「一起」
• tribute 貢物，貢金
• -ion 名 表「行為」

❷ The **contribution** Ms. Richer made to our community was greatly appreciated. 瑞奇兒小姐對我們社區的貢獻備受讚嘆。

20 **credit** [ˋkrɛdɪt] 名 U ❶ 信用，信譽；❷ 信賴；❸ 榮譽，功勞
動 ❹ 把……歸於

❶ Matt should have no trouble getting a loan if his **credit** is good.
麥特的信用要是夠好的話，要申請貸款應該不難。

❷ Sam's trustworthiness and good reputation made him a witness of **credit** in the murder case. 山姆的信用和聲譽都好，所以在謀殺案中出面作證。

❸ People thought the director deserved all the **credit** for the movie's success, but he said it should be shared with everyone on the team.
人們認為那齣電影的成功全歸功於導演，但導演表示應該歸功於團隊中的每一個人。

❹ The basketball team won the important game; the players **credited** the victory to hard work.
棒球隊贏得了這場重要的比賽，球員將勝利歸功於他們的努力。

補充 credit card 信用卡；credit rating 信用評等

21 **deposit** [dɪˋpɑzɪt] 名 C ❶ 存款；❷ 保證金，押金，定金
動 ❸ 放置，寄存；❹ 把（錢）儲存，存放

❶ Every month, Kurt makes a $500 **deposit** into his parents' bank account. 柯特每個月都會在父母的銀行帳戶存進 500 美元。

❷ The landlord asked the tenant to give him one month's rent in advance and a **deposit** of NT$10,000.
房東要求房客先付一個月的租金和台幣一萬元的保證金。

❸ Before I entered the supermarket, a clerk asked me to **deposit** my bag at the counter. 在我進入超級市場之前，一個店員要求我將包包寄放在櫃台。

❹ Yesterday morning, the woman **deposited** NT$20,000 in the bank. 那名女子昨天早上在銀行存了台幣兩萬元。

22 **dime** [daɪm] 名 C（美國或加拿大的）一角硬幣

● To use up some of her change, Marcy gave the clerk 10 **dimes** instead of a dollar bill.
梅希給店員十個一角的硬幣，因為她不想給紙鈔，想把銅板用掉。

23 **discount** 名 [ˋdɪskaʊnt] ❶ 名 C 折扣，打折扣
動 [dɪsˋkaʊnt] ❷ 動 將……打折扣

・dis- 表「不」
・count 數

❶ Mr. Collins got a **discount** at the restaurant because the waiter gave him the wrong order.
餐廳服務生給柯林斯先生送錯菜，所以柯林斯先生得到一次折扣優惠作補償。

❷ To attract more customers, the bookstore has **discounted** all its books and magazines. 為了吸引更多顧客，書店削價出售所有的書籍和雜誌。

24 **earnings** [ˋɝnɪŋz] 名（複）❶ 收入，工資；❷ 利潤，收益

- earn 動 賺得
- -ing 名 表「結果」
- -s（複）

❶ Mr. Merril spent a quarter of his **earnings** this year on travel and recreation.
梅利爾先生今年在旅遊及娛樂上花了總收入的四分之一。

❷ As a result of the financial tsunami, the company's **earnings** dropped 15% in the first quarter of 2010.
由於金融海嘯的衝擊，這家公司的收益在 2010 年的第一季下降了 15%。

25 **economic** [ˏikəˋnɑmɪk] 形 經濟上的

● Ashlee expected political stability to bring a period of sustained **economic** growth. 艾許麗期待政局穩定能帶來一段持續的經濟成長。

26 **economical** [ˏikəˋnɑmɪkḷ] 形 節約的，節儉的

- economic 經濟上的
- -al 形 表「關於……的」

● The woman is very **economical**; she never spends more money than necessary.
這名婦女很省，不需要花的錢就不花。

37 Money & business
金錢與商業 (2)

73

01 **economics** [ˏikəˋnɑmɪks] 名 U 經濟學

- economic 經濟上的
- -s 名 表「學說」

● Roger's fascination with **economics** has helped him successfully operate his own business.
羅傑對經濟學的熱愛，幫助他成功經營自己的事業。

02 **economist** [iˋkɑnəmɪst] 名 C 經濟學家

- economy 經濟
- -ist 名 表「做……的人」

● Some **economists** believe that free international trade can facilitate global peace.
一些經濟學家相信，自由的國際貿易可以促進全球和平。

03 **economy** [ɪˋkɑnəmɪ] ❶ 名 U 經濟　❷ 形 經濟的，平價的

❶ Few consumers realize how their choices affect the **economy**.
大部分的消費者很少意識到他們的選擇會如何影響經濟。

❷ Per unit, the large **economy** pack is much cheaper than the single packs. 量販的經濟包裝比買單包來得便宜很多。

04 **employ** [ɪm`plɔɪ] 動 ❶ 雇用；❷ 使用，利用　名 employment 雇用

❶ Mr. Jansen intends to expand his company, so he wants to **employ** about 10 extra people.
詹森先生想要擴展公司的規模，所以他想再多應徵十名員工。

❷ Albert has **employed** his charm and good looks to become a top salesman. 艾伯特靠著個人魅力和俊秀的外表，成為了一名頂尖推銷員。

相關片語 **employ oneself in** 忙於，從事於

- When Alina is not at the office, she employs herself in volunteering at the homeless shelter. 愛蓮娜不上班的時候，都會去庇護收容中心當志工。

05 **employee** [ˏɛmplɔɪ`i] 名 C 受雇者，雇工，雇員

- How many **employees** are there in your company? 你公司裡有多少員工？

・employ 雇用
・-ee 名 表「與……有關的人」

06 **employer** [ɪm`plɔɪɚ] 名 C 雇主，雇用者

- The automobile factory is a major **employer** in this city. 這家汽車製造廠是這座城市的主要雇主。

・employ 雇用
・-er 名 表「人」

07 **employment** [ɪm`plɔɪmənt] 名 U ❶ 雇用，受雇；❷ 職業，工作；❸ 使用，運用

・employ 雇用
・-ment 名 表「狀態」

❶ After graduating from college, Benson was offered **employment** at a computer company.
班森大學畢業後受雇於一家電腦公司。

❷ Doris is looking for **employment** after relocating to a small village in the mountains. 多莉絲搬到山中的一座小村莊後，正在找工作。

❸ The **employment** of the Internet as a teaching tool has aroused students' interest in learning.
使用網路來當作教學工具，增加了學生學習的興趣。

08 **exchange** [ɪks`tʃendʒ] 名 U ❶ 交換；❷ 匯兌，匯率　動 ❸ 交換；❹ 兌換

❶ Gavin gave Fiona a novel in **exchange** for her magazine. 蓋文拿了一本小說和費歐娜交換她的雜誌。

❷ The **exchange** rate between U.S. dollars and U.K. pounds has been stable for the past month.
美元和英鎊之間的匯率從上個月開始穩定。

・ex- 表「由內向外」
・change 交換

❸ At the Christmas party, people **exchanged** gifts.
在耶誕派對上，人們交換禮物。

❹ Gina went to the bank this morning because she wanted to **exchange** some pounds for dollars.
吉娜今天早上去銀行，因為她想把一些英鎊兌換成美金。

[用法] in exchange for something 換成某物
[補充] exchange student 交換學生

09 **expense** [ɪk`spɛns] 名 C 費用，支出　形 expensive 昂貴的

・ex- 表「出」
・pens(e) 表「秤量；支付」

● For Chandra, redecorating the house represents a considerable, but worthy, **expense**.
對香卓而言，重新裝潢房子是一筆可觀的支出，不過很值得。

[相關片語] **at the expense of** 以……為代價
● James worked day and night to complete the project at the expense of his health. 詹姆斯日以繼夜地工作，工程雖然完成了，卻也損害了他的健康。

10 **export** [ɪks`port] 動 ❶ 輸出，出口　名 U ❷ 輸出，出口

❶ Larry's factory **exports** computer accessories to many countries.
賴瑞的工廠出口電腦零件到很多國家。

❷ These bananas have been sold to Japan; they are now packaged for **export**. 這些香蕉要賣到日本，現在正要包裝出口。

11 **finance** 名 [`faɪnæns] 名 ❶ C（常作複數）財務情況；❷ U 財政，金融
動 [faɪ`næns] 動 ❸ 供資金給

・fine 罰金
・-ance 名 表「狀況」

❶ Armando believes that his **finances** will improve greatly after he pays off his debts.
亞曼多相信只要把債還完，他的經濟情況就會大幅好轉。

❷ The **finance** minister's duties are to improve the economic conditions of the people and speed up the development of the country. 財政部長的職責是改善人民的經濟狀況，並加速國家的經濟發展。

❸ The construction of high-speed rail and MRT systems is **financed** by the government. 高鐵和捷運系統的興建都由政府供予資金。

12 **financial** [faɪ`nænʃəl] 形 財政的，金融的

・finance 財政
・-ial 形 表「具有……特性」

● The latest **financial** reports show Mr. Powell's company has been growing over the last three years.
最新的財務報告顯示，寶威先生的公司在過去三年來都持續成長。

13 **fortune** [ˋfɔrtʃən] 名 ❶ C 財產，財富；❷ U 好運，幸運；❸ C 命運

❶ The director adapted this year's bestseller into a movie and made a **fortune**. 這位導演將今年最暢銷的作品改編成電影，大賺了一筆。

❷ Melinda believes that **fortune** is always on her side.
梅琳達相信好運永遠與她同在。

❸ The old man read my palm and told my **fortune**; he predicted something good will happen to me in the near future.
那個老人看看我的手掌，幫我算命。他說我最近會好運臨頭。

14 **fund** [fʌnd] 名 C ❶ 資金，基金；❷ 專款

❶ When Julio was short of **funds** in college, he worked as a waiter on the weekends.
胡力歐剛上大學的那幾年因為缺乏資金，週末時會去當服務生打工。

❷ After the earthquake, a restoration **fund** was set up; most of the buildings in the quake-stricken area were restored or rebuilt with the money. 在地震過後，設立了一筆重建專款。有了這筆錢，災區大部分的建築物很快展開了修復和重建。

補充 fund-raiser 募款聚會（餐會）

15 **goods** [gʊdz] 名（複）商品，貨物

- Today, many consumer **goods** are manufactured in countries with low labor costs. 今日的許多消費品都是在勞力較低廉的國家製造的。

74

16 **import** 動 [ɪmˋport] 名 [ˋɪmport] ❶ 動 進口，輸入 ❷ 名 C 進口商品

❶ Since the country is not rich in natural resources, businesses have to **import** most of their raw materials. 這個國家因為天然資源不豐富，所以企業的原物料大都是進口的。

- im- 表「向內」
- port 港口

❷ Some young people love Japanese **imports** and think they are better than goods made in Taiwan.
有一些年輕人喜愛日本進口商品，並認為它們比台灣製造的商品更好。

17 **inflation** [ɪnˋfleʃən] 名 U 通貨膨脹

- **Inflation** pushes the value of most goods upward; the relative value of money is one exception.
通貨膨脹導致大部分的物價都漲價，只有幣值是下滑的。

- inflate 膨脹
- -ion 名 表「行為的狀態」

18 **insurance** [ɪnˋʃʊrəns] 名 U 保險

- Wesley has no medical **insurance** to cover his visit to the doctor. 衛斯理沒有投保醫療險來幫忙負擔看病的錢。

- insure 動 投保
- -ance 名 表「狀況」

補充 life insurance 壽險；health insurance 健保

19 **invest** [ɪnˋvɛst] 動 投資　名 investment 投資

・in- 表「向內」
・vest 使穿上

● If you don't have money to invest, be sure to **invest** your time wisely.
如果你沒有多餘的金錢可以投入，那麼就把你的時間用在刀口上。

20 **investment** [ɪnˋvɛstmənt] 名 C 投資（物）

・invest 投資
・-ment 名 表「結果」

● Just as factories and equipment are **investments** for manufacturers, stocks and bonds can be investments for individuals. 一如廠商投資廠房與設備，個人也可以投資股票與債券。

21 **loan** [lon] ❶ 名 C 貸款　❷ 動 借出，貸與

❶ Marisa took out a **loan** from the bank and opened a coffee shop.
瑪麗莎向銀行貸款開了一家咖啡店。

❷ The bank **loaned** a large sum of money to the factory for expansion. 銀行貸了一大筆錢給那家工廠來擴張。

22 **luxurious** [lʌgˋʒʊrɪəs] 形 豪華的，非常舒適的

・luxury 名 奢侈
・-ious 形 表「有……特性」

● Lonnie invited his family and friends to a **luxurious** hotel for dinner to celebrate his 60th birthday.
隆尼邀請親友到一家豪華飯店吃飯，慶祝自己的六十大壽。

23 **luxury** [ˋlʌkʃərɪ] 名 ❶ U 奢侈，奢華；❷ C 奢侈品；❸ U 享受，樂趣

❶ The rich man lives in **luxury**; everything he uses is special and expensive. 這個有錢人生活奢華，他用的東西都很特別而且昂貴。

❷ Very few people can afford a **luxury** such as a private jet.
像私人噴射機這種奢侈品只有極少數的人能買得起。

❸ I am studying so hard for the upcoming entrance exam that I do not have the **luxury** of resting this weekend.
我正在為即將來臨的入學考試努力念書，這個週末沒有那個命休息啦。

24 **manage** [ˋmænɪdʒ] 動 ❶ 處理，管理，經營；❷ 設法做到；❸ 安排（時間）做

❶ Mr. Coleman could not **manage** his heavy work schedule without his secretary. 科曼先生沒有祕書的協助，就處理不了大量的工作行程。

❷ They finished the task on time; I don't know how they **managed** to do that. 他們準時完成了任務，真不曉得他們是怎麼辦到的。

❸ Mr. Brown is so busy at work that he can't **manage** a two-day holiday with his family.
布朗先生的工作這麼忙，無法排出兩天的假期和家人去渡假。

25 **management** [ˋmænɪdʒmənt] 名 ❶ U 管理，經營；❷ C 資方，管理部門；❸ U 管理手段

❶ Kelly relied on her family's help for the successful **management** of her business.
凱莉的事業全仰賴家人的成功管理。

▪ manage 管理
▪ -ment 名 表「方法」

❷ Hoping to bring an end to the strike, the **management** is talking with the labor representatives. 資方正在和勞方代表交涉，期待罷工能結束。

❸ Good time **management** allows you to make better use of your precious time. 良好的時間管理能幫助人善用寶貴的時間。

26 **manufacture** [ˌmænjəˋfæktʃɚ] 動 ❶（大量）製造，加工　名 ❷ U 製造；❸ C（常作複數）製品，產品

▪ manus 手
▪ fact 事實
▪ -ure 名 表「動作」

❶ Clifton can't tell which of the three crystals is **manufactured** and which is natural.
克里夫頓看不出這三顆水晶哪一顆是人工製造，哪一顆是天然的。

❷ The **manufacture** of these cars was done in the United States, whereas those automobiles were produced in Germany.
這些車子是在美國製造的，而那些車子是在德國生產的。

❸ Some people prefer Japanese **manufactures**; they think the goods made in Japan are better.
某些人比較喜歡日本產品，他們認為在日本製造的商品比較好。

27 **manufacturer** [ˌmænjəˋfæktʃərɚ] 名 C 製造業者，廠商，製造公司

● **Manufacturers** should be responsible for the quality of their products. 廠商應該對產品的品質負責。

▪ manufacture 製造
▪ -er 名 表「人」

28 **needy** [ˋnidɪ] 形 貧窮的

● Pinkie collects used books and donates them to **needy** children. 萍琪收集舊書捐給貧童。

▪ need 需要
▪ -y 形 表「有……的」

29 **occupation** [ˌɑkjəˋpeʃən] 名 ❶ C 工作，職業；❷ U 占領，占據

❶ Joan is an accountant by **occupation**. 瓊在當會計師。

❷ Taiwan was under **occupation** from the end of the first Sino-Japanese War in 1895 to 1945.
中日甲午戰爭之後，台灣在 1895 年到 1945 年期間被占領。

▪ occupy 使從事
▪ -ation 名 表「狀態」

30 **owe** [o] 動 ❶ 欠（債等）；❷ 虧欠；❸ 把……歸功於

❶ Yesterday, Grace gave $100 to her brother, but she still **owes** him $200. 葛蕾絲昨天還給她哥哥一百元，但是她還欠他兩百元。

❷ Besides the money I loaned him, Marty also **owes** me an apology for causing all this trouble.
馬爾迪除了欠我錢，他也惹了這麼多麻煩，應該跟我道個歉。

❸ Glen **owed** his success to his colleagues. Without their help, he couldn't have made it.
葛蘭把他的成功歸功於同事。沒有他們的幫忙，他也不可能做到。

31 **penny** [ˋpɛnɪ] 名 C ❶（英）便士，（美）一分（硬幣）；❷ 一小筆錢

❶ There are 100 **pence** in one pound. 一英鎊是一百便士。

❷ Mr. Jameson's new car cost him a pretty **penny**.
傑姆森先生的新車花了他一大筆錢。

複數形 pence

38 Money & business 金錢與商業 (3)

75

01 **poverty** [ˋpɑvətɪ] 名 U 貧窮，貧困　形 poor 貧窮的

● Milton's family lived below the **poverty** line when he was born.
米爾頓出生時，家境貧苦。

02 **precious** [ˋprɛʃəs] 形 貴重的，寶貴的，珍貴的

● That diamond necklace is Vicky's most **precious** possession.
那條鑽石項鍊是薇琪最珍貴的財產。

03 **proceed** [prəˋsid] 動 ❶ 繼續進行；❷ 開始，著手；❸（沿特定路線）行進，移動

・pro- 表「先，前」
・cede 讓與

❶ After the crying child was removed from the courtroom, business **proceeded** as usual. 哭鬧的小孩被帶出法庭後，程序就照常繼續進行。

❷ The teacher said there were some misspellings in my paper, and he **proceeded** to point them out.
老師說我的報告有一些拼字錯誤，接著就把錯誤指出來。

❸ All the passengers on Flight 616 **proceeded** to Gate 65.
所有搭乘 616 班機的乘客都往 65 號登機門移動。

04 **product** [ˋprɑdəkt] 名 C 產品，產物

- Cheese, powdered milk, and yogurt are common milk **products**.
  起司、奶粉和優格是常見的奶製品。

05 **production** [prəˋdʌkʃən] 名 U ❶ 生產，製作；❷ 產量

- product 產品
- -ion 名 表「行為的結果」

❶ The old model went out of **production** five years ago; it is no longer on the market.
這個舊的型號在五年前就停產了，現在在市面上買不到了。

❷ Our factory's **production** of handbags has steadily decreased in the last six weeks. 我們工廠手提袋的產量，在過去六個星期逐步減產。

06 **productive** [prəˋdʌktɪv] 形 多產的，富饒的，富有成效的

- product 產品
- -ive 形 表「有……特性」

- Odell realized that he would be more **productive** at his job if he could take some time off.
  歐戴爾知道，自己如果能休息一段時間，工作會更有效率。

07 **profession** [prəˋfɛʃən] 名 C 職業　形 professional 專業的

- professed 專業的
- -ion 名 表「行為」

- Tabitha intended to make playing golf her **profession**. 塔碧莎打算當職業高爾夫球員。

08 **professional** [prəˋfɛʃən!] 形 職業的，專業的

- profession 職業
- -al 形 表「……的」

- As a **professional** photographer, Phillip has spent a fortune on cameras.
  菲利浦是專業攝影師，他在相機器材上投資了很多錢。

09 **profit** [ˋprɑfɪt] 名 ❶ C 利潤，收益；❷ U 利益，益處　❸ 動 得益於

❶ Dona made a **profit** of half a million dollars by selling the properties she inherited. 唐娜賣掉了繼承而來的房產，獲利 50 萬美金。

❷ There is no **profit** in postponing the project; that will only cause a great loss. 將計畫延期一點好處也沒有，那只會造成很大的損失。

❸ Johnny is **profiting** from his part-time job; for example, he is gaining some practical work experience.
強尼從打工中受益良多。舉例來說，他獲得了一些實用的工作經驗。

補充 nonprofit 形 非營利的；profit margin 利潤率

10 **profitable** [ˋprɑfɪtəb!] 形 有利潤的，贏利的

- profit 利潤
- -able 形 表「有……特性的」

- Selling fried chicken at the night market doesn't appear to be a respectable business, but it is actually quite **profitable**.
  在夜市賣炸雞看似不是什麼稱頭的行業，但實際上是很賺錢的。

11 **program** [ˋprogræm] 名 C ❶ 課程；❷ 節目

・pro- 表「在前」
・-gram 名 表「……寫的東西；圖像」

❶ Northern Michigan University offers many practical academic **programs**; you can get more information about them by visiting the school's website.
北密西根大學有很多實用課程，你可以上學校的網站了解更多資訊。

❷ I like to watch the TV **program**, but I'm not sure what time it's on. 我想要看這個電視節目，但是我不確定它是幾點播出。

12 **promote** [prəˋmot] 動 ❶ 促進；❷ 晉升；❸ 推銷

❶ Ms. Orford is **promoting** world peace in her global lecture tour.
歐福爾女士在世界巡迴演說中呼籲促進世界和平。

❷ Marian used to be a clerk in the store; after years of hard work, she has been **promoted** to shop supervisor.
瑪莉恩過去是這家店的店員，經過幾年的努力工作，她現在被晉升為店長。

❸ The pop singer is going on tour to **promote** her latest album.
這位流行歌手正在巡迴宣傳她的最新專輯。

13 **promotion** [prəˋmoʃən] 名 ❶ C 升遷，晉升；❷ U 促銷，推銷

・promote 晉升；推銷
・-ion 名 表「行為」

❶ Even though Salvador has worked very hard to get a **promotion**, his supervisor promoted his colleague instead.
沙華多為了能晉升職務而努力工作，但他的主管卻提拔了別的同事。

❷ To sell a new product, manufacturers often invest a large sum of money on its **promotion**.
為了能讓新產品賣得好，廠商常會投資一大筆錢來做促銷。

14 **property** [ˋprɑpətɪ] 名 ❶ U 財產，資產；❷ U 財產權，所有權；❸ C 特性

・proper 適當的
・-ty 名 表「性質」

❶ This flat is my **property**; I own it.
這間公寓是我的，我是屋主。

❷ An intellectual **property** such as a copyright or registered trademark is protected by law.
像著作權和商標之類的智慧財產權，是受法律保障的。

❸ The Chinese medicine doctor uses herbs with healing **properties** to cure many diseases. 這位中醫師運用具有療效的草藥來治療許多疾病。

76 15 **rate** [ret] 名 C ❶ 費用，價格；❷ 比例，比率；❸ 速度，速率
動 ❹ 認為，列為

❶ Our new promotional plan offers the lowest **rate** for long-distance calls at any time of the day.
我們的新促銷方案，提供客戶在任何時段撥打長途電話都享有最低價格。

❷ Fewer people in Taiwan want to have children, so the birth **rate** is declining. 在台灣越來越少人想要生小孩，所以出生率下降。

❸ The sports car is traveling at the **rate** of 150 kilometers an hour.
這輛跑車正以每小時 150 公里的速度行駛。

❹ Mr. Gates is **rated** one of the richest men in the world; he is also considered a genius.
蓋茲先生被列為世界上最富有的人之一，他也被認為是一個天才。

相關片語 ❶ **at this rate** 照這種情形看來；❷ **at any rate** 無論如何

❶ Another rainstorm is coming; at this rate, they won't be able to go mountain climbing. 暴風雨要來了，照這樣看來，他們無法去爬山了。

❷ At any rate, you must be on time for this important meeting. There will be no more delays.
無論如何，你一定要準時參加這個重要的會議，絕對不可以遲到。

16 **receipt** [rɪˋsit] 名 ❶ Ⓒ 收據；❷ Ⓤ 收到，接到

❶ You'll need the store **receipts** to show proof of purchase if you want to return any items you bought.
如果要退回所購買的商品，需要拿出商店的收據當作購物證明。

❷ The product will be mailed to you upon **receipt** of payment.
一收到付款，產品就會寄出給您。

17 **rent** [rɛnt] ❶ 名 Ⓒ 租金　動 ❷ 租用；❸ 租出；❹ 出租

❶ Stephen has leased his apartment to a young couple and gets NT$2,000 per week in **rent**.
史蒂芬把公寓租給一對年輕夫妻，每週可收租金台幣 2,000 元。

❷ Before Walter bought a house, he **rented** a small flat downtown.
瓦爾特在買房子之前，他在市區租了一間小公寓。

❸ After the Lins moved to their new apartment, they **rented** their old house out to their relatives.
林家人搬進新公寓之後，他們把舊房子出租給親戚。

❹ This warehouse **rents** for NT$20,000 a month.
這間倉庫一個月的租金是台幣兩萬元。

18 **salary** [ˋsælərɪ] 名 Ⓒ 薪資，薪水

• Steve always deposits a quarter of his monthly **salary** in his mother's bank account.
史帝夫每個月都會把四分之一的薪水存進媽媽的銀行帳戶裡。

- sal 鹽
- -ary 名 表「與……有關之物」

19 **saving** [ˋsevɪŋ] 名 ❶（常作複數）儲金，存款；❷ C 節儉，節約

❶ Edmund has saved as much money as possible; he plans to live on his **savings** after he retires.
艾德蒙盡可能存多點錢。他計畫在退休之後靠存款過日子。

▪ save 儲蓄
▪ -ing 名 表「結果」

❷ During the sale, I bought one product and got one free, giving me a **savings** of NT$250.
我在打折期間買了個買一送一的商品，讓我省了 250 元台幣。

20 **salesperson** [ˋselzˏpɝsn̩] 名 C 店員，售貨員（無男女性之分）

● How many **salespersons** work in this department store? 這間百貨公司有多少位店員？

▪ sale 販賣；出售
▪ -s（複）
▪ person 人

21 **tag** [tæg] 名 C 標籤，吊牌

● Greg keeps the sale **tags** from all the clothes he buys.
葛列格會收集所有他買的衣服的標籤牌子。

補充 price tag 價格標籤

22 **tax** [tæks] 名 C 稅

● After Mr. Gray's mother passed away, he had to sell her property in order to pay the inheritance **tax**.
葛雷先生在母親過世後，為了支付遺產稅，只好變賣母親的遺產。

23 **trader** [ˋtredɚ] 名 C 商人

▪ trade 做買賣
▪ -er 名 表「人」

● Traveling **traders** exchange modern goods for the villagers' handmade crafts. 旅行商人以現代化的商品跟村民交換手工藝品。

24 **valuable** [ˋvæljuəbl̩] 形 ❶ 有價值的；❷ 值錢的，貴重的

▪ value 價值
▪ -able 形 表「有……特性的」

❶ My experience as a teaching assistant has been very **valuable**. 助教的工作經驗對我來說非常實用。

❷ The diamond ring is **valuable**; it is worth $1 million.
這個鑽石戒指很值錢，值一百萬元。

25 **wages** [ˋwedʒɪs] 名（複）薪水

▪ wage 薪水
▪ -s（複）

● In Gloria's company, monthly **wages** are paid by check.
葛洛莉亞的公司用支票撥付月薪。

26 **wealth** [wɛlθ] 名 U 財富，財產　形 wealthy 富裕的

● Although Mercy has great **wealth**, her lifestyle remains plain and simple. 梅西雖然很有錢，但她的生活平實而簡單。

27 **wealthy** [ˋwɛlθɪ] 形 富有的，富裕的 同義 rich 富有的

- Penelope is from a **wealthy** family, so she never worries about money.
  潘妮洛普出身於富裕的家庭，所以從來就不用擔心錢的問題。

· wealth 財富
· -y 形 表「有……的」

39 Politics & government 政治與政府

77

01 **ambassador** [æmˋbæsədɚ] 名 C 大使，使節

- Christine toured Africa last month as an **ambassador** for the World Health Organization.
  克莉絲汀上個月以世衛組織的大使身分前往非洲訪問。

02 **authority** [əˋθɔrətɪ] 名 ❶ C（常作複數）官方，當局；❷ U 權力，職權；❸ C 權威人士，專家

❶ The residents wrote a letter to the local **authorities**, hoping the officials in charge would help them solve the problem.
居民寫了一封信給地方當局，希望負責的官員可以幫他們解決問題。

❷ The executive has the **authority** to finalize the annual budget for our company. 我們公司的經理對公司的年度預算擁有最終決定權。

❸ To solve the problem, we need an **authority** on criminal law and a specialist in information retrieval.
為了解決這個問題，我們需要一位刑事法的權威和一位資訊檢索專家。

03 **China** [ˋtʃaɪnə] 名 中國

- The Great Wall of **China** is one of the New Seven Wonders of the World. 中國的長城是世界新七大奇景之一。

04 **colony** [ˋkɑlənɪ] 名 C ❶ 殖民地；❷ 僑居地；❸（動物的）集群

❶ India was once a British **colony** and later became an independent nation under the leadership of Ghandi.
印度一度是英國的殖民地，後來在甘地的領導下成為獨立國家。

❷ This area is known as the Korean **colony** of Beijing; many immigrants from Korea live here.
這個地區是北京的韓國僑居地，有許多韓國移民住在這裡。

❸ A **colony** of penguins inhabits the rocky islet.
一群企鵝棲息於這個多岩石的小島上。

05 **congress** [ˋkɑŋgrəs] 名 C ❶ 國會；❷（正式）會議，代表大會

❶ A committee has been formed in the **congress** to supervise disaster relief efforts. 國會組成了一個委員會來監督救災成效。

❷ During the international **congress**, representatives from different groups will discuss the problem and decide how to solve it. 來自不同團體的代表將參加這個國際會議，針對這個問題進行討論，並決定出解決方法。

06 **democracy** [dɪˋmɑkrəsɪ] 名 ❶ U 民主，民主政體；❷ C 民主國家；❸ U 民主精神，民主作風

- demo- 表「人民」
- -cracy 名 表「統治」

❶ People throughout the country have asked for a return to **democracy** through free and fair elections. 那個國家的人民要求透過自由、公平的選舉回歸民主政治。

❷ In a **democracy**, people are allowed to speak freely.
在民主國家裡，人民擁有言論自由。

❸ The union's **democracy** made it popular among the workers.
工會的民主作風深得人心。

07 **democratic** [ˌdɛməˋkrætɪk] 形 民主的，民主政體的

- demo- 表「人民」
- -crat 名 表「……政治的擁護者」
- -ic 形 表「……的」

● People in a **democratic** country believe in and defend their right of free speech.
民主國家的人民相信並保衛言論自由。

08 **diplomat** [ˋdɪpləmæt] 名 C 外交官

● Edward Koch is a real **diplomat**; he knows how to deal with all kinds of people. 愛德華．科霍是位真正的外交人才，他具有與人交際的手腕。

09 **dynasty** [ˋdaɪnəstɪ] 名 C 朝代，王朝

● Paper was invented during the Han **Dynasty** in China.
紙是在中國漢朝時發明的。

10 **election** [ɪˋlɛkʃən] 名 C 選舉

- elect 選舉
- -ion 名 表「行為的結果」

● Ken Wright won the **election** and is our new mayor.
肯．萊特贏得選舉，現在他是我們的新市長了。

11 **embassy** [ˋɛmbəsɪ] 名 C 大使館

- The U.S. **embassy** grants visas to eligible foreigners who wish to travel to the country. 美國大使館核發簽證給欲赴美旅行、且符合條件的外國人。

12 **emperor** [ˋɛmpərɚ] 名 C 皇帝

- Do you know which **emperor** in China initiated the construction of the Great Wall? 你知道中國的長城是哪個皇帝下令建造的嗎？

13 **empire** [ˋɛmpaɪr] 名 C ❶ 帝國；❷ 大企業

❶ Alexander established an **empire** that extended from Greece to India; however, the great emperor died quite young.
亞歷山大建立了一個從希臘橫跨印度的帝國，但這位偉大的帝皇卻英年早逝。

❷ Joe started his manufacturing **empire** in his garage 20 years ago. 喬 20 年前就開始在自己的車庫建立他的工業王國。

78

14 **governor** [ˋgʌvɚnɚ] 名 C 州長

- Mr. Fisher was elected **governor** of our state three years ago. 三年前，費許先生選上了我們州的州長。

▪ govern 動 統治
▪ -or 名 表「人」

15 **lord** [lɔrd] 名 C 統治者，君王

- Sharks and whales are the **lords** of the ocean.
鯊魚和鯨魚是海洋的統治者。

16 **mayor** [ˋmeɚ] 名 C 市長，鎮長

- The **mayor** visited our school today and gave a speech on public health. 今天市長到我們學校，發表了有關公共衛生的演說。

17 **minister** [ˋmɪnɪstɚ] 名 C 部長

- Did you know that the **minister** of defense is going to visit our school? 你知道國防部長要來我們學校參觀嗎？

18 **ministry** [ˋmɪnɪstrɪ] 名 C（政府的）部

- The **Ministry** of Foreign Affairs is in charge of issuing visas.
外交部負責核發各項簽證。

19 **overthrow** 動 [ˌovɚˋθro] ❶ 動 打倒，推翻
名 [ˋovɚθro] ❷ 名 U 打倒，推翻

・over- 表「越過」
・throw 拋；摔下

❶ It is not easy to **overthrow** a current political power.
要推翻當前的政權並不容易。

❷ After the **overthrow** of the Ch'ing Dynasty in 1911 by Sun Yat-sen, many Chinese people envisioned a democratic nation.
在 1911 年孫中山推翻清朝之後，許多中國人就期待著能成為一個民主國家。

20 **political** [pəˋlɪtɪkḷ] 形 政治的　名 politician 政治家 名 politics 政治

・polity 政府
・-ic 形 表「具有……特性的」

● As a judge, Debra believes the court should never become a **political** institution.
黛博拉身為法官，她認為法院絕不可以成為政治機關。

21 **politician** [ˌpɑləˋtɪʃən] 名 C 政治家，政客

・political 政治的
・-ian 名 表「……的人」

● After serving for several years in Congress, the **politician** was elected to the U.S. Senate.
在國會服務了幾年之後，那位政治家當選了美國參議員。

22 **politics** [ˋpɑlətɪks] 名 U 政治

・polity 政府
・-ic 形 表「……的」
・-s 名 表「學說」

● After graduating from college, Bob thought of going into **politics**; he wanted to become a member of Parliament. 大學畢業之後，鮑伯考慮從政，他想成為一位國會議員。

23 **poll** [pol] 名 C ❶ 民意測驗；❷ U 投票
動 ❸ 對……進行民意測驗；❹（候選人等）獲得（若干票數）

❶ They are going to conduct a nationwide **poll** to find out people's opinions on racism.
他們即將進行一項全國性的民意測驗，調查人們對種族歧視的看法。

❷ Liz was disappointed to hear the result of the **poll**; the politician she supported lost the election.
莉茲對這次選舉的結果感到失望，她支持的政治家沒有勝選。

❸ More than 50% of those **polled** expressed concerns about high unemployment rates in recent years.
接受民意調查的人超過半數表示，擔心近幾年的高失業率。

❹ The politician **polled** more than 50% of the votes and won the election. 那位政治家以過半的票數贏得選舉。

相關片語 **go to the polls** 參加投票

● A high turnout was reported in the election; more than 70% of registered voters went to the polls.
根據報導，這場選舉的投票率很高，超過七成的登記選民參與了投票。

24 **republic** [rɪˋpʌblɪk] 名 C 共和國，共和政體　形 republican 共和國的

- The political leader of a **republic** is usually called the president rather than the prime minister.
共和政體的領袖通常稱為「總統」，而非「首相」。

25 **revolution** [ˏrɛvəˋluʃən] 名 C ❶ 革命；❷ 大革命性劇變，變革

❶ The Qing Dynasty was overthrown following the Xinhai **Revolution**. 清朝在辛亥革命之後被推翻了。

❷ The **revolution** in computer technology has changed our lives in many ways. 日新月異的電腦科技，在許多方面改變了我們的生活。

- revolute 參加革命
- -ion 名 表「行為」

26 **revolutionary** [ˏrɛvəˋluʃənˏɛrɪ] 形 ❶ 革命的；❷ 大變革的，完全創新的

❶ The **revolutionary** leader led the people in the overthrow of the monarchy.
那名革命領袖領導人民推翻帝制。

❷ The technology behind wireless communication is a **revolutionary** invention. 無線通訊科技是一項革命性的發明。

- revolution 革命
- -ary 形 表「與……有關的」

27 **territory** [ˋtɛrəˏtorɪ] 名 ❶ C 領土；❷ C 領域，地盤；❸ U（知識等的）領域，範圍

❶ This side of the lake is Germany's **territory**; that side is owned by Austria. 湖泊的這一邊是德國的領土，另一邊則屬於奧地利。

❷ Some animals have a strong sense of **territory**.
有些動物具有強烈的地盤意識。

❸ With these new digital cameras, the computer company steps into unfamiliar **territory**.
這家電腦公司推出這些新的數位相機，踏入了不熟悉的領域。

28 **vice president** [vaɪs ˋprɛzədənt] 名 C 副總統

- Since the president's schedule is tight, the **vice president** will attend the summit in his place.
由於總統的行程緊湊，副總統將代替他參加這場高峰會。

- vice- 表「副的」
- president 總統

40 Law & crime 法律與犯罪

79

01 **accuse** [ə`kjuz] 動 指控，控告 名 accusation 控告

- Cyril **accused** his neighbor of stealing the community property. 西瑞爾指控鄰居偷了社區的財產。

02 **burglar** [`bɝglɚ] 名 C 破門盜竊者，夜賊

- Some **burglars** broke into the department store during the riot last night. 昨晚有幾名小偷趁著暴亂闖入了那家百貨公司。

相關用法 名 **burglary** 盜竊罪

- The young man broke into the house and was later charged with burglary. 那名年輕人闖進房子，隨後以盜竊罪被起訴。

03 **capture** [`kæptʃɚ] 動 ❶ 捕獲，俘虜；❷ 獲得；❸ 引起（注意），迷住
名 ❹ U 捕獲，俘虜

❶ The escaped prisoner is still on the run; the police have not **captured** him yet. 那名越獄犯仍然在逃，警方尚未將他逮捕歸案。

❷ The candidate won the presidential election; he **captured** more than 55% of the vote.
那名候選人贏得總統大選；他獲得超過 55% 的選票。

❸ The teacher used posters to **capture** the students' attention in class. 老師在課堂中使用海報來吸引學生的注意。

❹ The convict had escaped **capture** by the police for five days; he was caught this afternoon.
那名罪犯五天以來都沒有被警方逮捕，但今天下午被抓到了。

04 **commit** [kə`mɪt] 動 ❶ 犯（罪），做（錯事等）；❷ 使承擔義務，使作出保證

❶ The man who had **committed** murder was sentenced to life imprisonment. 那個犯了殺人罪的男子被判終生監禁。

❷ Heather is **committed** to writing a weekly magazine column about urban life. 希瑟兒負責替雜誌專欄每週寫一篇有關都市生活的報導。

05 **constitution** [ˌkɑnstə`tjuʃən] 名 C 憲法，章程

- The **Constitution** of the United States was adopted in 1787. 美國憲法於 1787 年通過生效。

> ▪ constitute 設立
> ▪ -ion 名 表「行為的結果」

06 **criminal** [ˋkrɪmənḷ] 形 ❶ 犯罪的；❷ 刑事上的　名 ❸ Ⓒ 罪犯

❶ Theft and robbery are both **criminal** acts. 偷竊和搶劫都是犯罪行為。

❷ Each nation has its own **criminal** laws. 每個國家各自有其刑法法規。

❸ The drug dealer is a hardened **criminal**; he has been involved in drug dealing for a long time, and he is not sorry for what he does. 這個毒犯是個慣犯，他一直在從事毒品交易，而且毫無悔意。

07 **enforce** [ɪnˋfors] 動 實施，執行　名 enforcement 實施

・en- 表「使」
・force 力量

● The city will start to **enforce** the new recycling policy next year. 市政府明年會開始實施資源回收新制。

08 **enforcement** [ɪnˋforsmənt] 名 Ⓤ 實施，執行

・enforce 實施
・-ment 名 表「行為」

● One of the duties of the police is to ensure **enforcement** of the law. 警察的職責之一就是要確保法律的執行。

09 **gamble** [ˋgæmbḷ] 動 ❶ 賭博，打賭；❷ 冒險

❶ Many people in Hong Kong love to **gamble** on the horses; some of them do it just for fun.
許多香港人熱中賭馬，而其中有一些人只是為了好玩。

❷ Willard doesn't think he is **gambling** with his life by riding a motorbike across a field of fire.
威勒不覺得他騎機車越過火海是在玩命。

相關片語 **gamble away** 賭掉，輸光

● The rich man gambled away all his money; now he is as poor as a church mouse. 那個有錢人把錢全都輸光了，現在他身無分文。

10 **gang** [gæŋ] 名 Ⓒ（歹徒等的）一幫，一群

● Andre, the leader of a local **gang**, has to serve a three-year prison sentence. 本地一個幫派的頭頭安德瑞，即將入獄服刑三年。

11 **gangster** [ˋgæŋstɚ] 名 Ⓒ（結成團伙的）歹徒，流氓

・gang（歹徒等的）一幫
・-ster 名 表「與……有關者」

● An undercover detective was sent to investigate the crimes being committed by the **gangsters**. 一位密探被派去調查幫派分子所犯下的多起罪行。

12 **guilt** [gɪlt] 名 Ⓤ ❶ 有罪，犯罪；❷ 內疚　反義 innocence 無罪

❶ Although there is clear evidence that the politician took bribes, he denies his **guilt**. 雖然有明顯證據證明這個政客受賄，但是他仍然否認罪行。

❷ Karla was filled with **guilt** after she failed to keep her word.
卡拉因為守不住承諾而深感內疚。

13 **guilty** [ˋgɪltɪ] 形 ❶ 有罪的，犯……罪的；❷ 內疚的，自知有過錯的

・guilt 有罪；內疚
・-y 形 表「有……的」

❶ Dr. Walden was found **guilty** of medical malpractice. 華登醫生被查到犯下醫療失誤的過錯。

❷ I felt **guilty** about breaking my promise; I felt shame and embarrassment. 我對沒能信守承諾而感到內疚，我覺得又羞愧又尷尬。

14 **innocent** [ˋɪnəsn̩t] 形 ❶ 無罪的，清白的；❷ 純真的

❶ The jury spent more than five hours deciding whether the defendant was **innocent** or guilty.
陪審團花了五個多鐘頭的時間來裁定被告是否清白。

❷ They tried to protect the **innocent** boy, who has had few experiences in life. 他們想保護那個純真的男孩，他還涉世未深。

15 **jail** [dʒel] 名 ❶ Ⓒ 監獄，拘留所；❷ Ⓤ 監禁，拘留

❶ Whitney is planning to transform the abandoned **jail** into a retreat center. 惠特妮打算把那間廢棄的監獄改建成安養中心。

❷ The young man went to **jail** for drug dealing; he was sentenced to three years in prison. 那名年輕人因為販毒而入獄，他被判坐三年牢。

16 **justice** [ˋdʒʌstɪs] 名 Ⓤ ❶ 正義，公平；❷ 司法

・just 公平的

❶ All men and women should be treated with **justice**.
所有的男性和女性都應該受到公平的對待。

❷ The killer was caught last night; he will be brought to **justice**.
那名殺人犯昨天晚上被抓了，他將受到司法的制裁。

17 **lawful** [ˋlɔfəl] 形 合法的　同義 legal 合法的

・law 法律
・-ful 形 表「有……性質的」

● Is it **lawful** to hunt wild animals in this area?
在這個區域打獵合法嗎？

18 **murder** [ˋmɝdɚ] ❶ 名 Ⓤ 謀殺（罪），兇殺　❷ 動 謀殺，兇殺

❶ The **murder** that occurred last month is still under investigation.
上個月發生的兇殺案至今仍在調查中。

❷ The man was **murdered**; the police don't know who the killer is.
那名男子遭到殺害，警方還沒查明兇手是誰。

80

19 **murderer** [ˋmɝdərɚ] 名 C 謀殺犯；兇手

- murder 謀殺
- -er 名 表「人」

● **Murderers** must be punished to keep order in society. 兇手就必須接受制裁，以維持社會秩序。

20 **ought** to [ɔt tu] 助 應當，應該

● The youth **ought** to respect the elderly. 年輕人應該尊重長輩。

21 **penalty** [ˋpɛnl̩tɪ] 名 C ❶ 處罰，刑罰；❷ 罰款

- penal 刑罰的；應受刑的
- -ty 名 表「狀態」

❶ Those who maliciously destroy or damage property belonging to another are liable for a maximum **penalty** of five years in prison.
惡意損毀或損壞他人財產的人，最高可處五年的刑期。

❷ Angelo was given a **penalty** for hiring illegal foreign workers.
安傑洛因為雇用非法外勞而被罰款。

22 **pickpocket** [ˋpɪk͵pɑkɪt] 名 C 扒手

- pick 挖，扒
- pocket 口袋

● On the crowded bus, the **pickpocket** stole a wallet from a man's back pocket.
在擁擠的公車上，那個扒手從一個男子的後褲袋偷走了皮夾。

23 **pirate** [ˋpaɪrət] 名 C ❶ 海盜，劫掠者；❷ 剽竊者，侵犯版權者
動 ❸ 剽竊，非法翻印

❶ Bob is writing a fiction novel about the adventures of **pirates** in the Caribbean Sea. 鮑伯在寫一本虛構小說，是有關加勒比海海盜的冒險故事。

❷ Those **pirates** have made a lot of money by illegally copying CDs and computer software. 那些侵權者靠著非法複製 CD 和電腦軟體而大賺一筆。

❸ In the factory, the police found a lot of **pirated** computer games; the products had been copied in large quantities without permission.
警方在工廠裡發現許多盜版的電腦遊戲，這些產品未經授權就大量生產。

相關用法 **piracy** 名 ❶ 海盜行為；❷ 剽竊，著作權侵害

❶ Some ships have been attacked and hijacked in the Indian Ocean near Somalia; several countries are working together to fight Somali piracy. 一些船隻在印度洋接近索馬利亞的地方被攻擊並劫持，幾個國家現在正合力打擊索馬利亞的海盜行為。

❷ The man is charged with software piracy; he has been illegally copying computer programs and selling them for years.
這名男子被控侵犯軟體版權，他多年以來一直在非法拷貝和販賣電腦程式。

24 **plot** [plɑt] 名 C ❶ 陰謀，祕密計劃；❷ 情節　❸ 動 密謀，策劃

❶ A **plot** to kidnap the boss' son was uncovered by the police yesterday. 警方昨日瓦解了一起策動綁架老闆兒子的陰謀。

❷ The **plot** of the novel is very interesting; readers are curious about what will happen in the next volume.
這本小說的情節很有趣，讀者很好奇下一集會發生什麼事情。

❸ The criminals were **plotting** to rob the bank.
那些不法之徒在策劃搶劫銀行。

25 **proof** [pruf] 名 ❶ C 證據，物證；❷ U 證明

❶ The suspect had no **proof** that he was home on the night of the murder, so he was detained by the police.
那名嫌犯沒有證據證明他所說為真，所以被警方拘留了。

❷ Lorene designed some experiments that she hopes will offer **proof** for her theory. 蘿琳設計了一些實驗來證明她的理論。

26 **regulate** [ˋrɛgjə͵let] 動 ❶ 管理，規範；❷ 調整，調節　名 regulation 管理

❶ Schools have rules in order to **regulate** students' behavior.
學校制定校規是為了規範學生的行為。

❷ Pearl installed an air conditioner that **regulates** both the temperature and moisture level in her apartment.
珠兒在家中裝了一台可以調節溫度和溼度的冷氣機。

27 **regulation** [͵rɛgjəˋleʃən] 名 C 規章，條例

- regulate 規範
- -ion 名 表「行為的結果」

● Alberto doesn't like private schools because of their **regulations** on hair length and their strict dress codes.
艾伯托不喜歡私立學校限制頭髮長度和嚴格的服裝規定。

28 **release** [rɪˋlis] 動 ❶ 釋放；❷ 鬆開；❸ 發行，發表
名 C ❹ 釋放；❺ 發行，發表

- re- 表「再，重新」
- lease 租賃

❶ Jacqueline was found not guilty and will be **released** immediately. 賈桂琳被判無罪，會立即獲釋。

❷ Abigail asked the man to **release** her arm, but he refused to let her go. 愛碧凱要男子鬆開她的手臂，但男子拒絕放開她。

❸ When the pop singer's new album is **released**, I will buy one to show my support for him.
那位流行歌手發新專輯的時候，我會買一張來表示支持。

❹ The police questioned the suspect but let him go; many people were surprised to hear of his **release**.
警方審問那名嫌犯後就放他走了，許多人對他的釋放感到訝異。

❺ The **release** of her new album has earned the pop singer a fortune as well as worldwide fame.
那位流行歌手所發行的新專輯，讓她名利雙收，而且聞名全世界。

29 **restrict** [rɪˋstrɪkt] 動 限制　名 restriction 限制

・re- 表「再，更」
・strict 嚴格的

● Illegal drugs are a universal problem. Their use is not **restricted** to one country.
非法毒品是一個全球性的問題，不僅只出現在某個國家境內。

用法 restrict A to B　將 A 限制在 B 範圍內

30 **restriction** [rɪˋstrɪkʃən] 名 C（常作複數）限制規定

・restrict 限制
・-ion 名 表「行為」

● Filiberto is well-informed about the **restrictions** on opening a new restaurant. 菲力柏特很清楚開新餐廳的相關規定。

31 **rob** [rɑb] 動 ❶ 搶劫；❷ 剝奪（權利）　名 robber 劫匪　名 robbery 搶劫（案）

❶ A young man **robbed** Helen of her purse on the street this morning. 今天早上一位年輕人在街上搶了海倫的皮包。

❷ The war **robbed** the people of their freedom; it also took away their basic human rights.
那場戰爭奪走了人們的自由，也剝奪了他們的基本人權。

32 **robber** [ˋrɑbɚ] 名 C 搶匪，強盜

・rob 搶劫
・-er 名 表「人」

● The bank **robbers** escaped with millions of dollars in cash. 那幫銀行搶匪搶了數百萬的現金後逃逸。

33 **robbery** [ˋrɑbərɪ] 名 ❶ C 搶劫案，搶案；❷ U 搶劫罪

・robber 搶匪
・-y 名 表「狀態」

❶ In recent months, seven **robberies** have occurred in the neighborhood; the robber is still on the run.
近幾個月內，這個街坊已經發生了七起搶劫案，搶犯仍然在逃。

❷ Mr. Ward was arrested and charged with **robbery** last month.
華德先生上個月被捕，以搶劫的罪名被定罪。

34 **sin** [sɪn] 名 C（宗教或道德的）罪，罪過

● Teresa thinks it's a **sin** to waste food, energy, or time.
特麗莎認為浪費食物、能源或時間，都是一種罪過。

35 **suicide** [ˋsuə͵saɪd] 名 U 自殺

● It is not clear if Kurt committed **suicide** or if he was murdered.
柯特是自殺或是他殺，案情尚未明朗。

相關用法 形 **suicidal** 自殺的

- People who suffer from melancholia may have suicidal tendencies.
  罹患憂鬱症的人可能會有自殺傾向。

用法 commit suicide 自殺

36 **violate** [ˋvaɪə͵let] 動 違背，違反　名 violation 違反

- Driving faster than the speed limit **violates** traffic laws.
  超速開車是違反交通法規的。

37 **violation** [͵vaɪəˋleʃən] 名 U 違背，違反

- violate 違反
- -ion 名 表「行為」

- Celeste was charged with **violation** of a traffic regulation. 沙利斯特因為交通違規，吃了一張罰單。

41 Education & learning
教育與學習 (1)

81

01 **academic** [͵ækəˋdɛmɪk] 形 學術的

- Every scholar should respect and protect **academic** freedom.
  每位學者都應尊重並捍衛學術自由。

02 **adjective** [ˈædʒɪktɪv] 名 C 形容詞

- Doris learned how to use **adjectives** to modify nouns in her writing class today. 多莉絲今天在作文課裡學到怎麼用形容詞修飾名詞。

03 **admission** [ədˋmɪʃən] 名 ❶ U（學校、俱樂部等的）進入許可；❷ C 門票，入場券；❸ C 承認

❶ Taiwan applied for **admission** to the World Health Organization and eventually was accepted. 台灣申請加入世界衛生組織，最終被接受了。

❷ Miguel paid for his date's **admission** to the movie.
米格為約會的女伴付了電影票的錢。

❸ The woman made an **admission** that she broke the window; she also admitted that she did it on purpose.
女子承認她打破窗戶，也承認她是故意的。

04 **adverb** [ˋædvɝb] 名 C 副詞

- Many **adverbs**, including lovely and excitedly, end with the suffix -ly. 有許多副詞以 -ly 結尾，像是「lovely」或「excitedly」。

05 **biology** [baɪˋɑlədʒɪ] 名 U 生物學　形 biological 生物的

・bio- 表「生物」
・-logy 名 表「……學」

● Sophia wonders whether she should major in **biology** or mathematics. 蘇菲亞不知道該主修生物學還是數學。

相關用法 名 **biologist** 生物學家

● A **biologist** is a scientist who studies the life and structure of plants and animals. 生物學家是研究動植物生命和結構的科學家。

06 **chemistry** [ˋkɛmɪstrɪ] 名 U 化學

・chemist 化學家
・-ry 名 表「……類的事物」

● Fiona decided to change her major from biology to organic **chemistry**. 菲兒娜決定從生物系轉系到有機化學系。

07 **college** [ˋkɑlɪdʒ] 名 C 學院，大學　同義 university, academy 大學

● Henry has studied at this art **college** since last fall.
亨利從去年秋天開始在這間藝術學院念書。

08 **comma** [ˋkɑmə] 名 C 逗號

● The teacher said a **comma** should not be used before a clause beginning with because. 老師說以 because 開頭的子句前面不要使用逗點。

09 **conjunction** [kənˋdʒʌŋkʃən] 名 C 連接詞

・conjunct 結合的
・-ion 名 表「行為的結果」

● **Conjunctions** such as "and" and "but" connect units of speech, phrases, and clauses.
像是「and」、「but」之類的連接詞，用來連接一段話、片語和句子。

10 **consonant** [ˋkɑnsənənt] 名 C 子音

・con- 表「一起」
・sonant 有聲字母

● Can you tell the difference between a **consonant** and a vowel? 你能分辨子音和母音有什麼不同嗎？

11 **context** [ˋkɑntɛkst] 名 ❶ U 上下文，文章脈絡；❷ C 來龍去脈，背景

❶ It is very difficult to determine the meaning of a word without knowing its **context** or usage.
不先在上下文中了解詞彙的用法，要分辨詞彙的意義就很難。

❷ The book discusses the French Revolution in historical **context**, which helps the readers understand it.
這本書從歷史背景切入來討論法國大革命，這讓讀者更了解這場革命。

82

12 **cram** [kræm] 動 ❶（為應考）死記硬背塞進；❷ 擠進，塞滿；❸ 把……塞進，把……塞滿

❶ Alvin was up all night **cramming** for the test while his roommates partied. 在艾爾文為考試通宵猛 K 書的同時，室友們在大開派對。

❷ After 40 more people were **crammed** onto the bus, it was very crowded. 另外 40 人擠進公車後，公車裡頭變得很擠。

❸ The hungry boy **crammed** the food into his mouth so that he could hardly speak. 飢餓的男孩嘴巴塞滿食物，幾乎講不出話。

補充 cram school 補習班

13 **diploma** [dɪˋplomə] 名 C 畢業文憑，學位證書

● Briana obtained her college **diploma** in philosophy.
布蕾安娜拿到了大學的哲學文憑。

14 **drill** [drɪl] 名 C ❶ 訓練；❷ 鑽（機） 動 ❸ 鑽（孔）；❹ 訓練

❶ Elba did lots of **drills** in high school speech classes, so she never feels nervous speaking in public.
愛兒寶在高中的演講課上做過很多演講練習，所以公開演講時不會怯場。

❷ The worker used an electric **drill** to make a hole in the board.
工人用電鑽在板子上鑽出一個洞。

❸ It hadn't rained for weeks, so people in the village **drilled** wells for water. 已經好幾個星期沒下雨了，所以村民挖井來汲水。

❹ The teacher **drilled** the students on sentence patterns by making them do lots of exercises. 老師讓學生做很多練習，以熟悉句型。

15 **educate** [ˋɛdʒə͵ket] 動 ❶ 教育；❷ 培養，訓練 名 education 教育

❶ Elroy was born in Turkey but **educated** in Spain.
愛羅伊在土耳其出生，但在西班牙接受教育。

❷ The summer camp **educates** children about the importance of environmental preservation. 這個夏令營旨在培養兒童認識環保的重要性。

補充 well-educated 形 受過良好教育的

16 **educational** [͵ɛdʒʊˋkeʃənḷ] 形 ❶ 教育的；❷ 有教育意義的

- educate 教育
- -ion 名 表「行為的結果」
- -al 形 表「……的」

❶ Professor Varden shows us an **educational** documentary every Monday.
瓦爾登教授每週一都會播放教育記錄片給我們看。

❷ The TV program is **educational** and entertaining; it teaches us something as well as amuses us.
這個電視節目同時具有知識性與娛樂性，它能育教於樂。

17 **elementary** [͵ɛləˋmɛntərɪ] 形 初級的，基礎的

- element 基礎
- -ary 形 表「與……有關的」

● Eldridge did not go beyond an **elementary** education, but he has become a great artist.
葉爾居只有小學畢業，但他後來成為了一位偉大的藝術家。

18 **examinee** [ɪgˌzæməˋni] 名 C 應試者

- examine 測驗
- -ee 名 表「與……有關的人」

- These **examinees** are being tested to see how much they know about engineering.
  這些應試者正在接受考試，以測驗他們的工程學知識。

19 **examiner** [ɪgˋzæmɪnɚ] 名 C 主考人，檢查人，審查員

- examine 測驗
- -er 名 表「人」

- The **examiners** will write the questions and grade the papers for the college entrance exam.
  這些主考人負責大學入學考試的出題並批卷。

20 **expose** [ɪkˋspoz] 動 使暴露於，使接觸到　名 exposure 暴露

- The more one is **exposed** to an English-speaking environment, the more easily he or she will learn the language.
  越能在英文的環境中學習，就越能學好這個語言。

用法 expose A to B　將 A 暴露於 B 之下

21 **exposure** [ɪkˋspoʒɚ] 名 U 暴露，接觸

- expose 使暴露於
- -ure 名 表「動作」

- Linda's two-year stay in England increased her **exposure** to English, greatly helping her master the language.
  琳達在英國待了兩個月，她有了更多接觸英語的機會，英語能力突飛猛進。

22 **flunk** [flʌŋk] 動 ❶ 通不過（考試等）；❷ 給（某人）打不及格分數

❶ I didn't study for the exam; as a result, I **flunked** it.
  我考試沒準備，所以沒通過考試。

❷ The student did poorly on the exam, and the professor **flunked** him. 那個學生考試考得很差，教授給他打了不及格的分數。

23 **formation** [fɔrˋmeʃən] 名 C 構成物，形態，結構

- form 形成
- -ate 動 表「使成為」
- -ion 名 表「行為的結果」

- Ms. Norcross is a poet; she loves to experiment with the **formation** of her sentences. 諾克斯小姐是一位詩人，以創造各種的結構句為樂。

24 **freshman** [ˋfrɛʃmən] 名 C（大學等的）一年級生

- fresh 新鮮的
- man 人

- Delia made lots of interesting friends as a **freshman**.
  黛莉雅在大一時認識了很多有趣的朋友。

42 Education & learning 教育與學習 (2)

83

01 **graduate** 動 [ˋgrædʒʊˏet] ❶ 動 畢業
名 [ˋgrædʒʊɪt] ❷ 名 C 畢業生

❶ After **graduating** from the university, Natasha got a job with an insurance company.
娜塔莎畢業後在一家保險公司工作。

❷ Gina is a psychology **graduate** from the University of California.
吉娜畢業於加州大學心理系。

補充 graduate student 研究生；graduate school 研究所

- grade 階段
- -ate 動 表「使成為」

02 **graduation** [ˏgrædʒʊˋeʃən] 名 U 畢業

- Ignatius started working for his father as a plumber after senior high school **graduation**.
伊格內修斯高中畢業後就在當水電工，為父親工作。

- graduate 畢業
- -ion 名 表「行為」

03 **grammar** [ˋgræmɚ] 名 U 文法　形 grammatical 文法的

- **Grammar** can be used to either analyze a sentence or generate one. 文法可以用來分析句子或形成句子。

04 **grammatical** [grəˋmætɪkl̩] 形 文法的，合乎文法的

- Before turning in your essay to your English teacher, remember to proofread it for **grammatical** errors.
在交報告給英文老師之前，要記得先校對是否有文法上的錯誤。

05 **guidance** [ˋgaɪdn̩s] 名 U 指導，引導

- Beginners should not go rock climbing without expert **guidance**; it is too dangerous.
初學者沒有專家的指導就去攀岩，是很危險的。

- guide 引導
- -ance 名 表「動作」

06 **handwriting** [ˋhændˏraɪtɪŋ] 名 U ❶ 書寫，手寫；❷ 筆跡

❶ Jane prefers **handwriting** to typing when she writes letters. 珍寫信比較喜歡手寫，不喜歡用打字的。

❷ Anne scrawled the note; her **handwriting** was so scratchy I couldn't read it. 安匆促地寫了一張紙條給我，她的筆跡很潦草，我看不懂。

- hand 手
- write 寫
- -ing 名 表「動作」

07 **historic** [hɪs`tɔrɪk] 形 歷史上著名的，歷史上有重大意義的

- Parts of the Berlin wall are being allowed to stand as **historic** monuments.
  一部分的柏林圍牆沒有被拆掉，以作為歷史上的紀念。

> ‧history 歷史
> ‧-ic 形 表「具有……的」

08 **historical** [hɪs`tɔrɪkl̩] 形 ❶ 歷史的，史學的；❷ 有關歷史的，基於史實的

❶ Jonah conducted **historical** research on ancient kingdoms in Egypt.
約拿進行一項針對埃及古王國的歷史研究。

> ‧historic 歷史著名的
> ‧-al 形 表「關於……的」

❷ *Richard III*, one of the most famous **historical** plays by Shakespeare, tells how Richard becomes a king by ordering the murders of those around him.《查理三世》是莎士比亞最著名的歷史劇之一，內容描述查理三世如何剷除異己讓自己當上國王。

09 **idiom** [`ɪdɪəm] 名 C 慣用語，成語

- Rodney still remembers the English **idioms** he learned in senior high school. 羅德尼還記得高中時學過的英文慣用語。

10 **ignorance** [`ɪgnərəns] 名 U 無知，愚昧　形 ignorant 無知的

- Eli often says that **ignorance** is bliss.
  伊萊常愛說「傻人有傻福」。

> ‧ignore 忽視
> ‧-ance 名 表「狀況」

11 **ignorant** [`ɪgnərənt] 形 ❶ 無知的，不學無術的；❷ 不知道的

❶ Many people were **ignorant** of the dangers of smoking cigarettes, so they got into the habit at an early age.
有很多人不知道吸菸對身體的危害，所以年紀輕輕時就染上了這個惡習。

> ‧ignore 忽視
> ‧-ant 形 表「處於……狀態的」

❷ Albert is too **ignorant** to understand what is happening around him. 艾伯特對於周遭所發生的事情渾然不覺。

12 **instruct** [ɪn`strʌkt] 動 ❶ 教授，指導；❷ 指示，吩咐

❶ Before the speech contest, Ms. Tucker spent three days **instructing** her students on pronunciation.
塔克老師在演講比賽之前，花了三天的時間指導學生發音。

❷ The general **instructed** the soldiers to build a bridge across the river, and they followed the order.
將軍命令士兵築橋過河，士兵們奉命行事。

84

13 **instructor** [ɪnˋstrʌktɚ] 名 C 教練，指導者

- instruct 指示
- -or 名 表「人」

● Opal moved to an island in Southern Thailand and became a diving **instructor**.
歐寶兒搬去泰國南部的一座島上住，當起了潛水教練。

14 **intermediate** [ˌɪntɚˋmidɪət] 形 中等程度的，中級的

- inter- 表「在……之內」
- middle 中間
- -ate 形 表「有……性質或狀態的」

● Maxwell registered for an **intermediate**-level German class last week.
麥斯威爾在上週註冊了中級德語班。

15 **intonation** [ˌɪntoˋneʃən] 名 C 語調

- in- 加強語氣
- tone 語調
- -ate 動 表「使成為」
- -ion 名 表「行為的狀態」

● A question is asked with a rising intonation, while a statement is spoken with a falling **intonation**.
疑問句要用上升的語調，直述句要用下降的語調。

16 **learned** [ˋlɝnɪd] 形 有學問的，博學的

- learn 學習
- -ed 形 表「……的」

● The more **learned** a person is, the more modest he or she usually becomes. 一個人越是有學問，通常就會越謙虛。

17 **learning** [ˋlɝnɪŋ] 名 U ❶ 學習；❷ 學問

- learn 學習
- -ing 名 表「動作」

❶ Jacob's extensive **learning** has enabled him to become a brain surgeon. 雅各學習廣博，讓他得以成為腦外科醫生。

❷ Mr. Clinton is a man of great **learning**; he has a wide knowledge of history and literature.
柯林頓先生是個學識淵博的人，他在歷史和文學方面的學問很淵博。

18 **lecture** [ˋlɛktʃɚ] 名 C ❶ 授課，演講；❷ 訓斥，責備
動 ❸ 演講，講課；❹ 教訓，訓斥

- lection 經文
- -ure 名 表「動作」

❶ Professor Tilford is scheduled to give a **lecture** on Monday.
迪佛德教授安排了週一給我們上課。

❷ The teacher gave the student a **lecture** about cheating on exams. 老師因那個學生考試作弊而訓斥了他一頓。

❸ The professor used to **lecture** on social linguistics at Oxford University. 那位教授過去曾在牛津大學教授社會語言學。

❹ Parker's mother always **lectures** him about the way he talks and behaves; she doesn't think he is polite enough.
派克的媽媽總是訓斥他的言談舉止，認為他不夠禮貌。

19 **lecturer** [ˋlɛktʃərɚ] 名 C 講演者，講師

- lecture 授課
- -er 名 表「人」

● My daughter-in-law is a history **lecturer** at the community college. 我的媳婦在社區大學當歷史講師。

20 **mathematical** [ˏmæθəˋmætɪkḷ] 形 數學的，數學上的

- mathematics 數學
- -al 形 表「……的」

● Bernard was a **mathematical** genius, but he never learned to speak his mind.
柏納是個數學天才，但他卻不懂得如何表達自己心裡頭的事。

21 **mathematics** [ˏmæθəˋmætɪks] 名 U 數學　形 mathematical 數學的

● All senior high school students have to study the core subjects of Chinese, English, and **mathematics**.
所有的高中生都要學習國文、英文和數學這三門基礎課程。

22 **memorize** [ˋmɛməˏraɪz] 動 記住，背熟

- memory 記憶
- -ize 動 表「使」

● Casey has **memorized** all of the chemical elements in the periodic table. 卡希已經背熟了化學元素週期表上所有的元素。

23 **minor** [ˋmaɪnɚ] ❶ 動 副修　❷ 名 C 副修科目
形 ❸ 不重要的，次要的；❹ 較小的，較少的

❶ My brother is a college student; he majors in Chinese and **minors** in education. 我哥哥是大學生了，他主修中文，副修教育。

❷ Chinese is my brother's major, and education is his **minor**.
我哥哥主修中文，副修教育。

❸ Frances started out with some **minor** roles in TV dramas, but now she plays a major character.
法蘭西斯最初在電視上演出一些小角色，不過現在她已經是一線主角了。

❹ The mother gave most of the cake to her son; her husband got only a **minor** share. 媽媽把大部分的蛋糕給了兒子，她老公只分到一小部分。

24 **noun** [naʊn] 名 C 名詞

● In English, countable **nouns** are either singular or plural.
英文的可數名詞不是單數形，就是複數形。

25 **nursery** [ˋnɝsərɪ] 名 C ❶ 托兒所；❷ 苗圃

- nurse 護士；褓姆
- -ery 名 表「地方」

❶ This **nursery** takes children aged 14 months to 3 years. 這所幼兒園收 14 個月到 3 歲的兒童。

❷ Some new breeds of coconut trees were sent to Pat's **nursery**.
派特的苗圃收到了一些椰子樹的新品種。

26 **secondary** [ˋsɛkən͵dɛrɪ] 形 ❶（學校等）中等的；❷ 第二的，次要的，輔助的

❶ Children between the ages of 11 and 18 years should go to **secondary** school.
11 到 18 歲的孩子應該要上中學。

- second 第二的
- -ary 形 表「狀況」

❷ Elijah finally rose from a **secondary** position to team leader.
伊莉雅最後從團隊的副理升上了主管。

43 Education & learning 教育與學習 (3)

85

01 **major** [ˋmedʒɚ] 動 ❶ 主修　名 C ❷（大學中的）主修科目　形 ❸ 較多的，較大範圍的　❹ 主要的，重要的

❶ When Oscar was at college, he **majored** in social linguistics.
奧斯卡在念大學的時候主修社會語言學。

❷ My sister is a college student, and her **major** is history.
我姊姊是一名大學生，她主修的科目是歷史。

❸ Wayne's car needs **major** repairs because he was involved in a serious accident. 由於出了嚴重的車禍，偉恩的車子需要大整修。

❹ Shakespeare is a **major** English playwright; his contemporary, Ben Johnson, also has an important role in English literature. 莎士比亞是一位重要的英國劇作家，而跟他同代的班・強森在英國文壇的地位也是舉足輕重的。

02 **participle** [ˋpɑrtəsəpl̩] 名 C 分詞

- Using the correct **participle** in English sentences is challenging at first. 剛開始學習造英文句子時，想要正確使用分詞並不是件容易的事。

03 **philosopher** [fəˋlɑsəfɚ] 名 C 哲學家　名 philosophy 哲學

- Socrates was one of the greatest **philosophers** in the world.
蘇格拉底是世界最偉大的哲人之一。

04 **philosophical** [͵fɪləˋsɑfɪkl̩] 形 哲學的

- Calvin shares his **philosophical** views with people in his songs.
喀爾文透過他的歌曲和人們分享他的哲學觀。

- philosopher 哲學家
- -ic 形 表「具有……特性的」
- -al 形 表「……的」

05 **philosophy** [fə`lɑsəfɪ] 名 ❶ U 哲學；❷ C 人生觀

・philo- 表「愛好」
・-sophy 名 表「知識，學習」

❶ Augustine traced the term **philosophy** to its Greek origin, which means "love of wisdom."
奧古斯汀查出「philosophy」一詞的希臘字源語意是「熱愛智慧」。

❷ Ollie's **philosophy** of life is to seize the day.
奧利的人生觀是「把握現在」。

06 **physics** [`fɪzɪks] 名 U 物理學　名 physicist 物理學家

・physic 醫治
・-ics 名 表「一種科學」

● Bella has shown a great interest in **physics** ever since she was young. 貝拉從很小的時候就對物理學有濃厚的興趣。

07 **plural** [`plʊrəl] ❶ 形 複數的　❷ 名 C 複數形

❶ Children is the **plural** form of child.
「children」(孩子們)是「child」(孩子)的複數形。

❷ The **plural** of the noun teacher is made by adding -s to the singular form. 「teacher」(老師)這個名詞的複數形，是由單數形加「-s」所形成。

08 **preposition** [ˌprɛpə`zɪʃən] 名 C 介系詞

・pre- 在前的
・posit 安置
・-ion 名 表「行為的狀態」

● **Prepositions** such as "over," "on," "beside," and "in" indicate the place or position of a noun. 介系詞說明名詞的所在地方或位置，如「over」(在上方)、「on」(在上面)、「beside」(於旁邊)或「in」(在裡面)。

09 **professor** [prə`fɛsɚ] 名 C 教授

● Lewis Justice is a **professor** of computer science at Harvard University. 路易斯．賈斯汀是哈佛大學的資訊工程教授。

10 **pronoun** [`pronaʊn] 名 C 代名詞

・pro- 表「代替」
・noun 名詞

● I, you, and he are all **pronouns**.
「我」、「你」和「他」都是代名詞。

11 **pronunciation** [prəˌnʌnsɪ`eʃən] 名 U 發音

・pronounce 發音
・-ation 名 表「動作」

● After practicing for three months, Frederick finally improved his English **pronunciation**.
佛德瑞克練習英語發音三個月之後，總算有所進步。

12 **proverb** [`prɑvɝb] 名 C 諺語，俗語

● Have you ever heard the **proverb** "Don't count your chickens before they are hatched"? 你聽過「勿過早打如意算盤」這句諺語嗎？

86

13 **psychological** [͵saɪkəˋlɑdʒɪkl̩] 形 心理的，精神的

- Annie still needs both financial and **psychological** support from her parents.
  安妮還是需要父母在財務上和精神上給予支持。

> ‧psycho- 表「心理」
> ‧-logy 名 表「……學」
> ‧-ic 形 表「有……特性的」
> ‧-al 形 表「……的」

14 **psychologist** [saɪˋkɑlədʒɪst] 名 C 心理學家

- Lesley is a research assistant for a **psychologist** who is studying the effects of TV violence on children.
  蕾思麗擔任一名心理學家的研究助理，那位心理學家正在研究電視暴力對兒童的影響。

> ‧psycho- 心理
> ‧-logy 名 表「……學」
> ‧-ist 名 表「做……的人」

15 **psychology** [saɪˋkɑlədʒɪ] 名 U 心理學

- Ronald did not obtain a degree in **psychology**, but he talks like a psychologist.
  羅納德並沒有心理學的學位，但他講起話來就像個心理學家。

> ‧psycho- 心理
> ‧-logy 名 表「……學」

16 **recite** [rɪˋsaɪt] 動 ❶ 背誦，朗誦；❷ 歷數，列舉

❶ Bridget's granddaughter loves **reciting** poetry in public. 布麗姬特的孫女喜歡當眾誦詩。

❷ While showing me around the little town, the guide **recited** the list of local tourist spots. 嚮導帶我四處參觀小鎮時，列舉了一長串當地的觀光景點。

> ‧re- 表「再」
> ‧cite 引用

17 **repetition** [͵rɛpɪˋtɪʃən] 名 U 重複，反覆

- Children learn a language by hearing the **repetition** of their parents' words.
  孩子藉由反覆聽父母說過的話來學習語言。

> ‧repeat 動 重複
> ‧-ition 名 表「動作」

18 **scholar** [ˋskɑlɚ] 名 C 學者　名 scholarship 獎學金

- The governor consulted several **scholars** about his proposed education reform. 州長就自己所提出的教改方案，徵詢了幾位學者。

> ‧school 學校
> ‧-ar 名 表「人」

19 **scholarship** [ˋskɑlɚ͵ʃɪp] 名 C 獎學金

- Deborah won a **scholarship** to study abroad.
  黛博拉獲得了一份海外留學的獎學金。

> ‧scholar 學者
> ‧-ship 名 表「能力，技巧」

20 **system** [ˋsɪstəm] 名 C ❶ 制度，體制；❷ 系統

❶ Do you know the differences between the education **systems** in Taiwan and Britain? 你知道台灣和英國教育體制有何不同嗎？

❷ The MRT **system** consists of several lines; the Red Line is 28.3 km long. 捷運系統由數條路線組成，紅線長 28.3 公里。

21 **singular** [ˋsɪŋgjələ˞] ❶ 形 單數的；❷ 名 C 單數

- single 單一的
- -ar 形 表「……的」

❶ Datum is a **singular** noun, whereas data is plural.
「Datum」是單數名詞，「data」是它的複數形。

❷ The **singular** of geese is goose.
「geese」的單數形是「goose」。

22 **sophomore** [ˋsɑfmor] 名 C（大學或高中的）二年級學生

- James started learning French in his **sophomore** year of high school. 詹姆斯於高二開始學習法語。

23 **syllable** [ˋsɪləbl̩] 名 C 音節

- There are three syllables in the word **syllable**.
「syllable」這個字含 3 個音節。

24 **university** [ˌjunəˋvɝsətɪ] 名 U 大學

- universe 宇宙
- -ity 名 表「性質」

- Bruce said that he would never forget his life at the **university**. 布魯斯說他永遠不會忘記在大學的生活。

25 **verb** [vɝb] 名 C 動詞

- A **verb** is a word or phrase that describes an action.
動詞是用來形容動作的字或詞組。

26 **vowel** [ˋvaʊəl] 名 C 母音

- "An" is used before a noun with an initial **vowel** sound, whereas "a" is used before one with an initial consonant sound.
「An」用在母音開頭的名詞前面，「a」則用在子音開頭的名詞之前。

44 Military affairs & war 軍事與戰爭

87

01 **arms** [ɑrmz] 名 (複) 武器　同義 weapons 武器

- In Taiwan, selling **arms** such as handguns and rifles is illegal.
  在台灣，販賣手槍或來福槍一類的武器是違法的。

02 **barrier** [ˋbærɪr] 名 C ❶ 障礙物；❷ 障礙，阻礙；❸ 邊境，界線

❶ **Barriers** were put up to prevent the crowd from moving forward.
障礙物的架設是用來阻止群眾前進。

❷ Gender differences remain a **barrier** between men and women when it comes to understanding each other.
男女想要互相了解，性別的差異仍然是一個很大的障礙。

❸ Mountains and bodies of water made natural **barriers** for ancient kingdoms. 山脈河流是古代國家的天然屏障。

03 **blade** [bled] 名 C 刀身，刀片

- The hunter took out a knife and thrust the **blade** into the wild boar's heart. 那個獵人拿出一把刀，把刀身刺入野豬的心臟。

04 **bullet** [ˋbʊlɪt] 名 C 子彈，彈丸

- After a thorough search, the police found one **bullet** at the crime scene. 經過一番透徹的搜查，警方在犯罪現場找到了一顆子彈。

05 **clash** [klæʃ] 動 ❶ 發生衝突，抵觸；❷ 砰地相碰撞，發出鏗鏘聲

❶ Eyewitness accounts of the riot **clashed** with official government reports. 目擊者對暴動的描述與官方說法相互抵觸。

❷ The motorcycle **clashed** against the truck, making a loud noise.
那輛摩托車砰地撞上一輛卡車，發出很大的聲音。

06 **commander** [kəˋmændɚ] 名 C 指揮官，司令官

- command 命令
- -er 名 表「人」

- The **commander** in chief is hosting a meeting at headquarters. 總司令正在司令部主持一項會議。

07 **conquer** [ˋkɑŋkɚ] 動 ❶ 攻克，攻取；❷ 克服，戰勝

- con- 表「一起」
- query 表「調查」

❶ After the army **conquered** the city, the soldiers tried to take control of the entire country.
在軍隊攻下那座城市之後，他們企圖進一步掌控整個國家。

❷ Jetta finally **conquered** her habit of overeating and was able to lose some weight. 潔妲終於克服了暴食的問題，並且減輕了一些體重。

08 **defend** [dɪˋfɛnd] 動 ❶ 防禦，保衛；❷ 為……辯護

❶ The army was sent to **defend** the country and protect its people.
這支軍隊被派去保家衛民。

❷ Virginia **defended** herself from public criticism, but only her friends believed her.
維吉妮雅反駁公眾對她的批評，然而只有她的朋友才相信她。

09 **defense** [dɪˋfɛns] 名 U 防禦，保衛

● During the enemy attack, many soldiers died bravely in **defense** of their country. 在敵軍進攻的期間，許多士兵為捍衛國家而英勇地犧牲了。

10 **explode** [ɪkˋsplod] ❶ 動 使爆炸；❷ 爆炸；❸（情感）迸發；❹ 激增，迅速擴大

❶ The rebels **exploded** bombs in three subway stations yesterday.
反叛分子昨天在三座地鐵站引爆炸彈。

❷ The bomb **exploded** on the train, killing 10 passengers.
炸彈在火車上爆炸，奪走十名乘客的性命。

❸ Helen **exploded** with anger when she saw her boyfriend kissing an attractive girl. 當海倫看見她的男朋友親吻一個迷人的女孩時，她氣炸了。

❹ In the last five years, the country's population has **exploded**; now housing is a serious problem.
近五年來，這個國家的人口激增，現在住房供給是個很嚴重的問題。

11 **explosion** [ɪkˋsploʒən] 名 ❶ C 爆炸；❷ U 爆炸；❸ C 劇增

・explode 爆炸
・-sion 名 表「行為的狀態」

❶ The fire in the fireworks factory in Changhua set off a series of powerful **explosions** that killed four people.
彰化那間爆竹工廠的大火引發一連串威力強大的爆炸，造成四個人死亡。

❷ The **explosion** in the building could be heard from miles away.
在好幾英里之外，就可以聽到那棟建築的爆炸聲。

❸ There is an **explosion** of interest in learning Chinese; more and more American students are choosing Chinese as their second language.
現在掀起中文熱，有越來越多的美國學生選擇中文來當作他們的第二外語。

12 **explosive** [ɪkˋsplosɪv] ❶ 形 爆炸(性)的 ❷ 名 C 爆炸物，炸藥

❶ Ray is very careful when handling **explosive** substances. 雷在拿著易爆物時，非常地小心。

❷ The bus was completely destroyed by a powerful **explosive**. The explosion caused 20 deaths.
公車被一種威力強大的炸藥物整個炸毀。該起爆炸造成 20 人死亡。

- explode 爆炸
- -sion 名 表「狀態」
- -ive 形；名 表「有……的性質」

13 **fort** [fort] 名 C 堡壘，要塞

● Terry and his team held down the **fort** while the others went on a mission. 在其他隊員出任務時，泰利和他的小隊負責把守要塞。

14 **invade** [ɪnˋved] 動 ❶ 侵入，侵略；❷ 侵犯，侵擾 名 invasion 侵略

❶ Hitler's army **invaded** Poland on September 1, 1939.
希特勒的軍隊於 1939 年 9 月 1 日入侵波蘭。

❷ The paparazzi **invaded** the pop singer's privacy by taking pictures of him at his home. 狗仔隊偷拍那位流行樂手在家中的畫面，侵犯了他的隱私。

15 **invasion** [ɪnˋveʒən] 名 C ❶ 入侵，侵略；❷ 侵害，侵犯

- invade 侵入
- -sion 名 表「行為」

❶ Military **invasions** often kill many innocent civilians as well as soldiers.
軍事侵略往往不只會犧牲很多無辜的百姓，也會有很多軍人殉身。

❷ The superstar can no longer put up with the media's constant **invasion** of his privacy. 這名超級巨星無法再忍受媒體一再地侵犯他的隱私。

88

16 **missile** [ˋmɪsl̩] 名 C 飛彈，導彈

● We will all be in danger if the enemy attacks with nuclear **missiles**. 敵軍如果使用核彈攻擊，我們大家都會有危險。

17 **mission** [ˋmɪʃən] 名 C 任務，使命

● Larry has already completed more than 100 flight **missions**.
勞瑞已完成了上百件飛行任務。

18 **monitor** [ˋmɑnətɚ] ❶ 名 C 監聽器，監視器 ❷ 動 監控，監聽，監視

❶ All the ships near this area are displayed on the **monitor**.
這個區域鄰近的所有船隻都顯示在監視器上。

❷ The police **monitored** the suspect's phone conversations to uncover evidence of his crimes.
警方監聽了嫌犯的電話通話內容，找到了他犯罪的證據。

19 **navy** [ˋnevɪ] 名 C 海軍

- The **navy** has found the airplane that crashed in the South Pacific. 海軍找到了墜毀在南太平洋的飛機。

20 **occupy** [ˋɑkjə͵paɪ] 動 ❶ 占領，占據；❷ 占（時間、空間），占用；❸ 使忙碌，使從事

❶ The army **occupied** the city to take control of the main road.
為了控制主要幹道，軍隊占領了該城市。

❷ The student complained that studying **occupies** most of his time, leaving him with little time to do what he likes.
這名學生抱怨讀書占用他大部分的時間，讓他無法做他想做的事。

❸ Whitney **occupied** herself with some interesting projects this summer. 惠特妮今年夏天都在忙些有趣的計畫。

相關用法 形 **occupied** 已占用的，在使用的

- The bathroom is occupied. 浴室有人在用。

21 **odd** [ɑd] 形 ❶ 奇特的，古怪的；❷ 單隻的，不成對的；❸ 奇數的，單數的

❶ Among all the **odd** behaviors Mr. Lucas exhibits, walking backwards is the most acceptable.
在盧卡斯先生所有古怪的行徑中，倒著走算是最能讓人接受的。

❷ Douglas is wearing **odd** socks; he seems unaware that the socks do not match.
道格拉斯正穿著不成對的襪子；他似乎沒察覺他穿到了不同雙的襪子。

❸ Both 1 and 3 are **odd** numbers; neither can be divided evenly by 2.
1 和 3 是奇數，它們都不能被 2 整除。

22 **parachute** [ˋpærə͵ʃut] ❶ 名 C 降落傘　❷ 動 跳傘；❸ 傘投

- para- 表「側，旁」
- chute【口】降落傘

❶ Matthew always checks and folds his **parachute** himself before he jumps.
馬修在跳傘之前都會親自檢查並摺疊自己的降落傘。

❷ The soldiers **parachuted** from a large cargo plane into a remote mountain village inside enemy territory.
那些士兵從一架大型運輸機上跳傘，降落在敵軍領土內一個偏遠山區的村莊。

❸ Since all the roads leading to the mountain village were blocked, the government had to **parachute** supplies to the earthquake survivors.
由於所有通往山區村莊的路都被中斷了，政府不得不將補給品傘投給那些地震災民。

23 **radar** [ˋredɑr] 名 C 雷達

- An unidentified aircraft is showing up on the **radar**.
  雷達上出現一架不明飛行物。

24 **rebel** 名 [ˋrɛbl̩] 動 [rɪˋbɛl] ❶ 名 C 造反者，反抗者，反叛者　❷ 動 反抗

❶ According to recent reports, the **rebels** are supported by an overseas terrorist group.
根據最新情報顯示，叛軍受到一個海外恐怖集團的資助。

❷ The teenage girl **rebels** against her father and is unwilling to obey him. 這名少女反抗父親，不願意聽從父親的話。

25 **retain** [rɪˋten] 動 保留，保持　同義 preserve 保存

- The president struggled to **retain** control of the country after riots broke out in several cities.
  在數個城市發生暴亂後，總統努力維持對國家的控制權。

26 **retreat** [rɪˋtrit] ❶ 名 U 撤退　❷ 動 撤退　反義 動 advance 前進

▪ re- 表「離去」
▪ treat 對待

❶ After being defeated in the battle, the army was in full **retreat**. 在那場戰役被擊敗之後，軍隊全面撤退。

❷ Having suffered great losses, the army **retreated** from the battlefield to a safe distance.
由於蒙受重大損失，軍隊從戰場撤離到一個安全距離以外的地方。

27 **rocket** [ˋrɑkɪt] ❶ 名 C 火箭，飛彈　動 ❷ 迅速上升，猛漲

❶ The government decided to postpone the launch of the **rocket** this year. 政府決定今年要延後發射火箭。

❷ Research shows that the rate of obesity among children in the country has **rocketed** from 5% five years ago to 27% today.
研究顯示，這個國家兒童過胖的比例，在 5 年之內從 5% 激增到 27%。

28 **sword** [sord] 名 C 劍

- The **sword** hanging on the wall is a precious antique that Mr. Lane inherited from his father.
  掛在牆上的那把劍，是藍恩先生從父親那裡所繼承下來的一件稀世古物。

29 **troop** [trup] 名 C ❶ 部隊；❷ 一群

❶ The president declared the withdrawal of all the **troops** from Iraq. 總統宣布從伊拉克撤回所有的部隊。

❷ A **troop** of children rushed onto the playground after class was dismissed. 一群小孩下課後衝到操場上去玩。

30 **submarine** [ˋsʌbməˏrin] ❶ 名 C 潛水艇 ❷ 形 海底的

- sub- 表「底；下」
- marine 海的

❶ The nuclear-powered **submarine** sank in an unknown location. 那艘核子動力潛艇在一處不明海域沉沒。

❷ In the aquarium, you can see **submarine** creatures such as starfish and sea urchins. 在這個水族館，你可以看到一些像是海星和海膽等的海底生物。

31 **surrender** [səˋrɛndɚ] 動 投降，自首

- sur- 表「在上」
- render 放棄；讓與

● Ryan **surrendered** to the police after committing the crime. 里安在犯下罪行後，向警方自首。

Part 4 →

Science
科學

45 Technology 科技 (1)

89

01 **advanced** [əd`vænst] 形 ❶ 先進的；❷ 高級的，進階的

・advance 動 進步
・-ed 形 表「……的」

❶ In an **advanced** industrial society, you have access to modern technology and the latest innovations.
在先進的工業社會中，你可以接觸到現代科技和最新的想法。

❷ After a year of training in basic English, Colleen is ready for more **advanced** lessons. 在受過一年的基礎英語訓練後，蔻琳準備要上進階課程。

02 **agriculture** [`ægrɪˌkʌltʃɚ] 名 U 農業　形 agricultural 農業的

● Most undeveloped countries rely on **agriculture** as their main source of income. 大多數未開發國家倚賴農業為其主要的收入來源。

03 **atom** [`ætəm] 名 C 原子　形 atomic 原子的

● Everything in the world is made of **atoms**. 世上萬物皆由原子構成。

04 **atomic** [ə`tɑmɪk] 形 原子的

・atom 原子
・-ic 形 表「……的」

● The invention of the **atomic** bomb forever altered human history. 原子彈的發明，永久地改變了人類的歷史。

05 **automatic** [ˌɔtə`mætɪk] 形 自動的

● Whenever Ms. Pearson goes on vacation, she sets her e-mail server to send an **automatic** reply to anyone who sends her a message.
每當皮爾森小姐去渡假時，都會在電子郵件的伺服器上設定自動回覆寄件人。

06 **device** [dɪ`vaɪs] 名 C 裝置，設備　動 devise 設計，發明

● Randy invented a **device** that purifies sewer water.
朗迪發明了一項能淨化下水道汙水的設備。

07 **devise** [dɪ`vaɪz] 動 設計，發明

● Mr. Banks has **devised** a money-saving system to handle mail orders for his company.
班克斯先生替公司設計了一個省錢系統來處理郵購訂單。

08 **digital** [ˋdɪdʒɪtḷ] 形 數字的，數位的

- digit 數字
- -al 形 表「關於……的」

● Professor Cooper allows students to submit their papers in **digital** format. 庫柏教授允許學生以數位檔來繳交報告。

09 **download** [ˋdaʊn͵lod] 動（網路）下載　反義 upload 上傳

- down 向下
- load 裝載

● Now that my computer is connected to the Internet, I can browse e-papers, send and receive e-mail, and **download** software.
既然我的電腦連上了網路，我就可以瀏覽電子報、收發電子郵件和下載軟體。

10 **DVD** [di vi di] 名 C 多功能數位碟片，數位影音光碟

● The **DVD** for the movie Avatar is now available.
《阿凡達》的數位影音光碟已經上市了。

11 **electric** [ɪˋlɛktrɪk] 形 用電的，電動的　形 electrical 電的

● Since the power went out, the **electric** toy doesn't work.
因為沒電了，這個電動玩具不能玩了。

補充 electric shock 電擊，觸電

90

12 **electrical** [ɪˋlɛktrɪkḷ] 形 ❶ 與電有關的，電的；❷ 用電的

- electric 電的
- -al 形 表「關於……的」

❶ Andrew majored in **electrical** engineering in college. 安德魯在大學主修電機工程學。

❷ Before moving into the new flat, we have to buy some **electrical** appliances, such as an electric water heater, an electric oven, and an electric clothes dryer.
我們在搬進新公寓之前要買一些電器用品，像是電熱水器、電烤箱和電乾衣機。

13 **electrician** [͵ilɛkˋtrɪʃən] 名 C 電工，電氣技師

- electric 電的
- -ian 名 表「專家」

● The **electrician** has already finished wiring the house. 電工技師裝完了屋子裡的配線。

14 **electricity** [͵ilɛkˋtrɪsətɪ] 名 U 電，電力

- electric 電的
- -ity 名 表「性質」

● How much **electricity** can be generated by a solar panel? 一塊太陽能板可以產生多少電力？

15 **electronic** [͵ɪlɛkˋtrɑnɪk] 形 電子的　名 electron 電子

- electron 電子
- -ic 形 表「……的」

● **Electronic** watches do not have to be wound.
電子手錶不用上發條。

16 **electronics** [ˌɪlɛkˋtrɑnɪks] 名 U 電子學

- electronic 電子的
- -s 名 構成複數名詞

● How different would our lives be without **electronics**? 要是少了電子學，我們的生活會有什麼不同呢？

17 **email** [iˋmel] ❶ 名 U 電子郵件 ❷ 動 以電郵寄

- e- 表「電子的」
- mail 郵件

❶ Hobart turned on his computer and sent the file to his colleague by **email**. 霍伯特打開電腦，用電子郵件把檔案寄給同事。

❷ The tourist wanted to find an Internet cafe and **email** his photos to his family in the United States.
那名觀光客想找一家網咖，把他的照片用電子郵件寄給在美國的家人。

18 **engineering** [ˌɛndʒəˋnɪrɪŋ] 名 U 工程，工程學

- engine 引擎
- -eer 名 表「與……有關的人」
- -ing 名 表「職業，學說」

● Ms. Long majored in genetic **engineering**, and now she works at the National Medical Center. 隆小姐主修基因工程，她現在在國家醫學中心工作。

19 **experiment** [ɪkˋspɛrəmənt] ❶ 名 C 實驗，試驗 ❷ 動 進行實驗，試驗

❶ Are you willing to participate in our **experiment** involving new pain relievers? 你願意參與我們對新止痛劑所做的實驗嗎？

❷ In the lab, several scientists were **experimenting** on the animal; they did many scientific tests on it.
在實驗室中，幾位科學家對那隻動物進行實驗。他們對牠做了許多科學測試。

用法 experiment on A (with B) 在 A 身上實驗 B 方法

20 **experimental** [ɪkˌspɛrəˋmɛntl̩] 形 實驗性的，實驗用的

- experiment 實驗
- -al 形 表「關於……的」

● Long-term clinical tests by Quadar Company have shown that its new **experimental** drug can effectively treat depression.
魁達公司在經過長期的臨床試驗後，證明這個測試中的新藥可以有效治療憂鬱症。

21 **industrial** [ɪnˋdʌstrɪəl] 形 工業的

- industry 工業
- -al 形 表「……的」

● **Industrial** pollution has affected ecosystems all over the world. 工業汙染影響了全世界的生態系統。

22 **industrialize** [ɪnˋdʌstrɪəlˌaɪz] 動 使工業化

- industrial 工業的
- -ize 動 表「使形成」

● Most of the world has been **industrialized** over the past century. 世界上大部分的地區，在上一個世紀裡都已經工業化。

23 **Internet** [ˋɪntɚˏnɛt] 名 U 網際網路

- inter- 表「在⋯⋯之間」
- net(work) 網狀系統

● The room has **Internet** access, so you can send or receive e-mail. 這間房間可以上網，所以你可以收發電子郵件。

24 **keyboard** [ˋkiˏbord] 名 C ❶（電腦、鋼琴等的）鍵盤；❷ 鍵盤樂器

- key 鍵
- board 盤

❶ After resting his hands on the **keyboard**, the pianist started to play. 那位鋼琴家將手放在鋼琴鍵上，接著開始演奏。

❷ Alvin has played the **keyboard** with his band for years.
阿爾文已在樂團裡彈了幾年的鍵盤樂器。

46 Technology 科技 (2)

91

01 **laboratory** [ˋlæbrəˏtorɪ] 名 C **實驗室，研究室 (= lab)**

- labor 勞動

● Samuel works in a **laboratory** where he specializes in analyzing DNA. 山謬爾在一間實驗室工作，他專門負責分析 DNA。

02 **launch** [lɔntʃ] 動 ❶ 發射；❷ 發動，發起

❶ The space shuttle was successfully **launched** this morning.
今天早上，太空梭已經順利升空。

❷ Those bus drivers **launched** a strike to protest the low wages.
這些公車司機發動了一場罷工，抗議薪資太低。

03 **load** [lod] 名 ❶（電腦等的）負載；❷（車或船等的）裝載量；❸（精神方面的）負擔；❹ 工作量　❺ 動 裝載

❶ Owen's computer often breaks down when he tries to transfer excessive **loads** of data. 歐恩的電腦在傳輸大量資料時常會當機。

❷ The truck has a full **load**; it cannot carry any more goods.
那輛卡車已經滿載了，無法再運載更多的貨物。

❸ The mother was worried about her missing son; the news that he had been found took a **load** off her mind.
那個媽媽為他失蹤的兒子擔心不已。兒子被找到的消息，讓她鬆了一大口氣。

❹ The employees have been working too hard over the past few months; machines are being installed to lighten their **load**.
這些工人在過去幾個月中工作得太辛苦了，現在安裝了機器來減輕他們的工作量。

❺ Two young men are **loading** the truck with boxes of vegetables.
兩名年輕人正把一箱箱的蔬菜裝上卡車。

補充 workload 名 工作量；overload 動 裝載過量，超過負荷

04 **machinery** [məˋʃinərɪ] 名 U 機器，機械

- machine 機械
- -ry 名 表「……類的事物」

● Most consumer products are produced in large quantities by **machinery**. 大部分的消費產品都是用機器大量生產的。

05 **magnet** [ˋmægnɪt] 名 C ❶ 磁鐵；❷ 有吸引力的人或物

❶ The teacher placed a **magnet** on the desk, which caused the other metal objects to move toward it.
老師把一塊磁鐵放在桌上，磁鐵將其他的金屬物品吸引了過來。

❷ Flowers are **magnets** for bees and butterflies. 花兒會吸引蜜蜂和蝴蝶。

06 **magnetic** [mægˋnɛtɪk] 形 磁鐵的，磁性的，有磁性的

- magnet 磁鐵
- -ic 形 表「有……特性的」

● The needle of a compass points to the **magnetic** North Pole. 羅盤的磁針指向磁北極。

07 **mechanic** [məˋkænɪk] 名 C 機械工，修理工，技工

- machine 機器
- -ic 名 表「學術」

● Molly had her brother, who is a good **mechanic**, repair her car. 茉莉的哥哥是一名很好的機械工，幫她修好了車子。

08 **mechanical** [məˋkænɪkḷ] 形 機械的

- mechanic 機械工
- -al 形 表「……的」

● Bobby is a **mechanical** designer who might be able to help fix your car. 鮑比是一位機械設計師，他也許能幫你修車。

09 **network** [ˋnɛtˏwɝk] 名 C ❶ 電腦網絡；❷ 廣播網，電視網；❸ 網狀系統

- net 網狀物
- work 工作

❶ All the computers in the office are connected to form a **network**, which allows users to share information.
辦公室裡所有的電腦都被連結成一個電腦網路，讓使用者可以分享資訊。

❷ The baseball game will be broadcast on a national television **network**. 這場棒球比賽將由全國電視網聯播。

❸ Sean has developed extensive marketing **networks** for his retail business. 尚恩為自己的零售業務擴展出廣大的行銷網。

10 **nuclear** [ˋnjuklɪɚ] 形 原子核的，原子能的

- nucleus（原子）核
- -ar 形 表「……的」

● The government is researching alternative energy sources instead of building **nuclear** power plants.
政府正在研究替代能源，以取代興建核電廠。

補充 nuclear power plant 核能發電廠

11 **password** [ˋpæs͵wɝd] 名 C 暗語，密碼

- pass 通過
- word 口令，暗號

● Without a **password**, you can't open hotmail.com.
沒有密碼，就無法進入 hotmail.com。

12 **scientific** [͵saɪənˋtɪfɪk] 形 科學的 名 science 科學 名 scientist 科學家

● Edgar takes a **scientific** approach to solving his problems.
愛德格採用科學方法來解決問題。

92

13 **technical** [ˋtɛknɪkḷ] 形 科技的，技術的

- technic 技術
- -al 形 表「……的」

● Cheryl is a genius who can solve any **technical** problem we encounter.
綺麗兒是個天才，她能解決我們所遇到任何一種技術性問題。

14 **technique** [tɛkˋnik] 名 C 技術，技巧

● Mr. Welton will demonstrate different writing **techniques** in class today. 偉頓先生今天會在班上示範各種寫作技巧。

15 **technology** [tɛkˋnɑlədʒɪ] 名 U 技術，工藝

- techno- 表「技術」
- -logy 名 表「……學」

● As a specialist in information **technology**, Jean has a promising future. 珍是一位資訊科技專家，她的前程似錦。

補充 cutting edge technology 尖端科技；
IT=information technology 資訊科技

16 **theory** [ˋθiərɪ] 名 ❶ C 學說，理論；❷ U 原理，理論

❶ The **theory** of relativity caused a revolution in the scientific community. 相對論在科學界引發了一場大變革。

❷ The plan sounds good in **theory**, but I don't think it will work in practice. 這個計畫在理論上聽起來很好，但我不認為它實際上可行。

17 **tickle** [ˋtɪkḷ] ❶ 動 搔癢，使發癢 ❷ 名 C 搔癢

❶ Louis was **tickled** by his cat's tail as they relaxed together on the sofa. 路易士與他的貓在沙發上休息時，貓的尾巴搔得他發癢。

❷ I gave the little boy a **tickle** by moving my finger across the sole of his foot, and he laughed.
我用手指搔癢小男孩的腳底，然後他就笑了。

18 **X-ray** [ˋɛksˋre] 名 C X 光

- After the surgical procedure, Doctor Moore took an **X-ray** of Winona's lungs to check their condition.
  莫爾醫生替溫諾納照了肺部的 X 光以檢查手術後的情況。

19 **satellite** [ˋsætl̩ˏaɪt] 名 C 人造衛星

- Tomorrow morning, the space shuttle will send a weather **satellite** into orbit around the Earth.
  明天早上，這艘太空梭會把一顆氣象衛星送進地球軌道。

20 **software** [ˋsɔftˏwɛr] 名 U 軟體

- Christina predicted the computer **software** market would expand. 克莉絲蒂娜預測，電腦軟體的市場會擴大。

· soft 軟的
· ware 製品

21 **technician** [tɛkˋnɪʃən] 名 C 技術人員，技師

- Victor is the electrical **technician** who is responsible for the test. 維克多是負責今天測試的電機技師。

· technic 技術
· -ian 名 表「專家」

22 **technological** [ˏtɛknəˋlɑdʒɪkl̩] 形 技術的，工藝的

- **Technological** development has dramatically progressed in our time.
  我們這一代的科技發展進步神速。

· techno- 技術
· -logy 名 表「……學」
· -ical 形 表「……的」

23 **telescope** [ˋtɛləˏskop] 名 C（單筒）望遠鏡

- Planets such as Mars and Mercury can sometimes be seen at night without a **telescope**.
  像火星和水星等行星，有時不需要望遠鏡就可以在夜空中看到。

· tele- 表「遠距離」
· -scope 名 表「觀看的器具」

24 **upload** [ʌpˋlod] 動 上載　反義 download 下載

- The computer programmer **uploaded** files from his client's computer. 電腦程式設計師從客戶的電腦上傳檔案。

· up- 表「向上」
· load 裝載

25 **website** [ˋwɛbˏsaɪt] 名 C 網站

- Jim got a job designing **websites** for advertising companies. 吉姆的新工作是替廣告公司設計網站。

· web 網路
· site 地點，場所

47 Sound & light
聲光

93

01 **audio** [ˋɔdɪˏo] 形 聽覺的，聲音的

- It bothers Rita that some TV channels always raise the **audio** level during commercials.
  有些電視頻道會在廣告時間將音量放大，這讓麗妲覺得很討厭。

02 **bang** [bæŋ] 名 C ❶ 猛擊；❷ 砰砰聲
動 ❸ 發出砰的一聲；❹ 砰地敲；❺ 猛擊，猛撞

❶ The loud **bang** of the gun was heard across the field.
那聲巨大的槍響，傳遍了整個原野。

❷ The falling object hit the passerby with a **bang** on the head and knocked him out. 落下來的東西砰地一聲擊中他的頭，接著他就昏倒了。

❸ During the battle, the civilians could hear the soldiers' guns **banging** in the distance. 老百姓在戰爭期間可以聽見遠處士兵的槍響聲。

❹ After Mark quarreled with his parents, he went to his room and angrily **banged** the door shut.
馬克和爸媽吵架後就走進自己的房間，很生氣地砰的一聲關上門。

❺ As Peter hurried out of the room, he **banged** his knee on the table and cried out in pain.
彼得在匆忙走出房間時，膝蓋撞上了桌子，讓他痛得唉唉大叫。

03 **beam** [bim] ❶ 名 C 束，光線　動 ❷ 照耀；❸ 堆滿笑容，眉開眼笑

❶ **Beams** of sunlight are poking through the eastern sky.
陽光正從東方的天邊破曉而出。

❷ In the dark room, the man saw light **beaming** through a hole in the wall. 在黑暗的房間裡，男子看到光線從牆壁上的洞照了進來。

❸ When David heard that he had won the contest, he **beamed** with joy. 當大衛聽到自己贏得比賽時，他高興得眉開眼笑。

04 **brilliant** [ˋbrɪljənt] 形 ❶ 光輝的，明亮的；❷ 傑出的，出色的

❶ The sunshine is so **brilliant** that I can hardly open my eyes.
陽光太耀眼了，我幾乎張不開眼睛。

❷ Nicole is a **brilliant** linguist. Within a short time, she has developed a good command of both Chinese and Japanese.
妮可是一位傑出的語言學者。她在短時間之內就把中文和日文都學得很好了。

相關用法 名 brilliance ❶ 光輝，光彩；❷（卓越的）才華，才智

❶ The actress's evening gown glittered with the brilliance of crystals. 女演員的晚禮服在水晶飾品的光彩下閃閃發亮。

❷ Dr. Lee, a well-known physicist, is admired for his brilliance. 李博士是一位知名物理學家，他才智卓越，備受敬佩。

05 **buzz** [bʌz] ❶ 動（蜂等）嗡嗡叫 名 C ❷（蜂等的）嗡嗡聲；❸ 嘈雜聲

❶ Maggie was awakened several times last night by mosquitoes **buzzing** around her ears. 瑪姬昨晚被一隻在耳邊嗡嗡叫的蚊子吵醒了好幾次。

❷ I heard a **buzz** and then saw a bee flying over my head. 我聽到嗡嗡聲，然後就看到一隻蜜蜂在我頭上飛舞。

❸ The students chatted loudly in the classroom; the **buzz** of conversation stopped suddenly when the teacher showed up. 學生們在教室裡大聲地聊天，等老師一出現時，就立刻鴉雀無聲。

06 **chirp** [tʃɝp] 動（小鳥）發啁啾聲，（昆蟲）發唧唧聲

- My favorite season is spring, when the birds are constantly **chirping**. 我最喜愛有鳥兒啁啾不停的春天。

07 **crunchy** [ˋkrʌntʃɪ] 形 發嘎吱嘎吱聲的，易碎的

- crunch 嘎吱吱的聲音
- -y 形 表「有⋯⋯的」

- If you can't think of anything to talk about on your blind date, you could ask "Do you prefer **crunchy** or smooth peanut butter?" 第一次約會時你要是不曉得要說什麼，不如乾脆就問：「你喜歡有顆粒還是無顆粒的花生醬？」

08 **deafen** [ˋdɛfn̩] 動 使聾，使聽不見

- deaf 耳聾
- -en 動 表「使變為⋯⋯」

- During the air raid, the sound of the bombs exploding momentarily **deafened** them; they could barely hear any other sounds around them. 在空襲期間，轟炸聲震耳欲聾，他們聽不到周圍的其他聲音。

09 **dim** [dɪm] ❶ 形 微暗的，朦朧的 ❷ 動 變暗淡，變模糊

❶ **Dim** lights encourage a relaxing mood. 朦朧的光影有助於放鬆心情。

❷ The story was so sad that the woman's eyes **dimmed** with tears, and she couldn't continue reading. 這個故事好悲涼，女子看得淚眼朦朧，無法繼續讀下去。

10 **echo** [ˋɛko] 名 C ❶ 回聲，回響 ❷（輿論等的）反應，共鳴
動 ❸ 發出回聲，產生回響

❶ When Regina sings in the shower, she thinks the **echo** makes her voice sound better. 芮吉娜喜歡在洗澡時唱歌，因為回音可以讓歌聲聽起來更美。

❷ The speech set off an **echo** in the audience; everyone agreed with the speaker. 這篇演說在聽眾的心中引起共鳴，每個人都認同演講者。

❸ The climber's shout of joy **echoed** through the valley; he heard it again and again. 那位登山者喜悅的喊叫聲在山谷裡迴盪，不斷地傳回他的耳裡。

11 **fade** [fed] 動 ❶（聲音）變微弱，（光）變暗淡，逐漸消失；❷（顏色）褪去；
❸ 凋謝，枯萎

❶ The suspect was so overcome with guilt that her voice **faded** into a whisper; the police could barely hear what she was saying.
嫌疑犯講話的聲音因心虛而變得很小聲，警方聽不太清楚她在說什麼。

❷ The colors in the curtain **faded** after long exposure to the sun. 由於長時間曝晒在太陽下，窗簾都褪色了。

❸ The wildflowers have all **faded** as autumn approaches.
隨著秋天的腳步越來越近，野花都凋謝了。

12 **flame** [flem] 名 C 火焰，火舌

● The **flames** of our campfire danced with delight in the wind.
我們的營火在風中輕快地舞動著。

13 **giggle** [ˋgɪgḷ] ❶ 動 咯咯地笑，傻笑 ❷ 名 C 咯咯的笑，傻笑

❶ Blake listened to the comedian's absurd joke and started **giggling**. 布雷克聽著喜劇演員講了個很扯的笑話，咯咯地笑了起來。

❷ As the handsome boy entered the classroom, some girls burst into **giggles**; he didn't know why they laughed in that silly way. 當那個帥哥走進教室時，一些女孩突然咯咯地笑了起來；他不了解她們為什麼要那樣傻笑。

14 **glow** [glo] 動 ❶ 發光，發熱；❷（臉）發紅，容光煥發

❶ After sunset, the western sky continued to **glow** for some time.
日落後，西方的天邊仍短暫地泛著光。

❷ After Julia tripped over a stone in public, her face **glowed** with embarrassment. 茱莉亞當眾被石頭絆倒後，尷尬得滿臉通紅。

94 15 **hush** [hʌʃ] ❶ 動 使安靜，使沉默 ❷ 名 C 沉默，靜寂

❶ Antonio **hushed** his dogs as the mailman approached the house.
安東尼歐在郵差走向他家時，喝令狗狗安靜。

❷ As the curtain rose, a **hush** fell over the audience.
布幕升起時，觀眾安靜了下來。

補充 hush money 遮羞費

16 **laughter** [ˋlæftɚ] 名 U 笑，笑聲　動 laugh 笑

- Ms. Zimmerman enjoyed hearing the **laughter** after the jokes in her speech. 契摩曼小姐喜歡聽到觀眾對自己演講中的玩笑話回以笑聲。

17 **lighten** [ˋlaɪtn̩] ❶ 動 變亮，發亮；❷ 照亮；❸ 減輕（重量、負擔等）

- light 光亮
- -en 動 表「變為⋯⋯」

❶ After Sabrina painted her room white, it **lightened** up instantly.
莎賓娜把房間漆成白色之後，房間頓時明亮不少。

❷ The lamp **lightened** the dark room, and they could see the cat lying on the table. 那盞燈照亮了黑暗的房間，他們可以看到有一隻貓趴在桌上。

❸ The travelers **lightened** their backpacks by taking out the heavy bottles of mineral water. 旅行者從背包中拿出了幾瓶礦泉水以減輕重量。

18 **murmur** [ˋmɝmɚ] ❶ 動 私語，小聲說話　❷ 名 C 低語聲

❶ Abby **murmured** softly to the baby in her arms.
艾碧對懷中的寶寶輕聲說話。

❷ The shy boy spoke in a low **murmur**; I could hardly hear him.
那名害羞的男孩講話的聲音很小，我幾乎聽不到他的聲音。

19 **oral** [ˋorəl] 形 口頭的，口述的

- The legal durability of an **oral** agreement is much shorter than that of a written document. 口頭承諾比書面契約的法律效力來得低。

20 **ray** [re] 名 C ❶ 光線，電流；❷ 射線 ，輻射線

❶ Golden **rays** of sunlight broke through the heavy clouds.
金色陽光穿透重重雲霧。

❷ X-**rays**, which can go through solid objects, are used for photographing the inside of the human body.
X 光線可以穿透固體，用來拍攝身體內部。

21 **roar** [ror] 動 ❶（獅虎等）吼叫，（風浪等）呼嘯，（雷等）轟鳴；❷ 大聲叫喊，狂笑　名 C ❸ 吼叫，咆哮；❹ 大笑聲

❶ As the storm approached, the waves **roared** more intensely along the shore. 隨著暴風雨的逼近，岸邊的海浪也翻騰得更厲害了。

❷ After learning that he had been cheated again, the man **roared** with anger, shouting himself hoarse.
男子發現再度被騙之後，氣得大吼大叫，把嗓子都給喊啞了。

❸ The hunter was horrified by the **roar** of the tiger; the loud, deep sound echoed across the forest.
那名獵人被老虎的吼叫聲給嚇壞了，低沉的虎嘯聲迴盪在整片森林之中。

❹ The speaker had a good sense of humor; his speech was greeted with **roars** of laughter. 那位演講者很幽默，他的演講引來陣陣的哄堂大笑。

22 **scream** [skrim] ❶ 動 尖叫 ❷ 名 C 尖叫聲

❶ Whenever Zoe rides a roller coaster, she always **screams** at the top of her lungs. 柔伊坐雲霄飛車時都會尖聲狂叫。

❷ Gabriel heard a **scream**; he found that the loud, high cry had been made by an excited girl.
加百利聽到了一個尖叫聲，他發現那是一位興奮的小女孩所發出的尖銳叫聲。

23 **shade** [ʃed] ❶ 名 U 蔭，陰涼處 ❷ 動 遮蔽 形 shady 成蔭的

❶ Let's sit in the **shade** of this big tree to have our picnic.
我們坐在這棵大樹的樹蔭下野餐吧。

❷ The mother **shaded** the baby's eyes from the sun, blocking the direct light. 媽媽遮住小寶寶的眼睛，防止陽光直射。

24 **shadow** [ˋʃædo] 名 ❶ C 影子；❷ U 陰暗處；❸ U（負面的）影響

❶ A total eclipse of the sun occurs when the moon's **shadow** crosses the Earth's surface. 當月球的影子落在地球表面時，就會發生日全蝕的情況。

❷ The photographs showed the man's face in sunlight and in **shadow**. 照片上男子的臉龐一半在陽光下，一半在陰影下。

❸ All living things on Earth fall under the **shadow** of the greenhouse effect. 地球上的所有生物都受到溫室效應的影響。

相關片語 **without/beyond a shadow of a doubt** 毫無疑問

- Beyond a shadow of a doubt, William has a deep sense of integrity.
威廉的正直，是無庸置疑的。

25 **shady** [ˋʃedɪ] 形 成陰的，陰涼的

- shade 蔭
- -y 形 表「有……的」

- After walking in the sun for hours, they found a **shady** place to rest. 在太陽下走了幾個小時後，他們找了一個陰涼的地方休息。

26 **shiny** [ˋʃaɪnɪ] 形 發光的，閃耀的

- shine 發光
- -y 形 表「有……的」

- The rain makes all the cars look very **shiny**.
這場雨讓每輛車看起來都閃閃發亮。

27 **yell** [jɛl] 動 叫喊，吼叫

- After Joel scored a goal at the match, the crowd **yelled** with delight. 喬爾在比賽中得分後，全場觀眾一陣歡聲雷動。

用法 yell at somebody 對某人吼叫

28 **spark** [spɑrk] 名 C ❶ 火花，火星；❷ 微量，絲毫 ❸ 動 激起，鼓動

❶ A little **spark** can become a big flame with the help of the wind.
星星之火有了風的吹拂，也可燎原。

❷ Nydia didn't show a **spark** of interest in the idea; she didn't seem to like it at all. 妮蒂亞對那個主意毫無興趣，她看來是一點也不喜歡。

❸ The plan to build another nuclear power station **sparked** a storm of protest among the villagers.
興建另一座核能發電廠的提議，激起村民的一陣抗議聲浪。

29 **sparkle** [ˋspɑrkḷ] ❶ 動 發火花，閃耀 ❷ 名 U 閃耀，閃光

・spark 火花

❶ When Dolly's diamond ring **sparkled**, I forgot what I was going to say. 當我看到多莉的鑽戒閃閃發光時，一時之間忘了要說什麼了。

❷ The diamond's **sparkle** dazzled the woman.
鑽石閃閃發光，讓女子看得目眩。

30 **twinkle** [ˋtwɪŋkḷ] ❶ 動 閃爍，閃閃發光 ❷ 名 U 閃爍，閃耀

・twink 閃爍

❶ How are fireflies able to **twinkle** in the dark?
螢火蟲是如何在黑暗中閃閃發光的？

❷ We can see the **twinkle** of stars in the countryside at night.
在鄉下的夜裡，我們可以看到星星閃爍。

48 Transportation & traffic 運輸與交通 (1)

95

01 **accident** [ˋæksədənt] 名 C 意外，事故

- Emily witnessed a traffic **accident** last night.
愛蜜莉昨晚目睹了一場交通意外。

02 **alley** [ˋælɪ] 名 C 巷子，胡同

- Lelia drives very slowly and carefully when passing through narrow **alleys**. 蕾莉雅只要開車行經窄巷，就會開得很慢、很小心。

03 **automobile** [ˋɔtəmə͵bɪl] 名 C 汽車

- auto- 表「自動的」
- mobile 汽車

● The price of imported **automobiles** has risen 10% over the last six months. 進口汽車的價格，六個月以來已經漲了一成。

04 **avenue** [ˋævə͵nju] 名 C ❶ 大街，大道；❷ 林蔭大道；❸ 途徑，方法

❶ Ruth will go shopping on Fifth **Avenue**, as there are many great shops along the street. 露西要去第五街購物，因為那條街有很多不錯的商店。

❷ The **avenue** leading to the museum is wide and straight, with trees on both sides. 通往博物館的林蔭大道又寬又直，兩側都有樹木。

❸ Bonita has explored every possible **avenue** for publishing her book this year. 邦妮塔今年嘗試了各種可能的方法，尋求出書的機會。

05 **brake** [brek] ❶ 名 C 煞車 ❷ 動 煞住（車）

❶ When Jo took her car to the mechanic for a regular checkup, he found a problem with the **brakes**.
喬把車開到技師那裡做例行檢查，結果發現煞車有問題。

❷ The truck driver **braked** just in time to avoid a serious accident.
卡車司機及時煞車，避免了一起嚴重的交通事故。

06 **cabin** [ˋkæbɪn] 名 C ❶（飛機的）客艙；❷ 小屋

❶ Ten minutes after we got into the **cabin**, the flight attendant asked us to fasten our seat belts.
在我們進入客艙十分鐘後，一名空服員要求我們繫上安全帶。

❷ When Phoebe retired, she sold her apartment in the city and moved to a **cabin** in a rural community.
菲碧退休後賣掉城裡的公寓，搬進了鄉間社區的一間小屋。

07 **canoe** [kəˋnu] 名 C 獨木舟

● Jen brought her **canoe** and paddles on the camping trip with her friends. 珍帶著獨木舟和槳，與朋友一起去露營。

08 **cargo** [ˋkɑrgo] 名 C 貨物 同義 freight 貨物

● The ship carried a **cargo** of 2,000 tons and was headed for Vietnam. 那艘船載了兩千噸的貨物，航向越南。

09 **carriage** [ˋkærɪdʒ] 名 ❶ C 四輪馬車；❷ U 運輸

- carry 運載
- -age 名 表「行動的結果」

❶ These old-style **carriages** still work, but they are used only for making movies nowadays.
這些舊式的四輪馬車還能用，但現在只用來拍電影。

❷ They wanted to transport the goods from Taipei to Kaohsiung, but they didn't have the money to pay for the **carriage**.
他們想要把貨物從台北送到高雄，但他們沒有錢付運費。

10 **carrier** [ˋkærɪɚ] 名 C 運輸公司

- carry 運載
- -er 名 表「物」

● That airline **carrier** went out of business a few years ago. 那家航空運輸公司幾年前就停止營運了。

11 **cone** [kon] 名 C ❶ 錐形路標；❷（盛冰淇淋的）錐形蛋捲筒

❶ Jason placed some bright orange reflective **cones** behind his car when it broke down on the highway.
傑森的車子在公路上拋錨時，他在車子後方放置了一些橙色的反光路錐。

❷ The vendor took out a **cone** and put ice cream in it.
小販拿出一個錐形蛋捲筒，然後放進冰淇淋。

12 **convey** [kənˋve] 動 ❶ 運送；❷ 傳達，表達 同義 communicate 傳達

❶ A fleet of trucks will **convey** the produce to the market every morning. 每天清晨，一長列的貨車會運送農產品到市場。

❷ The man doesn't know how to express himself in words, so he uses paintbrushes and colors to **convey** his feelings.
男子不知道如何用言語表達自己，所以就用畫筆和顏料來表達他的感受。

13 **correspond** [ˌkɔrɪˋspɑnd] 動 ❶ 通信；❷ 符合，一致

- cor- 表「共同」
- respond 作出反應

❶ I have been **corresponding** with Lillian for two years; I e-mail her once a week.
這兩年來，我一直都有和莉麗安通信；我一星期會寄一封電子郵件給她。

❷ Hayden assured all the workers that his actions would **correspond** with his words. 海登向所有的員工保證，他會說到做到。

96

14 **craft** [kræft] 名 U 工藝，手藝

● Carlton started learning the **craft** of hairdressing as an apprentice three years ago. 卡爾頓三年前開始在美髮業作學徒。

15 **crash** [kræʃ] 名 C ❶ 相撞，墜毀；❷ 發出撞擊聲；❸（電腦）當機
動 ❹（發出猛烈聲音地）碰撞，墜落；❺ 相撞，墜毀；
❻ 發出撞擊聲，發出爆裂聲；❼（電腦）當機

❶ The investigation of the airplane **crash** will be conducted by experts. 墜機意外將由專家著手調查。

❷ As the two cars collided, passersby heard the **crash** of shattering glass. 在兩輛汽車相撞時，行人聽到玻璃粉碎的爆裂聲。

❸ This morning, a system **crash** caused serious flight delays.
今天早上，系統當機造成了班機嚴重延誤。

❹ A baseball **crashed** through the window and hit a vase on the table. 一顆棒球猛地砸進窗戶，擊中桌上的花瓶。

❺ Hit by lightning, the airplane **crashed** into the ocean soon after takeoff. 飛機在起飛不久後遭到雷擊並墜入大海。

❻ During the storm, lightning flashed and thunder **crashed**.
暴風雨中，閃電交加、雷聲大作。

❼ My computer **crashed** without warning, and I lost the file.
我的電腦毫無預警地當機，所以那個檔案就不見了。

16 **curve** [kɝv] ❶ 名 C **彎曲處，彎曲部分** ❷ 動 **彎曲**

❶ Drive safely. This mountain road has many **curves**.
小心開車！這條山路九彎十八拐的。

❷ As the girl smiled, her lips **curved** upward.
那個女孩微笑時，嘴唇會上彎。

17 **deck** [dɛk] 名 C **(船的)甲板**

● After spending several days sunbathing on the **deck**, Janetta has a deep tan. 珍娜妲在甲板上做了幾天的日光浴後，皮膚都晒成古銅色了。

18 **delivery** [dɪˋlɪvərɪ] ❶ 名 C **投遞，傳送**；U ❷ **交付，交貨**；❸ **分娩**

・deliver 傳送
・-y 名 表「狀態」

❶ The post office's special **delivery** service is very efficient. A package can be received in a few hours.
郵局的限時專送很有效率，寄出的包裹在幾個小時內就能收到。

❷ If you expect to have quick **delivery** of the goods, it is better to have them airmailed.
如果你想快速送達貨物，最好是用航空信寄出。〔91 年學測補考〕

❸ The pregnant woman has been taken to the **delivery** room, where she will give birth to her baby. 懷孕的婦女被帶去產房臨盆。

19 **dock** [dɑk] ❶ 名 C **碼頭，港區** ❷ 動 **使靠碼頭**

❶ When Troy's ship arrived at the **dock**, his family was waiting for him. 特洛伊坐的船抵達碼頭時，他的家人已經在岸邊等他。

❷ The harbor is near; the ship is going to **dock** in about half an hour. 就快到港口了，這艘船在半個小時內就會停靠碼頭了。

20 **fare** [fɛr] 名 U（交通工具的）票價，車資

- How much is the bus **fare** from Washington D.C. to New York City? 從華盛頓特區坐巴士到紐約的車資是多少？

21 **ferry** [ˋfɛrɪ] 名 C 渡輪

- Do you know when the last **ferry** will depart for the mainland today? 請問今天開往大陸的最後一班渡輪是什麼時候？

22 **freeway** [ˋfrɪˏwe] 名 C 高速公路

- free 自由
- way 道路

- Can you get off the **freeway** at the next exit and stop at a gas station? 你可以在下一個出口下高速公路，找間加油站停一下嗎？

23 **gasoline** [ˋgæsəˏlin] 名 U〔美〕汽油

- gas 汽油

- Monica's new car doesn't need **gasoline** because it runs on electricity. 莫妮卡的新車不需要汽油，因為它是電力發電的。

24 **harbor** [ˋhɑrbɚ] 名 C 港口，海港

- As the storm approached last night, several cruise ships were entering the **harbor**. 暴風雨在昨晚逼近時，數艘郵輪已經入港避風。

25 **helicopter** [ˋhɛlɪˏkɑptɚ] 名 C 直升機

- helico- 表「螺旋」
- -pter (n) 表「有翼之物」

- A serious car accident occurred on the highway, and the police **helicopter** arrived within minutes. 高速公路上發生了一起嚴重車禍，警方的直升機幾分鐘內便趕到現場。

26 **helmet** [ˋhɛlmɪt] 名 C 頭盔，安全帽

- Motorcycle riders must wear **helmets** whenever they get on the road. 機車騎士只要上路，就必須戴安全帽。

27 **jet** [dʒɛt] 名 C 噴射機

- When Kelsey first saw a **jet** flying across the night sky, she thought it was a shooting star. 凱希第一次看到噴射機飛過夜空時，以為那是一顆流星。

49 Transportation & traffic 運輸與交通 (2)

97

01 **license** [ˋlaɪsn̩s] ❶ 名 C 許可證，執照，牌照
❷ 動 許可，准許，發許可證給……

❶ After getting his driver's **license**, my brother started driving to work. 我哥拿到駕照之後，就開始開車上班。

❷ Sydney is **licensed** to practice law in the state of Rhode Island. 賽德尼獲准在羅德島州從事律師一職。

02 **lifeboat** [ˋlaɪf͵bot] 名 C 救生艇，救生船

- life 生命
- boat 船

● The coast guard dispatched a **lifeboat** to rescue the shipwreck victims. 海上防衛隊派遣救生艇救援船難受害者。

補充 life jacket 救生衣

03 **motor** [ˋmotɚ] 名 C 馬達

● Ralph's wheelchair runs on an electric **motor**. 瑞福的輪椅靠一具電動馬達來運轉。

04 **overtake** [͵ovɚˋtek] 動 ❶ 追上，超過；❷ 突然侵襲，壓倒

- over- 表「在……之上」
- take 取

❶ It is very dangerous to **overtake** a car when you are driving through a tunnel. 在隧道裡超車是非常危險的。

❷ After a hard day's work, exhaustion **overtook** the man; he fell asleep as soon as his head hit the pillow. 在辛苦工作一天後，男子累壞了，他頭一碰到枕頭就睡著了。

05 **pave** [pev] 動 ❶ 鋪，築（路等）；❷ 為……作準備，使容易

❶ All the paths in the park are **paved** with asphalt. 這個公園裡的小路都是用柏油鋪成的。

❷ The peace talks **paved** the way for the end of the war. 那場和平協議為停戰鋪路。

06 **pavement** [ˋpevmənt] 名 C ❶ 鋪過的道路或路面；❷ 人行道

- pave 鋪（路）
- -ment 名 表「結果，產物」

❶ Some people fell on the slippery **pavement**. 有一些人在滑溜的路面上跌倒了。

❷ You can't ride your bike on the **pavement**; it is meant for people to walk on. 你不可以在人行道上騎腳踏車，這裡是給行人走的。

07 **pedal** [ˋpɛdḷ] ❶ 名 C 踏板，腳蹬　❷ 動 騎腳踏車

- ped- 表「腳，足」
- -al 名 表「動作」

❶ Dolores pressed the **pedal** and sped up as she pulled onto the highway. 多洛莉絲一上公路便踩油門加速。

❷ After rushing out of her home, the girl jumped on her bicycle and **pedaled** away. 女孩衝出家後，便跳上腳踏車騎走了。

08 **porter** [ˋportɚ] 名 C 搬運工人，腳夫

- port 持，握
- -er 名 表「人」

● Eric used to be a **porter** at the airport, but he is now a certified airplane pilot.
艾立克以前是一位機場的搬運工人，但現在是一位正式的機師了。

09 **postage** [ˋpostɪdʒ] 名 U 郵資，郵費

- post 郵寄
- -age 名 表「費用」

● The **postage** for international mail and parcels is computed by weight. 國際郵件和包裹的郵資是以重量計算。

10 **route** [rut] ❶ 名 C 路線，航線　❷ 動（按規定路線）寄送或運送

❶ Marina works for an airline company; she plans alternative air **routes**. 瑪瑞娜在一家航空公司工作，負責擬定替代的飛航路線。

❷ The flight to Sydney is **routed** via Hong Kong.
這個航班被安排經香港飛到雪梨。

11 **tow** [to] ❶ 動 拖，拉　❷ 名 C 拖，拉

❶ Dorothy parked her car in a fire zone, so it was **towed** away by the police. 桃樂斯把車停在紅線上，所以車子被警察拖走了。

❷ Hunter's car broke down on the highway; a truck gave him a **tow**. 杭特的車子在高速公路上拋錨了，一台卡車幫忙拖著他的車子。

補充 tow truck 拖吊車

12 **trail** [trel] 名 C ❶（森林或荒野的）小徑；❷ 蹤跡　動 ❸ 跟蹤，追獵

❶ Ken followed his dog up an unmarked **trail** and found a natural spring. 肯跟著他的狗走到一條未標示的小路，發現了一處天然湧泉。

❷ The hound picked up the fox's **trail** by sniffing around the area.
獵犬藉由狐狸留下的氣味來尋找狐狸的蹤跡。

❸ The hunter was **trailing** the possum's paw marks in the fresh snow. 那名獵人正在剛下過雪的地面上追蹤負鼠的腳印。

98

13 **transport** 名 [ˋtræns͵pɔrt] 名 U ❶ 運輸；❷ 交通運輸系統
動 [trænsˋpɔrt] 動 ❸ 運輸，運送

- trans- 表「到……的另一邊」
- port 港

❶ The **transport** of supplies from the port to the central mountain is done by railway.
補給品的運輸是從港口以鐵路的方式運到中央山脈。

❷ The country is improving public **transport** so that people and goods can be carried from one place to another more quickly. 為了更快速地將人或貨物從一地運送到另一地，這個國家正在改善其大眾運輸系統。

❸ The goods will be **transported** from Taiwan to Los Angeles by sea. 貨物將從台灣海運到洛杉磯。

14 **trunk** [trʌŋk] 名 C ❶ 後車廂；❷ 樹幹

❶ Police officers check the **trunk** of every car that enters the capital. 警察檢查所有進入首府車輛的後車廂。

❷ The men chopped down the tree and used the **trunk** to make a canoe. 那些男子砍下樹木，用樹幹做了一艘獨木舟。

15 **van** [væn] 名 C **有蓋小貨車，箱形客貨兩用車**

- The police were chasing a **van** on the freeway while Olive was on her way home. 奧麗芙在回家的路上，看到了警方在高速公路上追逐一輛小貨車。

16 **vehicle** [ˋviɪkḷ] 名 C **車輛，運載工具**

- Every **vehicle** must pay a toll in order to cross the Golden Gate Bridge. 每輛車子都必須繳納通行費，才能通過金門大橋。

17 **wagon** [ˋwægən] 名 C（四輪）運貨馬車

- Jill built an old-style **wagon** to sell fruit at the farmers' market. 吉兒打造了一輛舊式的運貨馬車，用來在農莊市場販賣水果。

18 **shift** [ʃɪft] 動 ❶ 變（速），換（檔）；❷ 移動；❸ 變換，改變
名 ❹ C 輪班，輪班工作時間

❶ Don't forget to **shift** gears when you go down a steep hill. 在開下陡坡路段時，別忘了換檔。

❷ Since the speech was very boring, members of the audience were starting to **shift** uneasily in their seats. 因為那場演講很無聊，聽眾們開始在座位上不安地動來動去。

❸ Feeling very embarrassed, Thera **shifted** hastily to another topic. 席拉感到很尷尬，很快地換了個話題。

❹ At the factory, employees work eight-hour **shifts**; one group starts to work as another group finishes. 這家工廠的工人採八小時輪班制；一組工人開始工作時，另一組就可以休息。

19 **shuttle** [ˋʃʌtl̩] ❶ 名 C 接駁車輛 ❷ 動 短程穿梭般運送

❶ Free **shuttles** between the airport and the bus station are available from 9 a.m. to 6 p.m. Monday through Friday.
往返機場與公車站的免費接駁車，於週一到週五早上九點至晚上六點行駛。

❷ The bus **shuttles** the guests back and forth from the hotel to the airport. 巴士在飯店和機場之間往返穿梭，搭載旅客。

補充 space shuttle 太空梭

20 **smog** [smɑg] 名 U 煙霧

• sm(oke) 煙
• (f)og 霧

● All vehicles must pass annual **smog** tests; owners receive a sticker to put on the car's license plate.
所有的車輛都必須通過年度廢氣檢測，車主會收到一張要貼在車牌上的標籤。

21 **transfer** 動 [trænsˋfɝ] ❶ 動 換車，轉車；❷ 調動，轉換；❸ 改變，轉變
名 [ˋtrænsfɝ] ❹ 名 C 傳輸

❶ To get to the office, Mr. Wang has to take the bus and then **transfer** to the MRT. 王先生得先搭公車再轉搭捷運，才能到達辦公室。

❷ Darcy will be **transferred** from the sales department to another department. 達爾西將從業務部調往另一個部門。

❸ The town's historic image as a quaint fishing village has not been **transferred** to the new development, which is very modern and sleek.
這個小鎮自古以來就是一個古樸的漁村，尚未轉變為以現代和時尚為主的新發展。

❹ The instant **transfer** of vast amounts of data is possible with a high-speed Internet connection.
高速網路的連線，讓快速傳輸大量資料變得可能。

22 **transportation** [ˌtrænspɚˋteʃən] 名 U 運輸工具

• transport 運輸系統
• -ation 名 表「動作」

● With the completion of several public **transportation** projects such as the MRT, people living in the suburbs now have an easier commute to work.
隨著捷運等幾項大眾運輸工程的完成，通勤上班對住在郊區的人來說變得容易許多。

23 **underpass** [ˋʌndɚˌpæs] 名 C 地下通道

• under- 表「在……下」
• pass 穿過，經過

● It is too dangerous for us to cross the railroad tracks; let's take the **underpass**. 穿越鐵軌太危險了，我們還是走地下道吧。

24 **vessel** [ˋvɛsl̩] 名 C 船，艦

● Somali pirates attacked a fishing **vessel** about 300 miles out at sea, and they kidnapped the crew.
索馬利亞海盜在三百英里的外海攻擊一艘漁船，並綁架了船員。

25 **wreck** [rɛk] ❶ 名 C 失事船的殘骸 動 ❷ 使失事，使遇難；❸ 破壞，損害

❶ Divers have discovered the **wreck** of the Titanic.
潛水夫已經發現鐵達尼號的殘骸。

❷ The Titanic was **wrecked** in the Atlantic in 1912 when it hit an iceberg. 鐵達尼號在 1912 年撞上冰山後，於大西洋失事。

❸ Rufus's drinking problem has **wrecked** his career and family life.
魯佛斯的酗酒問題，毀了他的前途和家庭。

50 Media & communication 媒體與溝通

99

01 **accent** [ˋæksɛnt] 名 C 口音，腔調

- Mr. Snow speaks with a strong British **accent**.
史諾先生說話帶有濃重的英國腔。

02 **bulletin** [ˋbʊlətɪn] 名 C ❶ 公告；❷ 會報，期刊

❶ The teacher put a notice on the **bulletin** board.
老師把公告貼在布告欄上。

❷ This is the third time Earline has contributed an article to the foundation's monthly **bulletin**. 這是伊兒琳第三次為該基金會的月刊寫稿。

03 **channel** [ˋtʃænl̩] 名 C ❶ 頻道；❷ 海峽；❸ 途徑，管道，手段

❶ In Taiwan, some cable TV companies have up to 70 or 80 **channels**.
在台灣，一些有線電視台的頻道數多達七、八十個。〔91 年學測補考〕

❷ France and England are separated by the English **Channel**.
英吉利海峽將法國和英國分開。

❸ Painting provides a **channel** for Molly's creativity, and singing is a way for her to express her feelings.
繪畫是茉莉發揮創造力的管道，唱歌則是她表達情感的方式。

04 **chat** [tʃæt] ❶ 動 聊天，閒談 ❷ 名 C 聊天，閒談

❶ My parents often invite their friends over to **chat** and have tea.
我的父母常邀請朋友來家中聊天喝茶。

❷ My grandma often asks the lady next door to come over for a **chat**. They can talk for hours without a break.
我奶奶經常邀請住在隔壁的老太太來家裡聊天，她們可以不間斷地聊上幾個小時。

05 **clue** [klu] 名 C 線索，跡象

- For more than a week, the police have received no new **clues** regarding the missing child.
  一個多禮拜過去了，警方仍然沒有那名失蹤兒童的新線索。

06 **code** [kod] 名 C 代號，密碼

- Mr. Parrish sent a message to his partner using a secret **code** that only the two of them can understand.
  帕里士先生傳了一則簡訊給夥伴，簡訊中使用的代號只有他和夥伴才懂。

補充 zip code（美）／postcode（英） 郵遞區號

07 **communicate** [kəˋmjunə͵ket] 動 ❶ 溝通；❷ 通訊，聯絡

❶ Do your parents **communicate** with each other in a calm and respectful way? 你的父母是以冷靜與尊重的方式來和彼此溝通嗎？

❷ Since moving to the United States, Daphne has **communicated** with her sisters mostly by e-mail.
戴芬妮搬到美國後，大都是用電子郵件和姊妹們聯絡。

08 **communication** [kə͵mjunəˋkeʃən] 名 U 通訊，傳達，交流

- Satellites have an increasingly important role in global **communication**. 衛星在全球通訊中漸形重要。

・communicate 溝通
・-ion 名 表「行為」

09 **converse** [kənˋvɝs] ❶ 動 交談　❷ 形 相反的

・con- 表「一起」
・verse 韻文

❶ Domingo and Randy **conversed** for hours on the phone before they met. 多明哥和蘭迪在見面之前講了好幾個小時的電話。

❷ Maurice thought that the plan was workable, but his colleagues had a **converse** opinion.
摩里斯認為那項計畫可行，但是他的同事持相反的意見。

10 **detail** [ˋditel] 名 ❶ C 細節，詳情；❷ U 細部，局部

❶ Raymond gave us only a general picture of his plan; he didn't tell us all the **details**. 瑞蒙只大略地說了他的計畫，沒有告訴我們全部的細節。

❷ Diane told her friends about her project in **detail** and earned their support. 黛恩把自己的計畫一五一十地告訴朋友，並得到他們的支持。

11 **dialogue** [ˋdaɪə͵lɔg] 名 C ❶ 對話；❷（戲劇、小說等中的）對白

・dia- 表「徹底，完全」
・-logue 表「談話」

❶ The employer finally opened a **dialogue** with his employees in order to exchange views and solve the problem. 雇主終於和雇員們進行對話，以便交換看法並解決問題。

❷ Shakespeare's plays are written in **dialogue** and blank verse.
莎士比亞的劇本是用對白和無韻詩寫成的。

12 **fax** [fæks] ❶ 名 C 傳真 ❷ 動 傳真

❶ Have you received my **fax** regarding the updated schedule?
你有沒有收到我傳真給你的最新時刻表？

❷ Luke **faxed** the application form to the college.
路克把申請表傳真給那一所大學。

13 **gossip** [ˋgɑsəp] ❶ 名 C 閒話，聊天 ❷ 動 閒聊，傳播流言蜚語

❶ Mrs. Baxter didn't take her neighbor's **gossip** seriously.
巴克斯特太太沒有把鄰居的閒話當真。

❷ Those girls always **gossip** about pop singers, talking unkindly about their private lives.
那些女孩常閒聊流行歌手的八卦，缺德地談論他們的私生活。

100 14 **headline** [ˋhɛd͵laɪn] 名 C ❶（報紙等的）標題；❷ 頭條新聞 ❸ 動 給……加標題

- head 頭；上端
- line（詩文的）一行

❶ The front page carried a **headline** that read "A Star Idolized and Haunted, Michael Jackson Dies at 50." 頭版的標題這樣寫著：「受眾人仰慕且令人難以忘懷的超級巨星，麥克傑克遜於 50 歲辭世」。

❷ Mr. Best has been frequently mentioned in the **headlines** because of the scandal. 貝斯特先生常因醜聞出現在頭條新聞中。

❸ The news story was **headlined** "Earthquake Rattles Buildings and Nerves Across Island."
那篇新聞報導的標題是：「地震使建築物咯咯作響，全島都陷入緊張之中」。

15 **inform** [ɪnˋfɔrm] 動 通知，告知

- in- 表「形成」
- form 形狀

● Please **inform** Janet's husband of her safe arrival.
請告知珍妮特的先生，她平安抵達了。

16 **information** [͵ɪnfɚˋmeʃən] 名 U 消息，資訊

- inform 通知
- -ation 名 表「結果」

● The book Anne bought yesterday gives all sorts of useful **information** about nursing a baby.
安昨天買的書，介紹了育嬰的各種實用資訊。

17 **informative** [ɪnˋfɔrmətɪv] 形 提供豐富資料的，增進知識的

- inform 通知
- -ative 形 表「有……性質的」

● The book is not only **informative**, but it is also entertaining; it provides readers with many useful facts and ideas. 這本書不僅知性還很有趣，提供了讀者很多實用的資料和想法。

18 **interrupt** [ˌɪntəˋrʌpt] ❶ 動 打斷講話 動 ❷ 打斷（講話）；❸ 中斷

❶ It is impolite to **interrupt** when someone else is speaking. We should wait until the person finishes his turn.
打斷別人說話是不禮貌的，我們應該等別人先講完。〔92 年學測補考〕

❷ Please don't **interrupt** me. I haven't finished my story.
請不要打斷我，我還沒說完。

❸ The baseball game was **interrupted** by the heavy rain; all the players ran for shelter. 那場棒球比賽因大雨而中斷，所有的球員都跑去躲雨。

19 **interruption** [ˌɪntəˋrʌpʃən] 名 C ❶ 打擾，干擾；❷ 中止，阻礙

- interrupt 打斷
- -ion 名 表「行為」

❶ Harley's girlfriend called him every 20 minutes; the constant **interruptions** interfered with his work.
哈利的女友每 20 分鐘就叩他一次，這樣持續的干擾妨礙了他工作。

❷ The injury to the pitcher's shoulder caused only a minor **interruption** in his career; however, it prevented him from being ready on Opening Day.
肩傷只是稍稍中斷了那位投手的投球生涯，但卻讓他在開幕賽時無法上場。

20 **media** [ˋmidɪə] 名（複）媒體（medium 的複數）

● When the United States declared war on Iraq, the **media** flooded the White House with questions for the president.
美國向伊拉克宣戰時，媒體蜂擁至白宮詢問總統。

21 **medium** [ˋmidɪəm] 名 C ❶ 新聞媒介，傳播媒介；❷ 手段，工具
形 ❸ 中等的，適中的；❹（肉）中等熟度的

❶ The Internet has become a popular and widespread communication **medium**.
電腦網路已經成為最普遍、也最受歡迎的傳播媒介。

❷ They told the story through the **medium** of dance.
他們透過舞蹈的方式來傳達那則故事。

❸ Fred is of **medium** height; he is neither too tall nor too short.
佛瑞德是中等身高，不會太高也不會太矮。

❹ I want my steak **medium**; I don't want it rare or well-done.
我牛排的熟度要中等，不要半熟或全熟。

22 **messenger** [ˋmɛsn̩dʒɚ] 名 C ❶ 使者，信差；❷ 先兆，先驅

- message 訊息
- -er 名 表「人」

❶ In the past, letters were delivered by **messengers** on horseback or by boat. 在過去，信件是由信差騎馬或坐船來傳送。

❷ The wildflowers and other **messengers** of spring are already evident. 野花和其他春天的跡象已處處可見。

23 **poster** [ˋpostɚ] 名 C 海報，廣告畫

- Dolly's collection of film **posters** has grown over the years. 桃麗收藏的電影海報多年來持續增加。

> ・post 張貼
> ・-er 名 表「物」

24 **rumor** [ˋrumɚ] ❶ 名 U 謠言，傳聞 ❷ 動 謠傳，傳說

❶ Have you heard the **rumor** that the president will soon resign?
你聽到校長即將辭職的傳聞了嗎？

❷ It is **rumored** that the old house is haunted, but many people don't think that's true. 謠傳那間老房子在鬧鬼，但有很多人都不相信。

25 **signal** [ˋsɪgn!] 名 C ❶ 信號；❷ 號誌 ❸ 動 以動作向……示意

❶ The satellite suddenly stopped transmitting **signals** during the live broadcast.
在實況轉播期間，衛星通訊的訊號突然中斷了。

> ・sign 記號，符號
> ・-al 名 表「狀態」

❷ A red light is usually used as a warning **signal**.
紅燈通常被用來當作警告的號誌。

❸ The policeman raised his hand, **signaling** the truck to stop.
警察舉起手，示意卡車停下來。

26 **slogan** [ˋslogən] 名 C 口號，標語

- A good **slogan** is short, clear, and powerful.
好的標語應該要簡潔、清楚又有力。

27 **telegram** [ˋtɛlə͵græm] 名 C 電報

- Chad found some **telegrams** that his father had sent home during the war.
查德找到了父親以前在戰爭期間所拍回家的一些電報。

> ・tele- 表「遠距離傳送」
> ・-gram 名 表「……寫的東西」

28 **telegraph** [ˋtɛlə͵græf] ❶ 名 C 電報，電信 ❷ 動 打電報給

❶ Tragic news came by **telegraph** to the Frost family last night.
佛洛斯特家昨晚收到了用電報發送的不幸消息。

> ・tele- 表「遠距離傳送」
> ・-graph 名 表「寫的東西」

❷ Before the popularization of telephones, the siblings **telegraphed** their aunt, who lived far away, when they needed to contact her.
在電話普及之前，那些兄弟姊妹有事要連絡住在遠方的伯母時，就會發電報給她。

51 Medicine & sickness
醫學與疾病 (1)

101

01 **AIDS** [edz] 名 U **愛滋病，後天性免疫不全症候群**

- **AIDS** is a deadly disease caused by a virus that disables the body's defenses against infections.
  愛滋病是感染了會破壞身體防衛系統對抗其他感染的病毒，是一種致命疾病。

02 **aspirin** [ˋæspərɪn] 名 U **阿斯匹靈**

- Whenever Pedro has a headache, he takes **aspirin** for relief.
  裴卓只要一頭痛，就會吃阿斯匹靈鎮痛。

03 **bacteria** [bækˋtɪrɪə] 名（複）細菌（**bacterium** 的複數形）

- The doctor told Nelson that his skin rash is caused by pathogenic **bacteria**, and she prescribed some antibacterial cream.
  醫生告訴尼爾森，他的皮膚疹是由病菌引起的，並開了一些抑菌藥膏給他。

04 **bandage** [ˋbændɪdʒ] ❶ 名 C **繃帶** ❷ 動 **用繃帶包紮**

・band 帶
・-age 名 表「使用」

❶ Lydia applied **bandages** to the scrapes she incurred after riding her bike into the tree.
莉迪雅騎自行車時撞上了樹有擦傷，她在傷口上綁上了繃帶。

❷ The nurse carefully washed the patient's wound and then **bandaged** it. 護士仔細幫病人清洗傷口，然後進行包紮。

05 **bleed** [blid] 動 **流血，出血**

- Juan's finger is **bleeding** because he cut himself when preparing the vegetables. 璜切菜時不小心切到手指，一直流血。

06 **clinic** [ˋklɪnɪk] 名 C **診所** 形 clinical 臨床的

- Charlene felt dizzy this afternoon, so she called the local health **clinic** and made an appointment to see a doctor.
  查琳今天下午覺得頭暈，所以打電話到當地診所預約掛號。

07 **cripple** [ˋkrɪpl] 名 C ❶ **跛子，殘廢的人**
動 ❷ **使成跛子，使殘廢**；❸ **使陷入癱瘓**

❶ Today, it is considered offensive to refer to someone who cannot walk as a **cripple**. 在今天如果稱呼不能行走的人為「跛子」，被視為是一種冒犯。

❷ The man was **crippled** in a serious car crash; he is no longer able to walk. 那個男人在一場嚴重的車禍中殘廢了，從此再也無法行走。

❸ As a result of the accident, southbound traffic was **crippled** from about 9 p.m. to 12 a.m. 由於一場事故，南行交通從晚上 9 點到 12 點陷入癱瘓。

08 **crutch** [krʌtʃ] 名 C 丁形拐杖，（支在腋下的）撐拐

- Sherman is walking with a **crutch** because he broke his right leg last week. 謝爾曼上週摔斷了右腿，現在拄著拐杖走路。

09 **disease** [dɪˋziz] 名 C 疾病

- dis- 表「不」
- ease 安逸

- Rats and cockroaches that move from the sewer into the kitchen can spread **diseases**.
老鼠和蟑螂經由下水道進入廚房，能散播疾病。

10 **disorder** [dɪsˋɔrdɚ] 名 ❶ C 失調，不適，小病；❷ U 混亂，無秩序

- dis- 表「否定」
- order 秩序

❶ Sheldon has had a severe eating **disorder** for two years. 謝爾登這兩年來為嚴重飲食失調所苦。

❷ After the party, the living room was in a state of **disorder**; it took us three hours to tidy it up.
派對過後客廳一片混亂，我們花了三個小時才把它整理乾淨。

102 11 **dose** [dos] ❶ 名 C（藥物等的）一劑，一帖；❷（尤指苦事的）一次，一番 ❸ 動 給……服藥

❶ Dr. Roberts told Stanley to take a **dose** of the medicine three times a day for five days. 羅伯茲醫生要史丹利每天服藥三次，連續服用五天。

❷ I had a bad **dose** of flu last week, so I took three days off.
我上個星期得了嚴重的流感，所以請了三天假。

❸ Robert had a serious headache; he **dosed** himself up with painkillers and went to bed.
羅伯特頭痛得很厲害，他吃了止痛藥，然後上床睡覺。

12 **faint** [fent] 形 ❶ 頭暈的；❷ 微弱的；❸（希望等）微小的 ❹ 動 昏厥，暈倒

❶ Tanya felt **faint** for a moment after she stood up quickly.
譚雅忽然站了起來，隨即感到一陣暈眩。

❷ The patient's breathing has become **faint**; he is dying.
病人的呼吸逐漸微弱，瀕臨死亡。

❸ The woman held out **faint** hope that her husband would be cured, even though the doctor told her it was unlikely.
即使醫生告知可能性不大，女子抱著一絲希望，認為丈夫的病可以治癒。

❹ The poor woman **fainted** when she heard that her son was badly injured in the accident. 聽到兒子在事故中身受重傷，那位可憐的婦人暈了過去。

13 **fatal** [ˋfetl̩] 形 致命的，生死攸關的

・fate 命運
・-al 形 表「……的」

● Adrian survived a nearly **fatal** accident and recovered completely. 亞德安從幾近身亡的意外中完全康復了。

14 **formula** [ˋfɔrmjələ] 名 C ❶ 配方，處方；❷ 公式，方程式

・form 形成

❶ The **formula** Dr. Young uses to treat skin disease is the most effective cure. 楊醫生用來治療皮膚病的處方，是最有效的療法。

❷ When you know the circumference, you can use the **formula** to find the diameter. 如果你知道周長，就可以用這個公式算出直徑。

15 **germ** [dʒɝm] 名 C 微生物，細菌

● The surface of this table contains countless **germs** that are invisible to the naked eye. 這張桌子表面藏有無數用肉眼看不到的細菌。

16 **heal** [hil] 動 治癒，痊癒

● Randy believes that time can **heal** all wounds, but it doesn't stop him from seeing a doctor.
藍迪相信時間能夠療傷，但他生病時還是會去看醫生。

17 **healthful** [ˋhɛlθfəl] 形 有益健康的　名 health 健康 形 healthy 健康的

● A **healthful** diet keeps the waistline slim and the skin clear. 健康的飲食能保持身材苗條、肌膚有光澤。

・health 健康
・-ful 形 表「有……傾向的」

18 **infect** [ɪnˋfɛkt] 動 ❶ 傳染，感染；❷ 使受影響，感染（情緒）

❶ Thousands of people in Mexico were **infected** with the H1N1 virus. 在墨西哥，有數以千計的人感染了 H1N1 流感病毒。

❷ Ralph has a genuine and bright personality; his laughter easily **infects** people around him.
勞福的個性坦率開朗，他的笑聲能輕易感染週遭的人。

19 **infection** [ɪnˋfɛkʃən] 名 ❶ C 傳染病；❷ U 傳染

・infect 傳染
・-ion 名 表「行為的狀態」

❶ If you don't treat an **infection** right away, it can spread. 傳染病若不即時處理，疫情會擴大。

❷ Doctors suggest that people wash their hands more frequently to reduce the risk of **infection** from swine flu.
醫生建議民眾要經常洗手，以降低感染豬流感的風險。

20 **injure** [ˋɪndʒɚ] 動 傷害，損害，毀壞

- The police reported that two people who were **injured** in the car accident have been sent to the hospital.
  警方表示，在車禍中受傷的兩名傷者已經被送往醫院。

補充 the injured 傷者

21 **injury** [ˋɪndʒərɪ] 名 C 傷害，損害，毀壞 同義 harm 傷害

- injure 傷害
- -y 名 表「狀態」

- John sustained a serious **injury** to his head because of that woman's drunk driving.
  那名女性酒醉駕車，造成約翰的頭部受到嚴重損傷。

22 **itch** [ɪtʃ] ❶ 動 發癢 ❷ 名 C 癢

❶ After eating seafood, Grover **itched** all over. The doctor asked him not to scratch. 格羅佛吃完海鮮後全身發癢；醫生囑咐他不要抓。

❷ My father asked me to scratch his back, as he had an **itch**.
我爸爸叫我幫他抓背，因為他背上很癢。

相關用法 形 **itchy** 癢的

- The man felt itchy all over, so he kept scratching his skin.
  男子覺得全身發癢，所以一直抓皮膚。

52 Medicine & sickness
醫學與疾病 (2)

103

01 **medical** [ˋmɛdɪkḷ] 形 醫學的，醫療的 名 medication 藥物治療

- Cynthia plans to go to **medical** school because she is very concerned about the quality of human life.
  辛希雅關心人類的生活品質，所以打算就讀醫學院。

02 **nearsighted** [ˋnɪrˋsaɪtɪd] 形 ❶ 近視眼的；❷ 目光短淺的，沒有遠見的

❶ I'm **nearsighted**, so I have to wear eyeglasses when I'm driving.
我有近視，所以開車時得戴眼鏡。

- near 近
- sight 看
- -ed 形 表「有……特徵的」

❷ Their plan was **nearsighted**; they didn't think carefully about the possible effects. 他們的計畫短視近利，沒有慎重考慮可能的影響。

03 **operation** [͵ɑpəˋreʃən] 名 ❶ C 手術；❷ U 操作；❸ U 經營

- operate 操作
- -ion 名 表「行為」

❶ Eileen is going to have a minor **operation** on her shoulder this afternoon. 今天下午艾琳要動一個肩膀的小手術。

❷ The machine is designed for easy **operation**; just press the button, and it will start to work.
這台機器設計成簡單操作。只要按下按鈕，它就會開始運作。

❸ The **operation** of a company requires labor and capital.
一家公司的經營需要人力和資本。

相關片語 **come into operation 實施**

- The new traffic rule will go into operation next month.
新版交通規則將會於下個月正式上路。

04 **pale** [pel] 形 ❶ 蒼白的；❷（顏色）淡的 ❸ 動 使蒼白

❶ Kay must be sick, as she looked **pale** today.
凱一定是生病了，她今天臉色看起來好蒼白。

❷ Howard has dark brown hair and **pale** blue eyes.
霍爾有深棕色的頭髮，以及淺藍色的眼睛。

❸ The woman's cheeks **paled** with tiredness; she needed a good rest. 那個女人的臉頰因疲倦變得蒼白，她需要好好休息一下。

05 **physician** [fɪˋzɪʃən] 名 C 醫師，內科醫生

- physic 醫治
- -ian 名 表「專家」

- The **physician** hopes this new medicine will cure Jim's illness. 那位醫師希望這款新藥能治好吉姆的病。

06 **physicist** [ˋfɪzɪsɪst] 名 C 物理學家

- physic 醫治
- -ist 名 表「做……的人」

- Einstein is one of the most influential **physicists** in history. 愛因斯坦是歷史上最具影響力的物理學家之一。

07 **pill** [pɪl] 名 C 藥丸，藥片

- Jessica has trouble swallowing **pills**, so her doctor gave her liquid medicine instead. 潔西卡無法吞嚥藥丸，醫生就改開藥水給她。

08 **recover** [rɪˋkʌvɚ] 動 ❶ 恢復健康，復原；❷ 重新找到；❸ 恢復

- re- 表「重新」
- cover 覆蓋

❶ It took Samuel a long time to **recover** from the viral infection. 山謬經歷好長一段時間才從病毒感染中恢復健康。

❷ Baird lost his wallet at the MRT station this morning, but he **recovered** it a few hours later.
拜爾德今天早上在捷運站遺失了皮夾，不過他幾小時後就找到了。

❸ Since the operation, the patient has gradually **recovered** his health and will be released soon from the hospital.
手術過後，這個病人已經逐漸恢復了健康，很快就會出院了。

09 **recovery** [rɪˋkʌvərɪ] 名 C ❶ 恢復，復甦，痊癒；❷ 重獲，復得

- recover 恢復健康
- -y 名 表「狀態」

❶ It is unknown if the forest will have a full **recovery** from last year's wildfires.
那座森林去年遭野火侵襲，是否可以完全恢復還是未知數。

❷ The company offered a $10,000 reward for the **recovery** of the stolen money. 那家公司提供一萬美金當作尋回被盜金錢的報償。

用法 recover from 從……中恢復，復原

10 **remedy** [ˋrɛmədɪ] 名 C ❶ 治療，藥物；❷ 補救法 ❸ 動 補救，糾正

❶ The doctor gave me a **remedy** for headaches; after taking the medicine, I felt less pain.
醫生開給我治療頭疼的藥物。服藥過後，疼痛已經降低。

❷ Scientists are trying to find a **remedy** for global warming, but they know there's no simple solution to this problem.
科學家們正試圖找尋全球暖化的解決之道，但是他們知道這並非容易之事。

❸ Although the manager apologized many times for his poor decision, there was nothing he could do to **remedy** his mistake.
儘管經理再三為他不良的決策道歉，但已於事無補。

11 **resistance** [rɪˋzɪstəns] 名 ❶ U 抵抗力；❷（單數）抵抗，反抗

- resist 抵抗
- -ance 名 表「情況」

❶ René catches colds easily because his **resistance** is very low. 雷恩的抵抗力很差，很容易感冒。

❷ The rebels put up a stronger **resistance** than the government expected; it took the army a month to suppress the revolt.
反叛分子的抵抗比政府預期的更頑強，政府軍隊費時一個月才鎮壓住叛亂。

12 **sore** [sor] 形 疼痛發炎的

- Robert woke up this morning with a **sore** throat and runny nose.
羅伯特今天早上起床後，發現自己喉嚨痛又流鼻水。

補充 sore throat 喉嚨痛

13 **sprain** [spren] 動 扭傷

- Sally **sprained** her ankle playing basketball, and now she must rest it for six weeks. 莎莉打籃球時扭傷了腳踝，現在只好休養六星期。

104

14 **stiff** [stɪf] 形 僵硬的

- After typing for 10 hours, Sebastian rubbed his **stiff** neck with a warm towel. 賽巴斯丁打字打了 10 個小時後，用熱毛巾按按僵硬的脖子。

15 **stitch** [stɪtʃ] ❶ 名 C（縫合傷口的）針線　❷ 動 縫

❶ Allen fell down a stairway and had to have some **stitches** in his forehead. 艾倫從樓梯上摔落，額頭上縫了好幾針。

❷ Chloe cut her arm on the broken glass; the doctor **stitched** up the cut and left it to heal.
克羅伊的手臂被碎玻璃割破了。醫生縫合了傷口，等它自己癒合。

16 **suffer** [ˋsʌfɚ] ❶ 動 受苦，患病；❷ 遭受，經歷

❶ Pablo **suffered** from severe depression after he returned from the war. 帕布羅從戰場回來後，就罹患了重度憂鬱症。

❷ The soccer team **suffered** a major defeat in the match; it was an unpleasant experience for the players.
那支足球隊在比賽中遭受重大挫敗，對球員來說，那是一次很不愉快的經驗。

相關用法 名 **suffering**（身體、精神上的）痛苦，苦惱

- The war broke out and caused great hardship and suffering for the people in the area. 戰爭爆發了，並對那個地區的人們帶來了極大的艱難與痛苦。

17 **swell** [swɛl] 動 腫起，腫脹

- Jim's whole forehead **swelled** after a mosquito bit him.
吉姆的額頭被一隻蚊子叮咬後，整個腫起來了。

18 **tablet** [ˋtæblɪt] 名 C 藥片　同義 pill 藥片；藥丸

・tab 小片；小標牌
・-let 名 表「小的」

- Ray takes **tablets** made from Chinese herbal medicines for his skin problem. 瑞服用中藥錠來治療皮膚病。

19 **weaken** [ˋwikən] ❶ 動 使衰弱；❷ 變軟弱，動搖

・weak 衰弱的
・-en 動 表「變為……」

❶ The old man has been **weakened** by his long illness; he doesn't have much physical strength anymore.
這名老人因久病而變得衰弱，他現在沒有太多體力。

❷ No matter what problems arise, Raven's strong willpower never **weakens**. 瑞文不論遇到什麼麻煩，堅強的意志力從未動搖。

20 **shortsighted** [ˋʃɔrtˋsaɪtɪd] 形 ❶ 近視的；❷ 目光短淺的，無先見的

・short 短的
・sight 視力
・-ed 表「有……特徵的」

❶ The student is **shortsighted**; he has to wear glasses to see the board at the front of the classroom.
這名學生有近視，他連坐在教室前排都得戴眼鏡才看得清楚黑板。

❷ The policy is **shortsighted**; it seems good now, but it may cause some problems in the future.
這個政策缺乏遠見。現階段看來似乎不錯，但在未來可能會產生某些問題。

21 **sneeze** [sniz] ❶ 名 C 噴嚏（聲） ❷ 動 打噴嚏

❶ In the United States, saying "Bless you" is customary whenever someone **sneezes**. 在美國，有人打噴嚏時，旁人說句「願你受保佑」是項習俗。

❷ Having caught a bad cold, Myron coughed and **sneezed** all week. 麥倫得了重感冒，整週都在咳嗽、打噴嚏。

22 **stroke** [strok] 名 C ❶（病）突然發作，中風；❷（寫字等的）一筆；❸（幸運等的）機緣 動 ❹ 輕撫，撫摸

❶ The old man had a **stroke** last night; the doctor said an artery in his brain suddenly burst.
那名老人昨天晚上中風了。醫生表示他有一條腦血管突然破裂了。

❷ Kay always signs her full name in two **strokes**.
凱總是兩筆就簽完全名。

❸ By a **stroke** of luck, I found my lost purse in the park.
非常幸運的是，我在公園裡找回了遺失的皮包。

❹ The man put his hand on his dog's head and **stroked** it gently.
男子把手放在自己的小狗頭上，輕輕撫摸牠。

23 **surgeon** [ˋsɝdʒən] 名 C 外科醫生

- Steady hands and intense concentration are required to be a good **surgeon**. 要成為優秀的外科醫生，就必須做到手穩心定。

24 **surgery** [ˋsɝdʒərɪ] 名 U（外科）手術

- Cosmetic **surgery** can change one's outer appearance, but can it change one's heart? 整形手術可以改變外貌，但它可以改變內在嗎？

25 **virus** [ˋvaɪrəs] 名 C ❶ 病毒，濾過性病毒；❷【電腦】病毒

❶ Scientists are trying to understand how the **virus** mutates and spreads. 科學家正試圖了解病毒突變和散布的模式。

❷ The **virus** attached to the email may corrupt your hard disk.
附加在那封電子郵件的病毒可能會損毀你的硬碟。

Part 5 →

Nature
自然

53 Animals & plants 動物與植物 (1)

105

01 **beak** [bik] 名 C（鷹等的）鳥嘴

- The woodpecker's **beak** is so strong that it can penetrate hardwood trees. 啄木鳥的嘴非常堅硬，能夠刺穿堅硬樹木。

02 **beast** [bist] 名 C 野獸

- Some formerly wild **beasts**, including dogs and cats, have been domesticated by humans.
從前野生的動物包括犬類及貓類，已由人類馴養了。

03 **bloom** [blum] ❶ 名 C 花　❷ 動 開花　同義 名 動 blossom 花；開花

❶ In autumn, the tree produces white and pink **blooms**.
在秋天，這棵樹會開出白色和粉紅色的花。

❷ Many people visit the park to see the tulips that **bloom** in early March. 許多人造訪這座公園，為了觀賞從三月初就綻放的鬱金香。

相關片語 **in (full) bloom** 盛開

- Ian is planning to visit Japan when the cherry trees are in full bloom.
伊恩計畫在櫻花盛開時去日本玩。

04 **blossom** [ˋblɑsəm] 名 ❶ C（尤指果樹的）花　動 ❷ 開花；❸ 發展成

❶ When Richard walked home today, he noticed many **blossoms** on the magnolia trees. 理查今天走路回家時，發現木蘭樹上開了許多花。

❷ Last year, cherry trees in Tokyo **blossomed** earlier than usual because of global warming.
去年，由於全球暖化，東京的櫻花樹比以前更早開花。

❸ Since several casinos opened here, the desert town has **blossomed** into a famous tourist spot.
在幾家賭場開業之後，那個沙漠小鎮已經發展成為一個著名的觀光景點。

相關片語 **in (full) blossom** 盛開

- The apple tree in the backyard is in blossom; soon it will yield plenty of fruit. 後院裡的蘋果樹開花了，不久它就會結很多果實。

05 **bud** [bʌd] ❶ 名 C 葉芽，花蕾　❷ 動 發芽

❶ Betty won't pick the **buds** in the garden until they are in full bloom. 在花園裡的花蕾盛開前，貝琪不會把它們摘下來。

❷ As spring approaches, all the trees are **budding**.
隨著春天的腳步接近，所有樹木都在發芽。

06 **buffalo** [ˋbʌfḷˏo] 名 C 水牛，（北美）野牛

- The African **buffalo** is similar to a large cow with long curved horns. 非洲水牛的樣子貌似大型牛隻戴著又長又彎的角。

07 **bull** [bʊl] 名 C 公牛

- The rancher selects the strongest **bull** to father the next generation of cattle. 牧牛人挑選最強壯的種牛來生小牛。

08 **bush** [bʊʃ] 名 C 灌木叢

- Evelyn has great fun playing hide-and-seek in the **bushes** of her neighborhood park.
伊芙琳在住家附近公園的灌木叢中，玩捉迷藏玩得很高興。

相關片語 **beat about/around the bush** 拐彎抹角

- Don't beat around the bush. Get to the point! 不要拐彎抹角。說重點！

09 **caterpillar** [ˋkætɚˏpɪlɚ] 名 C 毛毛蟲

- Joy was amazed to watch a **caterpillar** spin a cocoon and then emerge as a butterfly. 喬伊看到毛毛蟲結繭後，蛻化成了蝴蝶，覺得很神奇。

10 **cattle** [ˋkætḷ] 名（集合名詞）（總稱）牛

- Cowboys use dogs and horses to help them herd **cattle**.
牧牛人利用狗和馬幫忙牧牛。

11 **creature** [ˋkritʃɚ] 名 C 生物，動物

- There are various kinds of microscopic **creatures** in a drop of water. 一滴水裡包含多種微生物。

> ▪ create 創造
> ▪ -ure 名 表「動作，過程」

12 **cricket** [ˋkrɪkɪt] 名 ❶ C 蟋蟀；❷ U 板球

❶ The sound of **crickets** chirping on an otherwise quiet country night is very peaceful.
在特別安靜的鄉間夜晚，蟋蟀的唧唧聲，顯得十分祥和。

❷ **Cricket** is a well-known English outdoor game.
板球是英國盛行的一種戶外球賽。

13 **feather** [ˋfɛðɚ] 名 U 羽毛

- Amy is used to sleeping on pillows and comforters stuffed with goose **feathers**. 艾咪睡覺時，習慣蓋鵝毛棉被、睡鵝毛枕頭。

106

14 **fertile** [ˋfɝtḷ] 形 多產的，肥沃的 名 fertility 肥沃 名 fertilizer 肥料

- Adam's **fertile** vineyard enables him to make a large annual profit. 亞當的葡萄園產量豐盛，讓他賺進一筆可觀的年收益。

15 **fossil** [ˋfɑsḷ] 名 C 化石

- Paleontologists study **fossils** to learn more about dinosaurs. 古生物學家研究化石，以便進一步了解恐龍。

16 **fragrance** [ˋfregrəns] 名 U 芬芳，香味 同義 scent 香味

- fragrant 芳香的
- -ance 名 表「狀況」

- Ann enjoyed going to the flower market. She believes that the **fragrance** of flowers refreshes her mind. 安很喜歡去花市，她認為花香能幫她重新提振精神。

17 **fragrant** [ˋfregrənt] 形 香的，芳香的 名 fragrance 香味

- From as far away as the bridge, I could smell the **fragrant** scent of incense burning in the Buddhist temple. 遠遠在橋的那端，我就能聞到佛寺中焚香的香味。

18 **fur** [fɝ] 名 ❶ U（獸類的）毛；❷ C 毛皮製品

❶ **Fur** coats and hats are required for the cold northern winters. 北方的寒冬裡，必須穿上毛皮大衣、戴上毛製帽子。

❷ Today, more and more people are against wearing furs; they think killing animals just for their **fur** is cruel and inhumane. 今天有越來越多人反對穿皮草。他們認為，只是為了毛皮而殺害動物既殘酷又不人道。

19 **grasshopper** [ˋgræs͵hɑpɚ] 名 C 蚱蜢

- grass 草
- hopper 跳蟲

- On summer evenings, male **grasshoppers** rub their back legs against their front wings, like the sound of a thousand violins. 夏夜裡，雄蚱蜢一齊用後腳摩擦前翅，猶如上千支小提琴齊聲演奏。

20 **harvest** [ˋhɑrvɪst] ❶ 名 C 收割，收穫 ❷ 動 收割

❶ The six-month drought in the central valley has severely decreased this year's bean **harvest**. 中央谷地遭逢六個月的乾旱，導致今年的豆類收成慘澹。

❷ The farmer tried to **harvest** the vegetables before the typhoon came. 農夫企圖在颱風侵襲之前收割蔬菜。

21 **hatch** [hætʃ] ❶ 動 孵化；❷ 孵（蛋）

❶ Stephanie enjoys visiting her grandmother's chicken farm to watch the baby chicks **hatch**. 史蒂芬妮喜歡去祖母的雞舍看小雞孵化。

❷ It will take the hen a few more hours to **hatch** her eggs. 母雞還需要幾個小時才能將蛋孵化。

22 **hawk** [hɔk] 名 C 鷹，隼

- The feathers of **hawks** are used by Native Americans for decoration. 印地安人用老鷹羽毛做裝飾。

23 **hay** [he] 名 U 乾草

- Four bales of **hay** are sent to Holly's farm every month to feed the horses. 荷莉的農場每個月都會進四大捆餵馬用的乾草。

24 **herd** [hɝd] 名 C 畜群，牧群

- The **herd** of sheep stays close together whenever danger appears. 羊群遇到危險時，會緊靠一起。

25 **hive** [haɪv] 名 C 蜂巢

- Every so often, Roger harvests the fresh honey made by the bees in the **hives**. 羅傑偶爾會從蜂巢內採集新鮮蜂蜜。

54 Animals & plants 動物與植物 (2)

107

01 **horn** [hɔrn] 名 C 角

- Buying or selling the **horns** of rhinos is illegal because the animals are endangered. 犀牛瀕臨絕種，所以買賣犀牛角是非法的。

02 **jungle** [ˋdʒʌŋg!] 名 C 叢林

- Many valuable medicines come from plants that grow in the **jungle**. 許多珍貴的藥材產自叢林植物。

補充 concrete jungle 水泥叢林（都市建築雜亂無章）

03 **kangaroo** [ˌkæŋgəˋru] 名 C 袋鼠

- A **kangaroo** is a large Australian animal with a strong tail and powerful back legs that it uses for leaping.
  袋鼠是澳洲一種大型動物，有強壯的尾巴和用來跳躍的有力後腿。

04 **lobster** [ˋlɑbstɚ] 名 ❶ C 龍蝦；❷ U 龍蝦肉

❶ A **lobster's** shell is black but turns bright red when it is boiled.
龍蝦的殼是黑色的，但是當煮熟後就變成亮紅色。

❷ Since Bill loves to eat **lobster**, he opened up his own seafood restaurant. 比爾愛吃龍蝦，所以自己開了一家海鮮餐館。

05 **oak** [ok] 名 C 橡樹

- **Oaks** can be found in many northern countries; they can live to be hundreds of years old. 北方許多國家都有橡樹生長。它們可以活上數百年。

06 **organic** [ɔrˋgænɪk] 形 有機的　名 organism 有機體

- organ 器官
- -ic 形 表「有……特性的」

- Cheryl's greenhouse produces tons of **organic** vegetables every year. 琪莉兒的溫室每年生產上噸的有機蔬菜。

07 **paw** [pɔ] 名 C 爪子

- Jenny has trained her dog to keep its **paws** off her guests' clothes. 珍妮訓練她的狗不要用爪子抓客人的衣服。

08 **pest** [pɛst] 名 C ❶ 害蟲，有害的植物；❷ 討厭鬼，害人精

❶ Some of the crops are being destroyed by **pests**; the farmer is using chemicals to kill the bugs.
有些作物遭到害蟲危害，農夫正在用農藥除蟲。

❷ Whenever Rebecca gets together with her friends, she treats her little brother like he is a **pest**.
芮貝卡只要和朋友在一起，就會嫌小弟是討厭鬼。

09 **petal** [ˋpɛtḷ] 名 C 花瓣

- Laura collected some rose **petals** from her garden to make greeting cards. 蘿拉從自家花園採來一些玫瑰花瓣做賀卡。

10 **pine** [paɪn] ❶ 名 C 松樹　❷ 動 憔悴，消瘦

❶ Jason used some fallen **pines** to build a small cabin close to the lake. 傑森利用一些倒下的松樹木材，在鄰近湖泊處建了一座小屋。

❷ The widow **pined** away; she missed her husband so much that she became very sick and weak.
那名寡婦日益消瘦。她太思念她的丈夫，以致於生病又衰弱。

11 **pony** [ˋponɪ] 名 C 矮種馬，小馬

- Ronnie will never forget the first time he rode a **pony** and fell off. 羅尼永遠忘不了，他第一次騎小馬摔下來的事。

補充 ponytail 名 馬尾（髮型）

12 **scrub** [skrʌb] ❶ 名 U 矮樹叢，灌木叢　❷ 動 用力擦洗

❶ The **scrub** behind Steve's backyard is home to wild rabbits and mice. 史蒂夫後院外的矮樹叢，是野生兔子與老鼠的家。

❷ Doreen **scrubbed** the kitchen floor hard to remove the stains.
多琳用力刷洗廚房地板，想要除去汙跡。

108 13 **spin** [spɪn] 動 ❶（蜘蛛等）吐（絲），結（網）；❷ 使旋轉

❶ Spiders **spin** webs to catch flying insects. 蜘蛛結網來獵食飛蟲。

❷ Lester is good at **spinning** a basketball on his fingertip.
里斯特擅長用指尖旋轉籃球。

14 **sting** [stɪŋ] 動 ❶ 刺，叮；❷（心靈、感情上的）刺痛　❸ 名 C 刺，螫針

❶ While picking flowers, the boy felt a sharp pain; he had been **stung** on the hand by a bee. 男孩在摘花時被一隻蜜蜂叮到手，感到劇烈疼痛。

❷ Those harsh words from Cedric **stung** his friends.
賽德里克說的重話，深深刺痛了朋友的心。

❸ Some insects, such as bees and scorpions, have **stings**.
像蜜蜂和蠍子這類昆蟲有刺。

15 **tortoise** [ˋtɔrtəs] 名 U 陸龜，烏龜

- The desert **tortoise** can live for more than 100 years.
沙漠陸龜能活一百多年。

16 **tulip** [ˋtjuləp] 名 C 鬱金香

- A bouquet of violets and yellow **tulips** was sent to Miranda on Valentine's Day. 情人節當天，米蘭達收到一束紫色和黃色的鬱金香。

17 **twig** [twɪg] 名 C 細枝，嫩枝

- Teresa used **twigs** and shredded newspapers to start a campfire.
泰瑞莎用小樹枝和碎報紙生營火。

18 **web** [wɛb] 名 C **網狀物，蜘蛛網**

- The trees cast a complex **web** of shadows on the lawn.
  樹林在草地上倒映出一片複雜的網狀樹影。

補充 www=World Wide Web 全球資訊網

19 **weed** [wid] 名 C **雜草，野草**

- After returning from her six-month journey, Jill found her garden overrun with **weeds**. 吉兒在結束六個月的旅行後，發現她的花園中雜草蔓生。

20 **wheat** [hwit] 名 U **小麥**

- **Wheat** is a grain that can be milled into flour for bread and cakes. 小麥是一種穀物，可以磨成麵粉來製作麵包或蛋糕。

21 **willow** [ˋwɪlo] 名 C **柳樹**

- Alex enjoys reading books under the shade of the **willow** in the park. 艾力克斯喜歡在公園的柳樹蔭下閱讀。

22 **seagull** [ˋsigʌl] 名 C **海鷗**

- sea 海
- gull 鷗

- When Louis has his lunch on the beach, he always feeds the **seagulls**. 路易斯在海灘上享受午餐時，都會餵食海鷗。

23 **sparrow** [ˋspæro] 名 C **麻雀**

- Outside of Anita's window, a couple of **sparrows** have made a nest. 有一對麻雀在雅妮妲的窗外築了一個巢。

24 **species** [ˋspiʃiz] 名 C **【生】(物)種**

- Humans are the only **species** that has developed written language. 人類是唯一發展出文字的物種。

25 **stem** [stɛm] ❶ 名 C **莖** ❷ 動 **起源於** 同義 名 stalk 莖

❶ Leaves and flowers have grown from the long, thin **stem**.
葉子和花從細長的莖裡長了出來。

❷ Ellen's career as a chef **stemmed** from her fond memories of cooking with her mother.
艾倫的廚師職涯，源自於和媽媽一起做飯的快樂回憶。

55 Religion & supernatural 宗教與超自然

109

01 **angel** [ˋendʒḷ] 名 C ❶ 天使；❷ 天使般的人　反義 devil, demon 惡魔

❶ It is said that there are many **angels** in Heaven.
據說天堂裡住著許多天使。

❷ Little Millie smiles like an **angel**. 小米莉笑得像個天使。

02 **Bible** [ˋbaɪbḷ] 名 C 聖經

- Valerie finds daily inspiration in reading the Holy **Bible**.
法樂莉每天讀聖經，從中找到了啟示。

03 **bless** [blɛs] 動 ❶ 為……祝福；❷ 保佑；❸ 使有幸得到

❶ At the end of the mass, Father **blessed** the congregation.
在彌撒的最後，神父為會眾祈福。

❷ Whenever a person sneezes, people around him or her always say "**Bless** you." 只要有人打噴嚏，周圍的人就會說「祝福你」。

❸ Mozart was **blessed** with great musical talent. When he was little, he could pick up a tune instantly on the piano.
莫札特的音樂天分十分優異，小時候他能隨即彈奏出一首鋼琴曲。

用法 be blessed with 幸運地被賜予

04 **devil** [ˋdɛvḷ] 名 C 魔鬼，惡魔

- In a sixteenth-century German folktale, Faust sells his soul to the **devil**. 在一則十六世紀的德國民間故事裡，浮士德把他的靈魂賣給了魔鬼。

05 **divine** [dəˋvaɪn] 形 神聖的

- When Danielle meditates, she is often absorbed in **divine** bliss.
丹妮兒冥思時，常沉浸在神聖的至善至樂中。

06 **fairy** [ˋfɛrɪ] 名 C 小妖精，仙女

- Ruby has believed in the existence of **fairies** since she was a child. 盧比從小就相信仙女的存在。

補充 fairy tale 童話故事

- fay 仙女，妖精
- -ery 名 表「……類的事物」

07 **faith** [feθ] 名 U ❶（宗教）信仰；❷ 信任，信念

❶ Alice is very religious; she never loses her **faith**, no matter what happens. 愛麗絲非常虔誠。不管發生什麼事情，她都不曾失去她的宗教信仰。

❷ After being treated wrongly, Eleanor lost her **faith** in humanity, but not her personal morality.
艾琳諾在受到不公平的對待之後，失去了對人性的信任，只相信自己的個人道德。

用法 have faith in 對……有信心

08 **fate** [fet] 名 U 命運

● Do you believe we can change our **fate**?
你相信我們能改變自己的命運嗎？

09 **heaven** [ˋhɛvən] 名 U ❶ 天堂；❷ 極樂，極樂之地 形 heavenly 天國的

❶ **Heaven** is believed to be the home of God and the place where good people go when they die.
有人相信天堂是上帝的家，也是善良之人死後去的地方。

❷ Bertha felt like she was in **heaven** when she had a massage last night. 波莎昨夜享受按摩時，感覺好像身在天堂。

10 **hell** [hɛl] 名 U ❶ 地獄，冥府；❷ 悲慘境地，極大的困境；❸（用於加強語氣）究竟，到底

❶ **Hell** is believed to be the home of devils and the place where bad people go after they die. 地獄被認為是惡魔的家，也是壞人死後會去的地方。

❷ The patient with terminal cancer suffered greatly; the last two months of his life were **hell**.
那位癌末病人受到極大折磨。他在生命的最後兩個月處境痛苦。

❸ What the **hell** are you doing? 你到底在做什麼？

11 **holy** [ˋholɪ] 形 神聖的

● Edna considers any church to be a **holy** place.
埃德娜認為教堂是神聖之地。

110

12 **magical** [ˋmædʒɪkḷ] 形 ❶ 魔術的，魔法的；❷ 神秘的，迷人的

- magic 魔法
- -al 形 表「關於……的」

❶ In the novel, Harry Potter is a wizard who has **magical** powers. 在小說裡，哈利波特是一位有魔法力量的巫師。

❷ After the shaman performed the **magical** ritual, Gail was completely healed. 蓋兒在巫僧舉行神秘儀式後，完全痊癒了。

13 **miracle** [ˋmɪrəkḷ] 名 C ❶ 奇蹟；❷ 奇蹟般的人或物 形 miraculous 奇蹟的

❶ Do you believe that **miracles** can happen at any time?
你相信隨時都可能發生奇蹟嗎？

❷ The construction of the Hsuehshan Tunnel is considered an engineering **miracle**. 雪山隧道的興建，被認為是工程學上的一個奇蹟。

14 **monk** [mʌŋk] 名 C 僧侶，和尚，修道士

● After serving for 10 years as the minister of defense, Gabriel finally became a **monk**. 加布列當了十年的國防部長後，最終成為了一名修士。

15 **mysterious** [mɪsˋtɪrɪəs] 形 神祕的，不可思議的

● A **mysterious** event changed Yvonne's life when she was only five years old.
在伊芳年僅五歲時，一樁神祕事件改變了她的一生。

・mystery 神祕的事物
・-ious 形 表「有……特性的」

16 **mystery** [ˋmɪstərɪ] 名 ❶ C 神祕的事物，難以理解的事物，謎；❷ U 神祕，祕密

❶ After years of investigation, the cause of Michael's death has remained a **mystery**. 麥可的死因經過多年調查，仍是一個謎。

❷ That crash has been shrouded in **mystery** for a long time; people still find it difficult to understand or explain.
長久以來，那次墜機事件一直籠罩著神祕的色彩。民眾難以了解或對它加以解釋。

17 **nun** [nʌn] 名 C 修女，尼姑

● The **nuns** of Saint John's Church decided to build an asylum for homeless people. 聖約翰教堂的修女決定要為難民蓋間收容所。

18 **paradise** [ˋpærəˏdaɪs] 名 ❶ U 天堂；❷ U 極樂，至福；❸ C 樂園，像天堂一樣的地方

❶ The father has passed away. His children believe he has gone to **paradise**. 那個爸爸過世了，他的孩子們認為他去了天堂。

❷ After a hard day at work, Claude thinks a hot bath is just like **paradise**. 辛苦工作了一整天，克勞德認為洗個熱水澡快樂似神仙。

❸ The tropical island is a **paradise** to tourists; it is extremely beautiful and perfect for water activities.
那座熱帶島嶼對遊客而言就像是天堂，十分美麗而且非常適合水上活動。

19 **prayer** [prɛr] 名 ❶ U 禱告，祈禱；❷ C 祈禱文

・pray 祈禱
・-er 名 表「人」

❶ Inside the church, many people knelt down in **prayer**. 教堂內，很多人跪下祈禱。

❷ Roland says his **prayers** before each meal and at bedtime.
羅倫在用餐前和睡前都會禱告。

20 **priest** [prist] 名 C **神父，牧師**

● As a **priest**, Chris has devoted his whole life to God.
克里斯身為神父，把一生都奉獻給上帝。

21 **religion** [rɪˋlɪdʒən] 名 C ❶ **宗教**；❷ **宗教信仰**　形 religious 宗教的

❶ Buddhism is a **religion** founded by Buddha in North India around 500 BC. 佛教是由佛陀在西元前 500 年左右於北印度創立的一個宗教。

❷ Wilbur is a person without **religion**; he doesn't believe in the existence of a god. 韋爾伯是個沒有宗教信仰的人，他不相信神的存在。

22 **religious** [rɪˋlɪdʒəs] 形 ❶ 宗教的；❷ 虔誠的

- religion 宗教
- -ous 形 表「有……特性的」

❶ Viola believes all **religious** conflicts will be overcome. 薇拉相信所有的宗教衝突都能獲得解決。

❷ Beatrice is a **religious** person; she believes strongly in the Christian religion and obeys its rules carefully.
碧翠絲是一位虔誠的教徒。她篤信基督教並且謹慎地遵守教規。

23 **witch** [wɪtʃ] 名 C **女巫，巫婆**

● Have you ever wondered how **witches** can ride on broomsticks?
你曾經想過巫婆是如何騎在掃帚上的嗎？

24 **wizard** [ˋwɪzɚd] 名 C 男巫，術士

- wiz 鬼才，天才
- -ard 名 表「沉溺於……的人」

● The **wizard** saved Alicia's life by chasing the demon away. 那名術士把愛麗西雅身上的邪靈驅走，救了她一命。

56 Water & weather 水與天氣 (1)

111

01 **absorb** [əbˋsɔrb] 動 ❶ **吸收**；❷ **使全神貫注**　同義 engross 使全神貫注

❶ Just like a sponge **absorbs** water, Lenny is absorbed in learning new skills. 藍尼就像海綿吸水一樣，全心學習新的技術。

❷ The boy is completely **absorbed** in the comic book; he isn't paying any attention to the people around him.
男孩全神貫注地看著漫畫書，絲毫沒注意週遭的人。

02 **breeze** [briz] 名 U ❶ 微風

- The gentle ocean **breeze** blows through the windows in the late afternoon. 向晚時，清柔的海風吹拂過窗櫺。

03 **bubble** [ˋbʌbḷ] 名 C 泡泡，泡沫

- Feeling very bored, the little boy blew **bubbles** into his juice through a straw. 因為感到很無趣，小男孩用吸管在果汁裡吹氣泡。

補充 bubble gum 泡泡糖；bubble wrap 汽泡包裝紙

04 **chill** [tʃɪl] 名 C ❶ 風寒，寒顫；❷ 寒冷，寒氣
形 ❸ 冷的 動 ❹ 使變冷，使感到冷

❶ If Bernard drinks too much chilled water, he will catch a **chill**.
伯納德要是喝了太多冰水，很容易著涼。

❷ As winter approaches, I can feel the **chill** in the air.
隨著冬天的腳步接近，我可以感受到空氣中的寒意。

❸ A **chill** wind was blowing as the hikers hurried down the trail.
一陣冷風吹來，這群健行者急忙走上小徑。

❹ The night air in the mountains **chilled** their bones, so they had to make a fire to warm themselves.
山區夜間的空氣冷冽刺骨，所以他們得生火取暖。

05 **chilly** [ˋtʃɪlɪ] 形 ❶ 冷颼颼的；❷ 冷淡的

- chill 寒冷
- -y 形 表「……的」

❶ The draft coming through the window is too **chilly**. 從窗外吹進來的風太冷了。

❷ The visitor received a **chilly** welcome when he entered the village; the people seemed unfriendly.
當那名遊客來到村莊時，他受到冷淡的對待；村莊居民似乎不太友善。

06 **damp** [dæmp] ❶ 形 潮濕的 ❷ 動 把……弄濕

❶ When it rains in the winter, the air is **damp** and cold.
冬季的雨天，空氣又濕又冷。

❷ The man **damped** the cloth in some water before wiping his car.
在擦車子之前，男子先把布弄濕。

07 **dip** [dɪp] 動 ❶ 浸，泡；❷ 把（手等）伸入

❶ After **dipping** the brush into the paints, Ellis splashed the colors on the canvas. 艾里斯將畫筆沾滿顏料後，在畫布上揮灑自如。

❷ Before taking a bath, Rita **dipped** her finger in the water to see if it was too hot. 在泡澡之前，芮塔將手指浸入水中，看水會不會太燙。

08 **drain** [dren] 動 ❶ 排出（液體），使排出；❷ 耗盡；❸（土地）排水，（衣物等）滴乾 名 ❹ Ⓒ 排水管

❶ To clean the swimming pool, they first have to **drain** the water from it. 要清洗游泳池，他們得先把水排掉。

❷ Running the marathon **drained** Sharon of all her energy. 馬拉松賽跑讓雪倫耗盡了體力。

❸ After coming home, Mona left the umbrella in the hall to **drain**. 回到家後，夢娜把雨傘放在走廊滴乾。

❹ The **drain** is leaking; it needs to be repaired. 排水管在漏水，需要修理。

09 **drift** [drɪft] 動 漂流

• Dandelion seeds can **drift** for miles in the wind. 蒲公英的種子可以在風中飄飛好幾哩。

10 **drip** [drɪp] ❶ 動 使滴下；❷ 滴下 ❸ 名 Ⓤ 滴水聲

❶ Bob always **drips** sauce on his shirt when he eats a hamburger. 鮑伯每次只要吃漢堡，醬汁就會滴到襯衫上。

❷ Blood was **dripping** from the head wound. 血從頭部的傷口流下來。

❸ In the quiet room, I heard the steady "**drip**, **drip**" in the basin. 在安靜的房間裡，我聽到水槽傳來滴滴答答的水聲。

112

11 **drown** [draʊn] 動 ❶ 淹死，溺死（某人、物）；❷（聲音等）壓過，蓋過；❸ 解（憂愁等）；❹ 淹死，溺死

❶ The farmer's horses were **drowned** by the tidal wave. 那名農夫的馬群被海嘯淹死了。

❷ The rumbling of thunder **drowned** out Mom's voice; I didn't hear what she said. 隆隆的雷聲掩蓋了媽媽的聲音，我聽不到她說什麼。

❸ Polly used to **drown** her troubles in drink, but now she tries hard to overcome them. 波莉以前習慣藉酒澆愁，但現在她努力嘗試克服煩惱。

❹ When the ferry sank, many people fell into the water and **drowned**. 當那艘渡輪翻覆時，許多人掉進水裡淹死了。

12 **float** [flot] 動 漂浮，飄動

• Sally was sad to see her red balloon **float** away in the sky. 莎莉看到她的紅氣球飄向天空飛遠，很傷心。

13 **foam** [fom] ❶ 名 U 泡沫　❷ 動 起泡沫

❶ There is a layer of **foam** atop the glass of beer.
這杯啤酒上面有一層泡沫。

❷ Pouring fresh beer into a glass mug makes it **foam**, creating a white head. 將新鮮啤酒倒進啤酒杯時會冒泡泡，形成白色的酒沫。

14 **fountain** [ˋfaʊntɪn] 名 C ❶ 噴水池；❷ 根源；源泉

❶ All the neighborhood children love to play in the water **fountain** in the park. 附近所有小孩都愛去公園的噴水池玩。

❷ Ancient Greece has been described as a **fountain** of philosophy.
古希臘是被認為是哲學的源泉。

補充 drinking fountain 飲水機

15 **freeze** [friz] 動 ❶ 凍死；❷ 結冰，凝固；❸ 感到極冷，凍僵；❹（因恐懼等）呆住，變僵硬；❺ 使結冰，使凝固

❶ Tropical plants could **freeze** in sub-zero temperatures.
熱帶植物在零下低溫中，可是會凍死的。

❷ On the Celsius scale, water **freezes** at 0°and boils at 100°.
水在攝氏零度時結冰，攝氏一百度時沸騰。

❸ It is very cold outside; I'm **freezing**! 外面好冷，我凍僵了！

❹ Michael **froze** at the sight of the snake; he stayed completely still and quiet for a few seconds.
麥克一看到那隻蛇就呆住了，有幾秒鐘他完全安靜動也不動。

❺ Last night, the cold weather **froze** the pond; water in the ditch also turned to ice. 昨晚，寒冷的天氣讓水池凝結成冰，溝裡的水也結冰了。

16 **frost** [frɑst] 名 U 霜

● The morning sun has melted away all the **frost** that covered the ground. 朝陽融化了遍地寒霜。

17 **humidity** [hjuˋmɪdətɪ] 名 U 濕氣，濕度

・humid 潮濕的
・-ity 名 表「性質」

● In this high **humidity**, it may take several days for the clothes to dry. 溼度太高，衣服要好幾天才會乾。

18 **hurricane** [ˋhɝɪˏken] 名 C 颶風，暴風雨

● More than 10 **hurricanes** formed in the Atlantic Ocean last season. 上一季，大西洋有十多個颶風形成。

19 **hydrogen** [ˋhaɪdrədʒən] 名 U 氫

- hydro- 表「水的，氫的」
- -gen 名 表「產生」

● Water is composed of oxygen and **hydrogen** atoms. 水由氫氧原子所組成。

20 **iceberg** [ˋaɪs͵bɝg] 名 C 冰山，浮在海洋上的巨大冰塊

- ice 冰
- berg 冰山

● As global temperatures rise, many **icebergs** are melting, and sea levels are gradually rising.
許多冰山隨著全球氣溫升高而消融，海平面因此漸升。

21 **icy** [ˋaɪsɪ] 形 ❶ 冰的；❷ 寒冷的；❸ 冷淡的，冷漠的

- ice 冰
- -y 形 表「性質」

❶ Try drinking some **icy** water to cool down in the heat of the tropical sun. 喝點冰水，消消熱帶豔陽的暑氣吧。

❷ In the early morning, an **icy** blast of wintry wind made me shiver.
在冬天的清晨，一陣寒風讓我全身發抖。

❸ Teresa was still angry with Stanley; she gave him an **icy** look and turned around. 泰瑞莎還在生史丹利的氣。她冷冷地看了他一眼便轉過身。

22 **landslide** [ˋlænd͵slaɪd] 名 C ❶ 山崩，坍方；❷（選舉中的）壓倒性勝利

- land 土地
- slide 山崩；滑動

❶ A mass of earth and rock fell down the slope; several houses were buried by the **landslide**.
大量的土石掉下陡坡，幾間房子被那坍方埋了。

❷ Our party is forecast to win by a **landslide**, but the election results are not in yet. 預測顯示我們黨將會大勝，但選舉結果尚未揭曉。

57 Water & weather
水與天氣 (2)

113

01 **leak** [lik] ❶ 動 滲，漏　名 C ❷ 漏洞，裂縫；❸（水、瓦斯等的）漏出

❶ Diana's carpet was damaged by water that **leaked** from the ceiling. 黛安娜的地毯因為天花板漏的水損壞了。

❷ There must be a **leak** in the roof, since the ceiling gets wet when it rains. 屋頂一定有裂縫，因為下雨時雨水一直滴下來。

❸ The mother walked into the kitchen and smelled the gas **leak**, so she opened the windows right away.
那位媽媽走進廚房就聞到滲出的瓦斯味，所以她立刻打開窗戶。

02 **melt** [mɛlt] 動 ❶ **融化，熔化；**❷ **熔解；**❸ **使融化，使熔化**

❶ The snow **melted** soon after the sun came up this morning.
今早太陽升起後不久，雪就融化了。

❷ Put salt on the ice, and it will **melt**. 鹽巴放進水裡會溶解。

❸ By noon, the sun had **melted** the snow on the street.
中午的時候，陽光將街上的雪融化了。

03 **mist** [mɪst] ❶ 名 U **薄霧** ❷ 動 **起霧，被蒙上薄霧**

❶ Through the **mist**, the driver could see only the outline of the car ahead; he couldn't see very far at all.
在薄霧中，那名駕駛人只能看見前面車輛的輪廓，沒辦法看太遠。

❷ When Austin ate hot noodles, his glasses **misted** up and he couldn't see anything.
當奧斯丁吃熱麵的時候，他的眼鏡起霧而看不到任何東西。

04 **moist** [mɔɪst] 形 **潮濕的，多雨的** 名 moisture 濕氣

• Irene frequently applies a balm to keep her lips **moist** during the dry season. 在乾季時，艾琳常在唇上擦護唇膏來保濕。

05 **moisture** [ˋmɔɪstʃɚ] 名 U **濕氣，潮氣**

• moist 潮濕的
• -ure 名 表「狀態」

• When it rains, the **moisture** in the air makes Bradley's window fog up. 下雨時，空氣中的水分讓布德利的窗戶蒙上霧氣。

06 **mudslide** [ˋmʌdˏslaɪd] 名 C **坍方，山崩**

• mud 泥
• slide 滑動

• The typhoon brought heavy rains, which caused floods and **mudslides**. 颱風帶來了豪雨，造成洪水和坍方。

07 **oxygen** [ˋɑksədʒən] 名 U **氧，氧氣**

• There is only enough **oxygen** in the tank to breathe underwater for one hour. 氧氣筒的氧氣只夠在水中用一小時而已。

08 **pour** [por] 動 ❶ **倒，灌；**❷ **傾注；**❸ **傾瀉，湧流；**❹ **(雨)傾盆而降**

❶ The waiter **poured** coffee into my empty cup.
服務生把咖啡倒進我的空杯。

❷ They have **poured** a great deal of money and energy into the project to make it successful. 他們投入了大筆的錢和精力來讓計畫成功。

❸ The crowds **poured** out of the stadium and into the streets after the game ended. 比賽結束後，人群從體育館魚貫而出湧入街道。

❹ The sky turned dark; all of sudden, the rain **poured** down.
天空變暗，突然之間，雨水開始傾盆而下。

09 **rainfall** [ˋren͵fɔl] 名 U 下雨，降雨量

・rain 雨
・fall 降

● The recent heavy **rainfall** caused several landslides.
近日的豪雨，引發了好幾起山崩。

10 **reflect** [rɪˋflɛkt] 動 ❶ 反射，照映出；❷ 反映，表現；❸ 思考，反省

❶ The red maple leaves on the shore were **reflected** in the green water of the lake. 綠色的湖水映照出岸邊的紅色楓葉。

❷ The clothes you wear may **reflect** your taste, whereas the colors you wear may show your emotions.
你穿的衣服可以反映你的品味，而穿著的顏色可以表現你的情感。

❸ When Carla **reflects** on her previous mistakes, she often learns something. 卡拉在反省之前犯的錯誤時，常能有所領悟。

114

11 **reflection** [rɪˋflɛkʃən] 名 C ❶ 映象，倒影；❷ 反映，表現

・reflect 反射
・-ion 名 表「行為(的結果)」

❶ The **reflection** of the setting sun creates a golden path on the lake. 落日的倒影在湖面上拖曳出一條金色的斜影。

❷ The way Jesse talks is a **reflection** of his changeable moods.
傑西的講話方式反映出他多變的性格。

12 **sip** [sɪp] ❶ 動 啜飲　❷ 名 C 小口

❶ Be careful when **sipping** the soup because it is extremely hot.
湯很燙，喝的時候要小心。

❷ After taking a **sip** of her coffee, Dolores continued to talk.
喝下一小口咖啡，多洛莉絲繼續講話。

13 **spill** [spɪl] ❶ 動 使溢出，使濺出；❷ 溢出，濺出

❶ Thomas accidentally **spilled** some wine on his new white sofa.
湯瑪斯不小心把一些紅酒灑在新的白色沙發上。

❷ Coffee **spilled** from Joanna's cup and stained her dress.
咖啡從喬安娜的杯子中濺了出來，弄髒了她的洋裝。

14 **splash** [splæʃ] 動 ❶ 潑，濺(某人，事)；❷ 濺汙，潑濕；❸ 濺，潑

❶ During the water festival, the townspeople **splash** water on everyone in the streets. 潑水節期間，所有鎮民會朝街上行人潑水。

❷ Last evening when Malcolm walked in the rain, a passing truck **splashed** his white pants.
昨天傍晚，當麥爾肯在雨中行走時，一輛駛過的卡車把他的白褲子濺髒了。

❸ When the severe earthquake struck, the water **splashed** out of the fishbowl and onto the floor.
當強震侵襲時，魚缸裡的水濺了出來，灑在地板上。

15 **spray** [spre] ❶ 動 噴　名 U ❷ 水花，浪花；❸ 噴液，噴霧

❶ Before going out, Marilyn likes to **spray** a little perfume on her neck. 瑪莉琳出門前，喜歡在脖子上噴一點香水。

❷ My hair is getting wet because of the **spray** from the shower.
我的頭髮因為淋浴時的水花而弄濕了。

❸ My mother often uses a styling **spray** to keep her hair looking beautiful. 我媽媽經常用造型噴霧來讓她的頭髮保持美麗。

16 **sprinkle** [ˋsprɪŋkl̩] 動 ❶ 噴灑；❷ 使星星點點地分布於；❸ 下毛毛雨
名 ❹ C 毛毛雨；❺（單數）少量

❶ The gardener is **sprinkling** water over the plants.
園丁正在幫植物灑水。

❷ Temples of different sizes are **sprinkled** throughout Taiwan.
大大小小的廟宇分布臺灣各地。

❸ Since it was only **sprinkling**, I decided not to put up my umbrella. 因為只是毛毛雨，我決定不撐傘了。

❹ We had only a few **sprinkles** this morning, but it started to rain heavily this afternoon.
我們這邊今天早上只有些毛毛雨，但是下午就開始下起豪雨。

❺ The man put a **sprinkle** of cinnamon in his coffee.
男子在他的咖啡上灑了少量的肉桂。

17 **stir** [stɝ] 動 ❶ 攪拌，攪動；❷ 喚醒，喚起　❸ 名 C 騷動，轟動

❶ After Stanley tasted the soup, he added some seasoning and **stirred** it again. 史丹利嚐了一口湯後，加了一點調味料，再加以攪拌。

❷ Wesley began to **stir** as the smell of freshly brewed coffee wafted into the bedroom. 隨著剛烹煮好的咖啡香味飄進房間，衛斯理醒了過來。

❸ The speaker's words caused a **stir** among the audience as people whispered to one another excitedly.
演講者的一席話引起聽眾的一陣騷動，他們興奮地交頭接耳。

18 **stormy** [ˋstɔrmɪ] 形 ❶ 暴風雨的；❷ 激烈的，猛烈的

- storm 暴風雨
- -y 形 表「有……的」

❶ Alice insisted on looking for her dog in spite of the **stormy** weather. 即使風雨交加，愛麗絲堅持要找尋她走失的狗狗。

❷ After having a **stormy** quarrel, they stared at each other angrily.
在激烈爭吵過後，他們憤怒地瞪著對方。

19 **suck** [sʌk] 動 吸，吮

- Carolyn uses a handheld vacuum to **suck** the dirt out of her rug.
卡洛琳用手持吸塵器吸地毯。

20 **tide** [taɪd] 名 C ❶ 潮水，潮汐；❷（常作單數）潮流，趨勢

❶ The high **tide** has washed away all of Billy's sand castles.
高漲的潮水沖毀了比利所有的沙堡。

❷ The politician paid attention to the **tide** of public opinion; he wanted to know what most people thought about the issues.
這名政治家注意輿論的趨勢，他想了解大多數人對某些議題的想法。

相關片語 **swim/go with the tide** 隨波逐流

- Nancy was the kind of person who swam with the tide; she did not oppose what most people thought.
南西是那種隨波逐流的人，她不會反對多數人的想法。

21 **tropical** [ˋtrɑpɪkl̩] 形 熱帶的

- tropic 熱帶
- -al 形 表「……的」

- When Janet takes a vacation, she likes to travel to **tropical** islands. 珍妮特渡假時喜歡去熱帶島嶼玩。

22 **warmth** [wɔrmθ] 名 U ❶ 溫暖；❷ 熱情，親切

- warm 熱的，溫暖的
- -th 名 表「性質，狀態」

❶ The **warmth** of the sun melts the frozen rivers.
太陽的溫暖融化了結冰的河水。

❷ Kind words create **warmth** and make the heart soar.
體貼的言語帶來溫暖，讓人內心雀躍。

Part 6 →

Abstract concepts
抽象概念

58 Thoughts & ideas 想法與意見 (1)

115

01 **abstract** [ˋæbstrækt] ❶ 形 抽象的 ❷ 名 C 摘要 ❸ 動 抽取，提取

❶ These philosophical concepts are too **abstract** for Virgil to understand.
這些哲學觀對維吉爾來說太抽象了，無法理解。

❷ Hermosa read the **abstract** first in order to get the main ideas of the essay. 艾爾蒙莎先讀了摘要，以便了解這篇論文的主要論點。

❸ Every day, the factory **abstracts** a great deal of water from the river. 這家工廠每天都從這條河裡抽取大量的水。

- abs- 表「離開」
- tract 延伸；廣闊

02 **acceptable** [əkˋsɛptəbl̩] 形 ❶ 可接受的；❷ 令人滿意的

❶ After retirement, Mr. Schmidt found his life was not only **acceptable**, but also very satisfying.
史密特先生發現他的退休生活不僅過得去，還非常如意。

❷ The plan is **acceptable** to all the people; no one is opposed to it.
這項計畫令大家都很滿意，沒有人反對它。

- accept 接受
- -able 形 表「可……的」

03 **acceptance** [əkˋsɛptəns] 名 U ❶ 接受；❷ 歡迎，贊同

❶ Reap wrote a letter of **acceptance** to the company, stating that he agreed to take the job.
雷普寫了一封職務同意信給那家公司，表明他同意接受那份工作。

❷ Bradley's idea of setting up a flexible work schedule won wide **acceptance** among his colleagues.
布列德利提出的「彈性工時」構想，在同事間獲得廣泛的響應。

- accept 接受
- -ance 名 表「狀況」

04 **associate** [əˋsoʃɪˏet] 動 ❶ 聯想，把……聯想在一起；❷ 結交，交往

❶ It is helpful to **associate** vocabulary words with similar or related terms when trying to memorize them.
記單字時，一起背下相似或相關的詞條很有幫助。

❷ Scott spends a lot of time with those guys, but his father doesn't like him **associating** with them.
史考特很多時間都和那些小伙子混在一起，但是他爸爸不喜歡他和他們來往。

用法 associate A with B 將 A 和 B 聯想在一起

05 **association** [ə͵sosɪˋeʃən] 名 C ❶ 協會，公會；❷ 聯想

・associate 聯想
・-ion 名 表「行為的結果」

❶ Ms. Cook joined the writers' **association** years ago and has attended meetings regularly.
庫克小姐多年前加入作家協會，定期參與其例行會議。

❷ When asked to come up with an **association** for the color yellow, the boy said, "Banana."
老師問男孩想到黃色會聯想到什麼，男孩回答：「香蕉」。

06 **assume** [əˋsjum] 動 ❶ 認為，假定為；❷ 呈現出，顯出　同義 take on 呈現

❶ Robin is the kind of person who always **assumes** the worst about any unusual situation. 羅賓是那種發生任何特殊狀況就愛先往壞處想的人。

❷ After Vincent and Rita became engaged, they quickly **assumed** the style of a married couple.
文森和芮塔訂婚後，很快就表現得像是一對結婚夫婦。

相關用法 連 **assuming** 假設

● Assuming they don't accept the proposal, what should we do?
假設他們不接受這個提議，我們應該怎麼辦？

用法 assume that S+V 假定

07 **assurance** [əˋʃʊrəns] 名 U 把握，信心

・assure 擔保，確信
・-ance 名 表「狀況」

● Can you give me some **assurance** that my personal information will be protected once it's entered in your computer? 一旦我的個人資料輸入你的電腦後，你能對它們的安全性作出保證嗎？

08 **assure** [əˋʃʊr] 動 向⋯⋯保證，擔保　名 assurance 保證；把握

● Captain Kramer **assured** the passengers that it was safe to sail through the storm. 克威馬船長向乘客保證船隻可以平安通過暴風雨。

用法 assure somebody that/assure somebody of something 向某人保證某事

09 **attitude** [ˋætətjud] 名 C 態度，看法

● Lindsay has a flexible **attitude** toward unpredictable changes in her life. 琳賽總以平常心，來面對生活中難以預料的變化。

10 **comparison** [kəmˋpærəsn̩] 名 C 比較，對照

・compare 比較
・-ation 名 表「動作」

● Can you make any **comparisons** among the islands of the South China Sea?
你可以對中國南海上的各個島嶼作出比較嗎？

相關片語 **by comparison** 相比之下

● After my three-day visit to Harbin last winter, Beijing seemed warm by comparison. 相較去年冬季在哈爾濱逗留的三天，北京似乎比較溫暖。

11 **concentrate** [ˋkɑnsɛn͵tret] ❶ 動 集中，聚集；❷ 全神貫注，全力以赴

❶ The factories are **concentrated** on the east side of town, close to the railroad tracks and the highway. 工廠集中設在小鎮的東面，靠近鐵路與公路。

❷ Breton couldn't **concentrate** on his studies because it was very noisy outside. 因為外面很吵雜，伯頓無法專心讀書。

- con- 表「一起」
- center 中心
- -ate 動 表「使成為」

12 **concentration** [͵kɑnsɛnˋtreʃən] 名 U ❶ 集中；❷ 專心，專注

❶ The **concentration** of people in a big city leads to increased traffic. 大型都市人口集中，造成交通量增加。

❷ If you want to learn proper English, **concentration** is very important. You have to direct all your effort and attention to the task. 如果想學習正統英語，專心是不二法門。你必須全心努力並專注在學習上。

補充 concentration camp 集中營

- concentrate 集中
- -ation 名 表「狀態」

116

13 **concept** [ˋkɑnsɛpt] 名 C 概念，觀念

● Iola's and Jeremiah's **concepts** of family were too different for them to get along. 艾兒拉與傑若麥的家庭觀念南轅北轍，很難處得來。

14 **confuse** [kənˋfjuz] 動 ❶ 使困惑，把⋯⋯弄糊塗；❷ 把⋯⋯搞混，混淆

❶ Don't tell me the names of so many plants at one time; you'll **confuse** me. 不要一次告訴我那麼多植物的名字，我會被弄糊塗。

❷ I always **confuse** Angela with her twin sister; they are so alike. 我老是把安琪拉和她的雙胞胎姊姊搞混。她們看起來太像了。

15 **confusion** [kənˋfjuʒən] 名 U ❶ 困惑；❷ 混淆

❶ To avoid **confusion**, please speak loudly and clearly. 為了避免誤解，請你說得更大聲、更清楚一些。

❷ Emma created a lot of **confusion** by telling different lies to her classmates. 艾瑪對班上同學說了不同的謊話，造成一片混亂。

- confuse 使困惑
- -ion 名 表「行為」

16 **conscience** [ˋkɑnʃəns] 名 U 良心

● Margaret believes her **conscience** is her guide through all kinds of conflicts. 瑪格莉特堅信自己的良知，能引領自己度過所有衝突。

- con- 加強語氣
- sci- 表「了解；智慧」
- -ence 表「狀態」

17 **consideration** [kən͵sɪdəˋreʃən] 名 ❶ U 考慮；❷ C 需要考慮的事；❸ U 體貼

- consider 考慮
- -ation 名 表「動作」

❶ In **consideration** of Leona's poor eyesight, her sister read the menu aloud. 姊姊考慮到莉歐娜視力不佳，把菜單唸給她聽。

❷ When Emmy bought the dress, price was her chief **consideration**. 價格是艾咪買下那件洋裝的主要考量。

❸ Andrew shows no **consideration** for others. He never thinks about other people's feelings. 安德魯不體貼他人。他從來不理會別人的感受。

18 **creativity** [͵krieˋtɪvətɪ] 名 U 創造力

- create 創造
- -ive 形 表「有……特性的」
- -ity 名 表「狀態」

● It's important that children have opportunities to develop their **creativity**.
讓孩子有發展創意的機會是很重要的。

19 **define** [dɪˋfaɪn] 動 ❶ 說明，闡明；❷ 解釋，給……下定義

❶ Quentin **defined** the current market trends before he presented his business idea. 昆汀在提出業務上的構想之前，先說明了目前的市場趨勢。

❷ The word defeat is **defined** as "a failure to win or to be successful."
「defeat」這個字被解釋為「無法獲勝或得不到成功」。

用法 define A as B　把 A 定義為 B

20 **definition** [͵dɛfəˋnɪʃən] 名 C 定義

- define 下定義
- -ition 名 表「動作」

● The **definition** of happiness is different for everyone.「快樂」的定義因人而異。

21 **determination** [dɪ͵tɝməˋneʃən] 名 U ❶ 決心；❷ 果斷

- determine 下決定
- -ate 動 表「使成為」
- -ion 名 表「行為」

❶ The **determination** of salary adjustment in our company is Marshall's responsibility.
馬歇爾負責決定本公司的調薪幅度。

❷ In this difficult time, the man showed great **determination** to carry out the plan. 在艱困時期，那名男子展現出絕佳果斷力以執行計畫。

22 **determine** [dɪˋtɝmɪn] 動 ❶ 下決定，決心；❷ 是……的決定因素，影響；❸ 裁定

❶ You should let your daughter **determine** her own future.
你應該讓你的女兒自己決定未來。

❷ Management's bad attitude toward the employees **determined** the sad fate of the Newton Company.
管理階層對勞工惡劣的態度，決定了紐頓公司悲慘的命運。

❸ Finally, they made their decision. They **determined** that signing the contract was in their best interest.
終於，他們做出了決定，他們認定簽署合約才能為他們帶來最大利益。

相關用法 形 **determined** 已下決心的；
be determined to do something 下定決心做某件事

- Adrian is determined to take the job; no one can make him change his mind. 亞德里恩已經下定決心接受這份工作。沒有人可以讓他改變心意。

23 **distinguish** [dɪˋstɪŋgwɪʃ] 動 區別，識別　同義 differentiate 區別

- To avoid being misled by news reports, we should learn to **distinguish** between facts and opinions.
為了避免被新聞報導所誤導，我們應該學習區別事實和見解。

用法 distinguish A from B　區分 A 和 B

24 **expectation** [ˏɛkspɛkˋteʃən] 名 ❶ Ⓤ 期待，預期；❷ Ⓒ 期望，預期的事物

❶ Darlene looked at her parents with **expectation**; she clearly believed she was getting a birthday present.
達琳滿心期待地看著父母，顯然相信她會收到他們的生日禮物。

- expect 期待
- -ation 名 表「狀態，結果」

❷ Janet's parents want her to be a doctor; she has tried her best to live up to their **expectations**.
珍妮特的父母希望她將來成為一名醫師；她竭盡所能想要達成他們的期望。

相關片語 **against all expectation(s)/beyond expectation** 出乎意料地

- Against all expectations, the runner finished first in the race. No one thought he would win.
出乎意外的是，那名跑者在比賽中得到第一名，原本沒有人認為他會贏。

25 **fantasy** [ˋfæntəsɪ] 名 Ⓤ 空想，幻想

- Luke lives in a world of **fantasy**. 路克活在幻想世界裡。

26 **favorable** [ˋfevərəbḷ] 形 ❶ 贊同的，稱讚的；❷ 有利的，適合的

❶ The writer's latest novel has received **favorable** reviews; almost all the critics think it is a good book.
這名作家的最新小說贏得了好評，幾乎所有書評都覺得這是一部很好的作品。

- favor 贊成；有利於
- -able 形 表「有……特性的」

❷ The weather seems **favorable** today for camping in the wilderness. 今天的天氣很適合野外露營。

59 Thoughts & ideas 想法與意見 (2)

117

01 **hopeful** [ˋhopfəl] 形 ❶ 抱有希望的，充滿希望的；❷ 有希望的，有前途的

❶ Fanny was **hopeful** that she would pass the exam, and indeed she did.
芬妮覺得有希望通過考試，而她的確辦到了。

- hope 希望
- -ful 形 表「充滿……的」

❷ Abraham found a **hopeful** way of solving his long-term sleeping disorder. 亞伯拉罕找到了一個方法，有望讓自己擺脫長期的睡眠失調。

02 **image** [ˋɪmɪdʒ] 名 C ❶ 形象；❷ 影像，圖像

❶ Mr. Black will have to improve his **image** if he wants to win Ellen's heart. 布萊克先生如果想要贏得愛倫的心，就得改善他的形象。

❷ After hearing the witness' vivid description, the police officer had a mental **image** of what the robber looked like.
透過目擊者生動的描述，警官在腦海中構勒出搶匪的長相影像。

補充 self-image 名 自我形象；corporate image 企業形象

03 **imaginable** [ɪˋmædʒɪnəbl̩] 形 能想像的，可想像得到的

- Of all the **imaginable** locations where humans might live, Mars is the most unique.
在所有想像得到適合人類居住的地方，其中火星是最獨特的。

- imagine 想像
- -able 形 表「有……特性的」

04 **imaginary** [ɪˋmædʒəˏnɛrɪ] 形 想像中的，虛構的，幻想的

- As a child, Shelley always had an **imaginary** friend. 雪莉小時候，一直有一個幻想出來的朋友。

- imagine 想像
- -ary 形 表「與……有關的」

05 **imagination** [ɪˏmædʒəˋneʃən] 名 U 想像力

- Without **imagination**, no brilliant inventions are possible. 沒有想像力，就沒有傑出的發明。

- imagine 想像
- -ation 名 表「狀態」

06 **imaginative** [ɪˋmædʒəˏnetɪv] 形 有想像力的，有創造力的

- The writer has very **imaginative** ideas; you can always find some new and interesting concepts in his works.
這位作家極富想像力，你總是可以在他的作品中發現一些新鮮又有趣的想法。

- imagine 想像
- -ative 形 表「有……傾向的」

07 **inspiration** [ˌɪnspəˋreʃən] 名 ❶ U 靈感；
❷ C（常作單數）鼓舞人心的人或事物

❶ Jill finds **inspiration** for her novels in daily conversations with people.
吉兒在與人們的日常交談中找到寫小說的靈感。

❷ The musician said that the woman was a constant **inspiration** to him and that she was the reason why he created.
那位音樂家說，那名女子是他源源不斷的靈感泉源，是他創作的理由。

- inspire 鼓舞
- -ation 名 表「狀態，結果」

08 **inspire** [ɪnˋspaɪr] 動 ❶ 鼓舞，激勵；❷ 賦予……靈感　名 inspiration 靈感

❶ Jordan's performance **inspired** his teammates, and they finally beat their opponents to win the championship.
喬丹的表現鼓舞了他的隊員。最後他們擊敗了對手，贏得冠軍。

❷ The beautiful landscape in the Lake District **inspired** the romantic poets; it gave them ideas for writing poetry.
大湖區的美麗風景讓浪漫派詩人文思泉湧，賦予他們寫詩的靈感。

09 **intend** [ɪnˋtɛnd] 動 想要，打算

- Ms. Wooten **intends** to travel around the world after her retirement. 伍坦太太打算在退休後去環遊世界。

- in- 表「朝，向……」
- tend 趨向

10 **intention** [ɪnˋtɛnʃən] 名 C 意圖，意向

- Johnnie's **intention** is to improve cross-cultural understanding, which is totally admirable.
強尼想了解更多跨文化的知識，這點讓人十分佩服。

- intent 意圖
- -ion 名 表「行為」

11 **logic** [ˋlɑdʒɪk] 名 U 邏輯，邏輯學

- Can you understand the **logic** of Linda's decision to sell her house? 你能理解琳達為什麼會賣掉自己的房子嗎？

- logo- 表「字、語」
- -ic 名 表「學術」

12 **logical** [ˋlɑdʒɪkl̩] 形 合邏輯的，合理的

- Without a **logical** conclusion, Vicki's theory is still in doubt. 維琪的理論若無合理定論，還是會令人質疑。

- logic 邏輯
- -al 形 表「……的」

13 **mental** [ˋmɛntl̩] 形 ❶ 精神的，心理的；❷ 精神病的

❶ Zachary believes it is possible to increase your power of **mental** concentration while in the dream state.
柴克瑞相信人可以在睡夢狀態增進集中精神的能力。

- mind 精神，心
- -al 形 表「關於……的」

❷ The patient has a **mental** illness and cannot tell illusion from reality. 這名精神病患無法分辨幻覺和現實。

14 **misunderstand** [ˋmɪsʌndɚˋstænd] 動 誤會，曲解

・mis- 表「錯」
・understand 理解

● Preston was frustrated because his good intention was **misunderstood** by his peers.
派斯頓的好意遭到同事誤解，他感到很灰心。

相關用法 **misunderstanding** 名 誤解

● There must be some misunderstanding—I ordered coffee, but you brought me black tea. 一定是有些誤會。我點了咖啡，但是你剛剛給我的是紅茶。

118

15 **recall** [rɪˋkɔl] 動 ❶ 回想，回憶；❷ 召回 ❸ 名 U 回想，回憶

・re- 表「重新」
・call 呼喚，召喚

❶ Can you **recall** the last time you visited a local museum? 你記得上次去參觀本地博物館是什麼時候嗎？

❷ After testing, these cars were found to be unsafe; they will be **recalled**. 經過檢驗，這些車子因判定不安全，將被召回。

❸ The old man has total **recall** of the incident; he is able to remember all the details. 老人家回想起整件事件，他記得其中所有的細節。

相關片語 **beyond recall** 無法復原的

● According to the experts, the painting is damaged; it is beyond recall.
根據專家的說法，這幅畫遭到損毀，已經無法恢復原貌了。

16 **recognition** [ˏrɛkəgˋnɪʃən] 名 U ❶ 認出，識別；❷ 賞識，表彰

・recognize 認出；表彰
・-ion 名 表「行為」

❶ The witness looked at the suspects, but there was no sign of **recognition**. Therefore, the killer is probably still on the run.
目擊證人看著那些嫌疑犯，卻無法加以指認。因此，殺人犯可能還在逃。

❷ Alvina has received international **recognition** for her musical talent. 艾兒維娜的音樂才華已獲得國際認同。

相關片語 **beyond/out of (all) recognition** 無法認出

● The telephone has changed beyond all recognition in recent years. In both form and function, it is totally different from the telephones of years past.
近幾年來，電話已有大幅改變。在外形和功能上，現在的電話和過去的大不相同。

17 **recognize** [ˋrɛkəgˏnaɪz] 動 ❶ 認可，認定；❷ 認出；❸ 表彰；❹ 承認（事實）

❶ Vesta has been **recognized** as the smartest girl in her class.
薇絲塔是班上公認最聰明的女生。

❷ Jerry didn't **recognize** Mary, his primary school classmate, until she introduced herself.
傑瑞沒認出他的國小同班同學瑪莉，直到她開始自我介紹。

❸ The firefighter was **recognized** for saving several lives in the big fire. 那名消防隊員因為在大火中拯救了幾條人命的表現而受到表彰。

❹ Abbott **recognized** that he had made a mistake; he also admitted that he deserved blame for it.
艾布特承認自己犯下過錯，他同時也承認自己應該受到譴責。

18 **relate** [rɪˋlet] 動 ❶ 有關，涉及；❷ 認同，欣賞

❶ According to the research, the increase in the crime rate is **related** to the rise in unemployment levels.
根據研究顯示，犯罪率增加與失業率上升有關。

❷ Karen found it difficult to **relate** to the latest trend of eating raw foods. 凱倫難以接受吃生食的最新風潮。

用法 relate A to B　使 A 和 B 有關聯

19 **remind** [rɪˋmaɪnd] 動 提醒，使想起

- re- 再
- mind 注意，記住要

● This love song always **reminds** Paula of her ex-boyfriend. 這首情歌總是讓寶拉想起她的前男友。

用法 remind somebody to V　提醒某人做某事

20 **resolution** [ˌrɛzəˋluʃən] 名 U ❶ 決心；❷（單數）解決，解答

- resolute 堅決的
- -ion 名 表「行為（的結果）」

❶ We have made up our minds, and nothing can shake our **resolution**.
我們已經做了決定，沒有任何事可以動搖我們的決心。

❷ As a professional negotiator, Janice sees a potentially peaceful **resolution** in every conflict.
珍妮絲身為專業談判師，能看到每種衝突中可能的和平解決之道。

21 **resolve** [rɪˋzɑlv] 動 ❶ 決心，決定；❷ 解決，消除（疑惑等）　名 ❸ U 決心

- re- 加強語氣
- solve 解決

❶ The government **resolved** to cease construction on the proposed nuclear power plant.
政府決定停擺興建核電廠。

❷ The man's explanation **resolved** our doubts, and we came to realize that he meant it as a jest.
男子的解釋消除了我們的疑慮，我們這才發現他只是說著玩的。

❸ The difficulty didn't depress the man; on the contrary, it strengthened his **resolve**.
困難並未使男子心灰意冷；相反地，加強了他的決心。

22 **riddle** [ˋrɪdḷ] 名 C ❶ 謎，謎語；❷ 奧祕，費解之事

❶ Does anyone know the answer to this **riddle**?
有人知道這道謎題的謎底嗎？

❷ The man's death is a **riddle** to the police; they can't understand or explain how it happened.
那名男子的死對警方來說是一團謎，他們無法理解或解釋其發生的原因。

23 **sensible** [ˋsɛnsəbḷ] 形 明智的，合情理的

- sense 判斷力；理智
- -ible 形 表「可……的」

● With the worsening global economy, keeping cash in the bank seems wiser and more **sensible** than investing it in the stock market.
全球經濟環境惡化下，將現金存入銀行似乎比投資股市更為理性和明智。

24 **suppose** [səˋpoz] 動 ❶ 猜想；❷ 認為應該；❸ 假定

- sup- 表「在……下」
- -pose 表「安置，放」

❶ I **suppose** the airport will be closed because of the bad weather. 我猜想機場可能會因為天候不佳而關閉。

❷ You're not **supposed** to eat or drink on the MRT train, and you also shouldn't talk too loudly. 你不該在捷運車廂內飲食，也不應該大聲喧譁。

❸ **Suppose** it rains on that day—what can we do instead?
假設那天下雨了，我們該做什麼？

相關用法 連 **supposing** 假如，如果

● Supposing it rains tomorrow morning, what should we do?
假如明天早上下雨了，那我們該怎麼辦？

25 **suspect** 動 [səˋspɛkt] 名 [ˋsʌspɛkt] ❶ 動 懷疑 ❷ 名 C 嫌疑犯

❶ Bradford **suspected** that a gangster did the kidnapping, but he had no evidence. 布拉弗德懷疑是一名幫派分子犯下這起綁架案，但苦無證據。

❷ The man is a murder **suspect**; the police think he may have killed the poor man.
那名男子是一起謀殺的嫌疑犯，警方認為他可能殺害了一名無辜的男子。

用法 suspect somebody of V-ing 懷疑某人做某事
suspect somebody to be N 懷疑某人是

26 **suspicion** [səˋspɪʃən] 名 ❶ U 懷疑，嫌疑；❷ C 懷疑

- suspect 懷疑
- -ion 名 表「行為」

❶ Amos was suspended on **suspicion** of spying for the company's business competitor.
亞摩斯被懷疑是公司競爭對手派來的間諜，所以遭到停職。

❷ The father has a strong **suspicion** that his daughter is lying because she won't look him in the eye.
這位父親強烈懷疑他的女兒在說謊，因為她不敢看著他的眼睛。

相關片語 **under suspicion** 受到懷疑的

- The man is under suspicion for murder, though he claims he is innocent. 雖然男子聲稱自己的清白，不過他仍遭懷疑犯下了謀殺罪。

27 **thoughtful** [ˋθɔtfəl] 形 ❶ 細心的，體貼的；❷ 深思的，沉思的

❶ Tara is always **thoughtful** of other people's needs.
泰拉一向為他人的需求設想周全。

❷ My brother looks **thoughtful**; I wonder what he is thinking about. 我哥哥看起來若有所思，我很納悶他在想什麼。

- thought 思考
- -ful 形 表「充滿……的」

28 **voluntary** [ˋvɑlən͵tɛrɪ] 形 自願的，志願的

- Madonna, a doctor with a **voluntary** agency, travels to remote and undeveloped areas. 瑪丹娜身為一名志願性組織的醫師，前往偏遠與未開發地區。

相關用法 副 **voluntarily** 志願地

- They did the job voluntarily; no one forced them to do it.
他們志願從事那份工作，沒有人強迫他們。

29 **wit** [wɪt] 名 U（單數）機智，風趣　形 witty 機智的

- Mark has a quick **wit**, so people enjoy his company.
馬克為人機智風趣，人們都喜歡與他為伍。

相關片語 **be at one's wits' end** 全然不知所措

- The car hit an old man; the driver was at his wits' end and tried to escape. 那輛車撞到一名老人。肇事司機慌了分寸，企圖逃逸。

60 Expression
表達 (1)

119

01 **admit** [ədˋmɪt] 動 ❶ 承認（做某事）；❷ 准許進入；❸ 可容納 ❹ 承認；❺ 容許，有餘地

❶ Connie **admitted** cheating on the English exam.
康妮坦承在英文考試時作弊。

❷ Only the staff is **admitted** into the room; no one else can enter. 只有職員才准許進入這間房，其他人禁止進入。

❸ The gym **admits** 5,000 people. 這座體育館可容納五千人。

❹ After 10 hours' questioning, the man finally **admitted** to the murder. 歷經十小時的訊問，該名男子終於坦承犯下謀殺。

❺ The matter is urgent; it **admits** of no delay.
這件事很緊急，不容耽擱。

[用法] admit V-ing/admit that 子句　承認（做了）……

02 **advice** [əd`vaɪs] 名 U **勸告，忠告**　動 advise 勸告

- Drake gave Miranda some good **advice** on how to organize a conference. 德瑞克提供米蘭達一些籌備會議的好建議。

03 **advise** [əd`vaɪz] 動 ❶（給某人）**勸告，忠告**；❷ **勸告**

❶ Jason **advised** me to leave work early because the weather was getting worse. 傑森建議我提早離開，因為天氣開始轉壞了。

❷ We decided not to do as Jim **advised**, even though he had more experience than us. 我們決定不接受吉姆的提議，儘管他比起我們更有經驗。

04 **announce** [ə`naʊns] 動 **宣布，發布**　[同義] declare 宣布

- The results of the speech contest will be **announced** in one hour. 演講比賽的結果，將於一小時後宣布。

05 **announcement** [ə`naʊnsmənt] 名 ❶ C **宣布，通告**；❷ U **宣布**

❶ According to the spokesman, an **announcement** regarding a peace agreement will be made tomorrow morning.
根據發言人的說法，和平協議的言論將在明天早上宣布。

- announce 宣布
- -ment 名 表「結果」

❷ The audience was eager to hear the **announcement** of the winner. 觀眾期待快點聽到冠軍揭曉。

06 **apologize** [ə`pɑlə,dʒaɪz] 動 **道歉**

- Ms. Patrick, the guest speaker, **apologized** for being late for the meeting.
客座演講者派翠克女士，為會議遲到表示歉意。

- apology 名 道歉
- -ize 動 表「使形成」

07 **apology** [ə`pɑlədʒɪ] 名 U **道歉**

- On receiving my letter of complaint, the hotel manager sent me a written **apology**. 在收到我的抱怨信後，飯店經理寄了一封道歉信給我。

08 **appreciate**

08 **appeal** [əˋpil] 動 ❶ 呼籲，懇求；❷ 訴諸，求助；❸ 有吸引力，迎合愛好 ❹ 將 . . . 上訴，對 . . . 上訴
名 C ❺ 呼籲，請求；❻ U 吸引力

❶ The woman **appealed** to her abductor for mercy.
那女人向綁架犯懇求憐憫。

❷ No matter what happens, we should not **appeal** to force.
不管發生什麼事，我們都不應該訴諸於武力。

❸ The design of the jeans **appealed** to the teenagers; almost all of them wanted to buy a pair.
這款牛仔褲的設計迎合青少年的喜好，幾乎每個青少年都想買一條。

❹ The murderer **appealed** the death sentence he had received.
那名謀殺犯對死刑判決提出上訴。

❺ Corinne made an **appeal** for money to feed the starving children. 寇妮為飢餓孩童募款。

❻ Portuguese egg tarts have lost their **appeal** for many customers; they are no longer a popular dessert.
葡式蛋塔對許多消費者失去吸引力，它們已經不再是受歡迎的甜點了。

09 **appreciate** [əˋpriʃɪˏet] 動 ❶ 欣賞，賞識；❷ 感謝，感激；❸ 領會，查覺

❶ The boy's musical talent is widely **appreciated**; many people think he will become a great musician in the future.
男孩的音樂才能廣受賞識，許多人認為未來他將會成為一名偉大的音樂家。

❷ Ben deeply **appreciated** Ivy's help and kindness.
班非常感謝艾薇的幫忙與友善態度。

❸ They did not **appreciate** the urgency of the matter, so they failed to take immediate action.
他們沒有察覺到事態的緊迫性，所以沒有立刻採取行動。

10 **appreciation** [əˏpriʃɪˋeʃən] 名 U ❶ 感謝；❷ 欣賞，鑑賞

- appreciate 感謝；欣賞
- -ion 名 表「行為」

❶ Ms. Lin is a loving and caring teacher, but so far her students have shown little **appreciation** for what she has done for them. 林老師是一位仁慈而有愛心的老師，但至今學生們對她的付出仍不太領情。〔93 年指測補考〕

❷ My mother has no **appreciation** of rock and roll; she doesn't enjoy it or think it has any value.
我媽媽不喜歡搖滾樂，她覺得搖滾樂不好聽，也不具有音樂價值。

11 **approval** [əˋpruvḷ] 名 U ❶ 贊成，同意；❷ 認可，批准

- approve 贊成，同意
- -al 名 表「狀態」

❶ Mr. Patten has a very critical personality; words of **approval** seldom pass his lips.
派頓先生愛在雞蛋裡挑骨頭；他鮮少表示贊同之意。

❷ The project has won the **approval** of the committee; it will be carried out soon. 這項計畫剛剛獲得委員會的批准，很快就會開始執行。

120 12 **approve** [əˋpruv] 動 ❶ **贊成，同意；❷ 批准，認可；❸ 贊成，贊許**

❶ Johnny told his mother that he wanted to drop out of school to work, but she didn't **approve**.
強尼向媽媽表示自己想輟學去工作，但媽媽不贊成。

❷ After a two-month delay, Everett's research plan has been officially **approved** by his professors.
艾弗瑞特的研究計畫在延宕兩個月後，已由他的教授們正式審核通過。

❸ My parents don't **approve** of me going out late at night, as they think it is dangerous. 我父母不贊成我太晚出門，因為他們覺得很危險。

13 **blame** [ˋblem] 動 ❶ **責備，指責；❷ 把⋯⋯歸咎於，歸因於**
名 C ❸ **責備，指責；❹ 責任**

❶ Howard was **blamed** for making them late for school again.
霍華因一再害他們上學遲到而被責備。

❷ The police **blamed** the car accident on the bus driver, since he ran the red light. 警方把這場車禍意外歸咎給公車司機，因為他擅闖紅燈。

❸ The fans put the **blame** on the coach for losing the game; they thought he should resign at once.
支持者將輸球責任歸咎於教練，他們認為他應該立即辭職。

❹ The careless researcher should take the **blame** for the mistake; it was all his fault. 這名粗心大意的研究人員應該承攬全責，錯誤都是由他所造成。

相關片語 **be to blame** 應受責備

● The drunken driver is to blame for the car crash.
酒駕司機應該為這場車禍受到譴責。

用法 take the blame for something 對某事負責

14 **blessing** [ˋblɛsɪŋ] 名 C ❶ **祝福；❷ 幸事**

・bless 祈禱
・-ing 名 表「行動」

❶ Elias and his newly wedded wife happily accepted the guests' **blessings**. 艾萊斯與新婚妻子愉悅地接受賓客的祝福。

❷ It is a **blessing** that no passengers were on the train when the bomb exploded. 當炸彈爆炸時，所幸沒有乘客在火車上。

15 **boast** [bost] ❶ 動 **誇耀，吹噓；❷ 自吹自擂，吹噓說** ❸ 名 C **大話**

❶ Sylvester always **boasts** about how handsome he was 20 years ago. 塞維斯特老愛吹噓自己二十年前是帥哥。

❷ The father **boasts** that his daughter is very smart; he always talks about her with pride. 這名父親吹噓自己的女兒很聰明；他總是很驕傲地談論她。

❸ That man is full of **boasts**, so don't take his words too seriously.
這個男子滿口大話，所以別把他的話當真。

16 **clarify** [ˋklærə͵faɪ] 動 澄清，闡明

● Can you **clarify** this point? We simply cannot understand it.
請你就這一點加以闡明，我們還是無法了解。

17 **comment** [ˋkɑmɛnt] ❶ 名 C 評論，意見 ❷ 動 發表意見，評論；❸ 評論

❶ My teacher wrote several positive **comments** on my paper.
老師在我的報告中寫下了一些正面評價。

❷ I wanted to know the teacher's opinion of my paper, but she did not **comment** on it. 我想知道老師對我報告的意見，但是她沒有提出任何評論。

❸ The film critic **commented** that the lead actor's performance in the movie was excellent. 影評家評論表示，那部電影的男主角表現精湛。

補充 no comment 不予置評

18 **complaint** [kəmˋplent] 名 C 抱怨，抗議 動 complain 抱怨

- com- 完全
- plaint 訴苦

● Please direct all feedback and **complaints** to Customer Service. 請將所有顧客建議和投訴轉給客服部。

19 **conclude** [kənˋklud] 動 ❶ 結論，推斷出；❷（最後）決定

❶ From their observations, the researchers **concluded** that classical music can stimulate young minds.
研究人員從觀察中得知，古典樂可以刺激年幼兒童的心智。

❷ Ray **concluded** that he would establish a foundation with his inheritance. 雷決定要用繼承的遺產來成立一間基金會。

20 **conclusion** [kənˋkluʒən] 名 C ❶ 結論，推論；❷ 結尾

- conclude 結論
- -ion 名 表「行為（的結果）」

❶ After five minutes' discussion, they came to the **conclusion** that the offer should be accepted.
經過五分鐘的討論，他們達成接受提議的結論。

❷ The cease-fire negotiations came to a **conclusion** yesterday.
直到昨天，停火協商才有了結果。

相關片語 **in conclusion** 最後，總之

● The Oscar winner expressed appreciation to many people. In conclusion, he said he owed his success to his parents.
那位奧斯卡得主對許多人表示感謝。最後，他把他的成功歸功於他的父母。

21 **confess** [kənˋfɛs] ❶ 動 向⋯⋯坦白，承認；❷ 坦白，承認

❶ The man has **confessed** to the crime he was accused of committing. 那名嫌犯已就受指控的罪狀俯首認了。

❷ The young man **confessed** that he walked off with the MP3 player; his friends persuaded him to admit it to the police.
年輕男子承認自己偷走了 MP3 播放器，是他的朋友說服他向警方坦承。

22 **congratulate** [kənˋgrætʃə͵let] 動 恭禧，祝賀

- con 表「一起」
- grat- 表「感謝的」
- -ate 動 表「使成為」

● Dr. Freeman **congratulated** his patient, who just delivered a healthy baby.
弗里曼醫生祝賀他的病人剛生下了個健康寶寶。

23 **convince** [kənˋvɪns] 動 說服，使信服

● Becky has **convinced** her friends that she is from New Mexico.
貝琪讓朋友相信她是新墨西哥州人。

相關用法 **convincing** 形 有說服力的，令人信服的

● The man sounded convincing, so they believed what he said.
那名男子聽起來令人信服，所以他們決定相信他說的話。

24 **critical** [ˋkrɪtɪkḷ] 形 ❶ 批評的，評論的；❷ 必不可少的，緊缺而必須的；❸ 危急的，緊要的

- critic 評論家
- -al 形 表「關於⋯⋯的」

❶ Some parents were highly **critical** of the school; they thought the way the school treated the bullies was wrong.
部分家長大肆批評學校。他們認為學校處理惡霸的方式有瑕疵。

❷ The rescue team has delivered some **critical** food supplies to the shelter. 搜救隊運送了一些緊急供糧到避難所。

❸ After the operation, the wounded man remains in **critical** condition; he could die at any time.
手術過後，受傷男子的狀況依然十分危急，他隨時會有生命危險。

61 Expression
表達 (2)

121

01 **criticism** [ˋkrɪtə͵sɪzəm] 名 U 批評，評論

- critic 評論家
- -ism 名 表「行為」

● Senator Navarro faced severe **criticism** from his opponent in the debate yesterday.
納瓦洛參議員在昨天的辯論中遭到對手痛批。

02 **criticize** [ˋkrɪtɪˏsaɪz] 動 批評，評論

・critic 評論家
・-ize 動 表「使」

● The newspaper **criticized** Tom's new book for misleading the public. 報紙批評湯姆的新書誤導社會大眾。

03 **cue** [kju] ❶ 名 C 暗示 ❷ 動 暗示

❶ Bennett was supposed to get in the car at the director's **cue**, but he missed the signal. 班奈特原本應該依導演的指示上車，但他錯過了提示信號。

❷ The conductor **cued** the trumpeters when it was their turn to play. 指揮給予信號，提示小號手開始演奏。

04 **curse** [kɝs] 動 ❶ 咒罵；❷ 詛咒 名 ❸ C 咒罵

❶ Mr. Truman **cursed** loudly when he found the stranger had cheated him out of his money.
當楚門先生發現錢被陌生人騙走後，他大聲地咒罵。

❷ In the fairy tale, the prince was **cursed** by a witch and turned into a frog. 在這則童話故事中，王子被巫婆詛咒，變成了青蛙。

❸ Feeling angry with her neighbor, the elderly lady muttered a **curse** at him. 對他的鄰居感到很生氣，老婦人低聲咒罵他。

05 **damn** [dæm] 動 咒罵

● While watching the news, Harold **damned** the gangsters for the increasing street violence.
哈洛德看新聞時，咒罵那幫流氓惹出越來越多的街頭暴力。

06 **declare** [dɪˋklɛr] 動 ❶ 宣布，宣告；❷ 宣稱 名 declaration 宣告

❶ The police **declared** war on the drug dealers in the neighborhood. 警方向本區的毒販宣戰。

❷ The woman **declared** that she had nothing to do with it, but no one believed her statement.
那名女子宣稱她與這件事毫無關係，但是沒有人相信她的說法。

07 **demand** [dɪˋmænd] 名 U ❶ 要求，請求；❷ 需要 ❸ 動 要求，請求

❶ The workers asked for a pay raise, but the boss rejected their **demand**. 工人們要求加薪，但是老闆拒絕了他們的請求。

❷ The supply of bananas has exceeded the **demand**, so the price has dropped. 香蕉已供過於求，所以價格暴跌。

❸ The manager **demanded** that Camille finish the project on her own, but she thought the order was unreasonable.
老闆要求卡蜜拉自己完成企畫，但是她認為這項要求不合理。

相關用法 形 **demanding** 苛求的，高要求的

- The boy is a very demanding child; he needs a lot of attention.
這個小男孩很纏人，他希望得到很多的注意。

08 **demonstrate** [ˋdɛmənˏstret] 動 ❶ 示範操作，展示；❷（用實例等）說明；❸ 示威

❶ Hazel works in a department store **demonstrating** how to use a food processor. 海柔在一間百貨公司示範食物調理機的使用方法。

❷ Providing convincing evidence, the researchers **demonstrated** how smoking harms our health.
提出了具有說服力的證據，研究人員以實例說明吸菸如何傷害我們的健康。

❸ The workers **demonstrated** outside the factory, protesting the decision to lay off half the workforce.
工人們在工廠外面示威，抗議裁員一半的決定。

09 **demonstration** [ˏdɛmənˋstreʃən] 名 C ❶ 示威；❷ 實地示範

- demonstrate 示範
- -ion 名 表「行為」

❶ The **demonstration** ended peacefully around midnight. 這場示威活動在午夜時分和平落幕。

❷ They are going to give a brief **demonstration** showing how to use the machine. 他們將會簡短示範，展示使用這部機器的方法。

10 **description** [dɪˋskrɪpʃən] 名 C 描繪，敘述

- describe 描述
- -ion 名 表「行為」

- Bradley gave his friends a **description** of what he saw during the riot. 布萊德利向朋友描述自己在那場暴動中的所見所聞。

相關片語 **beyond description** 無法形容

- The destruction caused by the severe earthquake was beyond description. 這場大地震造成的破壞難以言喻。

11 **dispute** [dɪˋspjut] ❶ 動 爭論，爭執；❷ 動 爭論，爭執 ❸ 名 C 爭端，爭執

❶ Rolando's contribution to the project has been **disputed**; Maureen claims he did very little work.
羅納杜對企劃案的貢獻引發了爭議，莫琳主張他的付出不夠多。

❷ Last night, they **disputed** what to do next; today, they are still arguing about it. 他們從昨晚開始爭論下一步該怎麼做，到現在他們還沒吵完。

❸ Since the two companies can't reach an agreement, the **dispute** has not been settled. 因為兩家公司無法達成協議，這個爭端還沒有獲得解決。

用法 in dispute 有爭議的

12 **emphasis** [ˋɛmfəsɪs] 名 U 強調，重視

- em- 表「置於……上」
- phasis 事物某一面

● In his work, Brady puts **emphasis** on quality rather than quantity. 布萊迪對於工作是重質甚於重量。

122

13 **emphasize** [ˋɛmfə͵saɪz] 動 強調，著重

- emphasis 強調
- -ize 動 表「使成為」

● Nellie Bly **emphasized** what she was saying by using gestures. 乃麗．布萊利用肢體動作來強調她的言談。

14 **evaluate** [ɪˋvæljʊ͵et] 動 評估，估價　名 evaluation 估價

● Can you **evaluate** how well the mechanic did when repairing my car? 你是否能評估出當時技師對我車子的整修程度？

15 **evaluation** [ɪ͵væljʊˋeʃən] 名 C 估價，評價

- evaluate 評估
- -ion 名 表「行為」

● At the end of the term, the teacher wrote an **evaluation** for each of his students. 期末時，老師針對每位學生寫下評價。

16 **exaggerate** [ɪgˋzædʒə͵ret] 動 誇大，誇張　名 exaggeration 誇張

● Barlow **exaggerated** the difficulties of the job; in fact, it was quite easy. 巴洛誇大了那份工作的困難度。事實上，它很簡單。

17 **explanation** [͵ɛkspləˋneʃən] 名 ❶ C 解釋，說明；❷ U 辯解

- ex- 由內向外
- plane 平；水平
- -ate 形 表「……狀態的」
- -ion 名 表「行為」

❶ The student gave an **explanation** for why his homework was late, but the teacher didn't believe it. 那名學生提出為何無法準時交作業的解釋，但是老師不相信。

❷ What can you offer as an **explanation** for Percy's misbehavior? 你要如何為派西的不當行為辯解？

18 **expression** [ɪkˋsprɛʃən] 名 C ❶ 表達，表示；❷ 表情；❸ 措辭，用語

- ex- 由內向外
- press 擠，壓
- -ion 名 表「行為」

❶ Jeffrey had been a great help to them, so they sent him a watch as an **expression** of gratitude. 傑佛瑞過去幫了他們大忙，所以他們送他一支手錶以示感謝。

❷ Did you see the **expression** on Laura's face when she entered the room? 當蘿拉進來房間時，你有沒有看到她的表情？

❸ The **expression** in the pink means "in good health."「in the pink」這個用語表示「身體健康」。

相關片語 **beyond/past expression** 無法表達，無法形容

● The spectacular scenery on the mountaintop was beyond expression. 山頂上的壯麗景色無法以言語形容。

19 **expressive** [ɪk`sprɛsɪv] 形 ❶ 表現的，表示……的；❷ 表達豐富的，意味深長的

- ex- 由內向外
- press 擠，壓
- -ive 形 表「……的」

❶ The music is **expressive** of the composer's peace of mind while living in the country.
這支音樂表現出作曲者在鄉間生活的平靜心靈。

❷ Kent's mother gave him an **expressive** nod, showing that she was very proud of him. 肯特的媽媽向他意味深長地點了點頭，表示非常以他為榮。

20 **farewell** [`fɛr`wɛl] ❶ 名 U 告別 ❷ 形 告別的

- fare【古】行走
- well 很好地

❶ Bonnie waved **farewell** to her relatives as she stepped onto the train. 邦妮上了火車後，揮手向親戚道別。

❷ They held a **farewell** party for Mr. Wang, who was retiring.
他們為王先生舉辦了一場送別會，因為他要退休了。

21 **flatter** [`flætɚ] 動 ❶ 奉承，諂媚；❷ 使感到很榮幸，使受寵若驚

❶ Gene admired the girl's new dress, trying to **flatter** her.
吉恩稱讚那個女孩的新洋裝，試圖奉承她。

❷ Joanna was **flattered** by the invitation to visit the Ferrari factory in Italy. 瓊安娜受邀參觀義大利的法拉利工廠，感到受寵若驚。

22 **fluent** [`fluənt] 形 流利的，流暢的 名 fluency 流暢

- John, a native English speaker, is also **fluent** in Spanish after spending most of his childhood in Spain.
約翰在西班牙度過了童年，所以除了英文外，他的西班牙文也很流利。

相關用法 副 **fluently** 流利地，流暢地

- My cousin's English is very good; he can speak the language fluently.
我表哥的英文非常好。他可以流利地說英文。

23 **forbid** [fɚ`bɪd] 動 禁止，不許 反義 allow, permit 允許

- for- 表「禁止」
- bid 吩咐

- Rowena's father **forbids** her from going out before she has finished her homework. 蘿溫娜的父親不許她沒寫完功課就跑出去玩。

24 **forecast** [`for,kæst] ❶ 名 C 預測，預報 ❷ 動 預測，預報

- fore- 表「預先」
- cast 投

❶ The weather **forecast** predicts we will have no rain on the weekend. 氣象預報說，週末不會下雨。

❷ Heavy rain is **forecast** for tomorrow afternoon, and it will thunder, too. 天氣預測明天會有午後雷陣雨。

25 **furthermore** [ˋfɝðɚˋmor] 副 而且，此外

- further 進一步的
- more 更多的

- Douglas spends more money than he earns; **furthermore**, he has no savings plan.
道格拉斯入不敷出，而且毫無儲蓄計畫。

62 Expression 表達 (3)

123

01 **greeting** [ˋgritɪŋ] 名 C 問候，打招呼

- greet 迎接；問候
- -ing 名 表「行動」

- Renee opened the door and welcomed us with a cheerful **greeting**. 芮妮開了門，以愉快的問候歡迎我們到訪。

02 **guarantee** [ˏgærənˋti] ❶ 動 保證，擔保
名 U ❷ 商品保證；❸ 擔保品，抵押品

❶ Duncan **guaranteed** that we would enjoy staying at his place.
鄧肯向我們保證，我們會喜歡在他家過夜。

❷ The washing machine is still under **guarantee**; you can have it repaired for free. 這台洗衣機還在保證期內，你可以免費送修。

❸ They offered their apartment as a **guarantee** when they got the loan. 當他們申請貸款時，用公寓作為抵押品。

03 **hint** [hɪnt] ❶ 名 C 暗示 ❷ 動 暗示

❶ Ms. Harrell gave us some helpful **hints** on how to start a fire with twigs and paper. 哈瑞爾小姐教了我們一些以樹枝和紙生火的方法，很有幫助。

❷ The boss **hinted** at a possible solution that included a shorter workday for the secretary.
老闆向秘書示意一些可行的解決方式，包括較短的工時。

04 **illustrate** [ˋɪləstret] 動 ❶（用圖、實例等）說明；❷ 插圖於（書籍等），圖解

- il- 表「入，向」
- luster 光輝
- -ate 動 表「使成為」

❶ George **illustrated** the historic event with colorful maps and comprehensive charts.
喬治以各式彩色地圖和易於理解的圖表，來說明歷史事件。

❷ These children's storybooks are well **illustrated**; they contain many beautiful pictures. 這些兒童故事書插圖精美，書內有很多精緻的圖畫。

05 **illustration** [ɪˌlʌsˋtreʃən] 名 C ❶ 實例；❷ 圖解，插圖

- illustrate 說明，圖解
- -ion 名 表「行為的結果」

❶ This video provides a graphic **illustration** of how global warming affects our lives.
這段影片提供了圖解，說明全球暖化如何影響我們的生活。

❷ Children's books are always filled with full-color **illustrations**.
童書總是充滿了全彩的插圖。

06 **imply** [ɪmˋplaɪ] 動 ❶ 暗示；❷ 意味著 同義 suggest 意味著

❶ Bartley **implied** that he wanted to take me out for dinner without directly saying so. 巴特利沒有直接說出口，但暗示他想約我出去吃晚飯。

❷ Obedience does not **imply** approval. 順從不意謂贊同。

07 **indication** [ˌɪndəˋkeʃən] 名 ❶ U 指示；❷ C 徵兆，跡象

- index 索引；標誌
- -ate 動 表「使成為」
- -ion 名 表「行為的結果」

❶ After the incident, the girl gave no **indication** of her feelings; no one knew exactly what she was thinking.
意外發生過後，女孩沒有表現出她的感受，所以沒有人知道她的想法。

❷ Emilia can read subtle **indications** and detect changes in the weather. 艾蜜莉亞能解讀天候的細微跡象，覺察天氣的變化。

08 **insult** [ˋɪnsʌlt] ❶ 名 C 侮辱，羞辱 ❷ 動 侮辱，羞辱

❶ Enid couldn't forgive the terrible **insult**; she had never been accused of being a racist before.
伊妮德無法忘記這次羞辱，她從未遭指控為種族主義者。

❷ When they fight, they always say rude things to **insult** each other. 每當他們吵架的時候，總會說出粗魯無禮的話來侮辱對方。

09 **interpret** [ɪnˋtɝprɪt] 動 ❶ 詮釋；❷ 解讀，理解；❸ 做口譯，當翻譯

❶ This poem may be **interpreted** in several different ways, and each interpretation makes sense.
這首詩可以用不同方式來詮釋，而每一種方式都能解釋得宜。

❷ Benny **interpreted** his father's frown as a sign of disapproval.
班尼將父親皺眉視為反對之意。

❸ Since my parents can't speak English, I had to **interpret** for them when we traveled in the United States.
因為我父母不會說英文，所以我們一起在美國旅行的時候，我得當他們的翻譯。

10 **mention** [ˋmɛnʃən] ❶ 動 提及，說起 名 ❷ C 提及，說起

- ment- 提醒，警告
- -ion 名 表「行為」

❶ Brenda never **mentioned** that she has a twin brother. 布蘭達從沒提起她有個雙胞胎哥哥。

❷ Belinda has never made any **mention** of her job, so I don't know what she does for a living.
布蘭達從來沒提過她的工作，所以我不知道她的職業。

相關片語 **not to mention** 更不必說

- The shoes are too big for you, not to mention the price is unreasonably high. 這雙鞋子對你而言太大了，更不必說價錢高的不合理。

11 **mislead** [mɪsˋlid] 動 誤導，使產生錯誤想法

- mis- 表「錯」
- lead 引導

- The robber tried to **mislead** the police, but a witness identified him as the one who committed the crime.
搶犯企圖誤導警方，但一名證人指認他犯案。

相關用法 **misleading** 形 使人誤解的，騙人的

- The man's description is quite misleading; it gives people the wrong idea. 這位男子的陳述令人誤解，讓人們產生一些錯誤的想法。

124

12 **moreover** [morˋovɚ] 副 並且，此外 同義 in addition 另外

- more 更多
- over 多餘

- Rebecca is the director of this film; **moreover**, she is the scriptwriter. 芮貝嘉是這部電影的導演，同時也是編劇。

13 **namely** [ˋnemlɪ] 副 亦即，也就是說

- name 名稱
- -ly 副 表「在……方面」

- Only one man can solve this problem, **namely** you. 只有一個人能解開這道難題，那個人就是你。

14 **nevertheless** [ˌnɛvɚðəˋlɛs] 副 不過，然而 同義 nonetheless 但是，仍然

- Ms. Henderson did not want to relocate; **nevertheless**, she agreed to cooperate with the government and move to the new housing project. 韓德森小姐並不想搬家，不過她還是同意配合政府新頒布的遷屋計畫。

15 **nonetheless** [ˌnʌnðəˋlɛs] 副 但是，仍然

- none 沒有
- the 定冠詞
- less 較少地

- Nelson prefers to play baseball; **nonetheless**, he has been chosen as the captain of the basketball team.
尼爾森雖然比較喜歡打棒球，卻被選為籃球隊隊長。

16 **nonsense** [ˋnɑnsɛns] 名 U 胡說，胡鬧

- non- 表「無」
- sense 理智；道理

- Did you really believe Steve's **nonsense** and lend him money? 你真的相信史蒂夫的一派胡言，把錢借給他了嗎？

17 **objection** [əbˋdʒɛkʃən] 名 U 反對 動 object 反對

- object 反對
- -ion 名 表「行為」

- No one has any **objection** to the plan, so it will be carried out immediately. 沒有人反對這項計畫，所以它即刻會開始執行。

18 **objective** [əbˋdʒktɪv] ❶ 形 客觀的 ❷ 名 C 目的，目標

・object 物體；目標
・-ive 形 表「有……特性的」

❶ The man made an **objective** decision; he considered only the facts, not his personal feelings. 男子作了一個客觀的決定。他只看事實，而不將個人感受考慮在內。

❷ A self-fulfilled and contented life has been Mr. Seeton's **objective** over the years. 西頓先生多年來的目標是能志得意滿的過生活。

19 **oppose** [əˋpoz] 動 反對，反抗 名 opposition 反對

● Lena thinks the best way to **oppose** unfairness is to speak her mind. 蕾娜認為反對不公的最好方法，是說出她自己的想法。

20 **otherwise** [ˋʌðɚˏwaɪz] 副 ❶ 否則，要不然；❷ 在其他方面，除此以外

・other 另一個
・-wise 副 表「像……的樣子」

❶ Mrs. Jones is probably already asleep; **otherwise**, she would answer your call.
鍾斯太太大概已經睡了，不然她會接電話的。

❷ These jeans are a little too long; **otherwise**, they are satisfactory.
這幾件牛仔褲有點太長，除此以外都很令人滿意。

相關片語 **or otherwise** 或用其他方式

● Don't worry; they will get here on time, by taxi or otherwise.
別擔心，不論是搭計程車或其他交通工具，他們會準時到達這裡的。

21 **permission** [pɚˋmɪʃən] 名 U 允許，許可，同意

・permit 允許
・-sion 名 表「行為的狀態」

● Visitors can't enter our office without **permission**.
訪客未經允許，不得擅入本辦公室。

22 **permit** 動 [pɚˋmɪt] ❶ 動 許可；❷ 允許，准許
名 [ˋpɝmɪt] ❸ 名 C 准許証，執照

❶ Lucy's birthday party will be held outdoors if the weather **permits**. 如果天氣好的話，露西的生日派對會在戶外舉行。

❷ The girl is not **permitted** to date boys; her parents don't allow her to go out late at night either.
女孩不允許和男生約會，她的父母也不准她很晚才出門。

❸ You need a **permit** to camp in the national park.
要在這座國家公園裡露營需要准許證。

補充 parking permit 停車證

用法 permit somebody to do something (permit+sb+to V) 允許某人做某事

23 **persuade** [pɚˋswed] 動 說服，勸服

- The salesperson **persuaded** Oren to buy a new kitchen table and chairs. 店員說服歐恩買下新的餐桌椅組。

63 Expression 表達 (4)

125

01 **persuasion** [pɚˋsweʒən] 名 U 說服，勸說

- It will take a lot of **persuasion** to get the stubborn man to give up his plan.
必須要費盡唇舌才有可能說服這名固執的男子放棄他的計畫。

・per- 表「透過」
・suasion 說服

02 **persuasive** [pɚˋswesɪv] 形 有說服力的

- Jury members considered the evidence in Julian's case to be **persuasive**, but not conclusive.
陪審團認為，朱利安一案的證據雖具有說服力，但決定性不足。

・per- 表「透過」
・suasive 勸說的

03 **portray** [porˋtre] 動 描繪，描寫　同義 depict 描述；描寫

- Greg **portrays** an insane old man very well in this movie.
葛瑞格在電影中飾演患有精神病的老人非常到位。

04 **predict** [prɪˋdɪkt] 動 預言，預料，預報　同義 forecast 預報

- Jim thinks the only way to **predict** the future is to create it.
吉姆認為要預知未來，唯有去創造未來。

05 **proposal** [prəˋpozḷ] 名 C ❶ 建議，提議；❷ 求婚

❶ Controversy surrounds the **proposal** for building a casino in the Pearl Islands.
在珍珠群島設賭場的提議引起爭議。

❷ Julia has received a marriage **proposal**; I heard that one of her colleagues asked her to marry him a few days ago.
有人向茱莉亞求婚了。我聽說是幾天前她的某位同事向她開口的。

・pro- 表「先，前」
・pose 提出
・-al 名 表「動作；狀態」

06 **protest** [prəˋtɛst] ❶ 名 C 抗議，反對　❷ 動 抗議，反對；❸ 斷言，聲明

❶ The demonstration Ms. Osman organized last weekend was a **protest** against capitalism and globalization.
奧斯曼女士上週末發動的示威遊行，要抗議資本主義和全球化。

❷ Thousands of people took to the streets, **protesting** against the new tax law. 數以千計的人走上街頭，抗議那項新的稅制。

❸ The suspect **protested** that he was innocent, but no one believed him. 嫌犯堅稱他是清白的，但是沒有人相信。

[用法] make a protest against something 對某事提出抗議

07 **quarrel** [ˋkwɔrəl] ❶ 名 C 爭吵，不和 ❷ 動 爭吵，不和

❶ Tristan had a **quarrel** with the coach after he took her out of the game. 泰絲妲在比賽中被裁判判出場後，與他起了爭執。

❷ Anna **quarreled** with her boyfriend about money; after the angry argument, they stopped talking to each other.
安娜為錢的事情與男朋友發生爭吵。激烈爭吵過後，他們就不講話了。

[用法] quarrel with somebody about/over something 與某人為了某事起爭執

08 **refer** [rɪˋfɝ] 動 ❶ 涉及，有關；❷ 論及，談到；❸ 查閱，參考

❶ Many inquiries from patients have **referred** to the new medicine developed by Mr. Barnes' company.
已經有許多病人詢問巴奈斯先生公司發明的新藥。

❷ Hunter didn't want to talk about the matter anymore, so they agreed not to **refer** to it again.
因為杭特不想再講那件事了，所以他們同意不再提起。

❸ After you answer the questions, you may **refer** to page 90 for the answers. 在你回答問題之後，你可以查閱第 90 頁的答案。

09 **reference** [ˋrɛfrəns] 名 U ❶ 參考；❷ 提及

- refer 涉及
- -ence 名 表「性質，狀態」

❶ Ms. Nelke filed all the notes she took during her job interviews for future **reference**.
聶爾克小姐整理了所有的工作面試筆記，以備未來參考之用。

❷ The man made no **reference** to his family; he mentioned only his hometown. 那名男子沒有提及他的家庭，他只說到了他的家鄉。

10 **regarding** [rɪˋgɑrdɪŋ] 介 關於，就……而論

- regard 與……有關係
- -ing 表「行動」

● What is your opinion **regarding** the judge's decision in favor of the defendant?
你對於法官做出利於被告的判決有何看法？

11 **rejection** [rɪˋdʒɛkʃən] 名 U 拒絕，退回 動 reject 拒絕

- reject 拒絕
- -ion 名 表「行為」

● The proposal met with **rejection**; they not only refused to accept it, but they also were unwilling to take it into consideration. 那項提議被拒絕了。對方不接受，甚至不會加以考慮。

126

12 **remark** [rɪ`mɑrk] ❶ 名 C 談論，評論 ❷ 動 談到，評論

- re- 再
- mark 標記號

❶ John's rude **remarks** about obese people offended Wilma, who is overweight.
約翰侮辱肥胖者的言論讓威瑪頗感不快，因為她是胖哥胖姊一族。

❷ The critic **remarked** that the book lacked originality, but the writer thought the comment was unfair.
那名評論家評論這本書缺乏原創性，但是作者認為這番評論不甚公平。

13 **request** [rɪ`kwɛst] ❶ 名 U 請求，要求 ❷ 動 請求，要求

❶ Regarding your **request** to change your billing address, please call back during business hours.
有關您請求更改帳單地址之事宜，請於上班時間來電。

❷ In the museum, visitors are **requested** to dispose of any food or drinks; they are also asked to put their cameras away.
在博物館裡，參觀者要求禁止飲食和拍照。

補充 song request 點歌

14 **sigh** [saɪ] ❶ 動 嘆息，嘆氣 ❷ 名 C 嘆息，嘆氣

❶ When Matt realized his missing child was found, he **sighed** with relief. 麥特得知失蹤的孩子已尋獲時，如釋重負鬆了一口氣。

❷ As Isaac's girlfriend forgave him, he breathed a **sigh** of relief.
當艾薩克的女朋友原諒他的時候，他寬慰地鬆了一口氣。

15 **somehow** [`sʌm͵haʊ] 副 不知怎地

- some 某
- how 怎樣

● **Somehow**, elephants can locate water sources, even from a far distance. 不知怎地，大象就是可以找到水源，即使路程遙遠。

16 **suggest** [sə`dʒɛst] 動 ❶ 建議；❷ 暗示，顯示

❶ Julia **suggested** that we go to the playground on weekdays instead of weekends. 茱利亞建議我們應該平日去遊樂場，而不要假日去。

❷ According to the police, most of the evidence now **suggests** that the suspect is innocent. 根據警方表示，大部分證據都顯示這名嫌犯是清白的。

用法 suggest doing something (suggest+V-ing) 建議做某事

17 **swear** [swɛr] 動 ❶ 發（誓），宣（誓）；❷ 發誓要，起誓保證

❶ Before presenting the evidence in court, Abel was asked to **swear** an oath of truth. 亞伯在法庭上必須宣誓所言皆屬實，才能發言作證。

❷ My friend **swore** not to tell the secret to others, and I hope he keeps his promise. 我朋友發誓保證不把祕密告訴別人。我希望他會遵守承諾。

18 **threat** [θrɛt] 名 C ❶ 威脅；❷ 構成威脅的人（或事物） 動 threaten 威脅

❶ The train station was closed this morning because of a bomb **threat**. 火車站因為今早發生的炸彈威脅事件關閉了。

❷ Water pollution presents a **threat** to all the creatures in the lake; it is also a danger to the people living around the water.
水汙染對湖泊裡的所有生物造成威脅，同時也危害周圍居民的安全。

19 **threaten** [ˋθrɛtn̩] 動 威脅，恐嚇

• threat 威脅
• -en 動 表「變為」

• Ursula has **threatened** to break up with her boyfriend many times. 烏蘇拉已多次威脅要與男友分手。

20 **warn** [wɔrn] 動 警告，告誡

• Has your doctor **warned** you about the dangers of smoking?
你的醫生有沒有警告過你抽菸的害處？

相關用法 **warning** 名 警告

• Scientists have issued a warning about global warming.
科學家已經對全球暖化提出警告。

用法 warn somebody of something 警告某人某事

21 **scold** [skold] 動 責罵，嘮嘮叨叨地責備 同義 rebuke 指責

• Mr. Eaton **scolded** his children for eating candy given to them by strangers. 伊頓先生責備他的孩子不該吃下陌生人給的糖果。

22 **suggestion** [səˋdʒɛstʃən] 名 U 建議，提議

• suggest 建議
• -ion 名 表「行為的結果」

• What is your **suggestion** regarding our travel plans? 請問你對我們的旅遊計畫有何建議？

23 **urge** [ɝdʒ] 動 ❶ 極力主張，強烈要求；❷ 催促，力勸
名 C ❸ 強烈的慾望，衝動

❶ The workers' union **urged** the management to respect the laborers' rights. 工會強烈要求資方重視勞工權益。

❷ They **urged** Darren to stay longer, but they failed to persuade him. 他們說服戴倫留久一點，但是他們沒能成功說服他。

❸ I cannot resist the **urge** to eat chocolate, even though I need to lose weight. 我無法抗拒想吃巧克力的強烈念頭，儘管我需要減肥了。

64 Ability & personality
能力與個性 (1)

127

01 **aggressive** [ə`grɛsɪv] 形 ❶ 好鬥的，挑釁的；❷ 有進取心的，雄心勃勃的

❶ The man is very **aggressive**; he is always looking for a fight. 這名男子好勇鬥狠，老愛找人打架。

❷ Issac has an **aggressive** ambition and the initiative to start his own business. 艾薩克以強烈的企圖心和積極的進取心自行創業。

- aggress 侵略
- -ive 形 表「……的」

相關用法 動 **aggress** 侵略

- Japan aggressed against many Asian countries during World War. 日本在二次世界大戰期間，侵略了許多亞洲國家。

02 **ambition** [æm`bɪʃən] 名 ❶ U 雄心，抱負；❷ C 追求的目標

❶ The young actor is filled with **ambition**; he wants to win an Oscar. 這名年輕的男演員野心勃勃，目標贏得一座奧斯卡獎。

❷ Gretchen's **ambition** is to become a professional singer, so she practices every day. 格麗卿的目標是當歌手，所以每天都在練唱。

03 **ambitious** [æm`bɪʃəs] 形 有雄心的，野心勃勃的

- Lois completed various **ambitious** projects before reaching the peak of her career. 露伊絲在達到事業巔峰之前，就已經完成了各種雄心壯志。

- ambition 雄心
- -ous 形 表「有……特質的」

04 **bold** [bold] 形 ❶ 大膽的；❷（字的）粗體的

❶ Bernadine created a **bold** design for modifying her recreational vehicle. 蓓娜汀設計了一組大膽的圖案，用來裝飾自己的休旅車。

❷ The headline is in **bold** type so that it stands out for the readers. 標題用粗體，這樣讀者比較容易注意到。

相關用法 副 **boldly** 勇敢地，大膽地

- State your opinions boldly; don't be afraid. 勇敢說出你的意見，不要害怕。

05 **bravery** [`brevərɪ] 名 U 勇敢，勇氣　同義 courage 勇氣

- Geraldine showed great **bravery** when standing up for social justice. 嬌拉汀展現出高度勇氣，為了社會正義挺身而出。

- brave 勇敢的
- -ry 名 表「行為」

06 **brutal** [`brut!] 形 殘忍的，野蠻的

- Those boys threw stones at the dog; it was a **brutal** act. 那些男孩向那隻狗丟石頭，他們的行為很殘忍。

- brute 獸，畜生
- -al 形 表「……的」

相關用法 副 **brutally** 殘忍地，直截了當地

- To be brutally honest, you don't look good in that yellow dress.
  我必須很殘忍的告訴你，這件黃色洋裝你穿起來不好看。

07 **capable** [ˋkepəbḷ] 形 ❶ 能夠（做……）的；❷ 有能力的，能幹的

❶ After three months of intense physical training, Paula feels **capable** of climbing Mount Everest.
寶拉經過三個月的密集體能訓練後，自覺能夠攻克聖母峰了。

❷ Frank is a very **capable** man; he has the ability to do many things well. 法蘭克具有相當優秀的能力；他有能耐把很多事做得很好。

用法 be capable of V-ing 有能力做某事的

08 **capacity** [kəˋpæsətɪ] 名 C ❶ 能力；❷ 容量

❶ Kent has a great **capacity** for mathematics, but his language skills are relatively poor. 肯特的數學非常強，但語文能力則是有待加強。

❷ The bus has a **capacity** of 50 passengers, but it was carrying about 100 people when the accident took place.
那輛巴士可以容納 50 名乘客。但是當意外發生時，車內大約擠進了 100 人。

09 **challenge** [ˋtʃælɪndʒ] 動 ❶ 挑戰；❷ 質疑，對……提出異議
名 C ❸ 挑戰；❹ 艱鉅的事

❶ Oscar never **challenges** his father's authority, so their relationship is very smooth. 奧斯卡從不挑戰父親權威，所以父子倆非常和睦。

❷ Alice was brave enough to **challenge** her boss' view of the plan; she questioned whether the plan would work.
愛麗絲勇敢挑戰老闆對那項計畫的看法，她質疑計畫的可行性。

❸ The presidential candidate received a **challenge** to appear in a TV debate, but he turned down the invitation.
這位總統候選人接到電視辯論的挑戰，但是他拒絕了這項邀約。

❹ Digging a tunnel through a mountain is a major **challenge**; many architects think it is an impossible one.
在山裡築一條隧道工程浩大，許多建築師認為這是不可能的任務。

相關用法 形 **challenging** 有挑戰性的

- It is a challenging project; although difficult, it will be interesting and will test your ability.
  這項具有挑戰性的計畫雖然困難，但它很有意思，還能測試你的能力。

128

10 **charm** [tʃɑrm] ❶ 名 U 魅力 ❷ 動 吸引，使迷住

❶ Cliff's warm smile is his greatest **charm**.
克里夫的溫暖微笑是他的迷人魅力。

❷ Karen was so attractive that every man at the party was **charmed** by her beauty. 凱倫的魅力讓舞會中每個男生都被她的美貌迷住了。

相關用法 形 **charming** 迷人的

- The man is very charming; many women find him attractive.
這名男子非常迷人，他對很多女人具有吸引力。

補充 Prince Charming 白馬王子

11 **courageous** [kəˋredʒəs] 形 英勇的，勇敢的

- Harriet's **courageous** action proved her heart is indeed fearless. 哈莉特英勇的行為證明她的確心無所懼。

> ・courage 勇氣
> ・-ous 形 表「有……特質的」

12 **courteous** [ˋkɝtjəs] 形 謙恭的，有禮貌的

- Jack is a **courteous** person; he is polite and kind, and he always shows respect for others.
傑克為人謙恭有禮，他既客氣又善良，並總是尊敬他人。

> ・court 法庭
> ・-(e)ous 形 表「有……的」

13 **courtesy** [ˋkɝtəsɪ] 名 ❶ U 禮貌；❷ C 謙恭有禮的言辭或舉動

❶ Young regularly sends greeting cards to his relatives out of **courtesy**.
楊都會定期禮貌性地寄賀卡給親戚。

❷ When you enter a building, be sure to hold the door open for anyone coming through behind you. It is a common courtesy in many **cultures**.
當你走進大樓時，務必替在你身後的人扶住門，這在很多文化中是一般禮儀。

> ・courteous 禮貌的
> ・-y 名 表「性質」

14 **cruelty** [ˋkruəltɪ] 名 U 殘酷，殘忍　反義 kindness 仁慈

- Nothing can justify **cruelty** to the unfortunate.
別對遭逢不幸者報以冷漠的心。

> ・cruel 殘忍
> ・-ty 名 表「狀態」

15 **cunning** [ˋkʌnɪŋ] 形 ❶ 熟練的，靈巧的；❷ 狡猾的，奸詐的

❶ Sylvia has become a **cunning** saleswoman after years of practicing her trade. 希薇雅在磨練經驗多年後，終於成為一名熟練的銷售員。

❷ Stanley is as **cunning** as a fox; he is always able to get what he wants by trickery or cheating.
史丹尼像狐狸一樣的狡猾，他總是能藉由哄騙或行騙來得到他想要的東西。

16 **dare** [dɛr] ❶ 動 敢，膽敢；❷（助動詞）敢，竟敢

❶ Elisa **dared** not to dive into the ocean without any equipment.
艾莉莎沒帶潛水裝備，不敢潛進海洋中。

❷ The boy **dare** not go into the forest alone; he is afraid that he may get lost. 男孩不敢單獨走進森林，他害怕會迷路。

相關片語 **I dare say**（我想）大概，可能

- There is a ring around the moon. It will be a sunny day tomorrow, I dare say. 月亮有一圈月暈，我想明天大概會是晴天。

17 **defensive** [dɪˋfɛnsɪv] 形 防禦的，自衛的

- Ruth is a very **defensive** person. She cannot take criticism and always finds excuses to justify her actions. 露絲是一個防衛心很強的人。她無法接受任何批評，而且總是找理由為自己辯護。

> ▪ defense 保衛
> ▪ -ive 形 表「……的」

18 **dignity** [ˋdɪgnətɪ] 名 U 尊嚴

- Virgil showed a true sense of **dignity** when dealing with unfairness from those around him. 維吉爾在不公平的對待下，仍展現出他的真實尊嚴。

19 **diligence** [ˋdɪlədʒəns] 名 U 勤勉

- With patience and **diligence**, you can learn to speak English well. 耐心與勤勉能讓你學好英文口說。

> ▪ diligent 勤勉的
> ▪ -ence 名 表「性質，狀態」

20 **diligent** [ˋdɪlədʒənt] 形 勤勉的，勤奮的

- Tito is not very intelligent, but he is very **diligent** when it comes to studying. 狄托不怎麼聰明，但是他讀書非常用功。

65 Ability & personality 能力與個性 (2)

129

01 **distinguished** [dɪˋstɪŋgwɪʃt] 形 著名的，卓越的

- Mr. Gale is **distinguished** for his knowledge of Indian philosophy. 蓋爾先生以精通印度哲學聞名。

> ▪ distinguish 識別
> ▪ -ed 形 表「有……特徵的」

02 **earnest** [ˋɝnɪst] 形 認真的，誠摯的

- A handshake is an **earnest** gesture of goodwill in many cultures. 在許多文化中，握手是一種誠心表示友好的手勢。

03 **efficient** [ɪˋfɪʃənt] 形 效率高的，有效率的　反義 inefficient 無效率的

● An **efficient** worker knows how to avoid making the same mistake twice. 一名有效率的工作者知道如何避免重蹈覆轍。

04 **enable** [ɪnˋebḷ] 動 ❶ 使能夠；❷ 使成為可能

‧en- 表「使……」
‧able 能夠

❶ The Internet **enables** people to exchange information quickly; it also makes it possible to communicate easily. 網際網路讓人們能夠快速交換資訊，也讓彼此的通訊變得簡單容易。

❷ Clara finally raised **enough** funds to enable the construction of the new hospital. 卡拉終於募集到足夠的資金興建一間新醫院。

05 **endure** [ɪnˋdjʊr] 動 ❶ 忍受，忍耐；❷ 持續　同義 bear 忍受；last 持續

❶ The cancer patient **endured** the chemotherapy; although it was really painful, he never complained.
那名癌症病患忍受了化療帶來的痛苦。雖然疼痛無比，但是他從不抱怨。

❷ Arnold and Lucy's relationship has **endured**, even after years of living apart. 阿諾和露西的關係沒有因多年分隔兩地而中斷。

06 **faithful** [ˋfeθfəl] 形 忠實的，忠誠的

‧faith 信任
‧-ful 形 表「充滿……的」

● Hubert's dog is his most **faithful** companion.
休伯特的狗是他最忠實的夥伴。

相關用法 副 **faithfully** 忠實地

● The manager has served the company faithfully for more than 30 years; the boss considers him trustworthy.
這名經理忠實地在公司服務超過三十年，老闆認為他很可靠。

07 **familiar** [fəˋmɪljɚ] 形 ❶ 熟悉的，通曉的；❷ 常見的，普通的

‧family 家；家人
‧-ar 形 表「有……特性的」

❶ Laura is **familiar** with this town, as she has lived here for 10 years; she knows the place very well.
蘿拉很熟悉這座小鎮，因為她已經住在這裡十年了；她非常了解這個地方。

❷ Televisions and refrigerators are ordinary and **familiar** objects found in every home. 電視和冰箱是每戶人家常見的一般物品。

用法 somebody be familiar with something 某人對某事熟悉
= something be familiar to somebody 某事對某人來說是熟悉的

08 **fierce** [fɪrs] 形 ❶ 兇猛的，粗暴的；❷ 激烈的，猛烈的

❶ The dog looks **fierce**; it barks at and even tries to bite people who pass by. 那隻狗看起來很兇猛。牠對經過的人吠叫，還想要咬人。

❷ After a **fierce** argument, Phyllis decided to break up with her boyfriend. 菲莉絲與男友大吵一架後，決定要分手。

相關用法 副 **fiercely** 猛烈地

- The fire is burning fiercely; the firefighters can barely approach the building. 這棟建築物猛烈燃燒著，消防隊員幾乎無法靠近。

130

09 **generosity** [ˌdʒɛnəˋrɑsətɪ] 名 U 寬宏大量，慷慨

- generous 慷慨的
- -ity 名 表「性質」

- Gustavo received a scholarship funded through the **generosity** of anonymous donors. 古斯塔夫獲得一筆由匿名人士慷慨捐助的獎學金。

10 **gifted** [ˋgɪftɪd] 形 有天賦的，有天資的

- gift 天賦
- -ed 形 表「有……特徵的」

- Suzanne is a **gifted** vocalist who has been singing all her life. 蘇珊是天生的歌手，終其一生奉獻給歌唱。

11 **gracious** [ˋgreʃəs] 形 ❶ 親切的，和藹的；❷ 優裕的，優渥的

- grace 優雅
- -ious 形 表「有……特性的」

❶ Mrs. Smith is a **gracious** lady; she is always polite and generous, especially to people in lower social positions. 史密斯太太是一位優雅的女士。她總是有禮貌又慷慨，尤其是對低下階層的人。

❷ The old man has gotten used to the simple life of the countryside; the **gracious** life of the big city no longer suits him. 這名老人已經習慣了鄉下的簡樸生活，他覺得大城市裡的優裕生活不適合他。

12 **honesty** [ˋɑnɪstɪ] 名 U 正直，誠實

- honest 誠實的
- -ty 名 表「狀態」

- I must tell you in all **honesty** that your chocolate cheesecake was delicious. 我得實話實說，你的巧克力起司蛋糕實在美味極了。

13 **honorable** [ˋɑnərəbl̩] 形 ❶ 可尊敬的，高尚的；❷ 表示尊敬的，體面的

- honor 榮譽
- -able 形 表「有……特性的」

❶ Mr. Woods is an **honorable** man; many people respect and admire him. 伍茲先生為人高尚正直，很多人尊敬並欽佩他。

❷ The soldier fought bravely and died in the battle; to pay its respects, the government gave him an **honorable** burial. 那名士兵在戰役中奮勇作戰捐軀。為了表示對他的尊敬，政府為他辦了一場體面的葬禮。

14 **idle** [ˋaɪdl̩] ❶ 形 懶惰的，無所事事的 ❷ 動 閒混，閒逛；❸ 虛度（光陰）

❶ Having been unemployed for three years, Randolph has become used to an **idle** life. 朗道弗失業了三年，早已習慣無所事事的生活。

❷ The young man **idled** down the street with no particular purpose. 那名年輕人在街上漫無目的地閒逛。

❸ Instead of finding a job, the man **idled** the days away.
男子不找工作，反而虛度光陰。

15 **innocence** [ˋɪnəsn̩s] 名 U ❶ 天真無邪，純真；❷ 無罪，清白

・innocent 無罪的
・-ence 名 表「性質，狀態」

❶ As we grow older, we gain more experience in the world; but at the same time, we lose our **innocence**.
隨著年紀變大，我們獲得世上更多的經驗，但同時也失去了我們的純真。

❷ After a long investigation, new evidence has finally proved Jeffrey's **innocence**. 經過長時間的調查，新證據終於證明了傑佛瑞的清白。

16 **intellectual** [͵ɪntl̩ˋɛktʃʊəl] ❶ 形 智力的；理智的 ❷ 名 知識分子

・intellect 智力
・-al 形 表「……的」;「狀態」

❶ Ruben's tremendous **intellectual** power can't always solve his emotional problems.
魯本的高智商有時還是無法解決自己的情緒問題。

❷ Those **intellectuals** used to gather in cafés, pondering and discussing social problems.
那些知識分子過去常常聚集在咖啡廳，進行沉思並討論社會問題。

17 **intelligence** [ɪnˋtɛlədʒəns] 名 U ❶ 智能，理解力；❷ 情報

・intelligent 有才智的
・-ence 名 表「性質，狀態」

❶ Over the years, Debbie has developed different forms of artificial **intelligence**.
多年來，黛比已研發出不同的人工智慧模式。

❷ The U.S. Central **Intelligence** Agency is responsible for collecting information related to the country's security.
美國中情局負責蒐集關於美國國家安全的資訊。

18 **intelligent** [ɪnˋtɛlədʒənt] 形 有才智的，聰明的

● Ms. Hook is not only competent, but she is also **intelligent**.
胡克小姐不僅能力佳，也很聰穎。

66 Ability & personality 能力與個性 (3)

131

01 **loyal** [ˋlɔɪəl] 形 **忠誠的，忠心的** 同義 true 忠誠的 反義 disloyal 不忠誠的

- Mr. Sparks has been **loyal** to his wife for more than 50 years.
  史巴克斯先生五十多年來都忠於自己的妻子。

用法 be loyal to 對……忠誠

02 **loyalty** [ˋlɔɪəltɪ] 名 U **忠誠，忠心**

- The citizens lost any sense of **loyalty** to the dishonest politicians. 公民會離棄言行不一的政客。

・loyal 忠誠的
・-ty 名 表「狀態」

03 **might** [maɪt] ❶ 助動 **可能，可以** ❷ 名 U **力量，威力，能力**

❶ Billy told us that he **might** come to the party.
比利告訴我們，他可能會來參加派對。

❷ Bessie has tried with all her **might** to balance her family and career.
貝絲已試著盡全力解決家庭與事業難以兼顧的困境。

04 **mighty** [ˋmaɪtɪ] 形 ❶ **強大的，強而有力的**；❷ **巨大的**

❶ As a writer, Vincent believes the saying "The pen is **mightier** than the sword." 身為一名作家，文森相信「文勝於武」這句諺語。

❷ Look at the **mighty** Yangtze River! It is large and impressive.
看看那巨大的長江！它規模廣大，令人印象深刻。

・might 力量
・-y 形 表「有……的」

05 **modest** [ˋmɑdɪst] 形 **謙虛的** 反義 immodest, boastful 不謙虛的，自誇的

- Ms. Sawyer received the Citizen of Honor award, but she is too **modest** to mention it.
  索伊爾小姐受封為「榮譽市民」，但她極為謙虛，隻字不提。

06 **modesty** [ˋmɑdɪstɪ] 名 U **謙遜** 形 modest 謙虛的

- What I like the most about Darnell is his **modesty**.
  我最喜歡達尼爾的地方是他很謙虛。

・modest 謙虛的
・-y 名 表「狀態」

07 **obedience** [əˋbidjəns] 名 U **服從** 形 obedient 服從的

- The father demands **obedience** from his daughter; he wants her to do what she is told to do.
  這個爸爸要求他的女兒服從。女兒得要聽從他的所有指令。

・obey 服從
・-ence 名 表「狀態」

08 **obedient** [ə`bidjənt] 形 服從的，順從的

- obey 服從
- -ent 形 表「有……性質的」

● Tommy is an **obedient** boy; he does whatever his mother tells him to do.
湯米是一個順從的孩子。他媽媽要他做什麼，他就會照著做。

09 **patience** [`peʃəns] 名 U 耐心，耐性　形 patient 耐心的

- patient 耐心的
- -ence 名 表「狀態」

● Being an elementary school teacher requires **patience**. 當小學老師需要很有耐心。

10 **personality** [͵pɝsn̩`ælətɪ] 名 C 個性，性格

- person 人
- -al 形 表「……的」
- -ity 名 表「性質」

● Claire has a bright **personality** that gives her a positive outlook on life.
克萊兒的開朗個性，讓她能夠積極面對人生。

11 **pessimistic** [`pɛsə͵mɪstɪk] 形 悲觀的　名 pessimist 悲觀者

- pessimist 悲觀者
- -ic 形 表「具有……特性的」

● Elizabeth is so **pessimistic** that only negative events catch her attention.
伊莉莎白生性悲觀，只有負面消息能吸引她的注意。

12 **refusal** [rɪ`fjuzl̩] 名 U 拒絕

- refuse 拒絕
- -al 名 表「動作」

● In many cultures, a shaking head shows **refusal**, and a nodding head shows approval.
在許多文化中，搖頭代表拒絕，點頭代表贊同。

132

13 **reliable** [rɪ`laɪəbl̩] 形 可靠的，可信賴的

- rely 依靠
- -able 形 表「可……的」

● This information came from a very **reliable** source, so you don't have to worry about being cheated.
這個消息的來源很可靠，所以你不用擔心被騙。〔98 年學測〕

14 **respectable** [rɪ`spɛktəbl̩] 形 值得尊敬的

- respect 尊敬
- -able 形 表「可……的」

● The man standing over there is a very **respectable** scholar; many people admire him for his brilliant achievements.
站在那邊的男子是一位十分可敬的學者，許多人欽佩他傑出的成就。

15 **respectful** [rɪ`spɛktfəl] 形 恭敬的，尊敬人的，尊重人的

- respect 尊敬
- -ful 形 表「充滿……的」

● Those boys spoke to the astronaut in a **respectful** tone of voice.
幾個男孩以尊敬的口吻跟那名太空人講話。

16 **sincere** [sɪnˋsɪr] 形 ❶ 誠實的，正直的；❷ 真誠的，衷心的

❶ Kenneth is a nice guy; he is decent and **sincere**.
肯尼士是一個好人，他為人正派、誠實。

❷ Douglas offered Iris a **sincere** apology after their fight.
吵完架之後，道格拉斯真誠地向艾莉絲道歉。

相關用法 **sincerely** 副 真誠地，誠懇地，由衷地

- We sincerely hope that you will accept our apology.
我們真誠地希望你能接受我們的道歉。

17 **stubborn** [ˋstʌbən] 形 ❶ 倔強的，頑固的；❷（汙漬）難去掉的

❶ It is hard to persuade the old man, for he is very **stubborn**.
要說服那名老人非常困難，因為他很頑固。

❷ Ramona used a special detergent to remove the **stubborn** stains from her dress. 蕾夢娜用一種特別的洗潔劑，來去除自己洋裝上難洗的汙漬。

18 **tame** [tem] 形 ❶ 沒骨氣的；❷（動物）經馴養的，馴服的　反義 wild 野生的

❶ Parker is too **tame** to disobey his parents for his own gain.
帕克太沒骨氣了，為了自己的利益，竟然對父母唯唯諾諾的。

❷ The panda has been trained to live with humans and has become **tame**; it can no longer go back to the wild.
這一隻貓熊訓練要與人類同住，變得馴服了，再也無法回到野外生活。

19 **tricky** [ˋtrɪkɪ] 形 狡猾的

- trick 詭計
- -y 形 表「有……的」

- The man is very **tricky**; he is clever and likely to deceive people. 這名男子很狡猾。他腦筋清楚，而且很可能欺騙人。

20 **truthful** [ˋtruθfəl] 形 誠實的，坦率的　同義 honest 誠實的

- true 真實的
- -th 名 表「狀態」
- -ful 形 表「充滿……的」

- Shelby gave the police a **truthful** report of the accident. 謝爾比向警方說明事故的確實情形。

21 **wisdom** [ˋwɪzdəm] 名 U 智慧

- wise 智慧
- -dom 名 表「狀態」

- Reginald shows great **wisdom** and compassion in his actions and his words.
雷金納德在他的一言一行中，展現出無比的智慧與同情心。

22 **sincerity** [sɪnˋsɛrətɪ] 名 U 誠心誠意

- sincere 真誠的
- -ity 名 表「狀態」

- With absolute **sincerity**, Alicia confided that she's decided to study Buddhism. 艾莉希亞滿懷誠懇，透露她決定研讀佛學。

23 **stingy** [ˋstɪndʒɪ] 形 吝嗇的，小氣的 同義 mean 吝嗇的

・sting 刺
・-y 形 表「有……的」

● Albert Morse is **stingy** with his money.
艾伯特．摩斯對錢很小氣。

24 **timid** [ˋtɪmɪd] 形 **膽怯的，羞怯的**

● The girl is too **timid** to ask the handsome boy out; she doesn't even have the courage to talk to him.
那女孩太羞怯了，無法約那位英俊的男孩出去，她甚至沒有勇氣跟他說話。

相關用法 副 **timidly** 膽小地，羞怯地

● The girl smiled timidly; she appeared to be very shy.
那名女孩羞怯地微笑；她顯得十分害羞。

25 **vain** [ven] 形 ❶ **愛虛榮的，自負的；**❷ **徒然的，無益的**

❶ The rich woman is **vain**; she is too proud of her wealth.
那個女人很自負，她以自己的財富而驕傲自滿。

❷ The firefighter was seriously hurt in a **vain** attempt to save the woman from the burning house.
消防隊員嘗試將女子從燃燒的房子救出來，但他沒有成功並且受了重傷。

相關片語 **in vain** 徒勞

● After the flood, all the labor Lewis put into building the house in the sand canyon was in vain.
路易斯用心在沙谷中蓋了一棟房子。但水災過後，一切努力都泡了湯。

67 Feelings & emotions 感受與情緒 (1)

133

01 **admirable** [ˋædmərəbḷ] 形 **值得讚揚的，令人欽佩的**

・admire 欽佩
・-able 形 表「可……的」

● Mother Teresa's devotion to helping the poor and sick was **admirable**; people around the world respected her for this. 泰瑞莎修女獻身幫助窮困病人之舉令人欽佩。全世界的人都很尊敬她。

02 **admiration** [͵ædməˋreʃən] 名 ❶ U **欽佩，羨慕；** ❷ C **令人欽佩或羨慕的人（或物）**

・admire 欽佩
・-ation 名 表「動作」

❶ People have great **admiration** for Martin Luther King, Jr., who fought for equal rights for all humans.
人們都非常欽佩馬丁．路德．金恩二世，他是替全體人類爭取平等權利的一位偉大領袖。

❷ Abigail's garden won the **admiration** of the whole community.
艾碧嘉兒的花園是全社區居民都稱羨的。

03 **admire** [əd`maɪr] 動 **欽佩，欣賞** 同義 respect, honor 尊敬

● Chloe **admires** Mr. Walton's ability to envision the future of the computer industry. 克蘿伊很欽佩華頓先生展望未來電腦產業的能力。

04 **amaze** [ə`mez] 動 **使大為吃驚，使驚愕**

- a- 表「在某狀態中」
- maze 迷惑

● Tom was very ill a week ago, but now he looks healthy. We are **amazed** by his quick recovery. 湯姆一星期前病得很重，但他現在看起來很健康。我們對他迅速的康復能力感到驚訝。〔96 年學測〕

05 **amazement** [ə`mezmənt] 名 U **吃驚，詫異**

- amaze 大為吃驚
- 迷惑
- -ment 名 表「狀態」

● No one thought they would finish the job on time; however, to everyone's **amazement**, they did. 沒人認為他們可以準時完成這件工作；然而，令大家吃驚的是，他們辦到了。

06 **annoy** [ə`nɔɪ] 動 **❶ 打攪，困擾；❷ 惹惱，使煩惱**

❶ The sound of mosquitoes buzzing in my ear really **annoys** me, especially when I'm trying to sleep.
蚊子在耳邊嗡嗡叫真的很煩人，尤其是在我要睡覺的時候。

❷ The woman was **annoyed** with her son because of his rude behavior. 那名女子因為兒子的粗魯行為而惱怒。

07 **anxiety** [æŋ`zaɪətɪ] 名 **❶** C **焦慮的原因，令人焦慮之事；❷** U **焦慮，掛念**

❶ Tammie feels real **anxiety** when she travels on an airplane, especially during a thunderstorm.
對泰美來說，飛行是很令人不安的，尤其在暴風雨中更是如此。

❷ All the students are filled with **anxiety** about the exam; they are worried they might fail it.
所有的學生都為了考試的結果滿心焦慮。他們擔心會不及格。

08 **anxious** [`æŋkʃəs] 形 **❶ 焦慮的，掛念的；❷ 令人焦慮的**

❶ Anne dreaded giving a speech before three hundred people; even thinking about it made her **anxious**.
安很害怕要在 300 人面前演講，甚至只要一想到就讓她焦慮起來。〔95 年學測〕

❷ Angelo spent an **anxious** night waiting for the birth of his first child. 安傑洛整晚焦慮不安，等待他第一個孩子的誕生。

09 **arouse** [ə`raʊz] 動 ❶ 激起；❷ 叫醒

・a- 表「朝向」
・rouse 喚醒

❶ Connie's speech **aroused** the crowd; soon, the people were marching down the street, calling for reform.
康妮的演講激勵了群眾，很快地，他們群起上街遊行，訴諸改革。

❷ Early in the morning, I was **aroused** from a deep sleep by my mom. 一大早，我就被媽媽從沉穩的睡夢中叫醒。

134

10 **ashamed** [ə`ʃemd] 形 **羞愧的，感到難為情的**

● Agatha was **ashamed** to admit that she had failed the final examination. 艾葛莎覺得，承認自己期末考試不及格很難為情。

11 **attract** [ə`trækt] 動 ❶ **吸引；❷ 引起（注意或興趣等）**

❶ Bert never wears cologne because he believes it **attracts** bees.
伯特認為香水會招來蜜蜂，所以他都不噴香水的。

❷ Carl is very interested in the job offer; what **attracts** him most is the chance to travel to different countries.
卡爾對那份工作非常有興趣，而最吸引他的是有機會走訪不同的國家。

12 **attraction** [ə`trækʃən] 名 ❶ Ⓒ 吸引物，賣點；❷ Ⓤ 吸引力

・attract 吸引
・-ion 名 表「行為的結果」

❶ The main **attraction** of this movie is its special effects; the story itself is very dull. 這部電影的賣點是特效，它的劇情其實很無聊。

❷ Rome holds much **attraction** for me; I try to visit the city every year. 羅馬對我很有吸引力，我想每年都去拜訪這個城市。

13 **attractive** [ə`træktɪv] 形 有吸引力的，引人注目的

・attract 吸引
・-ive 形 表「有……特性的」

● Elbert couldn't resist the **attractive** offer made by his company's competitor.
艾伯特抗拒不了競爭對手開給他的誘人薪資。

14 **aware** [ə`wɛr] 形 ❶ **知道的，察覺的；❷ 防備的，警覺的**

❶ Although Barb is **aware** of the dangers involved in space flight, she still insists on going to the Moon.
即使芭貝了解宇宙飛行的高危險性，她還是堅持要登上月球。

❷ When a soldier stands guard, he has to be **aware** of his surroundings at all times. 士兵站崗時，必須隨時保持警覺。

相關用法 名 **awareness** 覺悟，體認

● There is a general awareness that smoking harms people's health.
人們普遍體認到吸菸對健康有害。

15 **awful** [ˋɔfʊl] 形 ❶ 可怕的，嚇人的；❷ 極壞的，極糟的；❸ 非常的，十分的

▪ awe 敬畏
▪ -ful 形 表「充滿……的」

❶ There was an **awful** earthquake last night, and we were scared for our lives.
昨晚發生一場可怕的地震，我們都快嚇死了。

❷ The student's pronunciation is **awful**, and his grammar is even worse. 那名學生的發音很差，但他的文法甚至更糟糕。

❸ We had an **awful** lot of rain last night, which caused floods in the low-lying areas. 昨晚雨下個不停，導致低窪地區淹水。

16 **awkward** [ˋɔkwɚd] 形 **尷尬的，令人困窘的**

● Jane felt **awkward** speaking in front of the class but was quite relaxed talking with her good friends.
珍覺得在全班面前講話很尷尬，但她在好朋友面前就可以放鬆說話。〔92 年學測補考〕

17 **blush** [blʌʃ] ❶ 動 **臉紅** ❷ 名 C **臉紅**

❶ Andrea **blushed** when a young man whistled as she walked by.
一名年輕男子在安德莉亞經過時吹了聲口哨，讓她滿臉飛紅。

❷ Feeling embarrassed, the little boy grew as red as a beet; he covered his face with his hands to hide the **blushing**.
因為感到尷尬，那個小男孩的臉紅得像甜菜根。他用手遮住自己的臉，想遮掩臉紅。

18 **bore** [bor] 動 ❶ **使厭煩，煩擾**；❷ **鑽孔，鑽洞**

❶ Lillian has finally realized how much her daily routine **bores** her.
莉莉恩總算了解，自己的日常工作是多麼無聊了。

❷ The worker is **boring** the ground with a drill.
那名工人正在用鑽床在地上鑽洞。

19 **burden** [ˋbɝdn̩] ❶ 名 C **負擔，重擔** ❷ 動 **加負擔於**

❶ The **burden** of supporting his whole family has caused Seth to overwork himself for years.
塞斯為了扛起養育全家大小的重擔，多年來都工作過量。

❷ The new government promised not to **burden** the people with heavy taxes. 新政府承諾不會使國民負擔重稅。

68 Feelings & emotions 感受與情緒 (2)

135

01 **cheerful** [ˋtʃɪrfəl] 形 興高采烈的，情緒好的

- cheer 高興
- -ful 形 表「有……性質的」

- With his **cheerful** nature, Spencer has joyful encounters all of the time. 史賓塞天性活潑開朗，遇到誰都能相處融洽。

02 **cherish** [ˋtʃɛrɪʃ] 動 珍惜，珍愛

- Eduardo and his wife **cherished** their adopted child as one of their own. 厄杜瓦多和妻子把領養的小孩當成親生骨肉般疼愛。

03 **complex** [ˋkɑmplɛks] 名 C ❶ 情結；❷ 複合物，集合體 ❸ 形 複雜的，難懂的

❶ Nicolas has an inferiority **complex**; he believes he is much less important and clever than others.
尼可拉斯有自卑感。他總是覺得比起其他人，自己微不足道又不聰明。

❷ Many people choose to live in the area because of its impressive leisure **complex**. 許多居民選擇住在這個地區，因為這裡的綜合休閒設施很棒。

❸ The process of human birth is a **complex** phenomenon.
人類的誕生過程是一種複雜難懂的現象。

補充 Oedipus complex 戀母情結；inferiority complex 自卑情結

04 **concern** [kənˋsɝn] 名 ❶ U 擔心，掛念；❷ C 擔心或關心的事 動 ❸ 關於；❹ 使擔心

❶ Sarah has growing **concerns** about her son's school life.
莎拉對於兒子在學校的生活十分關心。

❷ The cancer patient has some **concerns** about the side effects of the treatment; he is also worried about the expense.
這名癌症病人擔心治療的副作用；另外醫療費用也讓他很煩惱。

❸ The book **concerns** global warming; the first chapter is about the causes of the climate change.
這本書談論全球暖化現象。第一章是關於造成氣候變化的原因。

❹ The father's poor health **concerns** his daughters; they are very upset about his illness.
父親的健康狀況不佳，讓他的女兒們很擔心。每個人為他的病憂心忡忡。

相關片語 **as/so far as...be concerned** 就……而言

- As far as I'm concerned, gardening is a good way to relax.
就我而言，園藝是一種放鬆的好方法。

05 **confidence** [ˋkɑnfədəns] 名 U 信心

- Velma has the **confidence** to swim across Arrowhead Lake. 威瑪有信心能游泳橫渡箭頭湖。

・confide 信任
・-ence 名 表「狀態」

06 **confident** [ˋkɑnfədənt] 形 ❶ 有信心的，自信的；❷ 確信的

❶ Ivy is quite **confident** that she will meet the requirements of the teaching position. 艾薇有自信符合那項教學職位的一切要求。

❷ They are **confident** that everything will go as expected. 他們確信事情會如期望般進行。

・confide 信任
・-ent 形 表「在……狀態的」

07 **content** 形 動 [kənˋtɛnt] ❶ 形 滿足的，滿意的
名 [ˋkɑntɛnt] 名 ❷ C 容納的東西；❸ U 內容 ❹ 動 使滿足

❶ I am **content** with my life; I am happy and satisfied with what I have. 我很滿意自己的生活；我對於自己所擁有的感到高興並滿足。

❷ Ronald emptied the **contents** of his pockets before walking through the metal detector at the security checkpoint. 羅德走向安全檢哨站的金屬探測器前，將口袋裡的物品全部拿出來。

❸ The article lacks **content**; it contains no ideas at all. 這篇文章缺乏內容，一點見解也沒有。

❹ The job used to **content** Cedric, but now he is dissatisfied with it. 這份工作過去令賽德里克很滿意，但是現在他無法以此感到滿足。

08 **contentment** [kənˋtɛntmənt] 名 U 滿足，滿意

- I do my best every day to seek peace and **contentment**. 我全力以赴追求每日的平靜與滿足。

・content 滿足的
・-ment 名 表「狀態」

09 **curiosity** [ˏkjʊrɪˋɑsətɪ] 名 U 好奇心

- Owen believes **curiosity** is the fuel for acquiring knowledge. 歐文相信，好奇心是獲取知識的動力。

・curious 好奇的
・-ity 名 表「狀態」

136 10 **delight** [dɪˋlaɪt] ❶ 名 U 愉快，欣喜；❷ C 樂事，樂趣 ❸ 動 使高興

❶ The fans screamed with **delight** when they saw the superstar. 當粉絲看到那位超級巨星時，他們興奮尖叫。

❷ Kerry's greatest **delight** is her companionship with her granddaughter. 對凱莉來說，最愉快的事就是陪伴孫女。

❸ The magician performed a variety of tricks to **delight** the audience; his show gave them a lot of pleasure. 魔術師變了很多戲法來娛樂觀眾。他的表演帶給他們很多樂趣。

11 **delightful** [dɪˋlaɪtfəl] 形 令人愉快的，令人高興的

- delight 愉快
- -ful 形 表「充滿……的」

● Elvis is planning a **delightful** surprise for his wife on her birthday. 艾維斯計畫要在妻子生日時，給她一個開心的驚喜。

12 **depress** [dɪˋprɛs] 動 ❶ 使沮喪，使消沉；❷ 使蕭條

❶ It **depresses** me that none of my friends like my idea.
沒有任何一個朋友喜歡我的主意，這讓我很沮喪。

❷ Daphne worried that rising inflation would further **depress** the economy. 黛芬妮擔憂，惡化的通貨膨脹會進一步拖垮經濟。

13 **depression** [dɪˋprɛʃən] 名 U ❶ 沮喪，抑鬱；❷ 蕭條，不景氣

- depress 使沮喪
- -ion 名 表「行為的結果」

❶ Gabriel tried to bring his wife out of her **depression** after her miscarriage.
加百利在妻子流產後，試著帶她走出憂鬱。

❷ Many people lost their jobs during the Great **Depression**.
許多人在經濟大蕭條時期失業。

14 **desirable** [dɪˋzaɪrəbl̩] 形 值得嚮往的，合意的

- desire 渴望
- -able 形 表「有……特性的」

● We took a class vote and decided that Mark Andrea was a more **desirable** candidate for class president than Jacob. 我們舉行班投，決定馬克．安德利比傑各更適合當班長。

15 **desperate** [ˋdɛspərɪt] 形 ❶ 孤注一擲的；❷ 絕望的；❸ 極度渴望的

- despair 絕望
- -ate 形 表「有……性質的」

❶ Leopold made a **desperate** attempt to save his family business. 利奧波德孤注一擲，企圖挽救家族事業。

❷ The woman grew **desperate** when her lover left her; she felt that her life was a hopeless mess.
當那女子的愛人離開她的時候，她變得絕望，覺得自己的生活一團混亂、毫無希望。

❸ The poor man is **desperate** for a job, since he needs money to support his family. 那名可憐的男子急需找到工作，因為他需要錢來養家活口。

16 **disappoint** [ˌdɪsəˋpɔɪnt] 動 ❶ 使失望；❷ 使破滅，使挫敗

- dis- 表「不，相反」
- appoint 任命

❶ Kristy was **disappointed** that only half of her duck eggs hatched.
克絲蒂的鴨蛋只有一半孵化，讓她很失望。

❷ The bad weather **disappointed** us; we couldn't set off as planned. 壞天氣打亂了我們的計畫；我們無法按原計畫出發。

17 **disappointment** [ˌdɪsəˋpɔɪntmənt] 名 ❶ U 失望，掃興，沮喪；❷ C 令人失望的人，令人掃興的事

❶ As he left the office after getting fired, Mr. Lace's **disappointment** was very visible.
雷斯先生剛遭到解雇，垂頭喪氣地步出辦公室。

・disappoint 使失望
・-ment 名 表「狀態」

❷ The trip was a **disappointment**; it was not as exciting as we expected. 這次旅行真令人失望，沒有我們預期中的好玩。

相關片語 **to one's disappointment** 使某人失望的是

● To the boy's great disappointment, his mother did not make it to the baseball game to see him play.
讓那個男孩大失所望的是，他的媽媽沒能趕上棒球比賽看他打球。

18 **discourage** [dɪsˋkɝɪdʒ] 動 ❶ 使洩氣，使沮喪；❷ 阻擋，防止；❸ 勸阻

❶ The players were **discouraged** after losing the first game; they felt less enthusiastic about practicing after that.
球員們因為第一場比賽失利而沮喪，之後的練習也失去了熱情。

・dis- 表「不，相反」
・courage 勇氣

❷ The storm **discouraged** Echo from going out to meet her friends. 暴風雨讓愛蔻打消了出門和朋友聚會的念頭。

❸ Nora's father **discouraged** her from entering show business; he let her know often that he did not approve of the choice.
諾拉的爸爸勸她不要進入演藝圈。他一直對此表示反對。

用法 discourage somebody from V-ing　勸某人不要做某事

19 **discouragement** [dɪsˋkɝɪdʒmənt] 名 ❶ U 沮喪，氣餒；❷ C 使人洩氣的事物

❶ After the players lost the important soccer match, there was an atmosphere of **discouragement** around them.
在輸掉那場重要的足球比賽之後，球員間有一股沮喪的氣氛。

・discourage 氣餒
・-ment 名 表「狀態」

❷ Dylan failed in everything he did; despite all the **discouragements**, he didn't give up.
狄倫不管做什麼都失敗。儘管這一切讓人洩氣，他還是不放棄。

69 Feelings & emotions 感受與情緒 (3)

137

01 **disgust** [dɪsˋgʌst] 名 U ❶ 厭惡，憎惡；❷ 作嘔，噁心 ❸ 動 使作嘔

・dis- 表「不，相反」
・gust 一陣狂風

❶ People in the audience didn't hide their **disgust** at the speaker; they waved their fists at him to show their annoyance.
聽眾不掩飾他們對演講者的厭惡。他們對他揮舞拳頭，表示惱怒。

❷ Dominic was overwhelmed with **disgust** when he fell into an open sewer hole. 多明尼克跌進沒有蓋子的下水道口時，因惡臭難擋作嘔不止。

❸ The unrefrigerated fish had rotted, and the smell **disgusted** everyone. 擺在室溫下的魚腐爛了，那氣味讓大家作嘔。

相關用法 形 **disgusting** 令人作嘔的，十分討厭的

- The toilet is dirty, and the smell is disgusting. 這間廁所很髒，味道令人作嘔。

02 **dislike** [dɪsˋlaɪk] ❶ 動 不喜愛，厭惡 ❷ 名 C 不喜愛，厭惡

・dis- 表「不」
・like 喜歡

❶ Rebecca **dislikes** having to get up early to go to work.
芮貝嘉討厭必須早起去上班。

❷ The little girl has a **dislike** for carrots and onions.
這個小女孩不喜歡吃胡蘿蔔和洋蔥。

03 **doubtful** [ˋdaʊtfəl] 形 ❶ 懷疑的，疑惑的；❷ 令人生疑的

・doubt 懷疑
・-ful 形 表「充滿……的」

❶ Many people are **doubtful** about the existence of aliens. 許多人懷疑外星人是否存在。

❷ It is **doubtful** that Adeline will be chosen as the new leader of the research team. 愛德琳是否會選上研究團隊的新領導人仍是未知數。

04 **dread** [drɛd] ❶ 名 C（常作單數）畏懼，擔心 ❷ 動 懼怕，擔心

❶ Anna has a **dread** of walking home alone at night.
安娜很害怕要在深夜獨自走回家。

❷ Kelly **dreads** getting cancer, as both of her parents died of the disease. 凱莉很害怕得癌症，因為她的父母都死於這個疾病。

05 **eager** [ˋigɚ] 形 渴望的，急切的 同義 keen 渴望的

- When he travels, Cornelius is always **eager** to learn about different lifestyles. 寇尼里斯旅行時，總渴望能了解不同的生活方式。

06 **embarrass** [ɪmˋbærəs] 動 使困窘，使尷尬　同義 shame 感到羞愧

- Polly's childish behavior **embarrassed** her parents.
  波莉幼稚的行徑讓她父母感到很尷尬。

07 **embarrassment** [ɪmˋbærəsmənt] 名 ❶ U 困窘，難堪；❷ C 使人為難的人或事物

❶ The girl slipped and fell in front of the boy; she immediately blushed with **embarrassment**.
這名女孩在男孩面前滑倒，她立刻窘得臉紅。

・embarrass 使窘困
・-ment 名 表「狀態」

❷ Being slapped by his girlfriend in public was a real **embarrassment** to Horace, and he felt ashamed.
在公共場合被女朋友甩了一個耳光讓荷瑞斯十分難堪，他覺得很丟臉。

08 **emotional** [ɪˋmoʃənl̩] 形 ❶ 感情（上）的；❷ 易動情的，感情脆弱的

❶ My sister always provides **emotional** support for me; whenever I feel sad, she comforts me. 我的姊姊總是給予我情感上的支持。每當我感到悲傷，她便會安慰我。

・emotion 情感
・-al 形 表「……的」

❷ The woman is very **emotional**; she often cries when she watches soap operas on TV. 這名婦人感情脆弱。她看電視肥皂劇的時候，常常哭泣。

09 **enjoyable** [ɪnˋdʒɔɪəbl̩] 形 快樂的，有樂趣的

- Fern insisted that wearing wet shoes and clothes was not **enjoyable**. 芬恩覺得穿著溼鞋與溼衣很不好受。

・en- 表「使」
・joy 高興
・-able 形 表「可……的」

138

10 **enthusiasm** [ɪnˋθjuzɪˏæzəm] 名 U 熱心，熱情　形 enthusiastic 熱心的

- Elisabeth thinks that nothing great can be achieved without **enthusiasm**. 伊莉莎白認為，無熱忱不足以成大事。

11 **envious** [ˋɛnvɪəs] 形 嫉妒的，羨慕的　名 動 envy 羨慕

- Victor's classmates are very **envious** of him because he has just received a new cell phone for his birthday.
  維克多的同學很羨慕他，因為他生日剛收到一隻新手機。〔92 年指測〕

12 **envy** [ˋɛnvɪ] 名 ❶ U 妒忌，羨慕；❷ C 妒忌的對象，羨慕的目標；❸ 動 妒忌，羨慕

❶ Some of Steve's colleagues were green with **envy** when they learned that he had been promoted.
知道史蒂夫升職了，他的一些同事嫉妒得眼都紅了。

❷ Denny's new cell phone is the **envy** of his classmates; every one of them wants to have one.
丹尼的新手機成為同學的羨慕目標。他們每一個都想要擁有一支。

❸ Many girls **envy** Helen's beauty and wish they were as attractive as she is. 許多女孩忌妒海倫的美貌，希望能跟她一樣有魅力。

13 **exhaust** [ɪgˋzɔst] 動 ❶ 使精疲力盡；❷ 用完，耗盡 ❸ 名 U 排氣，排水

❶ A hard day's work completely **exhausted** the man; he needed a good rest. 在辛苦工作一天之後，男子精疲力竭。他需要好好休息一番。

❷ After being stuck in the mountains for three days, the lost climber had **exhausted** his supply of food; there was nothing left.
被困在山裡整整三天，那名迷路的登山者已經吃完了全部的食物，連一點也不剩。

❸ Eric bought a new car that produces less **exhaust** than a motorcycle. 艾立克買了一部比摩托車廢氣排放量更少的新車。

14 **flush** [flʌʃ] ❶ 動 臉紅；❷ 用水沖洗

❶ Every time Grace drinks wine, her face becomes **flushed**.
葛蕾絲只要一喝酒，就會滿臉通紅。

❷ After you use the toilet, remember to **flush** it.
在你用過廁所之後，記得沖水。

15 **fond** [fɑnd] 形 喜歡的，愛好的

● Roderick is very **fond** of his grandchildren, especially the four-year-old. 羅德瑞克非常喜愛自己的孫子，特別是那個四歲的孩子。

16 **frustrate** [ˋfrʌs͵tret] 動 ❶ 使感到灰心；❷ 挫敗，阻撓 同義 thwart 阻撓

❶ Antoinette has been **frustrated** by several failures, but she never gives up. 安朵娜特歷經數次挫敗，但她從未放棄。

❷ The approaching typhoon **frustrated** us by preventing us from going outside. 接近中的颱風阻礙了我們的計畫。我們無法外出了。

17 **frustration** [͵frʌsˋtreʃən] 名 ❶ U 挫折，挫敗；❷ C 挫折，挫敗

❶ Gilbert couldn't bear the **frustration** of failing the exam, as he had spent a lot of time preparing for it.
吉伯特無法接受考試不及格的挫敗，因為他花了很多時間做準備。

・frustrate 挫敗
・-ion 名 表「行為的狀態」

❷ Coco's life was full of difficulties and **frustrations**. Although she did feel down sometimes, she never gave up.
可可的一生充滿困難與挫折。雖然她有時會感到沮喪，但是她從不放棄。

18 **furious** [ˋfjʊərɪəs] 形 ❶ 猛烈的，強烈的；❷ 狂怒的

· fury 狂怒
· -ious 形 表「……特性的」

❶ The **furious** snowstorms have closed all the roads and bridges in the mountains. 猛烈的暴風雪封鎖了山區所有的道路和橋樑。

❷ My sister was **furious** at the decision. I didn't know why she was so angry. 我姊姊對這個決定大發雷霆。我不知道她為何會這麼生氣。

19 **grateful** [ˋgretfəl] 形 感激的，感謝的

• I am **grateful** to have James as my life partner.
我很感謝有詹姆斯當我的終生伴侶。

70 Feelings & emotions 感受與情緒 (4)

139

01 **gratitude** [ˋgrætə͵tjud] 名 U 感激，感恩，感謝　反義 ingratitude 忘恩負義

• The temple stages performances of Taiwanese opera every year as an expression of **gratitude** to the Goddess of Mercy.
這間廟每年演出歌仔戲，來表示對觀音的感謝之情。〔93 年指測〕

02 **grief** [grif] 名 U 悲痛，悲傷

• Ernesto's hysterical and alcoholic wife causes him endless **grief**.
恩內斯托的妻子情緒不穩又嗜酒，讓他痛心不已。

03 **grieve** [griv] ❶ 動 悲傷，哀悼；❷ 使悲傷，使痛心　同義 pain 痛苦

❶ The old couple **grieved** for their dead son; they held each other, weeping bitterly. 那對老夫婦哀悼他們過世的兒子。兩人互相擁抱，悲痛地哭泣。

❷ It **grieves** a mother to see her child in any kind of pain.
不管孩子受到什麼苦，做母親的看了，都會很捨不得。

04 **hatred** [ˋhetrɪd] 名 U 憎恨，敵意

· hate 憎恨

• The **hatred** between Chelsea and her family was dissolved by cultivating trust and respect in each other.
雀兒喜與家人之間的憎恨，在彼此互信互重後化解了。

05 **hesitate** [ˋhɛzə͵tet] 動 ❶ 有疑慮，不願意；❷ 躊躇，猶豫

❶ Penelope doesn't **hesitate** to ask for directions when she gets lost.
潘妮洛普迷路時，會毫不猶豫地向別人問路。

· hesitant 遲疑的
· -ate 動 表「使成為」

❷ Patrick was not sure whether he should accept the job. His friends told him not to **hesitate**, but to just take it.
派翠克不確定是否應該接受那份工作。朋友們告訴他不要猶豫，就接下去做吧。

[相關用法] 形 **hesitant** 躊躇的，猶豫不決的

● I am hesitant to tell the truth because I am uncertain what will happen afterward. 對於說實話，我感到很猶豫，因為我不確定之後會發生什麼事情。

[用法] hesitate about/over something 對……猶豫不決

06 **hesitation** [ˌhɛzəˋteʃən] 名 U 猶豫，躊躇

・hesitate 有疑慮
・-ion 名 表「行為」

● Dexter stopped his car without **hesitation** when an ambulance passed by. 一輛救護車經過，戴克斯特毫不遲疑剎了車。

07 **horrible** [ˋhɔrəbḷ] 形 ❶ 可怕的，恐怖的；❷ 極討厭的，糟透的

❶ One of Susan's most **horrible** experiences was a ride on a roller coaster. 蘇珊有過最恐怖的經驗之一，就是坐雲霄飛車。

❷ The food at the restaurant is **horrible**, and the service is bad.
這家餐廳的食物糟透了，服務也很差勁。

08 **horrify** [ˋhɔrəˏfaɪ] 動 使恐懼，使驚懼

● Reggie was **horrified** at the thought of getting lost in the desert. 瑞吉只要想到萬一在沙漠中迷了路，就心生恐懼。

09 **horror** [ˋhɔrɚ] 名 ❶ U 恐怖，毛骨悚然；❷ C 極端厭惡

❶ The audience watched in **horror** as the dancer fell off the stage; that was a terrible sight. 觀眾驚恐地看著舞者跌下舞台。那幅景象恐怖極了。

❷ The dance music that other people found tolerable was a **horror** to Mr. Poole. 一般人可以接受的舞曲，卻對普爾先生是種恐怖的折磨。

[補充] horror movie/horror film 恐怖片

10 **humorous** [ˋhjumərəs] 形 幽默的，滑稽的，可笑的

・humor 幽默
・-ous 形 表「多……的」

● In the eyes of our relatives and neighbors, my father is a **humorous** man. 在親戚和鄰居眼中，我父親是個幽默的人。

140 11 **impress** [ɪmˋprɛs] 動 ❶ 給……深刻的印象，使感動；❷ 使銘記

・im- 表「向……內」
・press 按，壓

❶ Vanessa dressed up in an attempt to **impress** her boyfriend's parents.
凡妮莎盛裝打扮，試圖要讓男朋友的父母親留下深刻的印象。

❷ Thomas' parents always **impressed** on him the importance of honesty. 湯瑪士的父母總是叮嚀他牢記誠實的重要性。

12 **impression** [ɪm`prɛʃən] 名 C 印象

- impress 給深刻印象
- -ion 名 表「行為」

• Thera wanted to make a good **impression** during her job interview, so she read everything she could find about the company.
席拉希望能在面試時留下好印象，所以她閱讀了各類與那間公司相關的資料。

13 **impressive** [ɪm`prɛsɪv] 形 予人深刻印象的，感人的

- impress 給深刻印象
- -ive 形 表「有……特性的」

• The ballet dancer's performance was very **impressive**; the audience watched with admiration. 那名芭蕾舞者的表演令人印象深刻，讓觀眾感到欽佩。

14 **instinct** [`ɪnstɪŋkt] 名 ❶ U 本能，天性；❷ C 直覺 同義 intuition 直覺

❶ Birds build nests and feed their young by **instinct**.
鳥類靠本能築巢、哺育幼鳥。

❷ Tammy always trusted her **instincts**; in this case, she had a feeling the statement was true.
泰美相信自己的直覺。現在這種情況，她相信那份聲明是真的。

15 **jealous** [`dʒɛləs] 形 ❶ 吃醋的；❷ 妒忌的

❶ Whenever Josephine kisses her daughter, it makes her elder son **jealous**. 每當喬瑟芬親吻女兒時，大兒子總感到非常嫉妒。

❷ Anthony is **jealous** of Blanche because she got the promotion he wanted. 安東尼忌妒白蘭琪，因為她得到了他所希望的升遷職位。

16 **jealousy** [`dʒɛləsɪ] 名 U 妒忌

- jealous 嫉妒的
- -y 名 表「狀態」

• Pandora rises above **jealousy** in close relationships because she has a liberal attitude toward love.
潘朵拉在親密關係中不會猜忌，因為她對愛的看法很開明。

17 **joyful** [`dʒɔɪfəl] 形 高興的，喜悅的 形 joyous 快樂的

- joy 高興
- -ful 形 表「充滿……的」

• Can you imagine how **joyful** Horace will be when the police return his stolen car?
你能想像當警方找回荷瑞斯失竊的車時，他會有多開心嗎？

18 **keen** [kin] 形 ❶ 熱心的，熱衷的；❷ 渴望的，極想的 同義 eager 渴望的

❶ Mrs. Hyde is **keen** on hosting a party next month for her daughter's wedding. 海德太太熱衷於張羅女兒下個月的婚禮。

❷ Arvin is very **keen** to get a new cell phone; he also really wants an MP3 player. 艾文非常渴望獲得一隻新手機。他同時也想要一台 MP3 播放器。

19 **mercy** [ˋmɝsɪ] 名 U **慈悲，仁慈，憐憫**

- Thanks to God's **mercy**, the whole Tess family survived the flood.
  感謝上帝憐憫，泰斯全家在水災中存活下來了。

相關片語 **at the mercy of** 受……所支配，任……擺布

- In spite of advanced technology, human beings still live at the mercy of nature. 儘管科技進步，人類仍舊任憑大自然擺布。

補充 mercy killing 安樂死

20 **merry** [ˋmɛrɪ] 形 **歡樂的，愉快的** 同義 cheerful, jolly 愉快的

- Bonnie spent a **merry** evening dancing with friends under the full moon. 邦妮和多位朋友在滿月下愉快地跳了一晚的舞。

補充 merry-go-round 旋轉木馬

21 **mood** [mud] 名 C ❶ **心情，情緒**；❷ **基調，氣氛**

❶ Freddie was not in the **mood** to chat when his girlfriend called this evening. 弗列迪的女友今晚打電話給他時，他無心談天。

❷ The **mood** of the meeting was warm and cordial; all of the attendees were pleased.
這場會議的氣氛溫暖真誠，所有的與會者都感到心滿意足。

相關用法 形 **moody** 喜怒無常的

- It is hard to get along with a moody person because you can never predict his or her reaction.
  要跟一個喜怒無常的人相處很困難，因為你無法預測他／她的反應。

71 Feelings & emotions 感受與情緒 (5)

141

01 **motivate** [ˋmotə͵vet] 動 刺激，激發，給……動機

- motive 動機
- -ate 動 表「使成為」

- Our team will certainly win this baseball game because all the players are highly **motivated**.
  我們隊伍肯定會贏得這場棒球比賽，因為所有的隊員都受到極大激勵。〔91 年學測〕

02 **motivation** [͵motəˋveʃən] 名 ❶ U 動力，積極性；❷ C 動機，原因

- motivate 刺激
- -ion 名 表「行為」

❶ The student is very smart, but he lacks **motivation**; therefore, his performance at school is so-so.
這名學生很聰明，但是不夠積極，所以他在校的表現馬馬虎虎。

❷ Adeline's **motivation** for giving up her career was not clear.
艾德琳離開職場的原因不是很清楚。

03 **nerve** [nɝv] 名 ❶ U 膽量；❷ C（常作複數）神經過敏，憂慮，焦躁

❶ Ryan doesn't have the **nerve** to tell his boss how much she gets on his nerves. 雷恩沒有勇氣告訴上司她已經把他惹毛了。

❷ The students are having an attack of **nerves** as the date of the college entrance examination approaches.
隨著大學入學考試的腳步接近，所有的學生變得非常焦慮。

04 **nervous** [ˋnɝvəs] 形 緊張不安的

- nerve 神經
- -ous 形 表「有……特質的」

● Sonia is going to perform in an opera, and she is very **nervous** about it.
索妮雅將在一齣歌劇裡演出，她為此感到非常緊張。

相關用法 副 **nervously** 緊張地，焦急地

● The boy looked at his mother nervously; he was afraid she would realize he had broken the vase. 男孩緊張地看著他的媽媽，怕她會發現自己打破了花瓶。

05 **offend** [əˋfɛnd] 動 冒犯，觸怒　名 offense 冒犯　形 offensive 冒犯的

● Mr. Holmes was **offended** by the immigration officer's direct questions regarding his personal affairs.
荷摩斯先生被移民局官員詢問的無禮私人問題所激怒。

06 **offense** [əˋfɛns] 名 ❶ U 冒犯，觸怒；❷ C 罪過，犯法

❶ Devin's words upset his friend, though he meant no **offense**.
戴文的話讓他的朋友很生氣，雖然他無意冒犯。

❷ For which **offense** was Wallace arrested? 沃雷斯是犯什麼罪被逮捕的？

07 **offensive** [əˋfɛnsɪv] 形 冒犯的

- offend 冒犯
- -ive 形 表「……的」

● Olivia often makes **offensive** comments about her classmates, so nobody likes her.
奧莉維雅常說錯話冒犯同學，所以沒人喜歡她。

08 **panic** [ˋpænɪk] ❶ 名 C 恐慌　❷ 動 使恐慌

❶ Rumors of bankruptcy started a **panic** in Ted's company.
泰德的公司倒閉流言四起，引起了一陣恐慌。

❷ The bloodless murder **panicked** the little town; people were frightened by it. 這起殘忍的凶殺案震驚了小鎮，鎮民十分驚恐。

09 **passion** [ˋpæʃən] 名 ❶ Ⓒ 酷愛；❷ Ⓤ 熱情，激情　形 passionate 熱情的

❶ Nathaniel has had a **passion** for soccer since he was a little boy.
納森尼爾從小就熱愛足球。

❷ Whenever we talk about Heidi's idol, she speaks with great **passion**. 每當和海蒂聊到她的偶像時，她總是滿懷熱情地談論。

補充 passion fruit 百香果

用法 have a passion for something 對……熱愛

10 **pity** [ˋpɪtɪ] 名 ❶ Ⓒ 可惜的事，憾事；❷ Ⓤ 憐憫，同情　❸ 動 憐憫，同情

❶ It is a **pity** that Patrice missed the chance to study abroad.
派翠絲錯過了留學的機會，真是可惜。

❷ Jessica took **pity** on the homeless man; she gave him some money out of sympathy. 潔西卡很同情那個遊民，所以出自憐憫給了他一些錢。

❸ We **pitied** those children who lost their parents in the severe earthquake and wondered what would happen to them.
我們憐惜在那場大地震中失去父母的孩子們。不禁想像他們的未來會如何。

142 11 **preferable** [ˋprɛfərəbḷ] 形 更好的，更合意的

- prefer 寧可
- -able 形 表「有……特性的」

● For Kelsey, living alone is **preferable** to having roommates. 對凱兒喜而言，比起擁有室友，她更喜歡一個人住。

12 **rage** [redʒ] 名 ❶ Ⓤ 狂怒　❷ 動 猖獗，肆虐

❶ Feeling offended, the man flew into a **rage** and began yelling angrily. 覺得受到冒犯，男子一陣盛怒，開始氣憤地大吼大叫。

❷ During the typhoon, it rained violently, and the wind **raged** furiously. 颱風來襲時，天降暴雨，風狂暴地肆虐。

相關片語 **be (all) the rage** 風行一時

● Orlando remembers that torn jeans were all the rage when he was in high school. 奧蘭多記得在他讀中學時，破洞牛仔褲曾經非常流行。

13 **regret** [rɪˋgrɛt] 動 ❶ 後悔，因……而遺憾；❷ 為……抱歉；
❸ 感到後悔，感到抱歉，遺憾
名 Ⓒ ❹ 懊悔，後悔，遺憾

❶ Laurence **regretted** not going to the alumni reunion and seeing his old friends. 勞倫斯很後悔沒去參加校友同學會，見見老朋友。

❷ I **regret** that I won't be able to come to your birthday party. I am really sorry about it.
很抱歉，我將無法參加你的生日派對。我真的覺得很遺憾。

❸ If we don't do something to solve the problem of global warming, we will surely **regret** it in the future.
如果現在我們不針對全球暖化應變出解決方案，未來我們一定會後悔。

❹ I have no **regrets** about turning down the offer; I would feel sorry now if I had accepted it.
我一點都不後悔拒絕了那項提議。如果當時我接受了，現在才會後悔莫及呢。

[用法] regret V-ing 後悔（做某事）；regret to V 感到遺憾

14 **relief** [rɪˋlif] 名 ❶ U 輕鬆，寬心；❷（痛苦等的）減輕，解除；❸ 救濟物品，救濟金

❶ When Mr. Osmond heard that his son had been rescued and was safe, he was finally able to feel some **relief**.
奧斯蒙先生聽到兒子獲救並且平安無事，他總算能寬心了。

❷ The medicine gave the wounded man some **relief** from his pain, and he fell asleep. 止痛藥減輕了那名受傷男子的一些疼痛，於是他便睡著了。

❸ Two days after the earthquake, **relief** was sent to the affected areas; the food and medicine were a great help to the people there. 救援物資在地震後兩天送達災區。這些食物和藥品對災區的人們幫助很大。

[相關片語] **to one's relief** 使某人鬆了一口氣

● Much to the mother's relief, the police have found her missing child.
警察找到了這位母親走失的孩子，讓她大大地鬆了一口氣。

15 **relieve** [rɪˋliv] 動 ❶ 使寬慰，使放心；❷ 緩和，減輕

❶ The anxious son was **relieved** to hear that his mother was safe.
焦急的兒子獲知母親安全無虞後大為寬心。

❷ Terra's doctor gave her some new medicine to **relieve** her heartburn and headaches. 泰拉的醫生開給她一些新藥，來減輕胃灼熱及頭痛。

16 **reluctant** [rɪˋlʌktənt] 形 不情願的，勉強的

・reluct 反抗
・-ant 形 表「處於……狀態的」

● Perla lives alone, rarely goes out, and is **reluctant** to socialize. 波拉獨居，很少出門，也不願融入社會。

[相關用法] **reluctantly** 副 不情願地，勉強地

● The boy reluctantly followed his mother out of the toy shop.
男孩不情願地跟著媽媽走出玩具店。

17 **satisfactory** [ˌsætɪsˋfæktərɪ] 形 令人滿意的，符合要求的

● Edwina tried on three skirts, but none was **satisfactory**. She left the store without buying anything. 艾德溫娜試穿了三條裙子，但是沒有一件令人滿意。她沒有買任何東西就離開那家店了。

18 **scary** [ˋskɛrɪ] 形 引起驚慌的，嚇人的

- scare 驚嚇
- -y 形 表「有……的」

● Don't you think this movie is too **scary** for children? 你不認為這部電影對兒童來說太可怕了嗎？

19 **sensitive** [ˋsɛnsətɪv] 形 ❶ 靈敏的；❷ 體貼的；❸ 易受傷害的

❶ Human ears are not **sensitive** enough to hear the sounds made by some whales. 人類的耳朵不夠靈敏，聽不到某些鯨魚發出的聲音。

❷ Heloise is a **sensitive** girl; she is always able to understand other people's feelings. 海洛伊絲是一位體貼的女孩。她總是能理解別人的感受。

❸ Ingrid is very **sensitive**; she is easily upset by what other people say. 英格麗是一個容易受傷的人。她很容易因為別人說的話而感到沮喪。

用法 be sensitive to 對……敏感

20 **shame** [ʃem] 名 ❶ Ⓒ 令人遺憾的事；❷ Ⓤ 羞恥；❸ Ⓤ 恥辱
動 ❹ 使感到羞愧

❶ It is a **shame** that Irving has to leave the company.
厄溫必須離開公司，真讓人遺憾。

❷ The student felt great **shame** at having been caught cheating on the exam; he felt guilty and embarrassed.
那名學生因為考試作弊被抓而感到非常羞愧。他很內疚也不好意思。

❸ The young man robbed an elderly lady of her money; his bad behavior brought **shame** on his family.
那名年輕人搶走一位老婦人的錢，其惡劣行徑給家人帶來恥辱。

❹ The girl felt **shamed** and humiliated when her father slapped her across the face in public.
當女孩的父親當眾賞了她一個耳光，她感到羞愧又丟臉。

21 **satisfaction** [ˌsætɪsˋfækʃən] 名 Ⓤ 滿意，滿足 形 satisfactory 令人滿意的

● The mother has the **satisfaction** of seeing her son become a promising young man. 這名母親眼見兒子成為大有可為的青年而感到心滿意足。

72 Feelings & emotions 感受與情緒 (6)

143

01 **sorrow** [ˋsɑro] 名 ❶ Ⓤ 悲傷，悲痛；❷ Ⓒ 傷心事，不幸的事

❶ Gustave felt great **sorrow** at the death of his father; every night, he cried himself to sleep.
父親的去世是葛絲塔芙沉重的傷痛；她每晚都哭著入眠。

❷ My best friends share my joys and **sorrows**; I cherish the times that we laugh and cry together.
我最好的朋友分享了我的快樂與悲傷，我很珍惜我們一起歡笑和哭泣的時光。

02 **spite** [spaɪt] 名 U **惡意** 　同義 malice 惡意

- Mr. Lloyd flattened his neighbor's tires out of **spite**.
洛依德先生因心懷怨恨，刺破了鄰居的輪胎。

相關片語 **in spite of** 不管

- They went to the beach in spite of the approaching typhoon.
儘管颱風即將來襲，他們跑到了海邊。

03 **temper** [ˋtɛmpɚ] 名 C **脾氣**

- Carlton's **temper** was well-known to all his friends and relatives.
卡爾頓的脾氣所有親朋好友都很清楚。

相關片語 **get/go/fly into a temper** 發脾氣

- I asked to speak to his boss and he just flew into a temper.
我要求直接跟他老闆談，結果他大發雷霆。

補充 good-tempered 形 好脾氣的；hot-tempered 形 性急的；
bad-tempered 形 脾氣不好的

04 **thankful** [ˋθæŋkfəl] 形 **感謝的，感激的**

- thank 感謝
- -ful 形 表「充滿……的」

- Tonia was **thankful** for her classmates' help on her science project. 塔妮雅很感謝同學協助自己的科學研究計畫。

05 **weep** [wip] 動 **哭泣，流淚**

- Lyle **wept** for his son, who was suffering from blood cancer.
萊爾為了飽受血癌折磨的兒子哭泣。

06 **shameful** [ˋʃemfəl] 形 **可恥的，丟臉的**

- shame 羞恥
- -ful 形 表「充滿……的」

- Saul thinks that abusing a child is the most **shameful** behavior. 索爾認為，虐待兒童是最可恥的行為。

07 **sob** [sɑb] 動 ❶ **哭得使……**；❷ **嗚咽，啜泣**

❶ Latasha **sobbed** herself to sleep on the night that her beloved cat died. 拉妲莎心愛的貓咪死掉的那一晚，她哭著入睡。

❷ After being scolded by her father, the little girl **sobbed**; she cried so noisily that the neighbors could hear her.
小女孩在被她爸爸責罵之後便放聲大哭。她的哭聲太大，鄰居都聽見了。

08 **sorrowful** [ˋsɑrəfəl] 形 悲傷的，傷心的

- With a **sorrowful** expression on his face, Neil told me that his pet was dead.
帶著悲傷的表情，尼爾告訴我他的寵物死掉了。

‧ sorrow 悲傷
‧ -ful 形 表「充滿……的」

09 **suspicious** [səˋspɪʃəs] 形 ❶ 可疑的，鬼鬼祟祟的；❷ 猜疑的，多疑的

❶ Terrell's **suspicious** behavior caught the police's attention.
特爾瑞鬼鬼祟祟的行為引起了警察的注意。

❷ They are **suspicious** of the man's intentions; they believe he is up to something. 他們懷疑這名男子的目的，認為他意圖不軌。

‧ suspect 懷疑
‧ -ious 形 表「充滿……的」

10 **sympathetic** [ˏsɪmpəˋθɛtɪk] 形 同情的，有同情心的

- Kendra, herself a mother, gave a **sympathetic** glance to the woman with the crying baby.
同樣為人母親，坎卓對一位抱著哭泣嬰兒的婦女投以同情的眼光。

‧ sym- 表「共同」
‧ pathetic 可憐的

144

11 **sympathy** [ˋsɪmpəθɪ] 名 U 同情

- Austin has no **sympathy** for thieves and robbers.
奧斯丁不同情小偷和搶犯。

12 **tense** [tɛns] ❶ 形 緊張的 ❷ 動 使拉緊，使繃緊

❶ After the bombing, international relations have become extremely **tense**. 發生炸彈攻擊後，國際關係變得極為緊繃。

❷ The soldier **tensed** up, preparing to attack.
那名士兵全身緊繃，準備發動攻擊。

13 **tension** [ˋtɛnʃən] 名 U ❶（精神上）緊張；❷ 緊張局勢，緊張狀況

❶ Robert's **tension** and stress are always relieved by a visit to the spa.
羅伯特做了 spa，消除緊張與壓力。

❷ The two countries could declare war on each other at any time, creating rising **tension** along the boundary.
因為兩國可能隨時會對彼此宣戰，所以邊界的氣氛越來越緊張。

‧ tense 緊張的
‧ -ion 名 表「行為的狀態」

14 **terrify** [ˋtɛrəˏfaɪ] 動 使害怕，使恐怖

- The horror film **terrified** Gabriela so much that she refused to stay home alone. 這部恐怖片讓嘉布麗娜受到不小驚嚇，她不敢獨自待在家了。

15 **terror** [ˋtɛrɚ] 名 U 恐怖，驚駭

- Glenna lives in **terror** of darkness and always sleeps with the lights on. 葛蓮娜很怕黑，所以都開著燈睡覺。

16 **tiresome** [ˋtaɪrsəm] 形 使人疲勞的，令人厭倦的

- Lisa considers watching sporting events to be a **tiresome** pastime.
麗莎覺得收看體育賽事是很無趣的嗜好。

- tire 疲勞
- -some 形 表「有……傾向的」

17 **tolerable** [ˋtɑlərəbl̩] 形 可忍受的，可寬恕的

- After Vanessa took some herbal medicine, her headache became **tolerable**. 凡妮莎服用了一些中藥後，頭痛就好多了。

- tolerate 忍耐
- -able 形 表「可……的」

18 **tolerance** [ˋtɑlərəns] 名 U ❶ 忍耐；❷ 寬容

❶ The teacher showed **tolerance** for the noise in the classroom and continued with his lecture as if he had not heard anything.
老師忍受著教室裡的噪音，繼續講課，好像什麼也沒聽見。〔92 年學測補考〕

❷ In a democratic society, people should show **tolerance** for different opinions. 在一個民主社會裡，我們應該包容不同的意見。

- tolerate 忍耐
- -ance 名 表「狀況」

19 **tolerant** [ˋtɑlərənt] 形 容忍的，忍受的

- Ms. Donovan is open-minded and tends to be **tolerant** of different opinions.
唐諾文小姐思想開放，對各種看法都予以尊重。

- tolerate 忍耐
- -ant 形 表「處於……狀況的」

20 **tolerate** [ˋtɑlə͵ret] 動 ❶ 忍受；❷ 容忍，容許　同義 bear, put up with 忍受

❶ Since our classroom is not air-conditioned, we have to **tolerate** the heat on hot summer days.
因為我們教室沒有空調，所以夏天的時候我們得忍受高溫。

❷ How can you **tolerate** evil deeds and avoid standing up for justice? 你怎能縱容惡行，不為正義挺身而出？

21 **troublesome** [ˋtrʌbl̩səm] 形 令人煩惱的，討厭的，麻煩的

- Kenny, who left home for his first job, found living alone to be quite **troublesome**.
肯尼為了第一份工作離家，覺得自己一個人在外面住很麻煩。

- trouble 麻煩
- -some 形 表「有……傾向的」

73 Measurement & numbers
測量與數字 (1)

145

01 **accuracy** [ˋækjərəsɪ] 名 U 正確（性），準確（性）

- ac-(=-ad) 向……
- cur- 表「照顧」

● Tony's electric scale measures lightweight items with great **accuracy**. 東尼的電子秤能精確測量出輕量物品的重量。

02 **accurate** [ˋækjərɪt] 形 **準確的，精確的** 反義 inaccurate 不正確的

● **Accurate** measurement requires appropriate tools.
工欲善其事，必先利其器。

03 **acre** [ˋekɚ] 名 C 英畝

● Ms. Rivera bought 90 **acres** of rain forest in Southeast Asia to preserve the land. 瑞弗拉女士在東南亞買下 90 畝雨林，要作為土地保護區。

04 **additional** [əˋdɪʃənl̩] 形 附加的，額外的

- add 附加
- -ition 名 表「行為」
- -al 形 表「……的」

● **Additional** information about joining our community is available on our website.
有關加入我們社團的其他詳情，可以參訪我們的網站。

相關用法 **additionally** 副 此外

● If you buy the machine, the company will provide free repairs during the period of guarantee; additionally, it will provide six months of technical support. 如果您購買這台機器，公司將會在保固內提供免費維修；此外，他們也會提供六個月的技術支援。

05 **adequate** [ˋædəkwɪt] 形 **足夠的** 同義 sufficient 足夠的

● Victoria has an **adequate** income to support her lifestyle.
維多利亞的收入足夠養活自己。

06 **angle** [ˋæŋgl̩] 名 C ❶ **角度**；❷ **觀點，立場**

❶ When you take photos, you can move around to shoot the target object from different **angles**.
拍照時，你可以更換位置，以不同角度來拍攝目標物。〔98 年學測〕

❷ After examining the problem from different **angles**, Elmer figured out a viable solution.
埃摩爾從不同的觀點看待問題後，想出了一個可行的解決方法。

07 **arithmetic** [əˋrɪθmətɪk] ❶ 名 U 算術 ❷ 形 算術的

❶ Brent excels in matters of **arithmetic**, but he is slow at analyzing the meaning of stories. 布恩特算術很厲害，但對故事的理解力卻反應遲鈍。

❷ The **arithmetic** problem is too difficult for the child; he can only count to 10. 這道算術題目對這個小孩子而言太困難了。他只會從 1 數到 10。

08 **average** [ˋævərɪdʒ] 形 ❶ 平均的；❷ 一般的，普通的
名 C ❸ 平均；❹ 一般，普通，中等 動 ❺ 平均達到

❶ The **average** age of the students in the class is 12 years.
這個班級的學生平均年齡是 12 歲。

❷ Some animals make sounds that are beyond the **average** human's ability to hear. 某些動物會發出人類聽不到的聲音。

❸ Angela spends an **average** of NT$10,000 a month on clothes.
安琪拉平均每個月花台幣一萬元在買衣服上。

❹ It is hotter than normal this summer. Temperatures are above **average** for this time of year.
今年夏天比較熱，氣溫比每年此時的平均溫度還要高。

❺ The businessman was very busy last month. He **averaged** 11 hours of work per day. 這名企業家上個月非常忙碌，平均每天工作 11 小時。

09 **barrel** [ˋbærəl] 名 C ❶ 一桶的量；❷ 大桶

❶ Lorene stores several **barrels** of high-quality wine in her basement; she drinks the wine only on special occasions.
蘿芮在地下室存放了幾桶高級葡萄酒，只在特殊場合才喝。

❷ The worker put the wine in the oak **barrels** and let it mature over time. 工人把葡萄酒放在橡木桶裡中，讓它陳釀一段時間。

10 **billion** [ˋbɪljən] 名 C ❶ 十億；❷（複）大量，無數

❶ Last year, the car manufacturer made a profit of just under $1 **billion**. 這家汽車商在去年賺進近十億美元的利潤。

❷ Merrilee was fascinated by the **billions** of stars twinkling in the clear night sky. 晴朗夜空中，閃爍的無數星點讓梅里莉著迷不已。

11 **bucket** [ˋbʌkɪt] 名 C ❶ 水桶；❷（一）桶

❶ The woman put some water into a plastic **bucket** and took it to the kitchen. 那名女子用塑膠水桶裝水，並把它拿到廚房裡。

❷ The monk came up the hill carrying two **buckets** of water.
這個和尚提著兩桶水上山。

12 **bunch** [bʌntʃ] 名 C ❶ 串，束；❷ 群，幫

❶ Edwin came back to the village with three **bunches** of bananas to share with his neighbors. 艾德溫帶了三串香蕉回到村莊，與鄰居分享。

❷ I saw a **bunch** of children playing games in the garden. 我看到一群小孩在花園裡玩遊戲。

146

13 **calculate** [ˋkælkjəˏlet] 動 ❶ 計算；❷ 估計，預測，推測

❶ Ashley **calculates** her income and expenses at the end of every month. 艾希莉每月底結算自己所有的收入和支出。

❷ It is difficult to **calculate** how the incident will influence the child in the future. 很難預測這起事件在未來會對這個小孩有什麼影響。

14 **calculation** [ˏkælkjəˋleʃən] 名 C ❶ 計算；❷ 估計

- calculate 計算
- -ion 名 表「行為的結果」

❶ To find the amount, we did a rough **calculation**. 為了知道總額，我們做了一個粗略的計算。

❷ By the scientists' **calculations**, sea level could rise an additional 1.1 feet by 2100 if the problem of global warming worsens. 如果全球暖化的問題惡化，根據這些科學家的估計，海平面到了 2100 年將上升 1.1 英尺。

15 **calculator** [ˋkælkjəˏletɚ] 名 C 計算機

- calculate 計算
- -or 名 表「物」

● Autumn can't work without a **calculator** because she has poor math skills. 歐婷的算數很差，沒有計算機就不能工作。

16 **centimeter** [ˋsɛntəˏmitɚ] 名 C 公分

- centi- 表「百分之一」
- meter 公尺

● Mendel was 168 **centimeters** tall when he was in junior high school. 曼得爾國中時的身高有 168 公分。

17 **countable** [ˋkaʊntəbl̩] 形 可計算的，可數的

- count 計算
- -able 形 表「有……特性的」

● Some things on this planet simply aren't **countable**, such as the grains of sand on all the beaches and deserts on Earth. 有些東西無法計算，像是地球上的海灘和大漠的滾滾黃沙。

18 **decrease** [dɪˋkris] ❶ 動 減少，減小；❷ 使減少，使減小
❸ 名 C 減少，減小

❶ During the last decade, the annual birth rate **decreased** in most of East Asia. 過去十年間，東亞大部分地區的出生率都降低了。

❷ One way to lose weight is to **decrease** the amount of fat that you eat. 為了減肥，你得減少所攝取的脂肪。

❸ The number of customers in the store has **decreased**, so the company is starting a sale next week to attract more shoppers.
光顧這家商店的顧客減少了，所以下個禮拜會展開拍賣，來吸引更多的顧客。

19 **deepen** [`dipən] 動 ❶ 使加深（了解）；❷ 使變深；❸ 使強烈，使變濃

▪ deep 深的
▪ -en 動 表「變為……」

❶ I want to **deepen** my understanding of Chinese opera before I see a performance.
欣賞表演前，我要先深入了解京劇。

❷ The farmer is **deepening** the well because he wants to get more water. 農夫正在挖深水井，因為他想要得到更多的水。

❸ The 10-day trip to Britain **deepened** Beryl's interest in English literature. 英國的十天旅行讓貝蘿對英國文學更有興趣。

20 **enlarge** [ɪn`lɑrdʒ] 動 ❶ 放大（照片）；❷ 擴大，擴展

▪ en- 表「變為」
▪ large 大的

❶ Adrian **enlarged** his favorite picture and framed it for display. 亞德里恩將最愛的照片放大裱框展示。

❷ Local government officials think the gym is too small; they plan to **enlarge** it. 地方政府官員覺得那間體育館太小了，他們計畫將它擴大興建。

21 **enlargement** [ɪn`lɑrdʒmənt] 名 C ❶ 放大的照片；❷ 擴大，擴展

▪ enlarge 放大
▪ -ment 名 表「行為，結果」

❶ Mr. Ansel made **enlargements** of his favorite photographs.
安索先生把所有自己最喜歡的照片放大。

❷ This year, the company is focusing on the **enlargement** of its overseas business; it plans to open more branch stores in Asia.
今年，這家公司著重於海外事業的擴展。他們計畫在亞洲開設更多分店。

22 **enormous** [ɪ`nɔrməs] 形 **巨大的，龐大的**

● The tree is more than 300 years old; it is so **enormous** that it shades almost an acre of land.
這棵樹的樹齡超過 300 歲了。這棵樹木如此巨大，幾乎可以遮蔽一英畝的土地。

23 **estimate** [`ɛstə͵met] 動 **估計，估量**

● Ms. Antonio consulted with financial experts in order to **estimate** the profit from her investment.
安東尼歐小姐請財經專家來評估自己的投資獲利率。

相關用法 名 **estimation** 估計

● Estimations of the total cost and duration were considered in the previous step. 應該要先進行的步驟包括整體費用與所需時間的估算。

24 **gallon** [ˋgælən] 名 C（單位）加侖

- According to the U.S. imperial system, a **gallon** is equal to about 3.8 liters. 依照美國英制單位，一加侖等於約 3.8 公升。

25 **gigantic** [dʒaɪˋgæntɪk] 形 巨大的，龐大的

- giant 巨人
- -ic 形 表「……的」

- The **gigantic** redwoods in the coastal areas of northern California are believed to be among the biggest trees in the world. 在北加州沿海的龐大紅杉木林，被認為是世界上體積最大的樹種之一。

26 **gram** [græm] 名 C（單位）克

- Julia added 50 **grams** of milk to her black tea.
茱利亞在她的紅茶裡加了 50 克的牛奶。

74 Measurement & numbers 測量與數字 (2)

147

01 **handful** [ˋhændfəl] 名 C ❶ 一把，一握；❷ 少量，少數

- hand 手
- -ful 名「充滿……」

❶ Seeing his granddaughter running toward him, the grandfather drew a **handful** of candy from his pocket.
看到孫女跑過來，祖父從口袋裡抓出一把糖果。

❷ Only a **handful** of students in Ms. Ward's class passed the final examination. 渥德老師的班上，只有少數學生期末考及格。

02 **heap** [hip] 名 C ❶ 一堆；❷ 大量，許多

❶ Loria was scared when she found a dead mouse under a **heap** of old newspapers in the garage.
蘿莉雅在車庫裡一疊舊報紙下發現一隻死老鼠，嚇得半死。

❷ Ruth was very busy; she had **heaps** of work to do.
露絲十分忙碌。她有很多工作要做。

03 **kilogram** [ˋkɪlə͵græm] 名 C 公斤

- kilo- 表「千」
- gram 克

- Pauline lost four **kilograms** in a month by exercising and staying on a healthy diet.
寶琳靠著運動與健康的飲食，在一個月內減掉四公斤。

縮寫 kg

04 **kilometer** [kəˋlɑmɪtɚ] 名 C 公里

- kilo- 表「千」
- meter 公尺

● The nearest hotel is about 30 **kilometers** away.
最近的旅館約在 30 公里外。

縮寫 km

05 **lengthen** [ˋlɛŋθən] ❶ 動 使加長，使延長；❷ 變長，延長

- long 長的
- -th 名 表「性質」
- -en 動 表「變為……」

❶ Tracy **lengthened** her skirt by attaching some lace at the bottom.
翠西在自己的裙襬上縫了一些蕾絲花邊，加長裙子長度。

❷ Whenever Pinocchio told a lie, his nose **lengthened**.
每當小木偶說謊時，他的鼻子就會變長。

06 **limitation** [͵lɪməˋteʃən] 名 ❶ U 限制；❷ C（進出口）限制；❸ C 局限，不足之處

- limit 動 限制
- -ation 名 表「行為」

❶ Several countries have reached an agreement on the **limitation** of nuclear warheads, hoping to control and reduce such destructive weapons.
幾個國家達成協議限制生產核彈頭，希望可以控制並減少這類型的毀滅性武器。

❷ To protect local farmers, the new policy will place **limitations** on rice imports. 為了保護當地農夫，這項新政策將會限制稻米的進口。

❸ There is a **limitation** to one's capacity; one should not make oneself overtired.
每個人的能力都有限。一個人不應該讓自己過度疲勞。〔91 年學測〕

07 **maximum** [ˋmæksəməm] ❶ 名 U 最大量，最大數
❷ 形 最大的，最多的，最高的

❶ Some experts suggest that people drink no more than a glass of wine a day; if they exceed this **maximum**, their brain cells may be damaged. 專家建議，人一天應該不要喝超過一杯紅酒。如果超過這個最大量，腦細胞可能因此受損。

❷ The theater has a **maximum** seating capacity of 500.
這間電影院最多可以容納 500 位觀眾。

08 **minimum** [ˋmɪnəməm] ❶ 名 C 最小量，最小數，最低限度
❷ 形 最小的，最少的，最低的

❶ The doctor suggests that people should exercise for a **minimum** of 20 minutes every day. 醫生建議大家每天最少運動 20 分鐘。

❷ Maida has saved enough money to cover the **minimum** down payment on a house. 美妲已存夠付房子頭期款的錢。

09 **multiple** [ˋmʌltəpḷ] 形 複合的，多樣的

- multi- 多
- -ple(x) 摺疊；倍

- When it comes to dates, Lance always has **multiple** choices, especially on the weekends.
說到約會，蘭斯總是有很多選擇，尤其週末時更是如此。

10 **numerous** [ˋnjumərəs] 形 許多的，很多的

- number 數字
- -ous 形 表「有……的」

- Rhonda visited her teacher **numerous** times after she graduated. 蘭妲在畢業後，去看過老師好幾次。

11 **pace** [pes] 名 ❶ C 一步；❷ U 速度，步調　❸ 動 踱步，慢慢地走

❶ Before the game started, the teacher asked the students to stand 2 **paces** from one another.
在比賽開始之前，老師要每個學生站在離彼此兩步寬的距離。

❷ After hours of office work, Connie goes swimming for a change of **pace**. 康妮在辦公室工作了幾個小時後，跑去游泳，調整一下工作狀態。

❸ Feeling very anxious, the husband **paced** up and down the corridor outside the delivery room. 丈夫感到十分焦急，在產房外的走廊來回踱步。

相關片語 **keep pace** 齊步並進，並駕齊驅

- When they go for a walk, Johnny has to take long steps to keep pace with his father.
當兩人去散步的時候，強尼得邁大步才能跟得上他的父親。〔91 年指測〕

12 **percent** [pɚˋsɛnt] 名 C 百分之……

- per 表「每一」
- cent- 表「百分之一」

- Sixty **percent** of Linda's salary is spent on rent, so she can never save any money.
琳達六成薪水拿來付房租，所以她永遠存不了錢。

13 **percentage** [pɚˋsɛntɪdʒ] 名 C 百分率，百分比

- percent 百分之……
- -age 名 表「成果」

- A recent survey shows that a high **percentage** of people own at least one mobile phone.
最近一項調查顯示，有很高比例的民眾擁有至少一支行動電話。

148

14 **pint** [paɪnt] 名 C 品脫

- Since Lizabeth's flight was delayed for an hour, she ordered a **pint** of beer at the sports bar in the airport.
麗茲貝絲的班機延後一個小時才飛，所以她在機場的運動酒吧點了一品脫的啤酒來喝。

15 **plentiful** [ˋplɛntɪfəl] 形 豐富的，充足的

- plenty 名 豐富
- -ful 形 表「充滿……的」

- Trees are **plentiful** in the forest; they grow in such large numbers that it is difficult to count them.
這座森林的木種豐饒，樹木數量多到數不清。

16 **plenty** [ˋplɛntɪ] ❶ 名 U 豐富，大量 ❷ 副 很，非常

❶ We have **plenty** of milk, but not many eggs.
我們有很多牛奶，雞蛋則沒幾顆。

❷ Adela was **plenty** busy with her career, so she didn't plan to have a baby. 艾黛拉工作忙碌，沒有生小孩的打算。

相關片語 **in plenty** 充足，大量

- They have food in plenty; there is much more than they need.
他們有十分充足的食物，供過於求。

17 **reduce** [rɪˋdjus] 動 減少，縮小，降低

- After Ms. Marlow started accounting for her daily expenses, she decided to **reduce** her spending.
馬爾洛小姐開始考量日常支出後，決定要減少花費。

18 **reduction** [rɪˋdʌkʃən] 名 C 減少，削減

・reduce 減少
・-tion 名 表「行為」

- Our members get an average **reduction** of 12 percent on each purchase in the stores listed in this flyer.
我們的會員只要在這張傳單上列出的商家購物，每次購物平均可享有 88 折的優惠。

19 **scarce** [skɛrs] 形 缺乏的，不足的

- Fresh vegetables were **scarce** during the drought, but now there are plenty to choose from.
新鮮蔬果在乾旱時極難買到，但現在可是有很多選擇。

20 **shallow** [ˋʃælo] 形 ❶ 淺的；❷ 膚淺的 同義 superficial 膚淺的

❶ Tommy stopped the boys from diving into the water because it was too **shallow**. 湯米阻止那群男孩跳水，因為水太淺了。

❷ The article is shallow, not showing any serious thought.
這一篇文章很膚淺，沒有表達任何重要的概念。

21 **shorten** [ˋʃɔrtn̩] 動 使縮短，使減少

・short 形 短的
・-en 動 表「變為……」

- Marcus had to **shorten** his trip because of illness, and he is still in the hospital.
馬庫斯因為生病只好縮短行程。他目前還躺在醫院裡。

22 **shrink** [ʃrɪŋk] 動 ❶ 收縮，縮小；❷ 變小，變少；❸ 使縮小，使減少

❶ When Robbie took the laundry out of the dryer, he found his sweater had **shrunk**. 羅比從烘衣機拿出洗好的衣服時，發現毛衣縮水了。

❷ Last year, the company had 68 employees, but now the staff has **shrunk** to only 23 people.
去年，這家公司有 68 位員工，但是現在只剩下 23 人。

❸ Airplanes have **shrunk** the world; people can travel from country to country in just one day.
飛機讓世界變小了。人們可以在一天內，從一個國家旅行至另一個國家。

23 **slice** [slaɪs] ❶ 名 C **薄片** ❷ 動 **把……切成薄片**

❶ Since I am not really hungry, can I share a **slice** of pizza with you? 我不是很餓，可以分你一片披薩嗎？

❷ The mother **sliced** the bread, and every child got a thin piece.
媽媽將麵包切成數片，每個孩子都拿到一薄片。

24 **sufficient** [sə`fɪʃənt] 形 **足夠的** 反義 insufficient 不足的

● Mika works relentlessly; she wants to have **sufficient** savings to retire comfortably some day.
米卡不斷工作存錢，希望等退休後，有足夠的存款能舒服度日。

相關用法 副 **sufficiently** 足夠地，充分地

● The problem is sufficiently serious to arouse people's attention.
這個問題極為嚴重，足以引起人們的注意。

補充 self-sufficient 自給自足的

25 **sum** [sʌm] 名 C ❶ **一筆（金額）**；❷ **總數，總和** ❸ 動 **總結，概括**

❶ Mr. Reed borrowed a large **sum** of money from the bank to expand his business. 瑞德先生向銀行借了一大筆錢，來擴大事業。

❷ The **sum** of 21 and 57 is 78. 21 加 57 的總和是 78。

❸ Can you **sum** up the article in one sentence?
你可以用一句話來總結這一篇文章嗎？

相關片語 **in sum** 簡言之

● In sum, if we don't try our best to prevent global warming from worsening, we may someday regret our inaction.
簡而言之，如果我們不盡力防止全球暖化繼續惡化，有朝一日我們會因為自己的袖手旁觀而後悔。

26 **ton** [tʌn] 名 C ❶ **噸（重量單位）**；❷ **大量，許多**

❶ A **ton** is a unit for measuring weight; it is equal to 2,000 pounds in the United States. 噸是秤重單位。在美國 1 噸相當於 2000 磅。

❷ Lois can't go on the trip with us tomorrow because she has **tons** of work to do. 蘿伊絲明天有一堆事要忙，不能跟我們去旅行了。

27 **tremendous** [trɪˋmɛndəs] 形 ❶ 巨大的，極大的；❷〔口〕極好的，很棒的

❶ As a single parent, Macie carries the **tremendous** burden of supporting her family. 梅西是單親媽媽，一肩扛起照顧家庭的重責大任。

❷ The show was **tremendous**; the audience stood up and applauded the performers for five minutes.
那場表演太精采了，觀眾起立向表演者鼓掌喝采長達五分鐘。

28 **vast** [væst] 形 廣闊的，巨大的，大量的　同義 huge 巨大的

- Malcolm bought the house in the seaside town because of its **vast** ocean view. 麥爾康因為遼闊的海景，在海濱鎮上買了一棟房子。

75 State & condition 狀態與情況 (1)

149

01 **accidental** [ˌæksəˋdɛntḷ] 形 偶然的，意外的

- accident 意外
- -al 形 表「……的」

- An **accidental** encounter helped Victor get back in touch with his old friends. 因為一次巧遇，維克多再度和老朋友有了聯繫。

相關用法 副 **accidentally** 偶然地，意外地

- When I was on my way to school, I accidentally dropped my notebook.
在去學校的路上，我不小心把我的筆電掉在地上。

02 **actual** [ˋæktʃʊəl] 形 實際的，事實上的

- Why do Lois's expenses always manage to exceed her **actual** income? 露絲怎麼會老是入不敷出呢？

相關用法 副 **actually** 實際上

- Robert looks pretty young, but he is actually over 40.
羅伯特看起來相當年輕，但是實際上他已經超過 40 歲了。

03 **apparent** [əˋpærənt] 形 ❶ 表面上的，外觀的；❷ 明顯的，顯而易見的

❶ The **apparent** cause of the accident was the driver's carelessness, but the real cause was his drunkenness.
這場事故乍看之下是駕駛粗心大意，但實際原因其實是酒駕。

❷ Dale has no friends because he frequently gets angry for no **apparent** reason. 戴爾經常無故發脾氣，所以沒有人要和他做朋友。

相關用法 副 **apparently** 顯然地

- The girl frowned at the sight of the stinky tofu; apparently, she didn't like it at all. 小女孩一看到臭豆腐就皺起眉頭，顯然她一點也不喜歡。

04 **appropriate** [əˋpropr ɪ͵et] 形 **適當的，恰當的**

- Mr. Anderson spent an hour picking out an **appropriate** outfit to wear on his date tonight.
  安德森先生花了一個小時，挑選適合今晚約會穿的衣服。

相關用法 副 **appropriately** 適當地，合適地

- Bruce is a capable man; his work is always appropriately thorough.
  布魯斯很有能力，他總是把每件事都做得恰如其分。

05 **atmosphere** [ˋætməs͵fɪr] 名 ❶ C **氣氛**；❷ U **大氣**

❶ The restaurant creates a friendly **atmosphere**, making the customers feel relaxed.
這家餐廳營造出一種友好的氣氛，讓顧客感到很放鬆。

❷ The **atmosphere** is a mixture of gases that surrounds Earth.
大氣是圍繞著地球的混合氣體。

06 **awake** [əˋwek] 動 ❶ **醒過來** ❷ **意識到**
形 ❸ **醒著的**；❹ **認識到的，意識到的**

- a- 表「處於某狀態」
- wake 醒來

❶ Last night, I **awoke** from a deep sleep to see my dog on the bed.
昨天晚上我從沉睡中醒來，發現我的狗在床上。

❷ After she almost died in the accident, Mariah **awoke** to the realization that life is short.
瑪莉安差點在意外中喪命，她這才明白生命很短暫。

❸ Justin stayed **awake** all night studying for his English test.
賈斯汀通宵準備英語測驗。

❹ People are **awake** to the importance of their health only when they lose it. 只有當人們失去健康時，他們才會意識到健康的重要性。

用法 awake to something 醒悟並覺察某事

07 **bald** [bɔld] 形 **無毛的，禿頭的**

- Although most babies are **bald**, Jimmy was born with some black hair. 雖然大部分嬰兒都沒有頭髮，但吉米出生時卻有帶點黑髮。

08 **circumstance** [ˋsɝkəm͵stæns] 名 C（常作複數）**情況，環境**

- Celina started her business just as the economy began to fall; she was a victim of **circumstances**.
  賽琳娜在景氣開始下滑時成立公司，她是大環境的犧牲者。

- circum- 表「環繞」
- stance 表「站」

相關片語 **in/under no circumstance** 決不，無論如何都不

- As the mother was leaving home, she told her son that under no circumstances should he open the door for strangers.
  媽媽從家裡出門時告訴兒子，無論如何都不可以幫陌生人開門。

09 **complicate** [ˋkɑmplə͵ket] 動 使複雜化，使費解 名 complication 複雜

- The unpredictable weather pattern **complicated** Martina's construction project. 瑪汀娜的建設案因多變的天氣而變得複雜。

10 **condition** [kənˋdɪʃən] 名 ❶ U 情況，(健康等)狀態；❷ C 環境，形勢；❸ C 條件

❶ After the treatment, the patient's **condition** improved.
治療過後，那名病人的身體狀況逐漸好轉。

❷ The working **conditions** in the mine were so dreadful that the miners suffered a great deal.
礦坑裡的工作環境十分惡劣，礦工們吃了不少苦頭。

❸ Compatibility is a necessary **condition** of a successful and long-lasting marriage. 相互包容是維持成功與長久婚姻的一項必要條件。

相關片語 ❶ **(up) on condition that** 只要，以……為條件
❷ **on no condition** 決不

❶ We will go on a picnic tomorrow on condition that it doesn't rain. 只要不下雨，明天我們就會去郊遊。

❷ The father warned his son that on no condition was he to swim in the lake. 父親警告他的兒子絕對不可以在那座湖裡游泳。

補充 hair conditioner 潤髮乳

11 **curl** [kɝl] ❶ 動 捲曲；❷ 使捲曲 ❸ 名 C 捲髮

❶ Marta's hair **curls** naturally when it is wet.
瑪兒塔的頭髮弄濕時，會自然捲起。

❷ The hairstylist **curled** the woman's hair with heated rollers.
髮形師用加熱過的髮捲，將女子的頭髮捲起來。

❸ The little boy looks like an angel; he has blue eyes and blonde **curls**. 小男孩看起來像是一位小天使；他有藍色的眼睛和金色的捲髮。

12 **dependent** [dɪˋpɛndənt] 形 依賴的，依靠的

- How many **dependent** children are there in your family? 你家裡有幾個小孩子要養？

> ・depend 依靠
> ・-ent 形 表「有……性質的」

13 **despite** [dɪˋspaɪt] 介 儘管 同義 in spite of 儘管

- Regina won the mountain bike championship again **despite** her illness. 蕾吉娜儘管生病，還是再次贏得越野單車賽的冠軍。

150

14 **dusty** [ˋdʌstɪ] 形 滿是灰塵的，灰塵覆蓋的

- It is best to wear a face mask in **dusty** conditions.
在塵煙滿布的環境中，最好戴著面罩。

> ・dust 灰塵
> ・-y 形 表「……的」

15 **dynamic** [daɪˋnæmɪk] 形 **有活力的，有生氣的，強有力的**

- Guy forecasted that the stock market would be more **dynamic** in the coming season. 蓋預測下一季股市會比較蓬勃。

16 **efficiency** [ɪˋfɪʃənsɪ] 名 U **效率，功效**

‧efficient 有效率的
‧-cy 名 表「狀態」

- The invention of new machines has increased our **efficiency**, yet profits have remained in the hands of the corporations.
新機器的發明提高了我們的工作效率，但錢還是都進了大公司的口袋。

17 **elegant** [ˋɛləgənt] 形 **優美的，雅緻的** 同義 stylish 漂亮的

- Tina's **elegant** handwriting impressed me.
汀娜的字跡娟秀讓我印象深刻。

相關用法 名 **elegance** 優雅，雅緻

- The elegance of the woman's evening dress attracted everyone's attention. 那名女子穿的晚禮服很優雅，吸引了大家的目光。

18 **emergency** [ɪˋmɝdʒənsɪ] ❶ 名 U **緊急情況**；❷ C **突然事件**

‧emerge 出現
‧-ency 名 表「狀態」

❶ After the terrorist attack, the government declared a state of **emergency**. 政府在恐怖攻擊過後，宣布進入緊急狀態。

❷ This exit can be used only in an **emergency**.
這個出口只在緊急狀況下使用。

補充 emergency room (=ER) 急診室；emergency exit 緊急逃生口

19 **equality** [iˋkwɑlətɪ] 名 U **平等**

‧equal 形 平等的
‧-ity 名 表「狀態」

- Darnell devoted his life to working for racial **equality** in his country. 達尼爾終生為自己國家的種族平等努力不懈。

20 **evident** [ˋɛvədənt] 形 **明顯的，明白的** 同義 obvious, apparent 明顯的

- It is **evident** that Mr. Coleman likes Sandra very much because he always sits next to her. 科曼先生總是坐在珊卓旁邊，他顯然非常喜歡她。

相關用法 副 **evidently** 明顯地，顯然

- The woman's face turned pale; she was evidently ill.
那名女子臉色變得蒼白，她顯然是病了。

21 **existence** [ɪgˋzɪstəns] 名 U **存在**

‧exist 動 存在
‧-ence 名 表「狀態」

- Norton does not believe in the **existence** of ghosts; he thinks they are just illusions in people's minds.
諾頓不相信鬼的存在，認為那只是人心中的幻象罷了。

相關片語 ❶ **come into existence** 成立，開始存在；
❷ **in existence** 存在的，現有的

❶ The Republic of China came into existence in 1911, bringing an end to imperialism. 中華民國成立於 1911 年，替帝王政治畫下句點。

❷ Taipei 101 is one of the tallest skyscrapers in existence.
台北 101 是現有最高的摩天大樓之一。

22 **exit** [ˋɛgszɪt] 名 C ❶ 出口，太平門；❷ 離去，退出
動 ❸ 出去，離去，退出

▪ ex- 向外

❶ This shopping mall has more than a dozens **exits**.
這間購物中心有十幾個緊急逃生口。

❷ When her ex-boyfriend entered the hall, Heidi made a quick **exit**, as she did not want to meet him.
當海蒂的前男友進入大廳時，因為不想見到他，於是海蒂很快就離開了。

❸ When the fire broke out, people in the movie theater **exited** via the fire door. 火災發生時，電影院裡的民眾從逃生門離開。

23 **functional** [ˋfʌŋkʃənḷ] 形 起作用的，有效的

▪ function 名 功能
▪ -al 形 表「關於……的」

● Eric was surprised that his mobile phone was still **functional** even after being dropped into a glass of water.
艾力克的手機即使掉進一杯水後還是能用，他感到十分訝異。

24 **grace** [gres] 名 U 優雅，優美

● Terry always moves with **grace** and speaks with precision.
泰莉舉止優雅，言語有分寸。

25 **graceful** [ˋgresfəl] 形 優美的，優雅的

▪ grace 名 優雅
▪ -ful 形 表「充滿……的」

● Ignatius is a **graceful** dancer who also shows incredible musical talent.
伊格內修斯的舞姿優美，音樂才華也很驚人。

26 **hardship** [ˋhɑrdʃɪp] 名 U 艱難，困苦

▪ hard 艱苦
▪ -ship 名 表「狀態」

● Vonda is very self-motivated; she accepts whatever **hardships** come to her and moves past them.
芳達能夠自我勉勵，她能夠面對挑戰並且克服逆境。

27 **harmony** [ˋhɑrmənɪ] 名 U ❶ 和睦，融洽；❷ 調和，協調

❶ We hope that there will be no more war in the world and that all people live in peace and **harmony** with each other.
我們希望世界上沒有戰爭。人類彼此都能和平、融洽地相處。〔98 年學測〕

❷ Bernadine captured the colorful **harmony** of autumn leaves in her painting. 貝娜汀將秋葉色彩繽紛的調和之美捕捉在她的畫中。

相關用法 形 **harmonious** 和睦的；副 **harmoniously** 和睦地

❶ Relations between the two countries are very harmonious, so there is no conflict on the border.
兩國之間關係非常和睦，因此邊境上也不再出現紛爭。

❷ Different ethnic groups worked harmoniously.
不同族群和睦地一起工作。

76 State & condition 狀態與情況 (2)

151

01 **leisurely** [ˋliʒəlɪ] ❶ 形 從容不迫的，悠閒的 ❷ 副 從容不迫地，慢慢地

❶ On Sunday afternoon, we had a **leisurely** meal at the café and then walked home at a slow and relaxing pace. 週日的下午時分，我們悠閒地在咖啡廳享用美食，然後踏上緩慢而輕鬆的步伐回家。

- leisure 空閒的
- -ly 副 表「在……方面」

❷ It takes about three hours to go through the museum at a **leisurely** pace. 悠閒地逛完博物館需約三個小時。

02 **liberty** [ˋlɪbətɪ] 名 U 自由

- Roy believes that every human being should have the **liberty** of expressing his or her opinion. 羅伊相信每個人都應該有言論自由。

補充 the Statue of Liberty 自由女神像

03 **loose** [lus] 形 ❶ 鬆的，鬆散的；❷ 未受束縛的；❸ 鬆掉了的
動 ❹ 解開；❺ 釋放

❶ With **loose** brushstrokes in the foreground, Celina vividly captured the high grass in her painting.
希琳娜以粗放的筆觸，在畫作前景生動描繪出瘦高的野草。

❷ The monkey escaped from its cage, running **loose** in the zoo.
那隻猴子從籠子裡逃了出來，在動物園裡無拘束地到處亂跑。

❸ The little boy has a **loose** tooth; it will fall out soon.
小男孩有一顆牙齒鬆動，很快就會掉牙了。

❹ Abraham **loosed** the shoelaces and took off his shoes.
亞伯翰鬆開鞋帶並脫掉鞋子。

❺ The little boy let his dog **loose** so that it could run freely on the lawn. 男孩放開小狗，讓牠可以在草地上自由地奔跑。

04 **loosen** [ˋlusn̩] 動 鬆開，解開

• Freddie stuffed himself with too much food at dinner and had to **loosen** his belt.
弗列迪晚餐吃太多了，所以將腰帶鬆開。

• loose 鬆的
• -en 動 表「變為……」

05 **manageable** [ˋmænɪdʒəbl̩] 形 可管理的，可處理的

• This company, with its serious financial problems, is no longer **manageable**.
這家公司有嚴重的財務問題，無法繼續經營管理。〔91 年學測〕

• manage 管理
• -able 形 表「可……的」

06 **mature** [məˋtʃʊr] 形 ❶ 成熟的；❷ 成年人的 ❸ 動 變成熟，長成

❶ Miguel picks the grapes in his vineyard only when they are fully **mature**. 米古爾會等到葡萄園內的葡萄全部熟成才採收。

❷ Since they are **mature** men, they should take responsibility for what they have done.
既然他們是成年人了，他們應該為自己的所作所為負責。

❸ Robert has **matured** over the years; he is starting to behave like a sensible adult.
羅伯特在過去幾年裡變得成熟。現在他的舉止開始像個明理的成年人了。

07 **maturity** [məˋtʃʊrətɪ] 名 U 成熟

• Everyone is surprised by Marissa's high level of **maturity**, as she is only a teenager.
瑪芮莎才十幾歲就表現得很成熟，讓大家感到相當驚訝。

• mature 形 成熟的
• -ity 名 表「狀態」

08 **mess** [mɛs] ❶ 名 U 混亂，凌亂 動 ❷ 弄亂，弄糟；❸ 弄糟，毀壞

❶ After the party, the room was a **mess**; the floor was especially dirty. 舉辦派對過後，那個房間亂七八糟，尤其地板髒得不像話。

❷ Those who **messed** up the room should tidy it.
把房間弄亂的人應該把它整理乾淨。

❸ Carina has been planning the trip for two months; she doesn't want anyone to **mess** it up.
卡琳娜已經花了兩個月計畫這次旅行，她不要任何人來搞破壞。

相關片語 **make a mess of** 把……弄糟

• Conrad made a mess of the final exam and flunked the course.
康拉德期末考試考得亂七八糟，那科被當掉了。

09 **messy** [ˋmɛsɪ] 形 雜亂的，骯髒的

- After I walked on the muddy road for 10 minutes, my shoes were really **messy**.
在泥濘的路上走了十分鐘之後，我的鞋子變得很髒。

・mess 混亂
・-y 形 表「……的」

10 **miserable** [ˋmɪzərəbḷ] 形 痛苦的，不幸的

- Cameron suffers from depression and appears to be equally **miserable** wherever he goes.
凱麥隆受憂鬱症所苦，不管去哪裡情況都未見好轉。

・misery 不幸
・-able 形 表「有……特性的」

11 **misfortune** [mɪsˋfɔrtʃən] 名 ❶ U 不幸，惡運；❷ C 災難，不幸的事

❶ Yesterday, Archer had the **misfortune** of stumbling on the way to the bus stop; he was also unlucky enough to lose his wallet on the bus.
昨天是阿爾齊的倒楣日。他在去公車站的路上跌倒了，更慘的是又在車上弄丟了皮夾。

❷ The hurricane was a **misfortune** for millions of people in the gulf area. 颶風讓海灣地帶的上百萬人民陷入了不幸。

・mis- 表「壞」
・fortune 命運

12 **missing** [ˋmɪsɪŋ] 形 ❶ 失蹤的，找不到的；❷ 缺掉的

❶ Eliza posted notices in hopes of finding her **missing** cat. 伊莉莎張貼布告，希望能找到走失的貓咪。

❷ A page is **missing** from the encyclopedia; someone must have torn it out. 這本百科全書缺了一頁，一定有人把它撕走了。

・miss 動 遺漏
・-ing 形 表「行為的」

13 **muddy** [ˋmʌdɪ] 形 爛泥的，泥濘的

- The man is wearing a pair of **muddy** boots; the bottoms of his trousers are also covered in mud.
男子穿了一雙滿是泥巴的靴子；他的褲腳也蓋滿了泥巴。

・mud 名 泥
・-y 形 表「有……的」

152

14 **normal** [ˋnɔrmḷ] 形 ❶ 正常的，標準的；❷ 精神正常的，身心健全的

❶ The doctor said the results of Anthony's blood tests were **normal**. 醫生說，驗血報告顯示安東尼的身體狀況一切正常。

❷ The young man doesn't look **normal**; he appears to have a mental illness. 那名年輕人看起來精神不正常，似乎有某種精神疾病。

・norm 規範
・-al 形 表「關於……的」

15 **obvious** [ˋɑbvɪəs] 形 明顯的，顯著的

- Robin puts **obvious** signs at the driveway entrance every time she hosts a party. 蘿冰只要舉行派對，就會在車道入口處豎立起明顯的指示牌。

相關用法 副 **obviously** 明顯地，顯然地

● The ground was wet this morning; obviously, it had rained last night.
今天早上地是溼的，顯然昨晚下過雨。

16 **optimistic** [ˌɑptəˋmɪstɪk] 形 **樂觀的**

- optim 表「好的」
- -ist 名 表「……主義的人」
- -ic 形 表「有……特性的」

● Chris is very **optimistic** about the future; he believes that he will have the perfect job someday.
克里斯對未來非常樂觀，他相信自己會找到一份完美工作。

相關用法 名 **optimist** 樂觀者，樂觀主義者

● My brother is an incurable optimist; he always expects good things to happen. 我弟弟是一個無可救藥的樂觀主義者。他總是期盼好事的來臨。

17 **phenomenon** [fəˋnɑməˌnɑn] 名 C **現象**

● Starr has been very curious about all kinds of natural **phenomena** ever since she was a child. 詩塔兒從小就對各種自然現象非常好奇。

複數形 phenomena

18 **popular** [ˋpɑpjələ] 形 ❶ **流行的**；❷ **受歡迎的**　反義 unpopular 不受歡迎的

❶ Bryan loves **popular** songs, while his brother loves classical music. 布萊恩愛聽流行音樂，不過他哥哥喜歡古典樂。

❷ The video game was once very **popular**, but now only a few people enjoy playing it.
這款電動玩具以前很受歡迎，但現在只有少數人還喜歡玩。

19 **popularity** [ˌpɑpjəˋlærətɪ] 名 U **普及，流行，廣受歡迎**

- popular 流行的
- -ity 名 表「狀態」

● I was always jealous of my big sister's **popularity** when we were growing up. 從小到大，我一直很忌妒我大姊的好人緣。

20 **possess** [pəˋzɛs] 動 **擁有，具有**

● Mr. Ross **possesses** several valuable assets in addition to his business. 羅斯先生除了經營自己的事業之外，還擁有其他幾項有價資產。

21 **possession** [pəˋzɛʃən] 名 ❶ U **擁有，占有**；❷ C **(常作複數) 所有物，財產**

- possess 擁有
- -ion 名 表「行為(的結果)」

❶ Isaac regained **possession** of the basketball and scored the winning point at the end of the game.
艾薩克再度搶回球權，並在槍響前一刻投籃得勝。

❷ The poor man does not have much; the old TV set is one of his few **possessions**. 這名貧窮男子只擁有幾樣物品，這台老電視機是他所剩的財產之一。

22 **pressure** [ˋprɛʃɚ] 名 U ❶（水）壓，大氣壓力；❷（工作等）壓力；❸ 按，壓
動 ❹ 對……施加壓力，迫使

- press 壓；按
- -ure 名 表「狀態」

❶ Fanny cannot tolerate the increased **pressure** of deep water, so she'd better not join our diving trip.
芬妮無法承受深水水壓，所以她最好不要參加我們的潛水之行。

❷ The **pressure** of the heavy workload so stressed the manager that he developed migraine headaches.
繁忙工作帶來的壓力讓經理過度緊張，所以他偏頭痛發作了。

❸ Those glasses were crushed by the **pressure** of the heavy box.
這些玻璃杯被沉重的箱子壓碎了。

❹ The study indicates that a lot of teenagers are **pressured** to smoke by their peers. 這份研究指出，許多青少年是因為同儕壓力而開始抽菸。

補充 pressure cooker 壓力鍋

23 **privacy** [ˋpraɪvəsɪ] 名 U ❶ 獨處，清靜；❷ 隱私

- private 形 私人的
- -cy 名 表「狀態」

❶ May I please have some **privacy**?
請讓我獨處一下好嗎？

❷ The celebrity protested that the report was an invasion of his **privacy**; he wanted to keep his personal life private.
那位名人對那篇報導侵犯隱私提出抗議。他希望保有自己的私生活。

24 **probable** [ˋprɑbəbḷ] 形 很可能發生的，很有希望的

- Sergio foresaw the **probable** outcome of his investment as positive, so he put in all of his savings.
塞吉爾預測自己的投資可能會大賺一筆，所以投入了所有積蓄。

相關用法 副 **probably** 很可能

- Emma will **probably** take the offer, so she is likely to become their superior. 艾瑪極可能會接受這個職位，所以她很有可能成為他們的上司。

25 **promising** [ˋprɑmɪsɪŋ] 形 有希望的，有前途的

- promise 承諾
- -ing 形 表「行動」

- The scandal threatened to end Lynn's **promising** political career. 那件醜聞可能會讓林恩的大好政治前程畫上句點。

26 **prosper** [ˋprɑspɚ] 動 繁榮，昌盛，成功

- Toby's company is **prospering** under his flexible and thoughtful management. 陶比的公司在他靈活和周詳的規畫下，蒸蒸日上。

27 **prosperity** [prɑsˋpɛrətɪ] 名 U 繁榮，昌盛，成功

‧prosper 繁榮
‧-ity 名 表「狀態」

- Many countries have been in recession for a long time; therefore, a lot of people look forward to economic **prosperity** in the coming year.
  許多國家長時間經濟衰退，因此很多人期盼來年經濟繁榮。〔93 年指測補考〕

28 **prosperous** [ˋprɑspərəs] 形 興旺的，繁榮的，昌盛的

‧prosper 繁榮
‧-ous 形 表「有……的」

- Computer technology is a **prosperous** new industry in our era. 電腦科技是我們世代的一項新興熱門產業。

77 State & condition 狀態與情況 (3)

153

01 **publicity** [pʌbˋlɪsətɪ] 名 U ❶（公眾的）注意，名聲；❷ 宣傳，宣揚

‧public 公眾的
‧-ity 名 表「性質」

❶ To gain more **publicity**, some legislators would get into violent physical fights so that they may appear in TV news reports. 為了得到更高的知名度，一些立委會涉入暴力肢體衝突，好讓自己登上電視新聞報導。〔94 年學測〕

❷ The company launched a **publicity** campaign for the new cell phone, hoping to attract the public's attention.
那家公司展開新手機的宣傳活動，希望吸引民眾注意他們的新產品。

02 **remain** [rɪˋmen] 動 ❶ 保持；❷ 剩下，餘留；❸（人）留下
名 ❹ C（常作複數）剩羹，殘餚；❺ 遺跡

❶ In the summer, Scott sleeps in the living room because it **remains** cool all night. 夏天史考特會睡在客廳，因為那裡整晚都很涼爽。

❷ We picked almost all the apples off the tree; only a few **remained**. 我們幾乎要摘光樹上所有的蘋果。樹上只剩下幾顆了。

❸ Almost all the guests have left; only Parker **remains** in the living room. 幾乎所有的客人都走了，只有帕克還留在客廳裡。

❹ Bonnie couldn't finish the fish; she fed the **remains** to her cat.
邦妮無法吃完整條魚；她把剩下的餵貓吃。

❺ The prehistoric **remains** survived and were recently discovered.
這處史前遺跡存留至今，直到最近才被發現。

03 **reputation** [ˌrɛpjəˋteʃən] 名 C **名譽，名聲**

- Eve has an excellent **reputation** in the interior design industry. 在室內設計這行，伊芙的名聲數一數二。

・repute 名聲
・-ation 名 表「狀態」

04 **ripe** [raɪp] 形 ❶ **成熟的**；❷ **準備妥當的，時機成熟的**

❶ Since the peaches will soon be **ripe**, Dionne called her friends to help her harvest them. 桃子的熟成期近了，黛恩叫朋友過來幫忙採收。

❷ The time is **ripe** for a strict no-smoking policy.
推行全面禁菸這項嚴格政策的時機已經成熟。

相關用法 動 **ripen** 變成熟

- The persimmons are ripening on the trees; soon they will be edible.
樹上的柿子漸漸成熟，很快就可以吃了。

補充 the time is ripe 時機已成熟

05 **romantic** [roˋmæntɪk] 形 **羅曼蒂克的，浪漫的**

- Roxanne appreciated the **romantic** atmosphere her boyfriend created on her birthday.
蘿珊娜對男友替她生日營造出的浪漫氣氛感動不已。

06 **rot** [rɑt] ❶ 動 **使腐壞，使腐爛**；❷ **腐爛，腐壞**

❶ The frequent flooding has **rotted** the walls of Crystal's house.
克莉絲朵的房屋牆壁因為經常性淹水都腐爛了。

❷ The food will **rot** and the milk will go sour if you don't put them in the refrigerator. 食物和牛奶如果不放進冰箱，會腐爛和變酸。

07 **rotten** [ˋrɑtn̩] 形 ❶ **腐爛的**；❷ **腐敗的**

❶ This house must be really old—all the window frames are **rotten**.
這棟房子一定很老舊了，所有的窗架都已經腐蝕。

❷ The government was **rotten** to the core; many officials were arrested on bribery charges.
那個政府徹底腐敗，許多名官員因賄賂遭到逮捕。

補充 rotten to the core 壞到骨子裡了

・rot 動 使腐壞
・-en 置於不規則動詞後形成形容詞性的過去分詞

08 **rust** [rʌst] ❶ 名 U **鏽，鐵鏽**　❷ 動 **生鏽**；❸ **使生鏽**

❶ There must be some **rust** in the water pipes because the tap water looks a little reddish. 自來水看起來有點紅紅的，水管一定是哪裡生鏽了。

❷ Through the action of water and air, the iron frame has **rusted**.
水與空氣交互作用之下，這個鐵架已經生鏽了。

❸ Don't put the iron bars in the yard, or the rain will **rust** them.
不要把鐵棒放在院子裡，雨水會使它們生鏽。

09 **rusty** [ˋrʌstɪ] 形 ❶ 生鏽的；❷（知識、能力等）荒廢的，不靈光的

- rust 鏽
- -y 形 表「有……的」

❶ Stainless steel will not get **rusty** as easily as regular steel does. 不鏽鋼不像一般鐵那麼容易生鏽。

❷ Jeffrey hasn't spoken English in years, so he is a little **rusty**. 傑弗瑞好多年沒說英語了，所以有點不靈光。

10 **security** [sɪˋkjʊrətɪ] 名 U ❶ 安全；❷ 防禦

- secure 形 安全的
- -ity 名 表「狀態」

❶ When Felix moved to the city, he left behind the sense of **security** that comes from living in a small town.
當菲利斯搬到城市，他不再像過去住在鄉間一樣不注重安全考量。

❷ The unidentified ship was not allowed into the port because it was considered a threat to national **security**.
這艘未經查明身分的船隻不允許進入港埠，以防它對國家安危造成危害。

11 **situation** [ˏsɪtʊˋeʃən] 名 C 狀況，情況

- site 地點
- -ate 動 表「使成為」
- -ion 名 表「行為的狀態」

● The unpleasant **situation** between May and her husband finally ended in divorce.
梅和她先生相處不睦，最終以離婚收場。

補充 sit-com 情境喜劇 (=situation comedy)

154

12 **slippery** [ˋslɪpərɪ] 形 滑的

- slip 滑跤
- -er 名 表「……之物」
- -y 形 表「……的」

● Be careful! This mountain highway is very **slippery** when it rains.
小心！這條山區公路下雨天很滑。

13 **stable** [ˋstebḷ] ❶ 形 穩定的 ❷ 名 C 馬廄

❶ The price of oil is not **stable**; it changes all the time.
油價不穩定，一直變動。

❷ Nick always leads all his horses back to the **stable** before sunset.
尼克總在日落前將所有馬兒趕回馬廄。

14 **steady** [ˋstɛdɪ] 形 穩定的，不變的 同義 constant 不變的

● The expert predicts slow but **steady** economic growth; he believes the economy will keep developing at an even pace.
專家預測經濟成長將是緩慢但平穩。他相信經濟會維持穩定發展。

15 **survival** [sɚˋvaɪv!] 名 U 倖存，殘存

- sur- 表「超過」
- viv- 表「活著」
- -al 名 表「……的」

● Charles Darwin believed that the evolution of species was based on the **survival** of the fittest.
達爾文相信，適者生存的原則促成了物種演化。

16 **tidy** [ˋtaɪdɪ] ❶ 形 整潔的，整齊的 ❷ 動 使整潔，整理

❶ Fran always keeps her desk clean and **tidy**.
法蘭總是把她的書桌整理地清潔又整齊。

❷ Barnett's room was a mess, so his mother asked him to **tidy** it up. 巴奈特的房間很髒亂，所以他媽媽要他整理一下房間。

17 **unity** [ˋjunətɪ] 名 U ❶ 和諧，融洽；❷ 團結，統一 動 unite 統一

❶ Lisa thinks all people should live together in **unity**.
麗莎認為，所有人類都應該和諧共存。

❷ The leader pleaded for **unity** in the party, saying that they needed to work together to solve the difficult problems.
那名領導人呼籲黨內團結，因為黨員必須一起努力解決棘手難題。

18 **unless** [ʌnˋlɛs] 連 除非

● Douglas never calls his friends **unless** he needs their help.
除非需要朋友協助，道格拉斯不會打電話給他們。

19 **vanish** [ˋvænɪʃ] 動 ❶ 絕跡；❷ 突然不見，消失

❶ Many species have **vanished** from Earth, but their fossils have been found. 地球上許多物種現在雖已絕跡，但留有化石遺跡。

❷ The rabbit **vanished** from sight. It just disappeared suddenly in a way that couldn't be explained.
那隻兔子消失了。牠就莫名其妙憑空消失不見了。

20 **violence** [ˋvaɪələns] 名 U ❶ 暴力；❷ 猛烈

- violent 形 暴力的
- -ence 名 表「狀態」

❶ The **violence** in video games might be having a negative impact on our children.
電玩充斥的暴力可能會對我們的孩子產生不良影響。

❷ The volcano erupted yesterday; the **violence** of the eruption was so great that it was heard from far away.
那座火山昨天爆發了。爆發程度之猛烈，從遠方都可以聽見。

21 **violent** [ˋvaɪələnt] 形 ❶ 暴力的；❷ 猛烈的，強烈的

❶ All of a sudden, the mob turned **violent**; they threw bricks and petrol bombs at the police.
突然之間，那群暴民變得凶暴。他們向警察投擲磚塊和汽油彈。

❷ During the **violent** storm, the rain poured down and the wind blew hard. 在強烈的暴風雨中，大雨傾盆而降，狂風猛烈亂吹。

22 **status** [ˋstetəs] 名 U 地位，身分

● Is it true that one's occupation determines his or her social **status** in our society? 我們的社會是否讓職業決定了個人的社會地位？

23 **tendency** [ˋtɛndənsɪ] 名 ❶ C 趨勢，潮流；❷ 傾向，癖性

- tend 傾向
- -ency 名 表「狀態」

❶ With rising oil prices, there is an increasing **tendency** for people to ride bicycles to work.
隨著油價上漲，人人騎單車上班成為流行的趨勢。〔98 年學測〕

❷ The girl has a **tendency** to lose her temper easily when she is hungry or sleepy. 那個女孩在肚子餓或想睡覺的時候，容易發脾氣。

24 **urgent** [ˋɝdʒənt] 形 緊急的，急迫的

- urge 催促
- -ent 形 表「……的」

● The **urgent** message left on Jeffery's answering machine caught his attention. 傑佛瑞注意到電話答錄機中有一則緊急留言。

78 Time & space
時間與空間 (1)

155

01 **a.m.** [e ɛm]（縮寫）上午　同義 A.M./AM　反義 p.m. 下午

● I got up at 8 **a.m.** and arrived at the office before noon.
我早上八點起床，中午之前抵達辦公室。

02 **aboard** [əˋbord] 副 ❶ 在船、飛機或車上；上船、飛機或車
介 ❷ 在（船、飛機或車）上；上（船、飛機或車）

- a- 表「在……」
- board 板；船舷

❶ All the passengers **aboard** the plane were killed in the crash. 機上所有乘客都在墜機意外中喪生。

❷ Are all the passengers **aboard** the train? 所有乘客都搭上了火車嗎？

03 **A.D.** [e di]（縮寫）公元，西元

- In **A.D.** 8, Ovid was banished to Tomis by Emperor Augustus for political reasons.
  西元前八世紀，奧維德因為政治因素被皇帝奧古斯都放逐到托米斯。

04 **afterward(s)** [ˋæftɚwɚd(z)] 副 之後，後來

- Henry finished his homework and **afterward** went to a movie.
  亨利寫完功課後，就去看電影了。

05 **amid** [əˋmɪd] 介 在……之間，在……之中

‧a- 表「在……」
‧mid 中間

- Ryan was shocked to find the remains of an ancient temple **amid** modern buildings in his city.
  萊恩在自己居住的城市裡，發現了一座處於現代建築之中的古寺遺跡，感到很震驚。

06 **anniversary** [ˏænəˋvɝsərɪ] 名 C 週年紀念日

- Jean and her husband's 20th wedding **anniversary** is next year.
  明年是珍和丈夫的結婚二十週年紀念。

07 **annual** [ˋænjʊəl] 形 ❶ 每年的；❷ 一年的，一年一次的

❶ Filing the **annual** income tax return requires some paperwork.
申報年度所得稅的退稅需要一些文書作業。

❷ Every year, Trista takes a trip with her family; it is an important **annual** event for them.
每年，翠絲特與家人都會一同旅行。對他們而言，這是一年一度的大事。

相關用法 副 **annually** 每年，每年一次

- We celebrate our grandfather's birthday annually.
  我們每年都慶祝爺爺的生日。

08 **apart** [əˋpɑrt] 副 ❶ 分開地；❷ 相間隔地；❸ 拆散地，散開地

‧a- 表「使變成」
‧part 表「離開」

❶ Devin has been living **apart** from his family since he was seven years old. 戴文從七歲開始，就沒和家人一起住了。

❷ The two trees are about a meter **apart**. 這兩棵樹相距大約一公尺。

❸ The boy took the alarm clock **apart**, but he didn't know how to put it back together. 這男孩將鬧鐘拆開卻不知道如何將它組合回去。

相關片語 **apart from** 除了

- Apart from Judy, who had to finish a report, they all went to the party.
  除了茱蒂因為要趕一篇報告沒去之外，他們都去參加了派對。

09 **aside** [əˋsaɪd] 副 在旁邊，到旁邊

- a- 表「向」
- side 邊，側

● After talking with the actors, the director stepped **aside** and started filming. 導演與演員交談後，退回旁邊開始拍片。

10 **beneath** [bɪˋniθ] ❶ 副 在下，向下 ❷ 介 在……之下，向……下面

- be- (= by) 表「在……」
- neath 表「在……之下」

❶ We stood on the suspension bridge and looked at the stream **beneath**.
我們站在吊橋上，看著下面的溪流。

❷ Little Johnny loves to hide **beneath** the table and play with his toy soldiers. 小強尼喜歡躲在桌子底下玩玩具士兵。

11 **cease** [sis] 動 停止，結束

● After the negotiations, General Rang ordered his troops to **cease** fire. 朗將軍在協商會談後，已下令部隊停火。

12 **childhood** [ˋtʃaɪld,hʊd] 名 U 兒時，童年時期

- child 名 小孩
- -hood 名 表「狀態」

● When I saw her pictures of long ago, they reminded me of my own **childhood**.
每當我看到她以前的照片，就回想起自己的童年時期。

13 **climax** [ˋklaɪmæks] 名 C ❶ 頂點，顛峰；❷ 高潮

❶ The **climax** of the ritual occurred when the barefooted devotees walked over the burning embers.
儀式在虔誠的信眾赤腳走過餘燼時達到高潮。

❷ The novel reaches a **climax** in the last chapter; it is the most exciting part of the whole story.
小說在最後一章進入高潮，那是整個故事中最精采的部分。

14 **consequent** [ˋkɑnsə,kwɛnt] 形 隨之發生的，因……的結果而起的

- con- 表「一起；完全」
- sequent 結果

● The **consequent** damage that would occur from the use of nuclear weapons is beyond calculation.
使用核武會帶來的後續影響將難以估計。

156

15 **constant** [ˋkɑnstənt] 形 ❶ 固定的，不變的；❷ 接連不斷的，持續的

- con- 加強語氣
- stant 表「站立不動」

❶ I am tired of the **constant** rain; it has rained for a week, and it may not stop until next week.
我受夠雨下個不停了！雨已經下了一星期，可能要到下星期才會停。

❷ After two weeks of **constant** work, Ray finally had a day off.
瑞在連續工作兩週後，終於放了一天的假。

相關用法 副 **constantly** 不斷地，時常地

- My brother has the radio on constantly; I can hear music all the time. 我哥哥時常開著收音機，我一直聽到音樂聲。

16 **continual** [kənˋtɪnjʊəl] 形 ❶ 多次重複的；❷ 連續的，不間斷的

❶ Tammy's **continual** complaints are repeated so many times that they have become really annoying.
泰美不停地抱怨。同一件事情她不斷重複，實在令人討厭。

❷ Our **continual** efforts to maintain global peace will eventually come to fruition. 我們為全球和平所作的不懈努力終將開花結果。

17 **continuous** [kənˋtɪnjʊəs] 形 連續的，不斷的

- After three days, the **continuous** rain finally stopped. 雨連續下三天之後終於停了。

- con- 表「完全」
- tin 表「連在一起」
- -ous 表「有……的」

18 **crack** [kræk] ❶ 名 C 裂縫 動 ❷ 使破裂；❸ 破解（密碼），解開（難題等）；❹ 裂開，斷裂；❺（嗓音）變粗，變啞

❶ Even though this mirror has a small **crack** in it, we can still use it.
這面鏡子雖然有一道小裂痕，還是可以用。

❷ My father used a hammer to **crack** the walnut, breaking it into pieces. 父親用榔頭敲擊胡桃，胡桃碎成好幾塊。

❸ Many people thought it would be difficult to find the killer; however, to everyone's surprise, the police **cracked** the case in three days. 許多民眾認為很難找到兇手。然而，出乎大家意料之外，警方三天內就偵破了這個案件。

❹ When Maggie poured hot water into the glass, it **cracked**.
當瑪姬把熱水倒進玻璃杯時，杯子突然裂開了。

❺ The old man's voice **cracked** with emotion as he told us how he suffered in the war.
當老人對我們訴說他在戰爭中的經歷，他的聲音因為情緒激動變啞了。

19 **current** [ˋkɝənt] 形 ❶ 當前的，現今的；❷ 通用的，流行的 名 C ❸ 水流，氣流；❹ 潮流，趨勢

❶ By reading newspapers or watching TV, you can keep up with **current** affairs. 報紙或電視都能讓你即時獲得最新消息。

❷ Languages change all the time. Many words that were found in Shakespeare's works are no longer in **current** use.
語言不斷演進。許多在莎士比亞作品中出現的字彙現在不再通用。〔95 年指測〕

❸ We couldn't cross the river because the **current** was strong and rapid. 我們無法渡河，因為這裡的水流又急又快。

❹ There is a strong **current** of public opinion against going to war; most people think it is wrong.
有一股強大的反戰趨勢輿論。大多數人認為開戰是錯誤的。

20 **cycle** [ˋsaɪkḷ] ❶ 名 C 週期，循環 動 ❷ 循環；❸ 騎腳踏車或摩托車

❶ The **cycle** of life carries all life-forms from birth to death.
生命形式從出生至死亡，周而復始。

❷ The water in the fountain is **cycled** through a device and reused.
這座噴水池中的水以一個裝置循環再利用。

❸ Today, **cycling** is becoming more and more popular; everyone wants a bike.
今天，騎腳踏車越來越受人們歡迎，每一個人都想要有一台自己的腳踏車。

21 **deadline** [ˋdɛd͵laɪn] 名 C 截止期限，最後限期

- dead 死
- line 界線

● When is the **deadline** for submitting the midterm report? 你知道期中報告最晚的繳交時間嗎？

22 **decade** [ˋdɛked] 名 C 十年

● The Internet has revolutionized human communication over the last **decade**. 過去十年來，網際網路已徹底改變了人類的溝通方式。

23 **due** [dju] 形 ❶ 到期的；❷（車等）預定應到的；❸ 應支付的

❶ Gloria's midterm papers are **due** next Monday.
葛洛莉亞的期中報告在下週一要繳交。

❷ The ship was **due** at 12:10 p.m., but it is delayed.
這艘船預定中午 12 點 10 分抵達，但它延誤了。

❸ The payment is **due** today; you must pay it immediately.
款項於今天到期，你必須立刻付錢。

相關片語 **due to** 由於

● Bob's absence from the meeting was due to the traffic jam.
由於塞車，鮑伯沒趕上出席會議。

24 **elsewhere** [ˋɛls͵hwɛr] 副 在別處，到別處

- else 其他
- where 在哪裡

● Eleanor owns property at the seashore and **elsewhere**. 愛蓮娜在海邊及別處置有房產。

25 **empty** [ˋɛmptɪ] ❶ 形 空的，無人居住的 ❷ 動 使成為空

❶ There are two **empty** rooms in this apartment.
這間公寓裡有兩個空房間。

❷ Alena **emptied** out her handbag but couldn't find her wallet; she must have lost it.
艾琳娜把手提包的東西都拿出來，但還是找不到她的錢包。她一定在哪裡搞丟它了。

用法 empty A of B　將 A 裡面的 B 都拿出消耗完

26 **era** [ˋɪrə] 名 C 時代，年代

- Michael Jordan is one of the best basketball players of his **era**.
麥可．喬登是他當代最傑出的籃球球員。

27 **eve** [iv] 名 U 前夕　同義 night before 前夕

- It is customary for Chinese families to enjoy a rich dinner on Chinese New Year's **Eve**.
在除夕夜和家人吃一頓豐盛的晚餐是中國人的一項習俗。

28 **eventual** [ɪˋvɛntʃʊəl] 形 最後的，結果的

- Robert's **eventual** decision to join the army shocked his friends and family.
羅伯特最後決定從軍，這讓親友感到震驚。

> ‧e- 表「從……」
> ‧vent 表「將來臨」
> ‧-al 形 表「……的」

相關用法 副 **eventually** 最後

- The soldier was badly wounded and eventually died. 那名傷重士兵最後死了。

29 **extend** [ɪkˋstɛnd] 動 ❶ 延長；❷ 延展

❶ Antony decided to **extend** his trip in Britain; he will stay there for another two weeks.
安東尼決定延長他在英國的旅行。他會在那裡多待兩個星期。

❷ Ralph **extended** his tripod and set up his camera to capture the sunset. 瑞夫展開三腳架，固定好照相機，捕捉日落的畫面。

> ‧ex- 表「由內向外」
> ‧tend 表「延伸」

79 Time & space
時間與空間 (2)

157

01 **farther** [ˋfɑrðɚ] 副 ❶（距離、時間）更遠地，再往前地；❷（程度上）進一步地，此外　形 ❸ 較遠的，再往前的

❶ The old man was exhausted; he couldn't go any **farther**.
老人筋疲力盡，無法走得更遠了。

❷ Since we still have some problems to overcome, we have not gotten any **farther** with the project.
由於一些困難尚未克服，我們在這項工程上沒有任何進展。

❸ A red barn stood at the **farther** end of town.
鎮上遙遠的一方座落著一間紅色穀倉。

02 **forever** [fɚˋɛvɚ] 副 **永遠**

- A friend who supports you in good times and bad times is a friend **forever**. 陪伴你走過飛黃騰達與失意落魄的朋友，才是永遠的朋友。

03 **forth** [forθ] 副 **向前，向前方**

- When the teacher asked for help, several students came **forth** and volunteered. 老師要求幫忙時，幾名學生主動趨前協助。

04 **gap** [gæp] 名 C ❶ **裂口，缺口**；❷ **分歧，隔閡**

❶ The earthquake caused a huge **gap** in Jill's driveway.
吉爾的車道被地震震出了一道大裂縫。

❷ Mr. and Mrs. Hardy bridged the **gap** between them and their son by communicating with him.
哈帝夫婦藉由溝通來消弭他們與兒子之間的分歧。

05 **halt** [hɔlt] ❶ 動 **停止，終止**　❷ 名 C **停止，終止**

❶ The government does its best to **halt** tax fraud. 政府盡力遏止逃稅。

❷ The accident brought traffic to a **halt**; no cars were moving on the road. 那起意外使得交通停滯，馬路上的車輛都動彈不得。

相關片語 **call a halt** 命令停止，下令停止

- Only 10 minutes into the baseball game, it started to rain cats and dogs; the referee had no choice but to call a halt.
比賽才開始十分鐘，就下起了傾盆大雨。裁判別無選擇，只能下令停止比賽。

06 **handy** [ˋhændɪ] 形 ❶ **手邊的，近便的**；❷ **便利的，方便的**

- hand 手
- -y 形 表「關於……的」

❶ Sara keeps her spare change and mobile phone in a **handy** spot in her backpack.
莎拉把零錢和行動電話放在背包方便拿取之處。

❷ The recipe gives many **handy** hints for cooking beef.
這本食譜提供了許多實用的牛肉烹飪訣竅。

07 **haste** [hest] 名 U **急忙，匆忙**　形 hasty 急忙的　同義 hurry 急忙

- Glen hurried out of the room; in his **haste**, he bumped his head against the door. 葛蘭匆匆離開房間。在匆忙中，他的頭撞上了門。

08 **hasten** [ˋhesn̩] ❶ 動 加速；❷ 趕緊，趕快

- haste 急忙
- -en 動 表「變為……」

❶ The research shows that nicotine **hastens** the growth of lung cancer. 研究顯示，尼古丁會加速肺癌的發展。

❷ After winning first prize in the contest, Avery **hastened** home to tell his mother the good news.
在贏得比賽第一名之後，艾瑞里趕緊回家告訴媽媽這個好消息。

09 **hasty** [ˋhestɪ] 形 ❶ 匆忙的，急忙的；❷ 倉促的，輕率的

- haste 急忙
- -y 形 表「……的」

❶ Since Peggy was late for work, she had a **hasty** breakfast before leaving home.
由於佩姬上班遲到了，她只好在出門前匆忙吃完早餐。

❷ Davis doesn't want to make a **hasty** decision to change his career. 戴維斯不想要倉促做出轉換職業跑道的決定。

10 **hollow** [ˋhɑlo] 形 ❶ 空的，中空的；❷ 空洞的，虛偽的

❶ Earline was surprised to find a rabbit living in the **hollow** tree trunk in her backyard. 伊爾琳發現後院的空心樹幹中住了一隻兔子，感到十分驚訝。

❷ Simon's promise rang **hollow**; he did not sound sincere at all.
賽門的承諾很空洞。他講話聽起來一點也不誠懇。

11 **honeymoon** [ˋhʌnɪˏmun] 名 C ❶ 蜜月旅行，蜜月假期；❷（建立新關係等後）短暫的和諧時期

- honey 蜂蜜
- moon 月

❶ Two days after their wedding, Barret and his wife went to Italy for their **honeymoon**.
在完婚第二天，巴里特就和妻子去義大利渡蜜月了。

❷ The **honeymoon** between the new president and the press will soon be over. 新總統與媒體之間的蜜月期很快要結束了。

12 **hourly** [ˋaʊrlɪ] ❶ 形 每小時的 ❷ 副 每小時地

- hour 名 小時
- -ly 形 副 表「……的（地）」

❶ After his promotion to manager, Sean's **hourly** pay increased. 西恩晉升為主管後時薪增加。

❷ The website is updated **hourly**, so Internet users can always find the latest news there.
這個網站每小時更新一次，所以網路使用者總是可以在那裡得知最新的消息。

13 **immediate** [ɪˋmidɪɪt] 形 ❶ 立即的，即刻的；❷ 當前的，目前的

- im- 表「不」
- medi- 表「居中」
- -ate 形 表「……狀態的」

❶ You should seek **immediate** attention if you start to feel faint or dizzy.
當你感到暈眩或頭昏時，應該馬上治療。

❷ The government should take action right away to meet the people's **immediate** needs.
政府應該馬上採取行動，滿足人民當前的需要。

相關用法 副 **immediately** 立即，馬上

● It is very late; you should go home immediately. 很晚了，你應該立刻回家。

14 **initial** [ɪˋnɪʃəl] 形 **開始的，最初的**

● Alan took an **initial** step toward a happier life by changing his occupation. 艾倫換了工作，踏出追求更快樂人生的第一步。

158

15 **inner** [ˋɪnɚ] 形 ❶ **內部的，裡面的；**❷ **精神的，內心的**

・in- 表「在內」

❶ When they left home, they locked the outer door and left the **inner** one wide open. 他們從家裡出來時，把外面大門鎖上，內門則是敞開著。

❷ Nothing is more valuable than **inner** peace. 什麼都比不上內心的平靜。

16 **internal** [ɪnˋtɝnl̩] 形 ❶ **內的，內部的；**❷ **體內的，內服的**

・inter- 表「在⋯⋯內」
・-al 形 表「⋯⋯的」

❶ Although the external wall of the building was severely damaged in the earthquake, the **internal** structure is intact.
雖然這棟建築物的外牆在地震中嚴重受損，但是內部結構未受影響。

❷ This medicine is for **internal** use only. 此藥只供內服。

17 **lag** [læg] ❶ 動 **走得慢，落後** ❷ 名 C **(時間)落差**

❶ After the first lap of the race, some cars began to **lag**.
幾部賽車在過了第一圈後，速度開始落後了。

❷ The customer complained to the manager that there was a long time **lag** between ordering the meal and being served.
那名顧客向經理抱怨，點餐和上菜的時間落差太大。

補充 jet lag 時差

18 **lately** [ˋletlɪ] 副 **近來，最近**

・late 形 最近的
・-ly 副 表「⋯⋯地」

● Have you heard from Carl **lately**?
你最近有卡爾的消息嗎？

19 **latter** [ˋlætɚ] 形 ❶ **後面的，後半的；**❷ **(兩者中)後者的；** ❸ **現今的，最近的**

❶ The **latter** half of our meeting will be reserved for group discussion. 我們下半場的會議將留作分組討論。

❷ Paul presented two plans; the former is time-consuming, and the **latter** is more workable. 保羅提出了兩個計畫，前者很耗時，後者則比較可行。

❸ In the **latter** years, more people have become concerned about the problem of global warming. 近幾年越來越多人關心全球暖化的問題。

20 **lifetime** [ˋlaɪf͵taɪm] 名 C 一生，終身

- life 一生
- time 時間

● Some opportunities come once in a **lifetime**, and only a few of us can seize them. 有些機會一生僅有一次，只有少數人可以把握住。

21 **margin** [ˋmɑrdʒɪn] 名 C ❶ 邊，邊緣；❷ 頁邊空白

❶ Some palm trees are planted along the **margins** of the field.
田四周種了幾棵棕櫚樹。

❷ During class, I wrote notes in the empty space at the side of the page; now, the **margin** is full of words.
上課的時候，我在這一頁的空白處做筆記，現在這頁的邊緣都是字。

22 **meanwhile** [ˋmin͵hwaɪl] ❶ 名 U 其時，其間 ❷ 副 其間，同時

- mean 中間的
- while 一段時間

❶ Robin will go to the United States next week; he will visit a friend in the **meanwhile** .
羅賓下禮拜要去美國。在這期間他會去拜訪一位朋友。

❷ My brother was mowing the lawn; **meanwhile**, I was doing the dishes. 我哥哥割草坪的同時我在洗碗。

23 **monthly** [ˋmʌnθlɪ] ❶ 形 每月的，每月一次的 ❷ 副 每月，每月一次

- month 月
- -ly 形 副 表「……的(地)」

● The two departments hold a meeting together once a month; their **monthly** meeting is always on a Monday. 這兩個部門每個月一起開一次會。他們的月會通常在星期一舉行。

24 **nowadays** [ˋnaʊə͵dez] 副 時下，當今

- now 現在
- a 每一
- day 一天
- -s 構成副詞

● Most people do not get enough sleep **nowadays**.
現代人大多都睡眠不足。

25 **occasion** [əˋkeʒən] 名 C ❶ 場合，時刻；❷ 重大活動，慶典

❶ In the United States, Thanksgiving is an **occasion** for families to get together. 在美國，感恩節是闔家團圓的時刻。

❷ The public memorial service for Michael Jackson was a great **occasion**; tens of thousands of people attended the important ceremony.
麥克傑克遜的公祭會是一場重大活動。數以萬計的人出席了這場重要的儀式。

相關片語 **on occasion** 偶爾；有時

- Charlotte visits her grandparents on occasion, but not very often.
  夏綠蒂偶爾會去探望她的祖父母，但不是常常去。

26 **occasional** [əˋkeʒənl̩] 形 **偶爾的，非經常的**

- Claude was very busy at work; he paid his parents **occasional** visits, but not often. 克勞德的工作十分忙碌。他偶爾會去探望他的父母，但是不常去。

・oc- 表「將近」
・cas 表「發生」
・-sion 表「行為的狀態」
・-al 形 表「……的」

27 **onto** [ˋɑntu] 介 **到……之上，向……之上**

- Carolyn can't help but jump **onto** a chair whenever she sees a cockroach.
  卡洛琳只要一看到蟑螂，就會忍不住跳到椅子上。

・on 表「在……上」
・to 表「到」

28 **opportunity** [͵ɑpɚˋtjunətɪ] 名 C **機會，良機**

- Alan took the **opportunity** to visit his Uncle Frank while he was in Australia.
  艾倫在澳洲時趁機去拜訪他的法蘭克叔叔。

・opportune 及時的
・-ity 名 表「狀態」

29 **opposite** [ˋɑpəzɪt] 形 ❶ **對面的**；❷ **相反的，對立的**
介 ❸ **在對面** ❹ 副 **在對面**
名 C ❺ **對立面，對立物**

・op- 表「反，逆」
・pos(it)- 表「置於」

❶ There is a coffee shop on this side of the market and a post office on the **opposite** side.
靠這條街這邊有一家咖啡店，對邊有一間郵局。

❷ Religions sometimes have **opposite** views concerning the afterlife. 不同的宗教對於來世有時抱持相反的見解。

❸ The post office is **opposite** the coffee shop. 郵局在這家咖啡店的對面。

❹ On the MRT train, a man stared at the woman who sat **opposite**.
捷運車廂內，一名男子盯著坐在對面的女子看。

❺ Denny is tall and thin, and his younger sister is just the **opposite**; she is short and chubby.
丹尼又高又瘦，而他的妹妹卻恰恰相反，又矮又胖。

30 **origin** [ˋɔrədʒɪn] 名 C ❶ **起源，起因**；❷ **(常作複數) 出身，血統**

❶ The **origin** of some English words is Latin. 某些英文詞彙源自於拉丁文。

❷ The man was born into a poor family; however, through hard work, he has risen from humble **origins** to wealth.
這名男子出生於一個貧苦家庭。然而藉由辛勤工作，他從低微的出身崛起成了富人。

80 Time & space 時間與空間 (3)

159

01 **original** [ə`rɪdʒənl̩] 形 ❶ 最初的，本來的；❷ 有獨創性的，新穎的；❸ 原作的，原本的 名 ❹ Ⓒ 原著，原畫

・origin 起源
・-al 形 表「關於……的」

❶ I bought the dress at a discount; the **original** price was a bit too high.
我打折的時候買了這件洋裝，它的原價太高了一點。

❷ Rollins is an **original** novelist; her works are full of new and interesting ideas.
蘿琳斯是一個有獨創性的小說家，她的作品充滿了又新又有趣的想法。

❸ Adam's **original** paintings have been carefully preserved by his children. 亞當的原畫作已由其後代小心收藏。

❹ This statue is a copy; the **original** is in the National Museum.
這個雕像是複製品，它的原作在國立博物館裡。

02 **outdoor** [`aʊt͵dor] 形 戶外的，野外的 反義 indoor 室內的

・out- 表「外」
・door 門

● Karl makes **outdoor** furniture with driftwood and sells it at the market. 卡爾用漂流木製作戶外家具，在市場上販售。

03 **outdoors** [`aʊt`dorz] ❶ 副 在戶外，在野外 ❷ 名 Ⓤ 戶外，野外

・outdoor 戶外的
・-s 形成副詞

❶ We stayed **outdoors** until it began to rain.
我們一直待在戶外，直到開始下雨。

❷ Since it was very hot **outdoors**, Fiona came into the house.
因為外面很熱，費歐娜走進了屋子。

04 **outer** [`aʊtɚ] 形 在外的，外面的 反義 inner 內部的

・out- 表「外」

● Even if the **outer** layer is slightly damaged, the onion will still taste delicious. 洋蔥即使外層輕損，仍不失美味。

05 **overnight** [͵ovɚ`naɪt] 副 ❶ 一夜間，突然；❷ 通宵，整夜 形 ❸ 一夜間的，突然的；❹ 一整夜的

・over- 表「越過」
・night 夜

❶ Because he won the talent show, the young man became famous **overnight**; soon everyone in the city knew him.
因為選秀節目，那名年輕人突然成名，很快地，城市裡每一個人都認識他了。

❷ How can Mary complete all her writing assignments **overnight**?
瑪莉怎麼可能只花一晚，就寫完所有的作業？

❸ The novel was an **overnight** success, and the writer won instant fame. 那本小說一夕成功，而作者也迅速竄紅。

❹ I took an **overnight** flight to Sydney and arrived there early the next morning. 我搭了一整夜的飛機去雪梨，隔天一早抵達當地。

06 **p.m.** [pi ɛm] 縮寫 **下午** 同義 pm/PM/P.M. 反義 a.m. 上午

- After eating lunch, they arrived home at 3 **p.m**.
午餐過後，他們下午三點到家。

07 **partial** [ˋpɑrʃəl] 形 ❶ **部分的，局部的**；❷ **不公平的，偏袒的**

- part 名 部分
- -ial 形 表「……的」

❶ Jack made a **partial** payment on the new computer because he did not have enough money for it.
傑克分期付款買了那部新的電腦，因為他沒有足夠的錢一次付清。〔92 年學測補考〕

❷ Miriam thinks that her mother is **partial** to her younger brother; she feels that is unfair. 蜜莉恩覺得她媽媽偏愛她的弟弟，很不公平。

08 **pause** [pɔz] ❶ 名 C **暫停，中斷** ❷ 動 **中斷，暫停**

❶ After a brief **pause**, Janet continued her speech.
珍妮特在稍微停頓過後，又繼續講下去。

❷ Gaby **paused** to think about the question before giving his answer. 蓋比停下來思考那個問題一陣子之後，講出他的答案。

09 **permanent** [ˋpɝmənənt] 形 **永久的，固定的**

- per- 表「完全地」
- remain 停留
- -ent 形 表「……的」

- If you don't have a **permanent** address, we may not be able to contact you.
如果你沒有永久地址，我們可能會聯絡不到你。

相關用法 副 **permanently** 永久地，長期不變地

- The elderly couple decided to settle permanently in New Zealand; they will spend the rest of their lives there.
這對老夫妻已經決定永遠定居在紐西蘭，並在那裡度過餘生。

10 **postpone** [postˋpon] 動 **使延期，延遲** 同義 put off 拖延

- The young couple decided to **postpone** their wedding until all the details were well taken care of.
這對年輕情侶決定要將婚禮延期，直到把所有的細節都處理好。〔92 年學測〕

11 **postponement** [post`ponmənt] 名 U **延期，延遲**

- postpone 動 延期
- -ment 名 表「行為」

- The approaching typhoon led to the **postponement** of our trip to the beach.
  逼近中的颱風使得我們去海灘的旅行延期了。

12 **previous** [`priviəs] 形 **先前的，以前的**

- Mrs. Marco reviewed the **previous** chapter before discussing the next one. 馬可老師在教下一章之前，先複習了前一章。

相關用法 副 **previously** 事先，以前

- The room was previously used as a study, but now it is my brother's bedroom. 這個房間以前用來當作書房，但是現在是我弟弟的臥室。

13 **prime** [praɪm] 名 ❶（單數）青年，壯年，全盛時期 形 ❷ 最初的，基本的；❸ 主要的，首位的；❹ 最好的，第一流的

❶ The 31-year-old man was killed in the accident. It was hard for his family to accept the fact that he died so suddenly in the **prime** of his life.
那名 31 歲的男子在那起意外中喪生，他的家人很難接受他在壯年時突然逝世。

❷ The **prime** need for medical facilities in remote villages is now recognized. 偏遠村莊對於醫療設備的基本需求，現已獲得重視。

❸ Excessive drinking is considered one of the **prime** causes of liver cancer. 酗酒被認為是導致肝癌的主要原因之一。

❹ The soap opera is on during **prime** time, when most people are watching television. 這齣肥皂劇在黃金時段播映，正是最多人在看電視的時候。

補充 Prime Minister 首相

14 **primitive** [`prɪmətɪv] 形 ❶ 原始的，遠古的；❷ 簡單的，未開化的

- prime 最初
- -itive 形 表「有……性質的」

❶ Millions of years ago, **primitive** people lived in caves and used stone tools.
幾百萬年前，原始人住在山洞裡面，用石頭當工具。

❷ Living conditions in the Amazon rain forest are still very **primitive**. 亞馬遜雨林的居住環境仍是很簡陋。

160 15 **prompt** [prɑmpt] ❶ 形 及時的，迅速的 ❷ 動 提示，給（演員等）提詞

❶ **Prompt** action is required before the situation gets worse; there is no room for hesitation. 在情況變得更糟之前，需要及時採取行動，不容遲疑。

❷ The director will **prompt** you when it's time to begin singing.
指揮會提示你開始唱歌。

相關用法 副 **promptly** 迅速地，立即地

- It is urgent; you must deal with it promptly. 事情很緊急，你必須立刻處理。

16 **remote** [rɪ`mot] 形 ❶ 遙遠的，偏僻的；❷ 久遠的

❶ Relatively few people have ever traveled into the **remote** Himalayas. 只有少數人曾攀上遙遠的喜馬拉雅山攬勝。

❷ Few people remember the incident, since it took place in the **remote** past. 很少有人記得這個事件，因為它發生在久遠的過去。

補充 remote control 遙控器

17 **schedule** [`skɛdʒʊl] 名 C ❶ 日程表，計劃表；❷（火車等的）時刻表，課程表 動 ❸ 安排，預定

❶ Sylvia has a very tight **schedule** during her tour of Japan.
希維雅去日本的行程非常緊湊。

❷ On the first day of school, every student receives a class **schedule**. 開學第一天，每個學生都拿到了課程表。

❸ Fitzgerald is **scheduled** to arrive in Taipei at 10 a.m. tomorrow.
費茲傑若預定於明天早上十點鐘到達台北。

相關片語 **behind/on schedule** 落後於／按照預定時間

- The train is supposed to arrive on schedule—not 1 minute earlier or later.
這班火車應該要準時到達——不提早一分鐘，也不延誤一分鐘。

18 **separation** [ˌsɛpə`reʃən] 名 U 分開，分離

- separate 分離
- -ion 名 表「行為」

- Alice admitted that the lengthy **separation** was a major challenge to her marriage.
愛麗絲承認，長期分隔兩地對她的婚姻是種嚴苛的考驗。

19 **shortly** [`ʃɔrtlɪ] 副 立刻，不久；簡短地

- short 形 短的
- -ly 副 表「……地」

- The man was severely injured in last weekend's tragic car accident and died **shortly** afterwards.
那個男子在上週末不幸的車禍意外中嚴重受傷，不久便死去了。〔92 年學測〕

20 **someday** [`sʌmˌde] 副 將來有一天，有朝一日

- some 某一
- day 天

- Marvin has been practicing basketball every day; he hopes to **someday** become an NBA player.
馬文每天都練習籃球，他希望有朝一日成為 NBA 選手。

21 **sometime** [`sʌmˌtaɪm] 副 在（將來或過去）某一時候

- some 某一
- time 時

- The train is supposed to arrive **sometime** soon, but I'm not sure exactly when.
火車應該很快就會進站，但我不確定確切時間。

22 **swift** [swɪft] 形 迅速的

- The **swift** movement of the squirrels in the tree caught Deanna's attention. 笛恩娜突然注意到樹上有多隻松鼠靈敏活動著。

相關用法 副 **swiftly** 迅速地，敏捷地

- The man walked swiftly; within minutes, he arrived at the bus stop. 那個男子快步走路，幾分鐘之內，他就抵達了車站。

23 **temporary** [ˋtɛmpə͵rɛrɪ] 形 暫時的，臨時的

- Robert has a number of **temporary** jobs, but no permanent employment. 羅伯特有許多臨時工作，但尚未找到一份固定工作。

相關用法 副 **temporarily** 暫時地，臨時地

- We will stay temporarily with a friend before moving into our new apartment. 在我們搬進新公寓之前，我們暫時住在一位朋友家裡。

24 **trace** [tres] 動 ❶ 追溯；❷ 追蹤；❸ 追溯自 ❹ 名 C 痕跡，遺跡

❶ George can **trace** his family tree back to the 18th century.
喬治的家譜可以追溯到十八世紀。

❷ The rescuers are trying to **trace** a child who is lost in the forest.
救難人員正試圖追蹤在森林裡迷路的孩子。

❸ Eunice's fear of water can be **traced** back to a near drowning experience in her childhood.
尤妮絲對水的懼怕可以追溯自她童年時期的一次溺水經驗。

❹ The hunter searched the path through the woods, but he couldn't find any **trace** of the wounded deer.
那名獵人沿著林間小路搜尋，但是他無法找到受傷的鹿的任何蹤跡。

25 **vacant** [ˋvekənt] 形 ❶ 空著的，未被占用的；❷（職位）空缺的

❶ We tried to find a **vacant** seat, but all of them were occupied.
我們試圖要找一個空位，但是所有的座位都有人坐了。

❷ Due to the yearly bonus system, the 100 **vacant** positions in this high-tech company have attracted many applicants from around the island. 由於年終分紅的制度，這家高科技公司的 100 個空職已經吸引了許多來自全島各處的申請者。〔94 年學測〕

26 **senior** [ˋsinjɚ] 形 ❶ 年長的，年紀較大的；❷ 地位較高的，年資較深的 名 ❸ C 前輩，上司，學長

❶ My brother is four years my **senior**. 我哥哥比我大四歲。

❷ The company started making profits after Victoria was promoted to **senior** manager. 該公司在維多莉亞升上資深經理後，開始轉虧為盈。

❸ Aries, my **senior**, has been with the company for 30 years.
我的學長亞力士已經在這家公司工作 30 年了。

27 **spare** [spɛr] 形 ❶ 多餘的，空間的；❷ 備用的 動 ❸ 撥出，騰出（時間等）；❹ 使免遭，免；❺ 饒恕，不傷害 ❻ 名 C 備用輪胎

❶ In her **spare** time after work, Elaine likes to do cross-stitch.
下班之後，伊蓮恩喜歡在空閒時間縫十字繡。

❷ After Ron moved out of his apartment, he slept in a **spare** bedroom at my house. 在朗恩搬出他家後，就住進我家的客房。

❸ Although the teacher was very busy, she **spared** some time for me. 雖然老師很忙，她還是為我撥出了一些時間。

❹ To **spare** your mother any anxiety, you should give her a call; otherwise, she will worry about you.
省得你媽媽焦急，你應該打個電話給她，不然她會很擔心你。

❺ The robber took the elderly lady's money but **spared** her life; he didn't want to hurt her.
那名搶匪搶走老婦人的錢，饒了她一命；他一點也不想傷害她。

❻ Their car had a flat tire; they had to replace it with a **spare**.
他們的車爆胎了，得用備胎來更換。

28 **weekly** [ˋwiklɪ] ❶ 形 每週的，一週一次的 ❷ 副 每週，每週一次 ❸ 名 C 週刊，週報

- week 名 星期
- -ly 形 副「……的（地）」

❶ Everyone in the sales department has to attend the **weekly** meeting, which is always held on Mondays.
業務部的每個人都得參加這個每週會議；會議總是在每週一舉行。

❷ They practice basketball three or four times **weekly**.
他們每週練習籃球三到四次。

❸ In the convenience store, the man bought a daily newspaper and two **weeklies**. 在便利商店裡，那名男子買了一份日報和兩份週刊。

29 **yearly** [ˋjɪrlɪ] ❶ 形 每年的，一年一次的 ❷ 副 每年，一年一度

- year 名年
- -ly 形 副「……的（地）」

❶ Last week, they paid their **yearly** visit to their parents in New York. 上個星期，他們一年一度探訪了在紐約的父母。

❷ The water bill is paid **yearly**; the bill is usually due in February.
水費一年支付一次，通常應該在二月支付。

30 **youthful** [ˋjuθfəl] 形 年輕的

- youth 名 年輕
- -ful 形「充滿……的」

● Marilyn's **youthful** appearance attracts many admirers. 馬莉琳的年輕外貌吸引了眾多的仰慕者。

81 Degree & frequency 時間與空間 (4)

161

01 **absolute** [ˋæbsə͵lut] 形 **完全的**

- Tyler has **absolute** trust in his business partner.
  泰勒完全信賴自己的事業夥伴。

相關用法 副 **absolutely** 絕對地，完全地

- It is absolutely not my fault. 這完全不是我的錯。

02 **barely** [ˋbɛrlɪ] 副 **幾乎沒有，僅僅** 同義 hardly 幾乎不

- When Ethel answered her mobile phone, she could **barely** hear the speaker because of the poor connection. 艾瑟兒接行動電話時，因收訊不好，幾乎聽不到對方的聲音。

- bare 僅僅的
- -ly 副 表「……地」

03 **considerable** [kənˋsɪdərəbḷ] 形 **相當多的，相當大的**

- After spending **considerable** time studying, Edgar did better on the test.
  愛德格花了很多的時間念書後，考試成績進步了。

- consider 考慮
- -able 形 表「有……特性的」

04 **extent** [ɪkˋstɛnt] 名 U **程度，範圍**

- Daniel was shocked at the **extent** of the flood damage shown on the satellite image. 衛星照片顯示的洪水肆虐範圍，讓丹尼爾十分震驚。

相關片語 **to a certain/some extent** 在某種程度上

- The driver was responsible for the accident to an extent; however, the pedestrian was also partly to blame.
  那位駕駛人在某種程度上要為意外負責，但是，那名行人也負起部分責任。

05 **extreme** [ɪkˋstrim] 形 ❶ **極度的**；❷ **末端的**
名 C ❸ **極端**；❹ **極度，最大程度**

❶ Gayle has an **extreme** aversion to sewer water.
家瑤極度討厭水溝的汙水。

❷ Just keep driving; the farm is at the **extreme** end of the county.
就一直走，那座農場就在郡的盡頭。

❸ The girl used to be very timid, but she has gone to the other **extreme**. Now she is so brave that she is always expressing herself. 那個女孩過去很羞怯，但她已經完全變了。現在她夠勇敢能自我表達。

❹ No one can tolerate Kathy anymore; she has become picky to an **extreme**. 沒有人能再忍受凱西了，因為她過度吹毛求疵。

相關片語 ❶ **go to extremes/carry...to extremes** 走極端
❷ **in the extreme** 極度，非常

❶ Never go to extremes, or you will become unreasonable.
不要走上極端，否則你會變得不講理。

❷ They were foolish in the extreme to believe such a liar.
他們會相信那個騙子真是愚蠢極了。

補充 extreme sport 極限運動

06 **fairly** [ˋfɛrlɪ] 副 ❶ **頗為，相當地；❷ 公平地，公正地**

- fair 形 公正的
- -ly 副「……地」

❶ Tammy is **fairly** sure that she can finish her homework tonight. 泰美很有把握，今天晚上能寫完功課。

❷ The soccer player felt he hadn't been treated **fairly**; he thought the referee was prejudiced against him.
那名足球員感覺沒有被公平對待，他認為裁判對他有偏見。

07 **frequency** [ˋfrikwənsɪ] 名 U **頻率，次數**

- frequent 頻繁的
- -cy 名 表「狀態」

- The **frequency** of our meetings has increased over time. 我們開會的次數越來越多。

08 **frequent** [ˋfrikwənt] 形 **時常發生的，頻繁的**

- Helen makes **frequent** telephone calls to her boyfriend.
海倫經常打電話給男友。

09 **gradual** [ˋgrædʒʊəl] 形 **逐漸的**

- grade 階段
- -al 形 表「……的」

- Mr. Hall has seen a **gradual** increase in customers at his hot dog stand. 霍爾先生的熱狗攤有越來越多人光顧。

相關用法 副 **gradually** 漸漸地

- Ida moved to Berlin six months ago; she has gradually gotten used to her new life there. 愛妲半年之前搬到柏林，現在她已經漸漸習慣在那裡的新生活。

10 **highly** [ˋhaɪlɪ] 副 **非常，很**

- high 形 高的
- -ly 副 表「……地」

- Angela is one of the few **highly** successful students at the university. 安琪拉大學時，是校內少數的頂尖學生。

11 **indeed** [ɪnˋdid] 副 **真正地，確實**

- We were **indeed** fortunate to have Ms. O'Neal as our guest.
我們有歐尼爾小姐這號貴客，真是三生有幸。

12 **intense** [ɪnˋtɛns] 形 **強烈的，極度的**

- It takes **intense** concentration to be a professional race car driver. 要當專業賽車手，就須心無二想。

13 **intensify** [ɪnˋtɛnsə͵faɪ] 動 ❶ **加強，增強**；❷ **使加強，變得激烈**

- intense 強烈的
- -ify 動「使……化」

❶ The search for the missing hikers **intensified** as dusk approached. 搜救失蹤健行者的行動隨著天色漸暗而加快救援。

❷ These two countries are trying to **intensify** trade and cultural exchanges between them.
這兩個國家企圖加強兩國之間貿易和文化的交流。〔91 年學測補考〕

14 **intensity** [ɪnˋtɛnsətɪ] 名 U（思想、感情、活動等的）**強烈，極度**

- intense 強烈的
- -ity 名 表「狀態」

- The **intensity** of Linda's love for music made her fly to Vienna to enter a music school.
琳達對音樂的熱愛，讓她飛到維也納就讀音樂學校。〔90 年學測〕

162

15 **intensive** [ɪnˋtɛnsɪv] 形 ❶ **加強的，密集的**；❷ **特別護理的**

- intense 強烈的
- -ive 形 表「有……特性的」

❶ The workers received three weeks of **intensive** training; they did a lot of activities in that short period.
那些工人接受了三個星期的密集訓練，他們在這短短的時間內進行了很多活動。

❷ After the surgical procedure, Mrs. Flynn received **intensive** care in the hospital. 福林太太在醫院開完刀後，留院接受特別照護。

16 **largely** [ˋlɑrdʒlɪ] 副 **大部分，主要地**

- large 大的
- -ly 副 表「……地」

- The number of earthquake survivors **largely** depends on the effectiveness of the rescue efforts.
地震的生還人數主要取決於救援的效率。

17 **mere** [mɪr] 形 **僅僅的，只不過是**

- Walter was disturbed by the **mere** idea that his car might have been stolen last night. 沃特只要想到自己的車子可能已在昨晚遭竊，就很不安。

相關用法 副 **merely** 只是，僅僅

- The treatment won't cure the cancer; it will merely kill some cancer cells. 這項治療無法治癒癌症，它僅能幫助殺死一些癌細胞。

18 **mild** [maɪld] 形 ❶ **溫暖的，溫和的**；❷ **輕微的，寬大的**

❶ Due to global warming, they had a **mild** winter last year.
由於全球暖化效應，他們去年過了個暖冬。

❷ Dante was given a **mild** punishment for the inconvenience he caused. 但丁因為自己造成的不便受到輕微的處罰。

19 **moderate** [ˋmɑdərɪt] 形 ❶ **適中的，適度的；** ❷ **有節制的**

❶ Mr. Hodge eats a **moderate** diet and has a regular exercise program. 哈吉先生飲食適中，並且規律地運動。

❷ My father is a **moderate** drinker; he never has more than a glass of wine a day. 我爸爸喝酒很有節制，他一天從來不喝超過一杯紅酒。

20 **mostly** [ˋmostlɪ] 副 **大部分地，大多數地**

- most 多數的
- -ly 副 表「……地」

● Can you believe that the landscaping was **mostly** done by Juanita, who is only 16 years old?
你相信大部分的造景工程是由當時年僅 16 歲的璜妮塔一手包辦的嗎？

21 **roughly** [ˋrʌflɪ] 副 **粗略地，大體上**

- rough 粗略的
- -ly 副 表「……地」

● I'm not sure exactly how much scholarship you'll receive, but it will **roughly** cover your major expenses.
我不清楚你會獲得多少獎學金，但是大體上會足夠支付你主要的開銷。〔96 年學測〕

22 **scale** [skel] 名 ❶ Ⓤ **規模，大小；** ❷ Ⓒ **比率；** ❸ Ⓒ **（常作複數）秤，天平**

❶ The melting of the ice cap may cause the sea level to rise on a global **scale**. 冰帽的融化會造成全球海平面上升。

❷ The map is drawn to a **scale** of 1 centimeter to 10 kilometers.
這張地圖是以 1 公分比 10 公里的比例繪製而成。

❸ Before weighing the goods, make sure that the **scales** are accurate. 在秤貨物之前，要確定這個秤是精準的。

23 **seldom** [ˋsɛldəm] 副 **不常，很少**

● Elaine **seldom** eats meat and has pretty much become a vegetarian. 伊蓮很少吃肉 ，簡直就是在吃素了。

24 **somewhat** [ˋsʌm͵hwɑt] 副 **有點，稍微**

- some 某
- what 多少

● Neoma realized she had been **somewhat** misunderstood by her friends. 妮歐瑪知道朋友們有點誤會了自己。

25 **scarcely** [ˋskɛrslɪ] 副 **幾乎不，幾乎沒有**

- scarce 缺乏的
- -ly 副 表「……地」

● Leslie **scarcely** ever went fishing after his father passed away. 萊斯利在父親去世後，就極少去釣魚了。

26 **severe** [sə`vɪr] 形 ❶ 嚴重的，劇烈的；❷ 嚴厲的，嚴肅的

❶ Since Mrs. Ramirez has a **severe** illness, she takes medication prescribed by the doctor.
雷米瑞茲太太患有重度疾病，所以服用醫生開的藥物。

❷ My grandfather is a **severe** old man; he seldom smiles.
我爺爺是一個嚴肅的老人，很少看到他笑。

相關用法 副 **severely** 嚴重地

- The city was severely damaged in the earthquake; most of the buildings collapsed. 那座城市在地震中嚴重損毀，大部分的建築物都倒塌了。

27 **slight** [slaɪt] 形 ❶ 輕微的，少量的 ❷ 動 輕視，怠慢 ❸ 名 C 輕視，怠慢

❶ Shannon left the office early to see a doctor because she has a **slight** fever. 香儂上班時有點發燒，所以提早下班去看醫生。

❷ They treated the man rudely, so he felt **slighted**.
他們很粗魯地對待那名男子，所以他感到被輕視。

❸ Sigrid took Murphy's rude remarks as a **slight**, even though he didn't mean to offend her.
西格莉德視摩菲粗魯的言辭為一種輕蔑，雖然他無意冒犯她。

相關用法 副 **slightly** 輕微地，稍微地

- The box is a little too small; we need a slightly bigger one.
這個箱子有一點太小，我們需要稍微大一點的。

28 **strengthen** [`strɛŋθən] 動 ❶ 加強，鞏固；❷ 使更為強壯

- strong 強壯的
- -th 名 表「狀態」
- -en 動「變為……」

❶ The failure didn't depress the scientist; instead, it **strengthened** his resolve to continue the experiment. 失敗沒有使那名科學家沮喪，反而增強了他要繼續實驗的決心。

❷ Doing push-ups **strengthens** our upper body and increases our endurance. 做伏地挺身可讓我們的上半身更強壯，同時增強耐力。

29 **thorough** [`θɝo] 形 徹底的，仔細的

- Nancy did a **thorough** search of her apartment, but still could not find her diary. 南西在家中徹底找過一遍，還是找不到日記本。

82 Good & bad
好與壞 (1)

163

01 **advantage** [əd`væntɪdʒ] 名 C ❶ 利益，好處；❷ 優點，優勢

❶ More people are aware of the **advantages** of wind power and believe it can benefit mankind.
越來越多人意識到風力發電的好處，並相信它可以造福全人類。

❷ Can you describe some of the **advantages** of this computer?
可以請你說明一下這台電腦的優點嗎？

相關片語 **take advantage of** ❶ 利用；❷ 占……的便宜

❶ Last week, we took advantage of the good weather and went picnicking in the woods. 上個星期，我們趁著天氣好去樹林裡野餐。

❷ The bully is always taking advantage of the younger kids, making them to do things for him. 那個惡霸老是占小朋友的便宜，要他們替他做事情。

02 **affect** [ə`fɛkt] 動 ❶ 影響，對……發生作用；❷（病）侵襲，罹患（病）

❶ The coming typhoon will probably **affect** our trip to Japan.
即將來襲的颱風可能會影響我們到日本的行程。

❷ The disease mainly **affects** the lungs, but it sometimes also attacks the liver. 這種疾病主要侵襲肺部，有時也損害肝臟。

03 **badly** [`bædlɪ] 副 ❶ 壞地，惡劣地；❷ 很，非常

- bad 形 壞的
- -ly 副 表「……地」

❶ Nicholas behaved **badly** in front of the guests and was sent to his room.
尼可拉斯在賓客面前放肆無禮，被帶回房間了。

❷ Those refugees need food **badly**; they are starving.
那些難民非常需要食物，他們快餓死了。

04 **benefit** [`bɛnəfɪt] ❶ 名 C 利益，好處 ❷ 動 有益於；❸ 得益，受惠

❶ The field trip to the national forest that Mr. Ramos organized was a great **benefit** for all his students.
雷蒙斯老師籌畫的國家森林原野之旅，讓他所有的學生獲益良多。

❷ Acting on his doctor's advice, the elderly gentleman is moving to the country, where the fresh air will **benefit** his health.
按照醫生的建議，那名老人即將搬去鄉下，因為那裡的新鮮空氣對他的健康有益。

❸ The students **benefited** greatly from Dr. Lee's lecture, which contained a lot of new information.
李博士的演講使學生們獲益匪淺，他們學到很多新資訊。

05 **consequence** [ˋkɑnsə͵kwɛns] 名 U 結果，後果

- Besides lung cancer, another **consequence** of smoking is wrinkles, a premature sign of aging.
  除了肺癌之外，抽菸的另一個後果是長皺紋，是提早老化的跡象。〔98 年學測〕

・con- 表「一起；完全」
・sequent 結果的
・-ence 名 表「狀態」

06 **deserve** [dɪˋzɝv] 動 應受，該得

- Bob's boss finally recognized that he **deserved** a promotion after all these years. 鮑伯的老闆在鮑伯工作多年後，終於認可他該獲得升遷了。

07 **destroy** [dɪˋstrɔɪ] 動 ❶ 毀壞，破壞；❷ 殺死；❸ 打破（希望、計劃），使失敗

❶ Ian believes that too much money can **destroy** a person, just as surely as too little money can.
伊恩認為，錢太多就像錢太少一樣可以毀了一個人。

❷ The horse has a broken leg and will be **destroyed**.
那匹馬的腿斷了，很快牠就要被安樂死了。

❸ The news that the wreckage was found in the mountains **destroyed** their last bit of hope.
在山區發現飛機殘骸的消息，摧毀了他們最後的一絲希望。

08 **destruction** [dɪˋstrʌkʃən] 名 U 毀滅，破壞

- Weapons that can cause the **destruction** of humankind should be prohibited.
  造成人類毀滅的武器應該被禁止。

・de- 表「分開」
・struct- 表「建造」
・-ion 名 表「行為」

09 **disadvantage** [͵dɪsədˋvæntɪdʒ] 名 C 不利（條件）

- The thunderstorm is a **disadvantage** for the rescue team. 那場大雷雨替救援隊造成了不利條件。

・dis- 表「沒有」
・advantage 好處

10 **disaster** [dɪˋzæstɚ] 名 C 災難，災害　形 disastrous 災難的

- Ignorant exploitation of the environment will eventually invite terrible **disasters**. 盲目開發環境最終會招致嚴重的災難。

11 **endanger** [ɪnˋdendʒɚ] 動 危及，使遭到危險

- Illegal hunting in Southeast Asia has **endangered** many of the jungle species.
  東南亞的非法狩獵活動，危及了許多的叢林動物。

・en- 表「使」
・danger 危險

相關用法 形 **endangered** 快要絕種的

- The Formosan black bear has been classified as an endangered species; soon, it may be extinct.
  台灣黑熊已經被列為瀕臨絕種的動物，牠們可能很快就不復存在了。

164

12 **evil** [ˋivḷ] ❶ 形 **邪惡的，壞的** ❷ 名 U **邪惡，罪惡**

❶ Cindy has an **evil** tongue, so no one wants to be her friend.
欣蒂的嘴巴很壞，所以沒有人想和她交朋友。

❷ The movie is about the eternal struggle between good and **evil**, and its ending shows that evil never prevails over good.
這部電影是關於正邪之間永恆的交戰；電影的結尾揭示了邪不勝正。

13 **excellence** [ˋɛksḷəns] 名 U **優秀，傑出**

- Darlene's **excellence** as a painter was discovered when she was very young. 達蓮娜很小的時候就展現出繪畫天分了。

・excel 優於
・-ence 名 表「性質，狀態」

14 **factor** [ˋfæktɚ] 名 C **因素，要素**

- Conrad's positive attitude is the primary **factor** in his success as a salesman. 康拉德的積極態度是他能成為一位成功銷售員的主因。

15 **fake** [fek] ❶ 形 **假的，冒充的** ❷ 名 C **冒牌貨，冒充者** ❸ 動 **假裝**；❹ **冒充**

❶ Do you have any **fake** teeth? 你有假牙嗎？

❷ The diamond was judged to be a **fake**; it was not genuine, but it had been made to look real.
這顆鑽石被判定為假貨；它不是真的，只是被仿製成像真的一般。

❸ The boy didn't want to go to school, so he **faked** an illness.
那個男孩不想去上學，所以他假裝生病了。

❹ The man used someone else's credit card and **faked** the signature in order to pay for the products.
那名男子冒充某人的簽名，使用那張信用卡刷他買的東西。

16 **fantastic** [fænˋtæstɪk] 形 **極好的**

- Vivien looks **fantastic** in the ivory wedding gown.
  薇薇安穿著象牙色的結婚禮服看起來美極了。

17 **fortunate** [ˋfɔrtʃənɪt] 形 **幸運的，僥倖的** 同義 lucky 幸運的

- Clara made a **fortunate** decision to buy this house before its value doubled. 這棟屋子的房價要漲雙倍前，卡拉做了一個幸運的決定將它買下了。

・fortune 幸運
・-ate 形 表「……狀態的」

相關用法 副 **fortunately** 幸運地

- The car crashed into the wall; fortunately, the driver wasn't hurt.
那輛車撞上了牆。幸運的是，司機沒有受傷。

18 **glorious** [ˋglorɪəs] 形 ❶ 光榮的，榮耀的；❷ 壯觀的，壯麗的

❶ Our team won a **glorious** victory and returned with the championship trophy.
我們隊贏得了光榮的勝利，帶著冠軍獎品凱旋而歸。

❷ Early in the morning, the climbers watched the **glorious** sunrise from the mountaintop; the sky was very beautiful.
一大早，那些登山客從山頂看到壯麗的日出，那片天空真是美麗極了。

- glory 名 光榮
- -ious 形 表「有……特性的」

19 **glory** [ˋglorɪ] 名 U ❶ 光榮，榮譽；❷ 壯麗，壯觀

❶ The Oscar winner stood on the stage, enjoying his moment of **glory**. 那位奧斯卡得主站在台上，享受這榮耀的時光。

❷ Every morning, Wilma enjoys the **glory** of the sunrise, which she watches from her bedroom window.
葳瑪喜歡在早上起床後，望著臥室窗外壯麗的晨曦。

20 **harm** [hɑrm] ❶ 動 損害，傷害 ❷ 名 U 損害，傷害

❶ The chemicals that farmers use to kill insects can **harm** the environment. 農夫用來撲殺害蟲的農藥對環境有害。

❷ Studies have shown that smoking causes **harm** to your health.
研究已經證明了，吸菸對健康有害。

補充 do more harm than good 弊多於利

21 **harmful** [ˋhɑrmfəl] 形 有害的

- Eating too much candy can be **harmful** to your teeth. 吃太多糖果可能對牙齒有害。

- harm 傷害
- -ful 形 表「有……的」

22 **honor** [ˋɑnɚ] 名 ❶ U 榮譽，名譽；❷ C 光榮的事或人；❸ C（大學的）優等成績

❶ Mr. and Mrs. Lin considered their son's award to be a great **honor**; they were very proud of him.
林氏夫婦認為，他們的兒子獲獎是一個莫大的榮耀，他們以他為榮。

❷ Chien-Ming Wang's accomplishments are considered an **honor** to Taiwan; many Taiwanese people are proud of his Major League Baseball career.
王建民被認為是台灣之光，許多台灣人欽佩他在大聯盟的表現。

❸ Ricardo was awarded his bachelor's degree with **honors** last year. 瑞卡多去年以優等成績獲頒學士學位。

23 **ideal** [aɪˋdiəl] 形 理想的，完美的，適合的

- The weather today is **ideal** for outdoor activities.
今天的天氣很適合戶外活動。

・idea 主意
・-al 形 表「……的」

83 Good & bad
好與壞 (2)

165

01 **impact** [ˋɪmpækt] 名 U ❶ 衝擊，影響；❷ 撞擊 ❸ 動 衝擊，影響

❶ Once the war ended, the government faced the **impact** of thousands of wounded veterans.
政府在戰爭結束後，面臨數以千計返鄉傷兵帶來的衝擊。

❷ The car crashed into the wall; the force of the **impact** caused the driver to lose consciousness.
那輛車撞上牆壁，撞擊的力道讓駕駛人失去了意識。

❸ Barton's mother abandoned him when he was five years old, which greatly **impacted** his childhood.
在巴頓五歲的時候，媽媽遺棄了他，這對他的童年衝擊很大。

02 **inferior** [ɪnˋfɪrɪɚ] 形 ❶ 次等的，較差的；❷（地位等）低等的，下級的
名 ❸ C 部屬，部下

❶ Nathan feels **inferior** to his elder brother in both sports and academic performance. 南森覺得自己在運動和課業上的表現不如哥哥。

❷ The **inferior** officer doesn't have the power to make decisions; you need to talk to someone with a higher rank.
這名低階公務員沒有職權做決定，你得跟更高階的人談。

❸ Although Mr. Collins has a very high position in the company, he is friendly to his **inferiors**.
雖然柯林斯先生在公司的階級很高，但是他對下屬都很友善。

03 **lousy** [ˋlaʊzɪ] 形 差勁的 同義 awful, terrible 很差的

- Sebastian thinks most of the soap operas on TV are **lousy** plays. 賽巴斯契認為，大部分的電視連續劇都是爛戲。

・louse 蝨子
・-y 形 表「有……特性的」

04 **marvelous** [ˋmɑrvələs] 形 非凡的，令人驚嘆的，極佳的

- Lou gave a **marvelous** presentation; his boss was very satisfied with it.
  路的簡報表現傑出，他的老闆覺得很滿意。

> ▪ marvel 令人驚奇的事物或人
> ▪ -ous 形 表「有……的」

05 **merit** [ˋmɛrɪt] 名 C ❶ 長處，優點；❷ 功績，功勞

❶ One **merit** of the book is that it is easy to read; it also has other advantages. 這本書容易閱讀是它的長處，它還有其他的優點。

❷ Mr. Skinner always judges people according to their **merits**.
史金納先生一向以功勞來評論他人。

06 **misery** [ˋmɪzərɪ] 名 U 痛苦，不幸，悲慘，窮困

- Neal refused to admit that he was in **misery**.
  尼爾不承認自己處境悲慘。

07 **moral** [ˋmɔrəl] ❶ 形 道德上的　名 C ❷ 道德上的教訓，寓意
❸（常作複數）道德，品行

❶ Ruben had the **moral** courage to stand up for justice.
魯本有道德勇氣為正義挺身而出。

❷ The **moral** of the fable "The Lion and the Three Bulls" is that union is strength.
寓言故事《獅子和三隻公牛》的寓意是「團結就是力量」。

❸ Owners of fast-food restaurants that don't change their frying oil regularly have no business **morals**.
那些不定期更換炸油的速食店沒有商業道德。

08 **nightmare** [ˋnaɪtˏmɛr] 名 C ❶ 惡夢；❷ 夢魘般的經歷

❶ Mr. Mason's sleeping disorder has given him terrible **nightmares** for many years.
麥森先生許多年來，因睡眠失調而惡夢連連。

❷ The boy was kidnapped, which was an absolute **nightmare** for his parents. 那名男孩被綁架了，這對他的父母親而言完全是一場惡夢。

> ▪ night 夜
> ▪ mare 引起夢魘的魔鬼

09 **obstacle** [ˋɑbstəkḷ] 名 C 障礙（物），妨礙

- Stage fright is an **obstacle** to Pam's dream of becoming a professional singer.
  潘姆會怯場，這是她實現歌手夢的一大阻礙。

> ▪ ob- 表「逆，反」
> ▪ sta 表「站；留著」
> ▪ -cle 名 表「物」

10 **outcome** [ˋaʊtˏkʌm] 名 C 結果，成果

- Jay was satisfied with the **outcome** of his dieting program. 傑很滿意自己努力節食的成果。

・out- 表「出」
・come 來

11 **outstanding** [ˋaʊtˋstændɪŋ] 形 顯著的，傑出的

- Mr. Briggs' **outstanding** speech was quoted in the newspapers this week.
本週的報紙新聞引用布格斯先生發表的精彩演說。

・out- 表「超過」
・stand 站
・-ing 形 表「……的」

166

12 **perfection** [pɚˋfɛkʃən] 名 U 完美，盡善盡美

- Leona has achieved **perfection** in figure skating.
李奧娜的花式溜冰技巧已臻完美。

・perfect 使完美
・-ion 名 表「行為的狀態」

13 **pollute** [pəˋlut] 動 汙染，弄髒　名 pollutant 汙染物；汙染源

- Bella did not want to **pollute** the environment, so she cleaned up the leftovers and plastic plates from the picnic.
野餐過後，貝拉把剩下的東西和塑膠碗盤清理了一下，以免汙染環境。

14 **pollution** [pəˋluʃən] 名 U 汙染

- Angie and Nora helped take samples of the West River to measure the **pollution** levels.
安姬和諾拉幫忙採集西河的樣本，以測量汙染物的程度。

・pollute 汙染
・-ion 名 表「行為的結果」

15 **proper** [ˋprɑpɚ] 形 適合的，恰當的　反義 improper 不恰當的

- Phyllis wondered if it would be **proper** to ask her boss for a promotion. 菲麗絲想知道，請求上司讓她升官是否恰當。

相關用法 副 **properly** 恰當地，正確地

- Your computer isn't working properly; you need to have it repaired. 你的電腦無法正確運作，你得送修了。

16 **risk** [rɪsk] 名 U ❶ 危險，風險
動 ❷ 使遭受危險，以……作為賭注；❸ 冒……的風險

❶ Unsupervised children are considered at **risk** for dropping out of school. 大家都認為，未受管教的孩子會有輟學的風險。

❷ It was brave of the young woman to **risk** her life to save the drowning boy. 那名年輕女子很勇敢，冒著生命危險試圖拯救快淹死的小男孩。

❸ People **risked** being arrested by throwing eggs at the presidential palace to protest the war.
為了抗議戰爭，人們冒著被逮捕的風險，朝總統府丟雞蛋。

[相關用法] 形 **risky** 危險的，冒險的

- It will be risky to go out once the typhoon hits land.
  當這號颱風登陸之後，外出是很危險的。

[相關片語] **take risks/a risk** 冒險

- Firefighters have to take lots of risks in their work; they can get hurt or even killed while putting out a fire.
  消防隊員工作時要冒很多風險，他們在滅火時可能會受傷、甚至死亡。

17 **ruin** [ˋruɪn] ❶ 動 **毀滅，毀壞**
名 ❷ Ⓤ **毀滅，毀壞**；❸ Ⓒ **（常作複數）廢墟，遺跡**

❶ A violent hurricane **ruined** Samuel's apple orchard.
一次強烈的颶風摧毀了山謬的蘋果園。

❷ The severe earthquake left the little town in a state of **ruin**; all the buildings were destroyed.
大地震毀滅了那座小鎮，所有的建築物都被摧毀了。

❸ They are going to visit the **ruins** of the school, as parts of the building remain after it was severely damaged in the flood.
他們將去參觀這所學校的遺跡。學校的部分建築受到洪水嚴重損毀後，便遺留在原地。

18 **superior** [səˋpɪrɪɚ] 形 ❶ **（在品質方面）較好的，優秀的；**
❷ **（在職位等）較高的，上級的**
名 ❸ Ⓒ **上司，長官**

❶ This new computer is obviously **superior** to the old one because it has many new functions.
這一台新電腦很明顯地比舊的好，因為它有許多新的功能。〔97 年學測〕

❷ To solve the problem, you need to talk to a **superior** officer or someone with a higher rank than mine.
要解決這個問題，你得跟上級或者比我職位更高的人說。

❸ Mr. Brown is my **superior**. It is certainly an honor to work under him. 布朗先生是我的上司，在他手下工作無疑是一種榮幸。

19 **wicked** [ˋwɪkɪd] 形 **壞的，缺德的** [同義] evil 罪惡的

- Lizzie denied that she had ever done anything **wicked**, but nobody believed her. 麗茲否認做過壞事，但沒人相信她。

20 **splendid** [ˋsplɛndɪd] 形 ❶ **顯著的，傑出的**；❷ **壯麗的，輝煌的**

❶ Gabrielle's **splendid** performance has attracted many viewers.
嘉波麗歐的精彩演出吸引了許多觀眾。

❷ In England, we visited a **splendid** cathedral that was very beautiful and impressive.
在英國，我們參觀了一座壯麗的大教堂，它很漂亮、令人印象深刻。

21 **triumph** [ˋtraɪəmf] ❶ 名 C 勝利；成功 ❷ 動 獲得勝利或成功

❶ The agreement to ban racial discrimination was a **triumph** for human rights. 禁止種族歧視的協議是在人權保障上的一大勝利。

❷ In the end, Taiwan **triumphed** 5 to 2 in the baseball game.
最後，台灣以 5 比 2 贏得那場棒球比賽。

22 **virtue** [ˋvɝtʃu] 名 C ❶ 美德；❷ 長處，優點 同義 advantage 優點

❶ My grandma always says, "Patience is a **virtue**."
我奶奶總是跟我說：「有耐心是一種美德」。

❷ Miranda always praises the **virtues** of practicality in solving problems. 米蘭達很欣賞務實解決問題的長處。

23 **welfare** [ˋwɛl͵fɛr] 名 U ❶ 福利，幸福，健康安樂；❷ 社會救濟（制度）

- well 好的
- fare 過活

❶ The volunteer cares about the **welfare** of children from poor families; she wants the boys and girls to be healthy and happy.
這名志工很在乎貧窮家庭兒童的幸福，她希望他們健康、快樂。

❷ Joshua lost his job recently and is now living on **welfare**.
約書亞最近失業了，現在靠社會救濟過活。

84 Quality 性質 (1)

167

01 **agreeable** [əˋgriəb!] 形 ❶ 令人愉快的，宜人的；❷ 欣然贊同、接受的

- agree 同意
- -able 形「可……的」

❶ They had an **agreeable** time together last night, chatting and laughing.
他們昨晚共渡了一段令人愉快的時光，有說有笑的。

❷ Ms. McClain was happy that her client was **agreeable** to her proposal. 麥克連小姐很高興地發現客戶欣然接受了自己的建議。

02 **artificial** [͵ɑrtəˋfɪʃəl] 形 人工的，人造的，假的 同義 fake 假的

● The organic food products are made of natural ingredients, with no **artificial** flavors added.
有機食品是由天然的原料製成，沒有添加人工香料。〔93 年學測〕

補充 artificial intelligence 人工智慧

03 **casual** [ˋkæʒʊəl] 形 ❶ 偶然的，碰巧的；❷ 非正式的

❶ After the elderly man passed out on the street, his wife sought help from a **casual** passerby.
那名老人在街上昏倒，他的妻子向碰巧路過的路人求助。

❷ Ms. Wiley had a **casual** meeting with one of her former employers. 魏利小姐與她以前一個老闆有個非正式的會面。

補充 casual wear 輕便（非正式）服裝

04 **changeable** [ˋtʃendʒəbl̩] 形 易變的，不定的

● Mr. Presley's easily **changeable** moods make it very difficult for him to get along with other people.
普萊斯利先生喜怒無常，跟誰都處不來。

・change 變化
・-able 形「可……的」

05 **characteristic** [͵kærəktəˋrɪstɪk] 名 C 特色，特徵

● Retta believes that personal **characteristics** such as intelligence and a sense of humor are more important than good looks and money.
芮妲認為個人特色，像是智慧和幽默感，比好看和有錢來得重要。

・character 特性
・-istic 名 表「性質」

06 **circular** [ˋsɝkjələ] 形 圓的

● From the windows to the chairs, everything in Bond's house is designed in **circular** shapes.
龐德家中的窗戶到椅子，每樣東西都設計成圓形。

・circul- 表「圓」
・-ar 形 表「有……特性的」

07 **clumsy** [ˋklʌmzɪ] 形 ❶ 笨拙的，手腳不靈活的；❷ 不得體的，不圓滑的

❶ Sue is so **clumsy** that she always breaks something when she is shopping at a store.
蘇笨手笨腳的，她在商店購物的時候，總是打破東西。〔97 年學測〕

❷ Who would think such a **clumsy** excuse could be true?
這種蠢藉口有哪個人當真過？

08 **coarse** [kors] 形 ❶ 粗的，粗糙的；❷ 粗俗的，粗魯的

❶ The poor man's pants are made of **coarse** cloth; the fabric is so rough that the pants are uncomfortable to wear.
那個窮人的褲子是用粗布做的。那布料相當粗糙，穿起來不舒服。

❷ Elma disagreed with the other students over their use of **coarse** language. 薇瑪不認同其他學生使用粗俗的語言。

09 **concrete** [ˋkɑnkrit] ❶ 形 具體的 ❷ 名 U 水泥

❶ The judge said Rocco needs to present **concrete** evidence to prove that he is innocent. 法官指出，羅科需要提出具體事證，來證明他自己是無辜的。

❷ Now, most of the buildings in the city are made of steel and **concrete**. 現在這個城市中的建築物，大部分是用鋼筋混凝土建成的。

10 **conservative** [kənˋsɝvətɪv] 形 保守的，守舊的

- conservation 保存
- -ive 形 表「……的」

● Julie recommends a **conservative** stance on the use of natural resources. 茱麗葉主張對大自然資源的使用採取保守的立場。

11 **consist** [kənˋsɪst] 動 組成，構成

● Molly's interior designs **consist** of simplistic furniture and futuristic decorations. 莫莉的室內設計由簡約風格的家具和具未來感的裝潢構成。

12 **consistent** [kənˋsɪstənt] 形 ❶ 與……一致的，符合的；❷ 始終如一的，前後一致的

- consist 組成
- -ent 形 表「有……性質的」

❶ Lewis's behaviors are always **consistent** with his words.
路易士向來言行一致。

❷ Parents should remain **consistent** when teaching their children good manners; they should not change their attitude.
父母對小孩的禮儀管教應該保持始終如一，他們不應該改變他們的態度。

168

13 **constitute** [ˋkɑnstə͵tjut] 動 組成，構成

● Freedom, liberty, and equality **constitute** the basic premises of human rights. 自由、自主與平等構成了人權的基

14 **constructive** [kənˋstrʌktɪv] 形 建設性的，積極的，有助益的

● Oleta offered **constructive** criticism of Stan's idea, for which he was very grateful.
歐麗達對史坦的構想提出建設性的批評，史坦非常感激。

- construct 建造
- -ive 形 表「……的」

15 **defensible** [dɪˋfɛnsəbl̩] 形 可辯護的 反義 indefensible 無可辯解的

● I don't think that the idea of abortion is **defensible**; most people won't support it.
我不認為墮胎的觀念是可以辯護的，大部分的人都不會支持。

- defense 保衛
- -ible 形 表「可……的」

16 **definite** [ˋdɛfənɪt] 形 明確的，確切的

● Without a **definite** travel plan, Bryan can't purchase a flight or book a hotel. 布萊恩沒有明確的行程，無法訂機票或飯店。

[相關用法] 副 **definitely** 明確地

- They can't say who is definitely at fault until they complete their investigation of the accident.
他們要在這起意外調查結束後，才能明確釐清肇禍者。

17 **delicate** [ˋdɛləkət] 形 ❶ 易碎的；❷ 精美的，雅緻的；❸ 纖細的；❹ 鮮美的，清淡可口的

❶ Please be careful when you move these **delicate** china teacups, or you may break them.
當你移動這些易碎瓷杯的時候，請小心，否則你可能會把它們打破。

❷ Look at the vase with the **delicate** floral pattern; it was skillfully made, with attention to the smallest details. 看看這個有精緻花卉圖象的瓶子；它以高超技巧製成，而且連最小的細節都注意到了。

❸ The pianist has long, **delicate** fingers.
這位鋼琴家有著又長又纖細的手指。

❹ Fannia knows how to use spices and herbs when cooking to create **delicate** flavors. 芳妮雅知道，煮菜時要用多少調味料和香草讓味道變鮮美。

18 **dense** [dɛns] 形 密的，濃的 名 density 稠密（度） 同義 thick 濃的

- **Dense** smoke from the volcanic eruption has been blackening the sky since last week. 火山爆發噴出的濃煙，上週起就持續遮蔽著天空。

19 **dependable** [dɪˋpɛndəbl̩] 形 可靠的，可信任的

- depend 依靠
- -able 形「可……的」

- **Dependable** companionship is based on mutual understanding and trust.
可靠的友誼是建立在互相了解和信任上的。

20 **differ** [ˋdɪfɚ] 動 不同

- Although they are twins, their interests **differ**. Their opinions can also be very different.
雖然他們是雙胞胎，彼此的興趣卻很不同，有時候他們的想法也很不一樣。

21 **distinct** [dɪˋstɪŋkt] 形 ❶ 有區別的，與其他不同的；❷ 清楚的，明顯的

❶ Although Ernesto and his twin brother look alike, they have **distinct** tastes.
恩斯托和他的雙胞胎哥哥長得雖像，但喜好截然不同。

❷ As the fog is dispersing, the outline of the lighthouse is becoming more **distinct**.
隨著霧氣消散，燈塔的輪廓也變得越來越清楚了。

22 **dominant** [ˋdɑmənənt] 形 **占優勢的，支配的**

- This well-known company plays a **dominant** role in the software industry.
這間知名公司軟體產業中扮演一個舉足輕重的角色。

· domin- 表「住家；主人」
· -ant 形 表「……的」

23 **durable** [ˋdjʊrəbḷ] 形 **耐用的，持久的** 名 duration 持續，持久

- Over millions of years, less **durable** rocks have worn away to form valleys and canyons.
幾百萬年以來，較鬆軟的岩石慢慢蝕化，形成了山谷與峽谷。

· dure- 表「持久的」
· -able 形 表「可……的」

24 **elastic** [ɪˋlæstɪk] 形 **有彈性的**

- Susan used an **elastic** band to tie her hair into a pony tail.
蘇珊用一個彈性髮圈，把頭髮綁成馬尾。

25 **essential** [ɪˋsɛnʃəl] 形 **必要的，不可缺的**

- We human beings may live without clothes, but food and air are **essential** to our life. 我們人類或許可以不穿衣服而生存，但是食物和空氣對我們的生活是不可或缺的。〔96 年學測〕

· essence 本質
· -ial 形 表「……的」

85 Quality 性質 (2)

169

01 **flexible** [ˋflɛksəbḷ] 形 ❶ **可彎曲的，柔韌的**；❷ **有彈性的，靈活的**

❶ The rubber tube is **flexible**; it can bend easily without breaking.
這條橡皮管是可以彎曲的；它很容易彎曲，而且不會折斷。

❷ We need a **flexible** plan that can be changed easily to suit any new situation.
我們需要一個彈性的計畫，可以因應任何突發狀況做出改變。

· flex 收縮
· -ible 形「可……的」

02 **fundamental** [ˏfʌndəˋmɛntḷ] 形 **根本的，主要的**

- The **fundamental** mistake Joseph made was to follow others blindly, ignoring his own judgment.
約瑟夫犯的重大錯誤，就是盲從他人、毫無主見。

· fund(a)- 表「建造；基本」
· -ment 名 表「行為」
· -al 形 表「……的」

03 **genuine** [ˋdʒɛnjʊɪn] 形 ❶ 真的，非偽造的；❷ 真誠的

❶ Lorraine doesn't know if this diamond is **genuine**.
蘿芮不知道這顆鑽石是不是真的。

❷ Alston is an honest and **genuine** man; we can trust him.
奧斯頓是一個誠實又真誠的人，我們可以相信他。

相關用法 副 **genuinely** 真誠地

- The boy is genuinely sorry for what he has done; I think he is really sincere. 這個男孩對自己所做的事真誠地感到抱歉，我想他是真心誠意的。

04 **harden** [ˋhɑrdn̩] 動 使變硬　反義 soften 使變軟

- Rosa **hardened** the butter by putting it in the refrigerator for 30 minutes.
蘿莎把奶油冰在冰箱 30 分鐘，讓奶油結凍。

- hard 硬的
- -en 動「變為……」

05 **harsh** [hɑrʃ] 形 ❶ 嚴厲的；❷ 嚴酷的，艱苦的　同義 severe 嚴厲的

❶ Evan's idea met with **harsh** criticism from his colleagues; he thought their words were cruel and unkind.
艾文的想法遭受同事的嚴厲批評，他覺得他們說的話既殘酷而又不客氣。

❷ Scott enjoys traveling in wild, **harsh**, and remote areas.
史考特喜歡去荒涼、環境惡劣和偏遠的地方旅行。

06 **identical** [aɪˋdɛntɪkl̩] 形 ❶ 同一的；❷ 完全相同的

❶ This is the **identical** dress that Freda wore to last week's party. 這是弗莉達上禮拜穿去參加舞會的同一件洋裝。

❷ Kurt lives in one of many **identical** apartment buildings on this street. 科特住的那條街上有很多同型的公寓大廈，他就住在其中一棟裡。

- identity 身分
- -ic 形 表「有……特性的」
- -al 形 表「……的」

07 **influential** [ˌɪnflʊˋɛnʃəl] 形 有影響力的，有權勢的

- Ms. Moran has been hosting an **influential** news program on public TV for many years.
摩倫小姐多年在公共電視主持一個很有影響力的新聞節目。

- in- 表「向」
- flu 表「流動」
- -ence 名 表「狀態」
- -al 形 表「……的」

08 **involve** [ɪnˋvɑlv] 動 ❶ 包含，需要；❷ 使捲入，牽涉

❶ Larry's work as a tour guide **involves** frequent travel, but he enjoys it very much. 勞瑞是一名導遊，經常需要旅遊各地，但他頗自得其樂。

❷ Do not **involve** me in your problem. I have nothing to do with it.
不要把我牽扯進你的問題中。那與我無關。

09 **involvement** [ɪnˋvɑlvmənt] 名 U 涉入，牽連

- involve 牽涉
- -ment 名 表「行為」

● The police suspected that the man killed his wife, but he denied any **involvement** in her death.
警方懷疑那名男子殺死了他的太太，但是他否認涉入妻子的死亡。

10 **lively** [ˋlaɪvlɪ] 形 ❶（色彩等）鮮明的；❷ 精力充沛的，活潑的

- live 活的
- -ly 副 表「……地」

❶ The bright colors that Peggy uses lend a **lively** touch to her floral paintings.
蓓姬的花卉畫使用明亮的色彩來增添生動感。

❷ The old man is still **lively**; he takes an active role in several clubs.
那名老人仍然精力充沛，他在一些社團中扮演活躍的角色。

11 **magnificent** [mægˋnɪfəsənt] 形 ❶ 壯麗的，宏偉的；❷【口】極好的

- magni- 表「大」
- -fic- 做；形成
- -ent 形「有……性質的」

❶ Ina visited a **magnificent** temple in the ancient city during the festival.
伊娜造訪那座古城中一座宏偉的廟宇時，適逢節慶。

❷ The performance was **magnificent**; it impressed everyone in the audience. 那場表演棒極了，讓所有的觀眾都印象深刻。

相關用法 **magnificence** 名 壯麗

● The magnificence of the sunrise was impressive; the colors were beautiful. 日升的壯麗令人印象深刻，顏色真是漂亮。

12 **meaningful** [ˋminɪŋfəl] 形 意味深長的，有意義的

- mean 意謂
- -ing 名 表「狀態」
- -ful 形 表「充滿……的」

● After the musicians' unexpected yet **meaningful** pause, the music resumed with full force. 在音樂家們出其不意卻意味深長的暫停後，充滿能量的樂聲再度響起。

170

13 **memorable** [ˋmɛmərəbl̩] 形 值得懷念的，難忘的

- memory 記憶
- -able 形「有……特性的」

● What was the most **memorable** experience in your journey to India? 你去印度旅行時，最難忘的事是什麼？

14 **noble** [ˋnobl̩] 形 高貴的，高尚的

● Kitty's **noble** deed deserves more attention.
凱蒂高尚的行為值得更多人的重視。

15 **oval** [ˋovl̩] 形 卵形的，橢圓形的

● The planets revolve around the sun in **oval** orbits.
所有繞日而行的行星軌道均呈橢圓狀。

16 **passive** [ˋpæsɪv] 形 **被動的，消極的**

- President Forbes remained **passive** on the issue of labor exploitation. 弗比斯總統在勞力剝削的議題上，仍採消極態度。

17 **peculiar** [pɪˋkjuljɚ] 形 ❶ **奇怪的**；❷ **獨有的，特有的**

❶ June looked at my new sports car with a very **peculiar** expression. 茱以非常奇特的眼神打量著我的新跑車。

❷ Kangaroos are **peculiar** to Australia. 袋鼠是澳洲特有的動物。

18 **poisonous** [ˋpɔɪzn̩əs] 形 **有毒的，有害的**

- The venom of some **poisonous** snakes is actually beneficial to humans. 某些毒蛇的毒液其實是對人體有益的。

> · poison 毒
> · -ous 形 表「有……特性的」

19 **portable** [ˋportəbl̩] 形 **便於攜帶的，手提式的**

- Julie wants to buy a **portable** computer so that she can carry it around when she travels.
  茱莉想買一台手提電腦，讓她可以在旅行的時候，帶著它到處走。〔93 年學測〕

> · port 港口
> · -able 形「可……的」

20 **practical** [ˋpræktɪkl̩] 形 ❶ **實際的**；❷ **實用的**；❸ **可實施的**

❶ Some students believe that part-time jobs provide **practical** work experience.
有一些學生相信兼差可以給他們實際的工作經驗。

> · practice 實行
> · -al 形 表「關於……的」

❷ Ronnie's approach to furniture design is completely **practical** yet artistically unconventional.
羅尼的家具設計風格完全是實用取向，兼具前衛感。

❸ I doubt if the plan is **practical**; to me, it seems unlikely to work.
我懷疑這個計畫的可行性，對我而言，它似乎不太可能實行。

21 **precise** [prɪˋsaɪs] 形 ❶ **精確的，準確的**；❷ **明確的，清晰的**

❶ The police have composed a **precise** description of the suspect based on eyewitness accounts.
警方根據目擊者的描述，精準地描繪出嫌犯的特徵。

❷ Your instructions are not clear enough. Can you make them more **precise**? 你的指示不夠清楚。你可以講得更明確一些嗎？

相關用法 名 **precisely** 準確地；精確地

- The conference will start at precisely 4 p.m.—not a minute earlier or later.
  這場會議將於四點鐘開始——一分不早，一分不遲。

22 **primary** [ˋpraɪˏmɛrɪ] 形 ❶ 主要的；❷ 初級的，初等的

- prime 最初
- -ary 形 表「……的」

❶ The **primary** factor in Matthew's success is his diligence. 麥修成功的主因在於勤奮。

❷ Every child starts **primary** school at age 7. 每個小孩七歲時開始讀小學。

相關用法 副 **primarily** 首要地，主要地

- This course is designed primarily for elementary school students, and that course is mainly for junior high school students.
這個課程主要是為小學生設計的，而那個課程則主要是給中學生上的。

23 **prominent** [ˋprɑmənənt] 形 ❶ 卓越的，重要的，著名的；❷ 突出的，顯眼的

❶ After numerous auditions, Mandy finally won a **prominent** role in a movie. 曼蒂經過無數次的試鏡後，終於在一部電影中擔綱演出。

❷ Taipei 101 is a **prominent** landmark in Taipei City; you can't miss it. 台北 101 在台北市是很顯眼的地標，你不會看不到它的。

24 **pure** [pjʊr] 形 ❶ 純淨的；❷ 純粹的；❸ 純潔的　反義 impure 不純淨的

❶ The air in high mountain areas is fresh and **pure**.
高山地帶的空氣十分清新。

❷ The ring is made of **pure** gold; it has not been mixed with anything else. 這只戒指是純金打造，沒有參雜其他任何材質。

❸ Those children are **pure** and innocent; they haven't seen evil in the world. 那些孩子純潔又天真，他們還未見過世上的邪惡。

25 **queer** [kwɪr] 形 奇怪的，古怪的　同義 odd 奇怪的

- The whales' **queer** behavior confused the scientists; it was strange and difficult to explain.
那些鯨魚的古怪行為讓科學家感到困惑，那真是奇怪又難以解釋。

86 Others 性質 (3)

171

01 **realistic** [ˏrɪəˋlɪstɪk] 形 現實的，注重實際的，實際可行的

- real 真的
- -ist 名「……主義的人」
- -ic 形 表「……的」

- Although your plans look good, you have to be **realistic** and consider what you can actually do.
雖然你的計畫看起來不錯，但是你得實際一點，想想確切的做法。
〔97 年學測〕

02 **reasonable** [ˋriznəbl̩] 形 ❶ 理性的，通情達理的；❷ 合理的

❶ Milton always comes up with **reasonable** solutions to his problems. 米爾頓一向能理性地解決自己的問題。

❷ The man made a **reasonable** offer for their apartment, so they sold it to him.
那名男子對他們的公寓出了一個合理的價錢，所以他們就把公寓賣給了他。

・reason 理性
・-able 形「有……特性的」

03 **remarkable** [rɪˋmɑrkəbl̩] 形 值得注意的，非凡的，卓越的

・re- 表「再」
・mark 標記號
・-able 形「有……特性的」

● Tony has accomplished **remarkable** achievements in modern theatrical performance.
湯尼在現代劇場表演的領域中成就非凡。

04 **resemble** [rɪˋzɛmbl̩] 動 像，類似 名 resemblance 相似

● Julian closely **resembles** his twin brother; I find it hard to tell them apart. 朱利安十分像他的雙胞胎哥哥，我很難分辨他們兩個。

05 **resist** [rɪˋzɪst] 動 ❶ 抗（酸），耐（熱等）；❷ 抵抗……的影響；❸ 抗拒；❹ 忍耐，忍住

❶ Mr. Orland applied a special layer of varnish on his wooden patio furniture so it **resists** weathering from rain and sunlight.
歐蘭德先生在自己陽台的木製家具上，塗了一層特殊亮光漆，以防日晒雨淋而變色。

❷ A good government official has to **resist** the temptation of money and make the right decision.
一名優秀的政府官員要能抵抗金錢的誘惑，並且做出正確的決定。〔94 年學測〕

❸ The president of the old college is very conservative; he **resists** any change and prefers traditional styles.
那所古老大學的校長非常保守，他抗拒任何改變，比較喜歡傳統的風格。

❹ The cake looked very delicious, so I couldn't **resist** taking a bite.
那個蛋糕看起來很美味，所以我忍不住要咬一口。

06 **rough** [rʌf] 形 ❶ 艱難的；❷ 粗糙的；❸ 粗略的 反義 smooth 光滑的

❶ Mr. Cole had a **rough** time as a single parent who also worked full-time. 柯爾先生曾是單親爸爸兼全職上班族，當時艱苦度日。

❷ After years of hard work, the skin on the farmer's hands is hard and **rough**. 因為多年的辛勤工作，那位農夫的雙手皮膚又硬又粗糙。

❸ The rescuers have a **rough** idea of where the missing sailor is; they are still trying to find his exact location.
救援者大略知道失蹤船員在哪裡，他們正試著找出他的精確位置。

07 **significant** [sɪgˋnɪfəkənt] 形 ❶ 有意義的；❷ 重要的，重大的

❶ Jerome gave me a **significant** look. It had a special meaning that was not understood by the others.
哲羅姆意義深長地看了我一眼，我知道那有特別的意義，雖然其他人不了解。

- signif 表「符號」
- fic 表「做」
- -ant 形 表「……的」

❷ In his autobiography, Bernardo recalled **significant** details of his childhood. 伯納度在自傳中，憶及兒時一些重要的往事。

08 **similarity** [ˏsɪməˋlærətɪ] 名 ❶ U 相似，類似；❷ C 相似點，類似點

❶ The **similarity** between these two dialects suggests they were related in recent history.
這兩種方言的相似度，顯示它們在近代歷史中相關。

- similar 形 相像的
- -ity 名 表「性質」

❷ Humans and apes both evolved from a common primate ancestor; they have other **similarities** as well.
人類和猿類都源自於同一個靈長類祖先，他們也還有其他相似之處。

09 **smooth** [smuð] 形 ❶ 平靜的；❷ 光滑的，平坦的　反義 rough 粗糙的

❶ As we drove along the seashore, the ocean looked calm and **smooth**. 我們沿著海岸開車時，大海看來是風平浪靜。

❷ Many years ago, the stone steps were quite rough, but now they have been worn **smooth**.
許多年以前，石階還是很粗糙，但是現在已經被磨得很光滑了。

10 **solid** [ˋsɑlɪd] 形 ❶ 固體的；❷ 堅固的

❶ The patient can't eat **solid** food; he is on a liquid diet.
這名病人不能吃固體食物，只能吃流質食物。

❷ The table is **solid**; it is strong and well made.
這張桌子很結實；它很牢固、做工精良。

11 **specific** [spɪˋsɪfɪk] 形 ❶ 特定的；❷ 明確的，具體的

- spec- 表「種，類」
- -fic 形 表「有……特性的」

❶ They raise funds for a **specific** purpose—providing poor children with food and education.
他們為了一個特定的目標而募款——為那些窮困的兒童提供食物和教育。

❷ Since setting up **specific** training goals, Mike has gradually transformed himself into a competitive athlete.
麥克設下具體訓練目標後，漸漸變成了一名有競爭力的運動員。

12 **suitable** [ˋsutəbḷ] 形 適當的，適合的

- suit 動 適合
- -able 形「有……特性的」

● Rich is not **suitable** for the job because he doesn't speak French. 李奇一點法文都不會說，所以不適合那份工作。

13 **tend** [tɛnd] 動 傾向，易於

● Roberta **tends** to exaggerate her personal experience to get our attention. 蘿蓓妲有誇大個人經驗的傾向，為的是要引起我們注意。

172

14 **typical** [ˋtɪpɪkḷ] 形 典型的，有代表性的

● Nelson grew up in a **typical** suburban, middle-class family. 尼爾森在一個典型的市郊中產階級家庭中長大。

用法 A be typical of B　A 是 B 的典型狀況

- type 類型
- -ic 形 表「有……特性的」
- -al 形 表「……的」

15 **variety** [vəˋraɪətɪ] 名（單數）種種

● Michele can make a **variety** of delicious dishes, so her friends like to join her for dinner.
蜜雪兒可以做出一道道美味佳餚，所以朋友總愛和她一起吃晚餐。

16 **various** [ˋvɛrɪəs] 形 不同的，各種各樣的　同義 diverse 不同的

● Nikki has received numerous awards for her **various** achievements in music, painting, and sculpture.
妮姬在音樂、繪畫和雕塑上，已領取了無數的獎項。

17 **vary** [ˋvɛrɪ] 動 變更　同義 differ 不同

● The supply of fresh fruit and vegetables in the market **varies** with the season. 市場供應的新鮮蔬果，隨季節而變換。

18 **violet** [ˋvaɪəlɪt] 名 ❶ Ⓒ 紫羅蘭；❷ Ⓤ 紫羅蘭色

❶ Bonnie has planted **violets** and morning glories in the small garden on her balcony. 邦妮在陽台上的小花園種了紫羅蘭和牽牛花。

❷ The singer is dressed in **violet**; the bluish-purple color suits her beautifully. 那位歌手穿得一身紫羅蘭色，紫帶藍的顏色非常適合她。

19 **vivid** [ˋvɪvɪd] 形 生動的，逼真的

● Steve's description of the place was so **vivid** that I could almost picture it in my mind.
史帝夫對那個地方的描述是如此生動，我幾乎可以在腦海中加以描繪。〔98 年學測〕

相關用法 副 **vividly** 生動地，逼真地

● Fred's memory of the event is so sharp that he is able to vividly recall every detail, including what people were wearing.
佛萊得對那件事記憶深刻，他可以生動地描述每個細節，包括人們的穿著。

20 **significance** [sɪgˋnɪfəkəns] 名 U ❶ 意義，涵義；❷ 重要性，重要

• signif- 表「符號」
• -ance 名 表「狀況」

❶ What is the **significance** of the rainbow in the poem? Does it represent something special?
那首詩裡的彩虹是什麼涵義？他代表了某件特別的事物嗎？

❷ This matter has no **significance** to them; they won't waste their time on such trivial things.
對他們而言這件事不重要，他們不會把時間浪費在這樣的瑣事上。

21 **spiritual** [ˋspɪrɪtʃʊəl] 形 精神上的，心靈的

• spirit 精神，心靈
• -al 形 表「關於⋯⋯的」

● **Spiritual** fulfillment is Shelly's ultimate goal in life. 對雪莉而言，最終的生活目標是精神得到滿足。

相關用法 副 **spiritually** 精神上

● I couldn't help my sister solve her problem; all I could do was support her spiritually. 我無法幫我姊姊解決那個問題，我所能做的就是在精神上支持她。

22 **systematic** [͵sɪstəˋmætɪk] 形 有系統的，有條理的

• system 系統
• -ic 形 表「有⋯⋯的」

● A **systematic** research agenda has been planned to uncover how different languages are structured.
一項系統化的研究計畫已完成，以了解不同語言的形成方式。

23 **tough** [tʌf] 形 ❶ 堅韌的，牢固的；❷ 不屈不撓的，剛強的；❸ 棘手的，費勁的；❹ 強硬的，嚴格的

❶ These glass fibers are as **tough** as metal, but they weigh less.
這些玻璃纖維像金屬一樣堅韌，卻輕多了。

❷ Alisa is a very **tough** woman; she is strong enough to deal with any difficult situation. 艾莉莎很堅強，她的強勁足以應付任何困難狀況。

❸ It is a **tough** task; I don't think I can do it alone.
這是一件棘手的工作，我不認為我一個人可以做得來。

❹ The government has taken a **tough** line on drunk driving; offenders will be punished severely.
政府將嚴懲酒駕，違法者將被重罰。

24 **unique** [juˋnik] 形 ❶ 獨特的；❷ 獨一無二

❶ Sophia thinks that the design of the British Museum is **unique**.
蘇菲亞覺得大英博物館的設計非常獨特。

❷ Fingerprints are **unique** to each individual.
每一個人的指紋都是獨一無二。

25 **universal** [ˌjunəˋvɝsl̩] ❶ 形 全體的，普遍的　❷ 名 U 普通性，普遍現象

❶ Darwin's theory of evolution had a great impact on the **universal** consciousness.
達爾文的進化論對普世想法衝擊很大。

- uni- 表「一，全」
- vers 表「轉」
- -al 形 表「……的；狀態」

❷ The concept is identified as the **universal** of the human mind.
這個觀念被視為是人類心智的普遍現象。

26 **visual** [ˋvɪʒuəl] 形 視力的，視覺　動 visualize 使看得見；使形象化

- Nowadays, teachers often use **visual** presentations in class to attract the students' attention.
現今在課堂上，老師常會使用視覺教材來吸引學生注意。

27 **vital** [ˋvaɪtl̩] 形 極其重要的，必不可少的　名 vitality 生命力

- E-mail plays a **vital** role in modern communication.
電子郵件在現代通訊上扮演一個重要的角色。〔90 年學測〕

Part 7 →

Others
其他

87 Others 其他

173

01 **access** [ˋæksɛs] 名 U ❶ 接近，使用（的權利）；❷ 通道，入口

❶ Mrs. Hurley doesn't have **access** to restricted data within the company. 赫利太太沒有權限使用公司裡的機密資料。

❷ The only **access** to the isolated cabin is by foot; there are no roads leading into the forest.
只有走路才能去到這間荒島小屋，沒有其他的通路能到森林裡了。

02 **aspect** [ˋæspɛkt] 名 C 方面

- After considering all the **aspects** of her situation, Laura decided to take legal action against her employers.
蘿拉全盤考量自身情況後，決定對老闆採取法律行動。

03 **concerning** [kənˋsɝnɪŋ] 介 關於

- concern 關於
- -ing 名 表「行為」

- Melissa made a documentary **concerning** wastefulness in capitalist societies.
梅莉莎拍的記錄片與資本主義社會中浪費資源的問題有關。

04 **confine** [kənˋfaɪn] 動 ❶ 限制，使侷限；❷ 使臥床，禁閉

- con- 表「完全」
- -fine 表「結束」

❶ Please **confine** your essay to the history of the telephone and keep it under 500 words.
請寫一篇與電話發展史有關的短文，文長勿超過 500 字。

❷ The patient is **confined** to his bed by pneumonia; he hasn't gotten up for 5 days. 這名病人因為肺炎臥病在床，他已經在床上躺了五天了。

05 **contrary** [ˋkɑntrɛrɪ] 名 相反的，對立的

- **Contrary** to what you think, our TV program has been enjoyed by a large audience.
跟你所想的恰恰相反，我們的電視節目一直有很多觀眾欣賞。〔91 年學測〕

相關片語 **on the contrary** 正相反

- I don't think the dog is cute; on the contrary, I think it is quite ugly.
我不覺得那隻狗可愛；相反地，我覺得牠蠻醜的。

174 06 **evidence** [ˋɛvədəns] 名 U **證據**

- The many awards that Professor Wang has won over the years are clear **evidence** that he is a distinguished scholar. 王教授這幾年獲頒很多獎，這就是他身為傑出學者的最佳證明。〔92 年學測補考〕

・e- 表「從……」
・vid 表「看，看見」
・-ence 名 表「狀態」

07 **fame** [fem] 名 U **聲譽，名望**

- Josefina has won **fame** as a director of international documentary films. 瓊絲芬娜已是國際知名的記錄片導演。

08 **including** [ɪnˋkludɪŋ] 介 **包括，包含** 動 include 包括

- June ordered some vitamins online, **including** vitamins C, E, and B. 茱恩在網路上訂了一些維他命，包括維他命 C、E 和 B。

・include 包括
・-ing 名 表「行為」

09 **outline** [ˋaʊtˏlaɪn] 名 C ❶ **外形，輪廓**；❷ **提綱，要點** ❸ 動 **概述，略述**

❶ From the plane, we could see the **outline** of the isle, which is shaped like a heart.
在飛機上，我們可以看到那座小島的輪廓，它的形狀像一個心形。

❷ Since they didn't have a lot of time, they just gave an **outline** of their plan and left out the details.
由於他們沒有足夠的時間，他們只給了他們計畫的大綱而省掉了細節。

❸ Herbert **outlines** a brief history of India in the first chapter of his dissertation. 赫伯特在博士論文的第一章概述了印度的簡史。

・out 外
・line 線

10 **rely** [rɪˋlaɪ] 動 ❶ **依賴**；❷ **信賴，指望**

❶ Jessica **relies** on radio reports for the latest traffic conditions before she gets on the highway.
潔西卡上公路前會收聽廣播，了解最新的路況。

❷ Prescott is always lying; he cannot be **relied** upon.
普萊斯考特老是撒謊，他不足以信賴。

11 **sake** [sek] 名 C **緣故，利益**

- Darlene helped out for her own **sake**, not for our benefit.
達蓮娜不是要幫忙我們，她是為了自身的利益而做。

相關片語 **for the sake of** 為了

- Herminia became a doctor for the sake of her father; her real interest is music. 荷蜜娜為了父親當了醫生，但她真正的興趣是音樂。

Index

Level 3

H

I~K

L

M

S

T